# QUICK *CASH* SECRETS

**COPYRIGHT, DISCLAIMER AND TERMS OF USE AGREEMENT**

# INTRODUCTION

## "You are ONE SECRET away from thousands of dollars and a new life..."

Let's face it. You bought this program because you want extra cash and you want it **NOW.** I know because I was once in your shoes. Seeking a way I could increase my income and live a better life. *Listen...*

I admit, back then, I wanted to get rich quick. However, I was willing to "work my butt off" to do it. *Regardless...*

I was a sucker for get rich programs. Because I really wanted to get rich. But I didn't care so much about the material things (like cars, homes and vacations). No. I wanted something else. Something **MORE** valuable (to me, anyway). *And that "thing" was...*

**"FREEDOM!"**

Freedom to wake up in the morning... when I WANTED TO WAKE UP! Freedom to go out to eat... when I WANTED TO GO OUT TO EAT! Freedom to visit with friends or family... when I felt like visiting with them!

Freedom to work... when I felt like working! Freedom to take a day off... when I wanted to take a day off! And yes... freedom to take a nap, when I felt like taking a nap!

*Have you ever desired these things?* Of course you have. And I know it... Because I started out like you. And the goal of this manual is to give you a **PROFITABLE RETURN ON YOUR INVESTMENT** by saving you time and money. *And...*

As you are about to discover, investing in this program "could" turn out to be one of the...

**"Best Investments of Your LIFE!"**

I say "could" because while people have saved and made millions with this package... if you choose **not** to study the material it will do you no good. Just like paying for a membership at a health club... and then never showing up to workout!

Except in this case, we aren't talking about busting your butt in the gym. No. **All we are talking about is two things** (both, simple and easy) which are...

**1.) Read the SECRETS.**

**2.) Act on the SECRETS.**

That's it. That's all that's required. And my God, if someone is **SO LAZY** they can't do that, then they have no one to blame and **NO RIGHT TO COMPLAIN** about their situation, right? So, let's get on with it because you are in for a surprise and here's why:

**Joe Karbo said it best back in 1970...**

*"You want to make enough money so the only problems you have in life... are the ones money won't solve."*

Decades later, I love that saying more then the day I first read it! But I bring it up for a reason. Because you are about to embark on a journey. *And this journey...*

Is about you creating a better life! After all, that's why you bought this program. Because you want a better life, right? **What I appreciate even more, is that you are "taking action" now.** *So here's the deal...*

I have been in your shoes and gone through all the **trial** and **error** to get the results and create what you are looking for...

Therefore, if you wish to ignore this fact (and reinvent the wheel by **not** studying this package) that's up to you, ok? However, if you want me to provide shortcuts to "save you" years of time and "tens of thousands of dollars" on the school of hard knocks... then you are in the **right** place!

Because I have likely read more books than you. Listened to more audio programs than you. Gone to more seminars than you, and... failed at more business ideas than you! So, if you want to succeed faster by **avoiding** the pitfalls, then I am more qualified than almost anyone to help you. *So listen...*

Because I'm here to help you. But if you want to do things the "hard way" I can NOT stop you. So, I suggest you listen closely to what I have to say, because (if you are open minded and teachable) your entire outlook on life is going to change - OVERNIGHT!

Listen... I don't gamble or bet on horse racing. But I have a saying. And that saying is this *"The horse which wins by a nose in a photo finish usually wins 10 TIMES the prize money of second place"* and you know what?

**"Life is NO DIFFERENT!"**

So, my goal is to give you THE EDGE to win... (even if by a nose). *So you can collect 10 times the prize money, ok?*

But with that said... all that glitters is not gold. Because the hardest part about changing your income is changing your thinking. Yes, that will be your biggest struggle... and mine as well. Because in order to *change* your life... you first must *change* things in your life. And the main thing, is your thinking. So please... listen closely, because what I am about to share is easy to miss. *So again (by the grace of God...) please, please, listen closely, ok?*

Like you, I started out buying *dozens* of money making programs. 98% turning out to be nothing but a bunch of "mumbo jumbo."

Before I share my story of wasting a small fortune (in time and money) let me show you something I think you will relate with. *Below is a picture of one weeks worth of junk mail...*

Again, this is only ONE WEEK. And each

piece promises the same thing...

**"A secret way to make thousands of dollars without working. All I have to do is order their program..."**

*Sound familiar?* Well, I can relate. Because for years I have been sending off for these plans. In fact, you might say it became my "hobby" to investigate money making programs. Except to me it was not a hobby.

**"It was a TOTAL OBSESSION!"**

I bought program after program. Went to seminar after seminar. And, invested in idea after idea. And then, when I wasn't rich within a year (after spending thousands of dollars) guess what happened?

**"My friends and family ALIENATED ME."**

Yup... they all thought I was crazy. But what they *did* to me... was even worse. Because they all IGNORED ME. After all, I kept telling them about these great plans I had... but when I wasn't rich by NEXT YEAR they all presumed

I was a loser. *And guess what?*

**"I felt like one..."**

But in the end... the joke was on them. Because it wasn't long after that... I met my mentor (*George*) who changed my life forever.

It was at a seminar. He sat their the entire day not taking a single note (while everyone was feverishly taking notes) *And guess what?* At the end he "bought" copies of two peoples notes.... genius!

Long story short... when I met George and he mentored me, all my years of failure quickly began transforming into **SUCCESS.**

It was like all the years of struggle quickly began PAYING OFF almost overnight. But the biggest thing I learned from *George* was two-fold...

**1.) Just ONE SECRET can change your life.**

and...

**2.) In most cases, you can "prosper" from that SECRET for 10 or 20 years!**

Let me give you an example. I went from failing at everything I touched to earning over $284,000 in a single year... getting completely out of debt... buying a new car... moving into a beautiful home with a gorgeous woman and...

**"All this happened for ONE reason."**

Not because I was smart (I wasn't). Not because I was super motivated (I'm not). And not because I was intelligent (I have no High School diploma). Nope. All this happened for ONE REASON...

Because I had **two** things.

1.) A mentor to GUIDE ME.

2.) Access to SECRETS.

And today, through this course (if you're not a lazy dog unwilling to work, or looking for a winning lottery ticket without buying one...) then I have good news for you.

Because if you can read and follow simple directions... the **"Quick Cash Secrets"** package will change your entire outlook on life overnight. And while not every secret in the package will apply to you... **it only takes one secret to change your life!** So don't be a lazy dog, ok? Please, please, read and apply the secrets! *Like these people did...*

**"Easily earns an EXTRA $10,000 a year..."**

*"One idea from your real cash secrets program earns me an extra $10,000 per year. I had always wondered what the truth was about Government seized merchandise. Your program explained it. And with that information I took care of the rest. Not only has it become a money maker, but it's also fun and I'm anjoying that at my age."*

*Scott*

**"One idea brings in over $3,180 every year..."**

*"I've saved thousands and made thousands with the help of your Real Cash Secrets manual. I think it's the first time I feel I received more than my moneys worth. I have benefited so much. My friends and family have benefited as well. But recently, one idea (about advertising on your car) is now earning me an extra $3,180 every year. And to think not finding this "one idea" three years ago has cost me over $10,000. If you work... this stuff works!"*

*Anita*

**"In less than an hour, qualifies for numerous programs with a cash value over $2,860..."**

*"One day I received a letter in the mail about Real Cash Secrets. Initially, I thought it was a scam. But the more I read, the more it made sense. So, I ordered it. In less than an hour of reading I discovered I qualified for numerous programs with a cash value of over $2,860. Words cannot describe the feelings of learning this... being on a fixed incomem, it came at a time when I really needed it. Can't wait to dig in to the rest of the course. Thanks again..."*

*Carl*

**"$2,000 in 20 minutes from ONE idea..."**

*"As a senior on a fixed income I am looking for all the help I can get. With Real Cash Secrets I discovered an IRS Program which seemed too good to be true. A 50% match to contribute to an IRA. In other words, $2,000 for a $4,000 IRA contribution. Probably the most profitable 20 minutes of my life. And that's only the first idea I have used..."*

*George*

To your future success...

*Tom Bentley*

P.S. Please, get started TODAY... one page at a time, because you will bless the day you did! And, if you have read this far, here is a **special recorded message** for you: **1-801-839-5988**

# Contents

## "Your Quick Cash Secrets Audio Programs.."

We took the best five hours of info from the manual and put it onto 4 audio programs. So you can listen when walking, driving, going to bed or even doing nothing. And, if you don't have an audio CD player, don't worry. We have a solution for that too. Because we had all five hours of the audio programs uploaded to a 24hr replay line and... they are in 20 to 30 minutes increments. So all you need is a telephone and you can CALL IN and here the audios anytime. 24 hours a day. 7 days week. *Simply call the number below and enter the "Access Codes" to hear each segment...*

**Quick Cash Secrets**
**24hr Audio Program**
**Replay Line**

**1-801-810-2020**

**Access Code: 1**
**Access Code: 2**
**Access Code: 3**
**Access Code: 4**
**Access Code: 5**
**Access Code: 6**
**Access Code: 7**
**Access Code: 8**
**Access Code: 9**
**Access Code: 10**
**Access Code: 11**
**Access Code: 12**

You can call anytime. If possible, have a pen and paper handy to take notes, because (like others) you may hear one idea which can change your life.

“

Our current problems cannot be solved with the same level of thinking which created them.

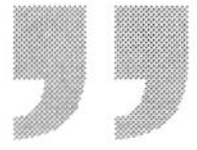

Albert Einstein

# Getting Started

- ☑ A simple way to make $1,700.00 for 3 hours work using your good credit…
- ☑ Math teacher reveals how to instantly reduce your debt $2,500.00 in 30 minutes
- ☑ 8 magic words anyone can use to save $8,000.00 in 4 years or less
- ☑ Ex-Geico employee reveals how to save $300 to $600 per year on insurance without changing carriers
- ☑ The one secret (99% miss) to successfully making money with a home based business
- ☑ The 8 best ways to legitimately earn a second income from home when you are over age 55
- ☑ 7 effective ways to raise up to $1,000.00 in one week or less
- ☑ And more!

TIME FOR ACTION

“

The Pessimist...
*Complains about the wind.*

The Optimist...
*Expects it to change.*

The Realist...
*Adjusts their sails.*

# A simple way to make $1,700.00 for 3 hours work using your good credit… (R001)

The inside strategy I am about to share is probably the easiest way I know to make $1700 (or more) for three hours work I've ever seen. Since you are probably wondering what "the catch" is, I will share it upfront before we proceed. And here it is. To make money with this technique you need one thing: good credit.

Before I get into the details of exactly how to take advantage of this incredible strategy, I would like to share the "back story" of how I discovered it because I think it's important. Why? Because many times in life the only thing which separates the winners from the losers (sadly) is one thing: knowledge.

### $1.5 Million Dollars

For example, did you know the average American will earn about **$1.5 million** during their working lifetime? However, less than 1 in 100 Americans will ever become wealthy. The key deciding factor, in my opinion, is knowledge.

A while back I had an American Express card which had accumulated about 500,000 credit card rewards points (a massive amount).

While at the golf course one day, a guy in our group was talking about how he SOLD his points and naturally my radar went on.

So I asked "who" he sold the points to and "how" did he do it.

In short order he put me on the phone with a 'point broker' in Las Vegas. They asked me how many points I had. I told him 500,000. They asked me what type of credit card they were on. I told them American Express. He asked to verify the points by emailing him a screenshot of my rewards portal via the Internet, and I did.

He informed me that my 500,000 points had a cash value of $7,500!

As you can imagine, I nearly fell out of my chair! I said "did you say $7,500?"

He replied "correct, $7500 yes."

All I had to do was transfer them the points, which was as easy as some clicks on the SmartPhone screen, and they would wire into my bank account the full $7,500 for the points!

### The secret to getting 100,000 points fast

But you don't have to wait years to accumulate points, because the next insider secret I'm going to reveal will take you only a few hours work.

First, if you're not familiar with credit card rewards points, they are basically a gimmick to get people to sign up for a credit card or to spend more money with a particular card. You've probably received credit card offers in the mail which offer you points just for signing up and that is the key here, **huge reward bonuses for simply getting a new card.**

Once you meet the criteria for the bonus points, you turn around and sell them on the secondary market like I did (fast and easy cash).

Now not all reward points can be sold, but of the ones that can, the most coveted are credit card rewards points in order to purchase flights at a discount. Because the best use of credit card rewards points is for first-class plane tickets and international travel. Remember this because it's a major key of how this works.

### American Express and Chase Sapphire Preferred

While the market is always changing, at the time of this writing the points you want to rack up are **American Express business points** as well as the **American Express Starwood** —

program. The other best program is **Chase — Sapphire preferred**. And most anyone with decent credit can obtain one of these credit cards.

And the way you get a ton of points fast is by applying for one of these cards and then meeting the minimum criteria, which usually means a couple months of using the card for a specific minimum amount because…

…an introductory offer for an American Express business or Starwood credit card, a Chase Sapphire preferred credit card or any other credit card you may find in the future has these 2 things in common.

1) Rewards points you can sell for cash.

and

2) A program which will bonus you 50,000 to 100,000 points as a new cardholder.

### How To Get These Cards

In the past, you could just go on the Internet. But today, that doesn't work because too many people have worn out the welcome mat by discussing these programs online (remember, we're telling you insider secrets and as soon as one door is barred, another opportunity opens up.)

Here's exactly what you'll need to do...

Both American Express and Chase tend to target **business owners with decent credit** to solicit new credit card offers. <u>These offers are delivered only one way: direct mail.</u> In fact, I have not seen 100,000 point bonus program to new cardholder's online in years. But I see them in direct mail all the time. Here's how to get one sent to you.

The first thing you need to do if you don't have a business is simply create one by taking your last name and adding the word "enterprises" onto it. Of course, if you already have a business you can skip this step.

The second thing you need to do is <u>subscribe to three business magazines</u>. I would suggest picking three which you're actually interested in. Don't just pick three that I give you. Although *Entrepreneur, Inc.* and *Fast Company* magazines are great examples, you could choose the *Wall Street Journal, Investor's Business Daily, Fortune* – you get the idea – subscribe to business publications and have them sent to Your Business Name.

As soon as you start your subscriptions, your name will be rented to direct mailers and all you have to do is wait for a great offer to come. And they will come fast.

When you receive a 50,000 to 100,000 point bonus credit card offer, simply apply for the card. If your credit is decent, you will be approved. The only thing you want to be careful about is the terms and conditions to qualify for the bonus points (every card will have them). Usually they work like this.

The credit card company will ask you to charge $500 per month for three months without missing a payment in order to qualify for your 50,000 to 100,000 bonus reward points. Just follow their program and you'll get rewarded handsomely with bonus points.

### How To Turn Your Bonus Points Into CASH

When you meet these criteria they will credit the points to your account. Once the points are credited you can do one of two things to sell your points for cash. If you wish, you can call us for a referral and we will gladly give you the company we sell our points to. I do not want to list it here because if circumstances change I cannot change it. We have been dealing with our contacts for years.

The other thing you can do is simply go online and search "earn rewards cash". My only caveat would be that you deal with the company which will pay you in advance for the points or have some type of written agreement in place. Like any business, there are some shady people in the credit card rewards game.

At the time of this writing the going rate for 100,000 points for the previously mentioned cards is a whopping $1,700.

Give it a go, as this will be the fastest and easiest $1,700 most people will ever make.

## Math teacher reveals how to instantly reduce your debt $2,500.00 in 30 minutes (R003)

What if I told you there was a legal way to reduce your debt by up to $2500.00 in less than 30 minutes and all it required was a telephone? Sound too good to be true? You are in for a pleasant surprise…

I once interviewed a man who is a banking executive for a large multinational corporation you would know the name of instantly if I told you. In fact, you probably drive by one of their locations every day. This man used to oversee the daily operations of over $10 billion in annual credit card revenue.

He also managed over 2500 customer service representatives located in the United States and two continents. He even wrote the security protocol for hiring these people. He was literally a billion-dollar banking executive.

I got to know him from a 3 hour interview during the creation of an audio cd for the **"Fight Debt and Win"** coaching program.

**http://FightDebtandWin.com**

One of the things he shared was that every financial institution which extends credit does so knowing a small percentage of customers will default.

More importantly, they know a percentage of these customers can be "salvaged" by placing them on payment terms so they do NOT go into default. This is *found money* for the corporation. As a result, every bank has programs to help consumers "who qualify" for some type of hardship program.

It makes sense, because banks want to save customers from going into default. They know customer "default" means the company gets nothing and nobody wins. This is a fact few people know about and even fewer take advantage of. But it can help them get out of debt at up to 10 times faster. Let me explain.

### How to Take Advantage of Secret Programs

You see, banks have programs—programs they don't advertise—programs which are designed to help people pay off their debt (instead of default) because default equals lost profits.

Obviously, it's better for the bank if you're in debt. But at some point the bank may realize that they will be better served in the long run by giving you a break. If they bury you in interest, it may eventually hamper your ability to pay them and reduce the likelihood that you will get loans from them in the future. Banks don't make money churning their customer base, they make money lending to the same customer again and again.

### How Steve saved $9,400.00 with nothing but his telephone

Here's an example.

Steve was a client we helped save $9,400 in interest with only a few phone calls. Here's what happened. Steve had a credit account he owed $13,000 on. The interest rate was 16.9%. By using the strategies (I'm about to share) he got that interest rate reduced to 4.5%.

This instantly saved him $9,400 in interest. And you, with a little bit of effort, can do the same thing. Here's why…

It's in the banks best interest to do everything they can to keep you from defaulting. The trick is, you have to communicate with them in a way to let them know you are sincere and telling the truth and not trying to scam them.

All you have to do is be persistent and follow the steps.

Write yourself a simple little script. A script makes it easy to say the right things, and harder to say the wrong things. Your script should say something like this:

"Hello, I've recently had a cut in pay and am working to manage my bills so that I don't fall behind. I would like to know if you can lower my interest rate."

Now take your script and call your credit card company by dialing the number on the back of the card. This is simple, honest, and quick… and your script immediately tells the person on the phone what it is you're after. They either will help you or they will not. If they can't, ask them to get someone who can. This might mean talking to a different department, or calling a different number.

Now, before I explain the next part, you should know that most banks have special programs for people in trouble. These programs may cut the interest rate in half, or even eliminate the interest altogether. As part of these special programs, the account may be closed or you may have to pay it off in a shorter time—but the benefit you get often outweigh these minor drawbacks.

Remember, you don't necessarily need a special program to come out ahead. Many times you can get your interest rate lowered substantially by just asking and proving your hardship case.

Now, one of two things typically happens. The bank says yes and lowers your interest rate, offering you a slightly higher fixed rate, a slightly lower variable rate, or some other combination. Or the bank will say "NO", but in a few short weeks you will get a letter informing you that they have lowered your interest rates!

**You Win… Banks Win… Here's Why…**

This is such a big winner for most people; you can hardly afford not to give it a try. One or two phone calls, a little patience, and you may save yourself thousands of dollars!

Proving your case is key, more proof equals better outcome faster.

Just look at how long it takes to pay off $13,000 in credit card debt with the interest rate at 16.9% versus calling the bank and getting it lowered to 4.25%.

In this case the few minutes it took to place a couple of calls to the bank resulted in saving $8,310.13 in interest. How often in life can you earn the equivalent of $1,000 per hour!

| | INTEREST RATE | DEBT AMOUNT | PAYMENT AMOUNT | MONTHLY INTEREST | TOTAL INTEREST | PAY OFF TIME |
|---|---|---|---|---|---|---|
| | 16.9% | $13,000.00 | $260.00 | $183.08 | $9,643.47 | 7 YEARS, 4 MONTHS |
| ➡ | 4.25 | $13,000.00 | $260.00 | $46.04 | $1,333.34 | 5 YEARS, 8 MONTHS |

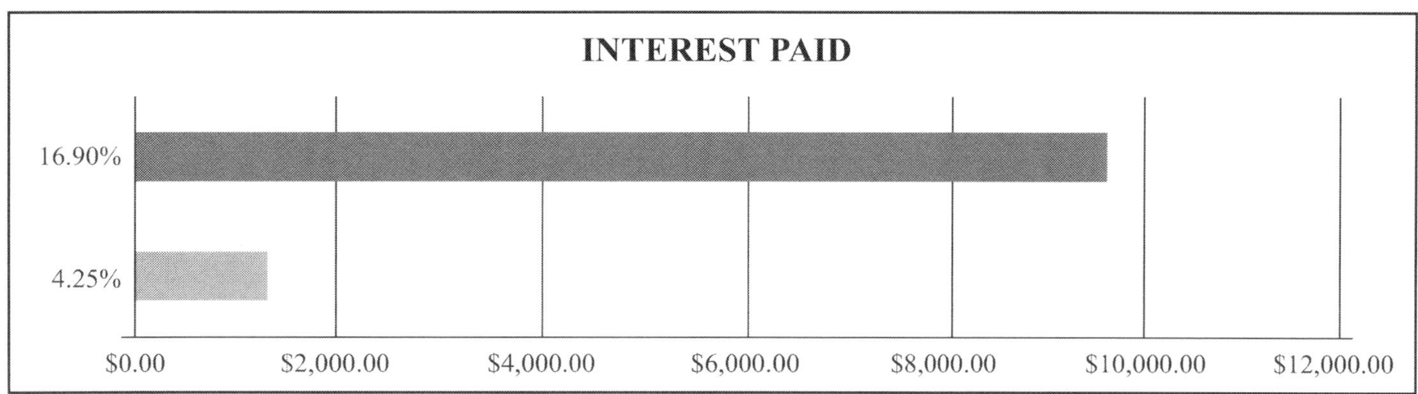


But remember, the key to getting your interest rate lowered this drastically is to be "pleasantly" persistent.

During your first call, the bank may budge just a little on the interest rate reduction, and thank them, but remind them that due to your current situation (job loss, work reduction, business setbacks, family health issue, etc.) you are still overburdened and may find it difficult to impossible to keep the payments up

When you call back again, your comments will have been noted on the account. If you asked the name and extension of the bank rep on the first call, try and reach them again, otherwise the notes on the account will back up your 'story.'

At many banks you can call and get the same rep who will be reviewing notes from the previous call. Speaking to the same rep will also help form an emotional bond, allowing the rep to exercise their leeway in giving you a break.

Remember, stick to your story. Don't change it unless there is something to add, such as after you lost your job your spouse had health issues. Be consistent, but do news updates that will support "why" you need your interest rate lowered.

Be 'pleasantly persistent.' Politely say, *"I'm trying as hard as I can but as I told you, because of (your story), I may not be able to pay this off without help. Can't you help me by lowering my interest rate?"*

Don't give up or be intimidated. The banks do this all the time, they just don't automatically – that's where your persistence comes into play.

Again, this is a **win-win** for everyone. Continuing to call, backing up your story with proof (job loss, medical condition, etc.) can even help drive your interest rate to <u>zero</u>. It happens every day in the U.S. for those consumers who take the time to pursue this strategy.

## 8 magic words anyone can use to save $8,000.00 in 4 years or less (R004)

There is a simple method I've used to save $150 at Best Buy of all places, and countless hundreds—even thousands—over the last several years. One friend of mine reported that he received an extra 10% ($300) on an automobile

insurance claim with this method. Here's how it works:

For any transaction where a price or quote is given, **do the following when you are given the quote/price:**

1. Flinch.

2. Immediately ask: "Is that the best you can do today?" Another variation is "Is that the best you can do for me?"

That's it. Your job is to ask a simple question. And that one question can save you thousands of dollars.

The key comes down to **understanding what negotiable expenses are** especially compared to non-negotiable expenses.

An expense should be considered *negotiable* if there is even the slightest chance that it might be changed or altered one way or the other. A negotiable expense is one you can do something about.

A lot of people feel hopeless with certain expenses. Sometimes they don't realize how negotiable their seemingly fixed expenses are. And you don't even have to ask if it's negotiable. You don't have to say, "Can you come down on the price?" You don't have to ask for more of this or less of that.

All you have to do is say:

***"Is that the best you can do today?"***

In many cases, when you ask this question, by the look on **the person's face or the sound of their voice you will quickly know the answer to the question**. You'll know that it is NOT, in fact, the best they can do for you.

What is even better is… when it isn't the very best they can do… Rather than simply say "No," many people will instead sweeten the offer so that it is indeed the **best** they can do.

Try it and see for yourself. Ask a simple question. Save thousands. It couldn't be any easier.

**Bonus: How to make the most of this strategy…**

Here's a "power-user" approach that will help you make the most of this strategy. It's still very simple. Here's exactly what to do:

1. Write down all of your expenses that might be negotiable. Even include ones that you're not sure about, but that it might be worth a try.
2. Total up the estimated annual cost of those expenses.
3. Apply this strategy systematically to each one of those expenses, and see how much money you can save.

For example, if you find you have $10,000 per year in negotiable expenses, even 10% savings across the board would give you $1,000 per year in savings. **Using this systematic approach, it is possible to save thousands of dollars for the long haul on everything from credit cards to cell phones to plumbers.**

## Ex-Geico employee reveals how to save $300 to $600 per year on insurance (R020)

Cedric, a former Geico employee and friend of the "Fight Debt and Win" program, sent us a letter recently offering some **helpful advice for those of us who would like to save some money on our homeowners and auto insurance costs.**

For those with full coverage car insurance or homeowner's policies, the **deductibles can make a huge difference in the amount of money you pay.** According to Cedric, there can be a substantial difference in premium with slightly higher deductibles, and it's smart to get quotes with several deductibles so that you can figure out where the real price breaks are.

For example, next time you get a homeowners insurance quote, find out the premium difference between $500 and $2500 deductibles. You could also check $500 or $1500 amounts, depending on what is offered. You'll be surprised at what a difference a larger deductible can make. **Savings of as much as $600 a year are possible if you apply this strategy across all of your insurance policies**.

And think about how those savings can add up:

$400/yr X 5 YEARS = $2,000

$500/yr X 5 YEARS = $2,500

$600/yr X 5 YEARS = $3,000

Want to see for yourself how much you can save? You can usually save a lot using this method without even changing carriers. **Call your insurance company right now and ask them for a quote at a higher deductible than what you currently have**. One short phone call could end up saving you thousands of dollars over time!

## The one secret (99% miss) to making money with a home based business (R027)

Having invested in dozens of opportunities myself, I can truthfully say, there is a **secret** which separates a money-maker from a scam.

If a person runs television ads lying to consumers and making fraudulent claims they usually wind up in prison (Kevin Trudeau was sentenced to 10 years for his diet book after being *repeatedly* warned by regulators).

But a person can put a video up on YouTube for free (a popular video sharing website) and blatantly **lie to consumers for years and get away with it.**

As an entrepreneur striving for a better life, you can feel compelled to research or investigate every opportunity which comes your way. But how do you find a money-maker while avoiding all the scams?

### The Secret to Making Money...

If you want the secret to making money, big money and creating real wealth, here it is: you need to focus on **SOLVING PROBLEMS**. Yes, solving problems is the <u>key</u> and here's why...

People only spend money to solve problems. And the greater the problem the **<u>more</u>** money they will spend. It may sound *simple*, but you won't believe how many entrepreneurs get this wrong. And when you get it wrong, it's not only painful, but also **very expensive**. Let me share a true story...

### $4,000.00 Water Machines from Japan...

I know a man who invested over $10,000 into a business which sold $4,000 water machines from Japan. I tried to advise him against this decision for a number of reasons.

The first was the fact he was investing this money into a multilevel or network marketing business. Studies have shown the **success rate of multilevel network marketing is less than 1% (about 0.3% to be exact)**. While for conventional business (based on statistics from the small business administration) the success rate is **over 50 times higher**.

The second issue was the $4,000 water machines did **<u>not</u>** solve problems other machines could not solve for one-tenth of the price.

Blinded by greed the man continued to argue. Because the problem he claimed to be solving was *"helping people make extra money by getting into the water machine business!"*

I advised him to do the math. To start with, *how many people can afford a $4000.00 water machine?* For most, it's like buying a car you can't drive. I also asked him how many other 'reps' selling the machines would he need to make any real money?

**Of course, the deadliest question (he could not answer) was how much money in marketing it would take to sell one of these $4000.00 water machines?**

He still didn't listen, because he was blinded by greed and the false promise of making big money fast. As a result, he lost $10,000.00 and still has a $4,000 water machine in his kitchen.

**Look for opportunities that solve real problems...**

The moral of the story? Look for opportunities that solve real problems and while many folks are truly concerned about the purity of their water, they are not likely to look for a solution that costs a month's pay.

If you are looking to start a full-time or part-time business, **look for real opportunities which solve real problems (not "get rich quick" schemes)**. Below are just a few opportunities you could start tomorrow with little cash and lots of upside potential.

- **Auto Detailing**
- **Carpet Cleaning**
- **House or Office Cleaning**
- **Personal Trainer**
- **Personal Debt Consultant**
- **Dog Grooming / Training / Sitting or Clean Up**

Each of these businesses have one thing in common, they solve a real problem for consumers. So the next time you get an offer in the mail or are emailed a link to a video about another "get rich quick" scheme... Ask yourself "what problem am I solving?"

One of the most repeated scams is the "stuffing envelopes" opportunity. What problem are you solving here? There is only one answer: to give the scammer money.

Or, you will rarely go a month without someone trying to recruit you into a multilevel or network marketing opportunity. **The fact is, only 0.3% of participants make money in MLM or Network Marketing.**

Your chances of becoming a professional blackjack player are over **five times higher** than making money in MLM or Network Marketing. Your chance for succeeding at one of the problem solving businesses mentioned above is over **50 times higher.**

So remember, to make money and create real wealth you do **NOT** want to focus on money. You want to focus on **solving problems**. Unless your market has a problem, it will be very hard to get them to spend money.

**$2.8 BILLION "Dog Poop" Market...**

Let me give you an example of how powerful and profitable this whole "solving problems" concept can be when applied to something as simple as cleaning up after dogs. Yep, dog poop.

DoodyCalls.com is in the pet "waste removal" business. The market is now estimated to be over **$2.8 billion per year**. That's billion, with a "B". Don't laugh. Jacob D'Aniello, Co-Founder and CEO of Doody Calls is cleaning up (no pun intended). He started by placing classified ads in local newspapers and guess what? The phone began to ring like crazy!

**Over 50 franchisees and 5 million in revenue!**

From the beginning his focus was to build the business into a national brand and franchise it. And franchise it he did (just 48 months later). Today Doody Calls has over 50 franchisees. And recently did over $5,000,000.00 in revenue. In many areas, dog poop cleanup is more profitable than pool cleaning for the simple fact there are more dogs than swimming pools and cleaning up dog poop doesn't require chemicals.

**No one has factored in the cost to get a new customer...**

Something else to keep in mind is your business margins. That's another way the MLM / Network Marketing people can blind you.

You are offered to buy a product for $100 which you can offer to the public for $150. Wow you think... I make a quick fifty bucks per unit. Sounds great on paper, but there's only one problem...

No one has factored in the cost to get a new customer. And in most businesses, the number one challenge you'll face is that of getting a new customer.

**Take Round Table Pizza or Starbucks Coffee.**

**How much do you think a large pizza from Round Table Pizza costs?**

The pizza sells for about $25. The cost (and this is coming from a friend who is a manager) is about one dollar. Yes, one dollar.

Now let's talk about Starbucks Coffee. What are their costs? As far as the cup and ingredients, it's about $.40. And they still sell it for around $4.00. That is a markup of ten-to-one. Of course, there are huge labor and energy costs as well as other overhead. But with a healthy market, operational costs are covered and there's profit left over.

**My point is simple:**

**Most businesses need margins of at least 3 to 1 or better.**

This is a reason why MLM / Network marketing has such a high failure rate. Have you ever noticed how overpriced the products are? We won't even talk about the small commissions.

Remember, thin margins and small commissions don't leave enough money for sales and marketing expenses to get new customers.

Still if you are convinced you have lucked upon a wonderful opportunity, do a little "test" marketing. Run a classified ad and gauge the response. Or buy just a handful of the product and set up at the local flea market.

Once you get real feedback from real customers you can reasonably evaluate any opportunity the market offers...

**The Truth?**

**You can make money in a home based business if it meets a few criteria.**

1. Your product or service solves a real problem the market has.
2. **You have a 3-to-1 margin (or better).**
3. The business can generate enough profit to sustain a marketing program.

There are also several current books on the subject including but not limited to;

- The Best Home Businesses for People 50+
- Home-Based Business For Dummies
- 5 Proven Methods For Making $1,000+ Per Month With Websites
- Making Money from Home: How to Run a Successful Home-Based Business
- How to Start a Successful Home Based Business
- Selling on eBay: 7 Steps to Selling $5,000 Per Month on eBay

A great place to get practical business advice is at **www.SBA.gov** and then search "Find a Mentor". Or you can call: **1-800-827-5722.**

## The 8 best ways to earn a second income from home when you are over age 50 (R056)

Who *doesn't* want to earn a "second income" working from home?

But to do so, you need to avoid the "get rich quick schemes" (and today) they are everywhere. If you buy into the hype, you will likely lose your money. The fact is – many people **do** "earn a second income" working from home.

But another fact is – almost all of them did not do an online search and buy into a "get rich quick" scheme such as *envelope stuffing, cash gifting or MLM/Network Marketing.*

Here's the good news…

**You Can Earn A Second Income Working At Home and Here's How to Do It...**

In order to work from home successfully, you need to meet a couple of requirements…

1. In order to work from home, you need to have some sort of **marketable skill**. It can be something like writing, editing, or creating graphics and logos. Others do well performing administrative tasks like organizing spreadsheets, compiling databases or formatting reports.

   Then there is the in-demand SmartPhone programming or website creation.

   Maybe you're a people person who is capable of providing good **customer service**.

   If you have a pleasant speaking voice and some basic equipment, you can even make money recording "voice-overs" for businesses. They are always looking for someone to sound professional for their **business voice mail** and often times they run radio commercials or videos on their website and need someone like you to do the announcing.

2. In most cases, you will need to be comfortable operating a computer and able to trouble shoot the normal day-to-day headaches like printer problems, software updates, etc. True, computers are getting easier to use, but you'll still need to handle some problems yourself or at least have someone near who can come fix the computer or do diagnostics over the Internet.

Now, let's talk about **specific work-at-home opportunities, many you can start doing as soon as you finish reading this report**.

**Freelancing.** There are numerous websites that specialize in helping freelancers find work, and helping people in need of help find the right freelancer. Go and study these sites:

- **www.Upwork.com**
- **www.Guru.com**
- **www.Odesk.com**
- **www.PeoplePerHour.com**

I'll warn you… the competition on the above websites is brutal in *certain* categories. But if you have the right skills, it is perfectly possible to make $500 to $1500, or more each month by doing work on freelance websites alone.

Although computer programming, graphics and other skills can be outsourced cheaply overseas, when it comes to writing and editing – employers have to use native English speakers.

You may ghost write a book. Or create a short report on dog training. Even create a flyer for the local landscaper. And on top of all that is everyone needing quality content for websites.

In fact, **thousands of people earn a FULL-TIME living working from home** on such sites. Just visit each site and look at the categories of jobs. Browse the job postings. Look at the freelancer profiles. You never know what may spark an idea that will change your life forever.

**In-demand work-at-home opportunities**

**Customer Service and Similar Jobs.** You may not know it, but there are a number of companies who hire at home workers for real "at home" jobs in the area of customer service and tech support. I have a friend that does tech support for **Oracle** from his home.

Some companies will want you to be an independent contractor (which they might call a "1099 employee") in which case you're responsible for paying all taxes. Other companies will want to hire you as an actual employee, and will offer benefits such as health insurance and vacation like Oracle does for my friend.

Here are three legitimate and tested companies that seek at-home customer service and tech support agents. These companies work with other large companies to provide quality customer service.

1. **Alpine Access - www.Sykes.com**
2. **LiveOps - Join.LiveOps.com**
3. **Arise - AriseWorkFromHome.com**

The pay can vary, but generally is in the range of **$10-$18 per hour.** For certain technical positions, the pay can be much higher.

*What should you be prepared for?* At any of these places, be prepared for **real** expectations like there would be at any other job. There will be applications, requirements, and other normal things you would do when applying for a job.

Also, **don't** expect to take customer service calls with a kid hanging on your hip, a dog barking in the background, or any other noise. You'll need a room where you can close the door unless you live alone and can totally control your environment.

**Transcription Jobs.** If you can type fast, have a good ear for English or a second language, and a good instinct for speech and the written word, you might consider doing transcription work from home.

**Here are three places that hire home-workers for transcribing audios and videos:**

- Tigerfish - **www.TigerFish.com/employment**
- UbiQus - **www.Ubiqus.com**
- Cambridge Transcriptions - **www.ctran.com/employment**

**Sales Jobs.** There are wide varieties of sales jobs that allow people to work from home. Two examples: Insurance agents and Real Estate agents. Certain other sales jobs offer at-home work with or **without** travel. While you may work "out of" your home, you have to leave to go on sales appointments and meet with clients.

For insurance and real estate jobs, your state will probably require licensing. This is usually a simple matter of studying independently or taking a class, and then taking a test to get your license.

And there are many other sales jobs that you can do **from home.**

The easiest way is to search your local classifieds or Internet job board for a sales position that interests you. One of the financial networks recently reported that as the U.S. continues to experience economic turbulence, the single biggest job they are having trouble filling is in sales.

**And Then, Consider Asking Your Present Employer if You Can Telecommute...**

This is a possibility that few people ever consider, but it's a big opportunity in the right circumstances. If you are at a job doing work that can be done on a computer, over the internet, or otherwise from home, then consider pitching the idea of "working from home" to your employer.

Many companies allow their employees to telecommute from home at least part of the time, and those same companies have found that people who work from home are happier, **more efficient,** and just all-around better workers. This will give you some "sales pitch" you might need to convince your employer to give it a shot.

**If you plan on approaching your employer, follow these steps.**

- **Have your ducks in a row in advance.** Make sure you can use and understand the technology (such as logmein.com) that may be needed to do your job from home.
- **Be open to compromises.** Don't say "Let me work from home or I'll quit." Instead, be open to working a day or two at home, or starting slow, or other arrangements that might make your employer more comfortable.
- **Prove yourself** as an honest and worthy employee first. When you mess up, tell someone. Don't let them find out on their own. Be transparent, honest, and most importantly… be a diligent worker.
- **If you do get the opportunity** to work from home, make it well-worth your employer's while. Show them that it wasn't a mistake by doing an amazing job.

I personally know of four people who have secured a "work from home" gig from their **current job** using the steps above. Give it a try and you may start enjoying working at home.

And at the time of this writing, a news story ran estimating that some **53 million** Americans are 'freelancing' either as additional income or their sole source of survival.

Because of computers, the Internet and smartphones – there has never been a better time to enjoy the freelance life from the comfort of your own home.

Plus, being a senior means you've got experience. Heck, you even have a lot of experience in your 'hobbies' and many people are searching online every single day looking for advice **you can provide.**

## 8 effective ways to raise up to $1,258.00 in one week or less (R016)

**If you need money fast**, then there are a few dependable ways you can get it. Most people are capable of coming up with a lot more money faster than they realize.

**First**, you should make it your goal to use your age and your place in life to your *advantage*. If you are young and in school, you will have advantages that others won't. If you are older and retired, you will have advantages that others won't.

**Second**, you should understand that raised money doesn't necessarily mean "earned" money. You can get money without earning it. And coming up with $1,000 in a few short days doesn't have to have anything to do with *earning* money.

**Third**, you must be willing to accept the opportunities right in front of you. Take stock of your situation, and then come up with a plan, rather than come up with a plan and try to bend and shape your situation to fit your "ideal" plan.

**Here are 8 creative ways to raise money fast:**

**1. <u>Liquidate Excess Items:</u>** Sadly, most people laugh at this one... but the reality is most people have lots of excess "stuff" they can liquidate for instant cash. Many have raised from $1,000.00 to $3,5000.00 in one week. The steps are easy...

First, gather ALL your excess stuff. This

means anything you can part with for instant cash. Second, research what each item is worth. You can start with searches on *eBay.com, Craigslist.org* and even *Amazon.com* but better tools for certain valauables will be listed later. Third, one you have assessed values, take pictures and list on eBay.com, craigslist.org or amazon.com. Or, sell locally.

Be careful of scams and always meet people in person if selling locally and only accept cash. With this method you will be amazed by **TWO** things. 1.) What some items are worth. And, 2.) How much all the "stuff" adds up to when sold. Again, many people have raised from $1,000.00 to $3,500.00 in one week... even more exciting is...

**2. Cashing in on antiques and collectibles:** Again, many will laugh at this. But one reader in his 60's earned **$1,200 in 5 days** without leaving his home. How? He learned how to **PROPERLY VALUE** antiques and collectibles which had been sitting in his garage. Turned out a "Tea Kettle" from the early 1900's was worth an instant $1,200.00 on ebay. And this was just the beginning...

Because there are a number of tools you can use. Many people are "sitting on a fortune" and don't even know it. One way to assess value is to search for items on eBay.com. But an even better way is to use a local expert as well as sites like: **http://ValueMyStuff.com - http://Lofty.com - http://Kovels.com http://BusaccaGallery.com.**

One woman found that by selling off her silver dollars she had collected, she was able to turn them into a quick $800! Another man had a vinyl record collection "conservatively" estimated to be worth over $5,000.00! What cash value are you sitting on? You will never know until research it...

**3. Hold a garage sale.** This is instant guaranteed "fast money" for cleaning up the house. In most cases $1,000.00 or more can be raised depending on the number of items you have around. The best part is that many local newspapers and websites (like Craigslist.org) accept free ads for sales. And never forget local signs on the street a few days before. Don't laugh and don't forget these online advertising sources when you are counting your cash **AFTER** your sale: *http://GSALR.com - http://GarageSalesTracker.com - http://YardSaleSearch.com*

**4. Back Pay.** Employers will often hold back a weeks pays when you start a new job. If you're comfortable asking, most times you can get them to **"release"** this pay to you. Some have raised $1,100.00 or more with this method.

**5. Create EXTRA employer value.** We just talked about getting "back pay" released. But one of the more exciting methods of generating instant cash is that of creating **EXTRA** employer value. Here's how it works. You find any problem your employer is failing to solve for current customers. You then offer to "create" this solution for a cut of the profits. It sounds complex but it's simple. One man created a **full-time** enterprise out of this single idea. He worked for a restaruant with great food and a loyal following. However, the establishment offered *nothing* in the way of catering or corporate events. So, he created that division of the business and shares in the profits with the owner. It's a win-win.

**6. Rent Out Rooms:** No. It's not what you think. I am talking about renting rooms out short term for premium prices. And you set the price. In the past 5 years over 575,000 people have turned to http://Airbnb.com to rent out all or a portion of their homes to its' **10 million** registered users. A room in your home may be worth $200 per night. That's $1,400.00 per week and you have control of how you screen the guests. Naturally, you want to do all you can to be comfortable with who you are short term renting to. But hundreds of thousands have been successful. *Why not you?*

**7. Get paid as a consultant or tutor.** You'd

be amazed how much quick cash can be made by just reaching out to those around you and offering your services as an expert in your field. One of the easiest ways is working as a consultant or tutor. It could be computers, cooking or calligraphy. One man earns **$35 per hour** tutoring a second language. Whatever you do for work is **YOUR SKILL** and someone is probably willing to pay you for it.

**8. Liquidating your silver and gold.** If you've received anything made of silver or gold as a gift—consider selling it as a way to get fast cash. In order to get the most for it you will need to do some **research** and get at least three opinions of the value. An excellent book to help you get **THE MOST** for your gold and silver is *"Protecting the Family Jewels" by Joe Brandt.*

## The easiest way to make up to $500 on a weekend without leaving home (R083)

*Need cash fast? Want to make money from home?* Then consider the humble (but mighty) **garage sale!**

The thing to understand about garage sales is that there is a definite **science to it**. Some garage sales make more money than others. And those that make more money do so *because* they have *certain characteristics*.

The best garage sales follow the rules below. Just follow these guidelines all the way to the bank. *(One stay at home mom raised over $900 for a new dishwasher using this strategy.)*

**Here's how it works:**

1. **Signs.** Place your garage sale signs at strategic intersections. Make sure that the location is clearly marked on the sign, and clearly readable from someone driving by in a car. Also post your garage sale on Craigslist, Facebook, and other applicable websites. And don't forget newspapers. Some newspapers will advertise a garage sale for free!
2. **Stuff.** The most successful garage sales have a LOT of *stuff*. If you don't have enough of your own, then ask your friends and family if they have anything you can take off their hands for them. Step 1 and rule 1 is that you need a LOT of STUFF.
3. **Organization.** Having lots of stuff is important. It should also be organized. You should have plenty of tables with stuff spread out on them so that people don't have to bend down to the ground or sift through boxes. Everything should be marked with a price. You should also have boxes of items where everything in the box is $2, $1, $3, etc. Clothes should be hanging up on clothes rods or sorted by size and type, and folded neatly on tables.
4. **Strategy.** You want to display your items to entice the most buyers—and the right buyers. Kids stuff, for example, should be at kid's level. All of the same rules apply for organization, but just do it on a smaller kid-friendly scale. Items of interest to men should be grouped with other items of interest to men, etc. Also, don't be afraid to bargain with people—but let them ask you first. If someone says "Will you consider taking less for this?" Answer "yes" if you can. Don't, however, try to offer them a lower price on an item that they are looking at. **Wait for them** to decide against it, or to ask you about it, and then you can start bargaining.
5. **Security.** Very expensive items should usually be closer to the cashier to discourage theft. The cash box should not have a large amount of cash in it. Have a trusted friend or relative take the cash from the cash box and lock it away safely inside or at a different location. Don't accept checks. Get

help from friends and family. Have several adults at your garage sale at all times if possible.

6. **Courtesy.** Offer plastic bags or paper bags, or even boxes for people coming to your garage sale. **If you give them a paper bag to shop with, they are more likely to put something in it.** Be friendly to all of your visitors—even the ones that don't buy. Always invite people back. Tell them you have more stuff coming if you do, or anything else that might interest them enough to bring them back.

7. **Timing.** Pay attention to the best garage sale times for your area. In some areas, the "big" garage sale day is Thursdays. Other areas it's Fridays. Others yet, Saturdays.

"You were the one who said we couldn't afford a new vacuum, so stop moaning and suck harder!"

In some areas it's customary to open the garage sale at 7:00 AM, and in other areas later starts are more common. Do what's right for your area, so that you will attract the most shoppers.

8. **Selling More.** Here's a powerful way to move more items and really go out with a bang. The last few hours of the last day of your garage sale, tell everyone who comes that they can fill up a bag for $1 or $2. If there is anything of high value that you would want to try selling on Craigslist or elsewhere, remove it from the sale before doing this. Many visitors will take you up on this offer, and some will even tell friends or family about it. <u>It's a great way to get rid of stuff in the last few hours of a garage sale.</u>

9. **Craigslist.** One final step to getting rid of your garage sale stuff is to offer everything left over on a website like Craigslist for a fixed price. Sometimes people will even come to your garage sale towards the end and offer to buy everything left for $100, or something like that. In either case, it's great. Move more stuff. Make more money. Make the most of the garage sale.

10. **Ad Text.** Any ad that mentions the words "Garage Sale" in conjunction with possibly high value words (i.e. "Jewelry", "Xbox", etc.) will usually get great results. People will flock to your garage sale!

**Helpful Hint:** Don't forget to check with your local city to make sure you get any permits required for a garage sale. <u>Some cities require permits, some do not.</u>

## The one proven way to get PAID to clean your house (R002)

*How much stuff do you have sitting in storage? How much storage space do you have in your house?*

For many people, the answer to both questions is "a lot!"

In America, we often find ourselves having too much stuff. In fact, some of us just plain-and-simple have too much *junk*. There is good news though. The government will pay you to get rid of your junk.

How do you get the government to pay you to clean your house and get rid of your junk?

There are two steps:

1. Itemize deductions.
2. Donate your junk.

Goodwill donations and donations to other non-profits are **tax deductible**. When you donate an item, the value of the donation is used for tax deduction purposes. The value that matters here isn't really the "garage sale" value. So don't think "my junk isn't worth enough." No, instead the value here is a reasonable estimate of the "fair market value" of the item. In other words, what might the market pay for it? Most goodwill and other stores offer guides for estimating the values of donated goods. Here are some examples:

- Computer monitors: $10 to $150
- Couches and Love Seats: $30 to $150
- Children's clothes: $1-$15
- CDs and DVDs: $1-$5

A lot of us have a lot of junk lying around. And you can donate it to get tax deductions. The key is to keep close track of the values, and to itemize deductions. If you don't itemize your deductions but take the standard one, then you won't be able to apply your charity giving.

The key to getting credit for deductions is keeping track of it all. You've got to keep track of the estimated value of things donated. And you've got to keep track of tax receipts from the non-profit that you donated to. If you can do this, you could lower your taxes by hundreds or even thousands of dollars—and effectively get the government to *pay you* to clean your house!

**Important Note:** In order for a donation to be tax deductible, it must be to a non-profit such as Goodwill or The Salvation Army and the donated item must be considered to be in "good condition".

**Helpful Hint:** Take a selection of quality items and either sell them at a garage sale or via eBay or Craigslist. Then donate the rest and keep track of your deductions. Also, be sure to check with your tax advisor before using this strategy. The average income from a garage sale is $500 to $700... add this to the tax savings, and you have a winner.

## City worker reveals sneaky (but legal) way to save thousands in property taxes (R023)

Have you ever challenged your property tax assessment? Only about 1% of property owners do. The other 99% are leaving money on the table. **Here's how we know.**

Rhonda is a county worker in the mid-west. She deals with various aspects of property tax assessments for the county. Rhonda says you'd be surprised how often people win property tax assessment challenges. 99% of property owners never challenge assessments they can win.

Here's what we learned from Rhonda:

- Like other interactions with the government, timing can be everything. In most cases, the best time to challenge your property tax will be shortly after the assessment has been issued.
- **But you have to do your homework.** Before you go to the time and effort of challenging the assessment, calculate an estimated difference between what the assessment is and what it should be.
- There are **certain circumstances** where you are likely to prevail. For example, when the size or other aspect of a property is lower or less than what the assessment is based on.
- If you plan on doing repairs for damage to the property, you should do so AFTER you challenge your tax assessment.

***Here are the sure-fire steps to challenging your assessment and winning!***

**1. Do your research first.** Before you plan a challenge, you should see what comparable homes in your area have been sold for recently. And don't forget the "old fashioned way" of just talking to your neighbors to see what kind of taxes they are paying. A lot can be learned from comparing notes with others in your neighborhood. You can also find out what your neighbors are paying by researching online.

You should also document anything that makes your property less valuable—any flaws or problems with the property. In any case, all this should take place BEFORE you think about challenging your assessment.

**2. Do the math.** Once you have some solid numbers for comparison based on your research, you can then estimate your savings and the cost of challenging the assessment.

You'll probably need to get an appraisal, which will generally run a minimum of $300. If you are currently getting any tax breaks on your property taxes (which are common for certain categories of people and for certain categories of property), you will want to consider the impact those will have.

For example, you may be getting tax breaks that do more for you than challenging the assessment would do. In this case, wait until the next assessment and enjoy the discount in the meantime.

**3. Decide on the basis of your challenge.** You should decide on the exact reason for your challenge. What is your argument? Was the assessment based on incorrect information? Is the property overvalued compared to others in the area? Are there problems with the property that would affect the assessment? Have values recently dropped?

**Here is a list of possible problems that could be the basis for your challenge:**

- Poor layout ("functional obsolescence"), or other features that are "neither practical nor desirable.
- Pre-bubble-burst assessments
- Assessed value is considerably higher than recent appraisal
- Location-related problems (something that makes the particular location of your property less desirable than others in the same area—such as being located at a bad intersection, at the end of a runway, or 30 feet from busy train tracks)
- The property information that the assessment is based on does not reflect reality (differences in square footage, design, size of the lot)

---

[1]Source: Bankrate.com

- Damage or deterioration that has not yet been repaired (important: if you plan on doing repairs, challenge the tax assessment FIRST!)

**4. Determine the proper procedures for challenges/appeals.** The procedures for appeals vary from place to place. You'll need to find out the exact procedure for your location.

**5. Challenge the assessment.** In some cases you can just walk into the assessor's office without an appointment and tell them about the mistake on your bill. And believe it or not—in some cases they'll adjust your tax bill right then and there!

Other times you'll have to go through an appeals process that will include hearings and other red tape. If you have decided to challenge your assessment, **don't let the red tape scare you off**.

Follow the procedures specific to your location for appeals and challenges. If the discrepancies are large enough, it could warrant enlisting professional help (i.e. appraisers, engineers, surveyors, and attorneys).

When you follow the steps outlined above,

you should have plenty of research and documentation to make a solid case. The key to winning is to follow the process through to the end.

A lot of people avoid it because they think it will be too difficult or because the process scares them. "There's nothing to be scared of, though," Rhonda assures us, "people challenge their assessments… and win!" Chances are, it will be worth the effort.

**Take a good hard look at your situation.** Just $500 in savings per year can really add up. In 10 years, that's $5,000.

And with all the various municipalities scrambling to make ends meet, you can bet they are counting on most folks simply paying the assessment without a challenge.

**Don't be afraid** to walk in their office and show proof why your assessment is too much, because in many cases, it is.

## Secret IRS Program gives taxpayers up to $8,000.00 to go back to school (R008)

What if I were to tell you there was a program where the IRS would literally pay you up to $8000 in cash to go back to school? And, if transportation or travel is a problem, don't worry! Because you can still qualify and get the cash even if you want to **go to school part-time and online from the comfort of your home!**

The program I am talking about not only exists, but is being underutilized by most everyone in the U.S. who wants to continue their education. So please, after reading this section, tell every hard-working American taxpayer you know about this opportunity!

So here's what it's all about...

**The American Opportunity Credit**

The American Opportunity Credit is a tax credit designed to help pay for the first 4 years of college. It means that if you are paying money to a college, you could have that money, up to certain limits, come straight off what you owe for taxes. Here are the details, from the IRS:

- Tuition, related fees, books and other required course materials generally qualify. In the past, books usually were not eligible for education-related credits and deductions.
- The credit is equal to 100 percent of the first $2,000 spent and 25 percent of the next $2,000. That means the full $2,500 credit may be available to a taxpayer who pays $4,000 or more in qualified expenses for an eligible student.
- The **full credit** is available for taxpayers whose modified adjusted gross income (MAGI) is $80,000 or less (for married couples filing a joint return, the limit is $160,000 or less). The credit is phased out for taxpayers with incomes above these levels. These income limits are higher than under the existing Hope and lifetime learning credits.
- **Forty percent** of the American opportunity credit is refundable. This means that even people who owe no tax can **get an annual payment** of the credit of up to $1,000 for each eligible student. Existing education-related credits and deductions do not provide a benefit to people who owe no tax. The **refundable** portion of the credit is not available to any student whose investment income is taxed at the parent's rate, commonly referred to as the kiddy tax.

An important thing to note about this credit is that only 40% is refundable. This means that if you are already getting a tax refund each year, and you want to take advantage of this credit—and really reap the rewards—then you will need to lower the amount being withheld from your paychecks for the years in which you intend to claim the credit. Again, from the IRS:

*"Eligible parents and students can get the benefit of this credit during the year by having less tax taken out of their paychecks. They can do this by filling out a new Form W-4, claiming additional withholding allowances, and giving it to their employer. For details, use the withholding calculator on IRS.gov"*

This tax credit can provide up to $2,500 per student per year the first 4 years of college. $2,000 per year of that is a dollar-for-dollar credit… meaning that every dollar you spend on education is one dollar in credit. Essentially, the government is giving you $8,000 for college… for your child.

And one of the great things about this tax credit is that **you can get it when you are taking classes online**. *One of our staff used it just last year to cover $2,500 of his costs for online classes. It's as if the tuition was free, after the tax credit.*

The American Opportunity Credit is a great way to get the government to pay for you (or your child's) education.

# Over $1 billion dollars was given to 6.1 million through this program (R011)

Here's another tax credit that's worth knowing about. It's the credit responsible for over a billion dollars in tax credits granted to over 6.1 million taxpayers in 2010. *What is this powerful tax credit that you shouldn't miss out on?* It's called the "Savers Credit".

You can get up to a $2,000 credit with the savers credit. That means that up to $2,000 of your retirement each year can be paid by the government!

*Want to find out if you're eligible?*

Here's what the IRS says about eligibility:

*You may be able to take this credit if you, or your spouse if filing jointly, made (a) contributions (other than rollover contributions) to a traditional or Roth IRA, (b) elective deferrals to a 401(k), 403(b), governmental 457, SEP, or SIMPLE plan, (c) voluntary employee contributions to a qualified retirement plan as defined in section 4974(c) (including the federal Thrift Savings Plan), or (d) contributions to a 501(c)(18)(D) plan.*

*However, you cannot take the credit if either of the following applies:*

- The amount on Form 1040, line 38; Form 1040A, line 22; or Form 1040NR, line 37, is more than $29,500 ($44,250 if head of household; $59,000 if married filing jointly).
- The person(s) who made the qualified contribution or elective deferral (a) was born after January 1, 1996, (b) is claimed as a dependent on someone else's 2013 tax return, or (c) was a student.

  You were a student if during any part of 5 calendar months of 2013 you:

- Were enrolled as a full-time student at a school, or
- Took a full-time, on-farm training course given by a school or a state, county, or local government agency.

(Note, tax laws are subject to change. Check with a qualified tax professional and the IRS website for the latest limits and information regarding this tax credit.)

A school includes technical, trade, and mechanical schools. It does not include on-the-job training courses, correspondence schools, or schools offering courses only through the Internet.

*"But my accountant hasn't told me about this credit!"*

This is a common complaint. Here's the thing you have to understand. Your accountant isn't there to save you money. Your accountant is there to run numbers and fill in the blanks. Most accountants manage finances for many businesses and/or individuals. *How much time do you think they can reasonably spend hunting down deductions and tax credits for you?* Obviously not much. It is up to you to hunt down the opportunities on your own, and **tell your accountant** about them. Accountants are great, but you can't depend on an accountant to do your saving for you. You've got to do your homework, and find the credits and deductions that you qualify for.

**Tax Credit versus Tax Deduction**

A tax *deduction* takes that amount of money off of your INCOME. So if you pay around 10% to the government in taxes each year, a $10,000 deduction would mean that $10,000 of your income isn't counted against you for tax purposes. If you're taxed at 10%, a $10,000 deduction would save you $1,000 in taxes.

A tax *credit* comes right off of the amount owed on your taxes. Let's say that you pay $3,000 in taxes in a year. Now, imagine that you use the credit I just told you about, and you have $2,000 of qualifying expenses. Instead of paying $3,000 in taxes, you pay $1,000 in taxes, and you get a $2,000 tax *credit* for the amount you spent on school!

## Six secrets to a larger social security check (R009)

Here are the 6 most powerful strategies for getting a larger Social Security check.

**1. Delay benefits as long as possible.**

You can start collecting benefits at age 62, but doing so will **reduce** your benefits by 25% or more (for the rest of your life). Generally speaking, the longer you wait the better off you will be. Waiting until age 70 is ideal because your monthly check will be **30% higher.** Obviously that isn't always an option, and in that case you should simply wait as long as you can to start collecting benefits.

For high income earners, waiting a little longer can also lead to the benefit of having your lower earning years "drop off" in the benefit calculation. This is because your benefits are calculated based on your **35 highest earning years.** So if you work more than 35 years—say 40 years—then the years you worked with the lowest earned amounts will be replaced by higher-earning years in the social security calculations.

**2. If you made the mistake of taking benefits early, undo it.**

Using social security **form 521** you can "undo" your decision to take benefits early if it turns out you made a mistake. This is considered a "loophole" by some and it's one of those options that the government will find a way to make less useful or even take away eventually. Until then, it is an option that may be available to you if you opted to take benefits before you should have. Here is how it works:

- First you must file social security **form 521**, to withdraw your application for social security benefits. Here's a snippet of information from the form:

*"This is a request to cancel your application. If we approve it, the decision we made on your application will have no legal effect. You will forfeit all rights attached to an application, including the rights of appeal. You will have to return any payment we made to you or anyone else on the basis of that application. You must then reapply if you want a determination of your Social Security rights at any time in the future. Any subsequent application may not involve the same retroactive period. We intend for you to use this procedure only when your decision to file has resulted, or will result, in a disadvantage to you. Your local Social Security office will be glad to explain whether, and how, this procedure will help you."*

- Once your application is processed, you must REPAY all of the benefits you received under social security (as of this writing, this is a tax deductible expense).
- Then, you can apply for social security again, and receive benefits at a much higher rate based on your current age (up to age 70).

The money you pay back to the government does **not** need to be paid back with interest (as of this writing), which makes the benefits you have received much like an interest-free loan.

While this strategy won't make sense for everyone, for some it can make a huge difference, especially if you live to a ripe old age. If you live to be 100 years old, it could amount to an extra $15,000 to $20,000 in spendable cash in your pocket over the remainder of your lifetime.

**3. Make the most of the options available to you.**

Did you know that it's possible to get help from your state with paying for Medicare premiums? Did you know that you may even qualify for financial assistance with deductibles, copays, and coinsurance?

Millions of seniors and disabled that may qualify fail to apply for these programs. To find out if you qualify, check the income and resource limits on the Medicare website, and click on "Get Help Paying Costs", then find the link for the Medicare Savings Programs:

http://www.medicare.gov/your-medicare-costs

And then, contact your state's Medicaid program, which can be found here:

http://www.medicaid.gov/Medicaid-CHIP-Program-Information/By-State/By-State.html

**4. Take a second job** – the amount of social security you receive is based on how much you've paid in during your **top 35 years** of income, so any year you can boost your income will in turn increase the amount of social security you receive.

**5. Claim your spouse's benefit** – for married folks, you can choose to claim the benefits based on *your earnings* or, if your spouse earned more, you can claim **half of their benefit** amount. Simply choose the *higher* number.

**6. Claim benefits twice** – this goes along with number 5. Say you are a working woman age 62 and your husband retires and claims Social Security at age 66. You can claim **half of his benefits** on top of what he receives and then after you retire, you can switch and claim benefits based on your earnings.

**7. Benefits for under age dependants** - Did you know that unmarried dependent children less than 18 years old may be able to qualify for up to half of your benefit amount. It doesn't matter if they are your biological child, a child you adopted, stepchildren or grandchildren who you claim as dependants. And there are other benefits reserved for children 18-19 years old and still in high school or, if they are over 18 and have a disability that arose *before* age 22.

## Alabama woman reveals secret to cutting grocery bill 50% in one week (R005)

For most people, groceries are a major expense. **Next to housing, groceries are the #1 expense in many households**.

Because of these facts, you should pay serious attention to your grocery bill. A lot of people complain about cable bills, utility bills, and phone bills… but somehow the grocery bill slips by unnoticed.

Not anymore. It's time to face the grocery expense head on. And lower your bill starting now.

One Alabama Housewife has **mastered the game of grocery savings**, and has offered a powerful selection of tips for those of us who would like to follow suit.

Here's what to do:

1. **Decide on a strategy.** Your strategy needs to match the grocery store you shop at most, or the area in which you shop. Possible strategies include: coupons, store hopping, price matching, or ad and coupon stacking. We'll talk more about these strategies in a moment.
2. Once you know what strategy you plan to use, **get organized**. Keep track of every dollar you spend on groceries in a week or a month. Get an average amount figured out. This will be the "base" from which you work. If you have a smart phone, there are many Apps available to help you track and categorize your spending, plus snag valuable coupons just for using the free App.
3. **Plan** to save money. Make checklists, folders and binders, and use clipboards as necessary.
4. Create a **system** for collecting ads and coupons. Again, there is no easier way to work your system than utilize a smart phone App. Most are free because they make money from advertisers giving instant access to coupons.

Now let's talk about the strategies for saving a LOT of money on groceries. First...

**Coupons**

Coupons are the bread and butter of grocery store savings. If you do nothing else, you should use coupons. But it's more than just clipping coupons from your local newspaper each week. In addition to the newspaper and what may show up on a smart phone App, also check out;

- Coupons.com and other coupon websites
- Blogs where "super shoppers" highlight valuable coupons and where to find them
- Coupons directly from the manufacturer. **Many companies will send you coupons for their products if you just ask.** Some even have places on their websites where you can register for their mailing list and get coupons delivered to your mailbox regularly. Proctor and Gamble is a big one, known for providing a lot of money-saving coupons if you know where to look. Here are are three places to check for valuable coupons:
  http://www.pgeveryday.com,
  http://savingspg.com/signup.
- Online coupons from your local grocery store chain
- Coupons from the mail, such as ValPak™ or other regular coupon mailers.

**Store Hopping**

Once you have your coupons in hand, the next thing to do is to research prices at the different stores in your area. Many people find that they can save hundreds of dollars each year by driving around just a little more when they grocery shop. The savings between stores on certain items can be substantial, so consider looking around to find out which store has the best prices and on what.

And then do what UPS automatically does for their driver's routes, maps out a drive that has only right turns to save time. For example, for my main grocery run every week I first go to Wal Mart, then to the local grocer to get a few items Wal Mart either doesn't stock or was out. And finally I'll stop by Whole Foods to get maybe 2 organic items not available anywhere else.

What are the price differences? Well here's an example. At Wal Mart a lemon is about 40 cents. At the local grocer a lemon is about 80 cents and at Whole Foods a lemon starts at $1.

Shop smart and drive efficiently so your savings don't go to operating a car.

**Price Matching**

Some stores offer price matching or ad matching. This is where they meet their competitors' prices that are advertised in ads (or not, in some cases). It's the equivalent of store hopping (above), but you only have to visit one store! You get the best of both worlds: shop at one place, and the best prices offered at all of them.

**Ad/Coupon Stacking**

This is where the savings really start to pile up. Some grocery stores have offers that can **double, even triple the value of your coupons**. Here's what to look for:

- Coupon stacking. Some stores let you use more than one coupon on a single item, "stacking" up the savings.
- Coupon/Ad stacking. Watch the store ads for items on sale at a good price—especially those items where you have good coupons. When the items go on sale, buy them and use your coupons and watch your savings add up!
- Double coupon days. Some stores offer to double the value of coupons on specific days of the week. Find out if a store in your area does this and what days they are offered.

**Bonus Grocery Savings!**

There is one more way to cut the grocery bill

that few people take full advantage of. **You can grow your own herbs and vegetables at home!** Many common herbs and veggies grow well in a variety of climates, and growing them at home can be much cheaper than buying them at the store. You can even chop them up, freeze them, and store them for use later in the year. We've seen grocery bills as low as $100 a month for people who grow their own food.

Another option to consider is **farmers markets and roadside stands**. Today more cities are encouraging, even subsidizing local farmers markets. Sometimes you can get in-season fruits and vegetables that taste better than the hot house grown or mass produced imports. Plus you'll save money buying directly from the farmer and cutting out the middle man. If you've never checked out your local farmers markets, give it a try—it could save you money, and you'll get better food.

And don't forget the Asian and other "ethnic" markets in your area. Often food that is quite expensive elsewhere can be found at these markets for cheap. One woman saved 90% on select items over the prices of her "regular" grocery store. That's substantial savings.

**What's it worth?**

So what's it all worth? When many families spend as much as $200 per week on groceries, a break on the grocery bill can be worth quite a bit. A 25% reduction in an $800 monthly grocery bill will add up to $2,400 per year in savings… or $24,000 over 10 years! A 50% reduction in your average grocery bill could double that to as much as $4,800 in a year or $48,000 in 10 years.

## Security expert reveals the best way to protect yourself from identity theft for free (R077)

Hackers and thugs are in the news every day clobbering powerhouse retailers like Target, Home Depot and even the big banks. So if they are not safe, what about you?

And worse now they are actively targeting children and the elderly. Why them instead of a big company with lots of data to steal?

"It's simple," says security expert Joe Vogel, "They are the least likely of all people to discover the identity theft, and the least likely to fight it."

The fact is that there is a period in life when we are most likely to pay attention to our credit and to apply for credit. It's when we're busy buying houses and cars and moving up the corporate ladder. For children, who have not yet reached that point, and elderly, who are past it, the reasons to check their credit report are often few and far between.

"Because they don't apply for loans as much, elderly people are easy targets. Children are easy targets because nobody suspects that their SSN could be used."

Regardless of your age, you should take steps to protect your credit from identity thieves. **Here is a method you can use to protect yourself for FREE.** (Yes, *really* free.)

Before we get started understand this important fact: about 40% of the identify theft risk that you face in your life will be from people you know—and even from those you love and trust. Another third of the risk will be from things like stolen purses and wallets.

And credit monitoring can only do so much. As few as 11% of identity theft cases are discovered through the user of credit monitoring services.

So what can you do to protect yourself? Follow this plan.

### Two Types of Identity Theft

First of all, there are two main types of identity theft:

1. Basic Identity Theft, and
2. Credit Hijacking Identity Theft

Basic identity theft occurs when a criminal steals your identity and then uses it to obtain new credit. Credit hijacking identity theft is when a criminal steals your identity in order to access and use your **existing** credit accounts.

Here's how you can defend yourself against each type of identity theft.

### Defending Against Basic Identity Theft

The best way to defend against basic identity theft is through the placement of an **"initial fraud alert"** on all three credit reports. What does this do for you?

It has the following 3 effects:

1. Credit bureaus can't sell your information to third parties anymore which means someone can't intercept your mail, fill out a credit card offer and then steal it when it arrives in the mail, if they didn't redirect to another address.
2. Nobody can be approved for credit in your name until the creditor calls you at the number listed on your credit report.
3. You get a free copy of all three of your credit reports from the major credit bureaus.

The initial fraud alert only lasts 90 days. You can **extend it for up to 7 years** by writing the credit bureaus at the address provided on the confirmation letters you received after filing your initial fraud alerts.

### Defending Against Credit Hijacking Identity Theft

Credit hijacking is a little trickier. In this form of identity theft, a criminal will call your banks and creditors posing as YOU, in order to change your address information on the account. Then they can order things in your name that get delivered to them, and by the time you find out they may have already spent thousands of dollars. This strategy bypasses an important security feature of credit cards known as "AVS", or "Address Verification Service". This is the security feature that requires your address to match that on the credit card. After they change it, it does.

**The best way to defend against this** is to add another layer of security to your communications with the banks and credit card companies. This can be done by setting up a personal security code with all of your bank accounts and credit cards. This "security code" is a unique number or combination of letters and numbers that only you know, and that an identity thief won't be able to guess. When you set up this number, it blocks thieves from making changes to your accounts without knowing the pass code. It is far better than using the last four digits of your SSN or your mother's maiden name, as that info is surprisingly easy for criminals to get a hold of.

### Identity Theft Proof

If you use both of the above techniques, you will be virtually identity theft proof. Of course, you should still use common sense and be vigilant with regards to your privacy and your personal information. Keep pin numbers and passwords in your head and nowhere else if possible. Shred documents with private information on them. Avoid giving out your SSN and other key security credentials whenever you can. (You'd be surprised how many places ask for your social security number that don't actually need it. Many will tell you it's optional if you resist or question it.)

“

When eating a fruit,
think of the person who
*planted* the tree.

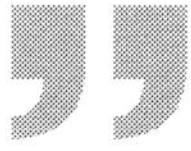

Vietnamese Proverb

# Saving Money

- ☑ **Energy consultant reveals secrets to save up to $1,800 per year on gas and electric**
- ☑ **HVAC repairman reveals how to turn a $500 investment into $5,000.00 of utility savings**
- ☑ **The dirty thief in your attic which is stealing up to $900 per year from you**
- ☑ **How to legally "slow down" your gas and electric meter and save thousands**
- ☑ **How to receive up to $6,500.00 in benefits to weatherize your home**
- ☑ **How to get $750 in rebates towards new household appliances**
- ☑ **A new way to watch your favorite television shows and save up to $600 per year**
- ☑ **The $10,000.00 coffee secret Starbucks (and cafes) don't want you to know…**
- ☑ ***And More***

“

All religions, arts and sciences are branches of the *same* tree.

Albert Einstein

## Energy consultant reveals secret to save up to $1,800 per year on utilities (R063)

"A ***programmable thermostat***, when used correctly, will instantly save a lot of people $300 or $400 a year. ***Better insulation*** in the weak spots could yield another $300 or more. Many people, when they work at it, will find that they can save as much as $2,000 per year on energy costs taking simple steps like these."

~Ron the Energy Consultant

My friend Ron is a professional energy consultant. I can't begin to tell you everything that he does. A lot of it is over my head. But Ron did have some simple advice for the "rest of us" folks when it comes to saving on energy costs.

The first thing Ron said to do is "TRY". Yes. It's that simple. He said a lot of people just don't put any effort into saving on electricity and gas. He recommends sitting down with a piece of paper and brainstorming ideas, and then trying just a few of them to see how much you can really save.

Ron says that most homeowners pay somewhere in the range of $0.60 to $0.90 per square foot for gas and electric. Multiplying your square footage by $0.90 to get a dollar amount and if your electric and gas run more than that each year, or are even close to it, taking a few simple steps can probably save you a lot of money.

Ron also told me about a cheap **$20 device** that you can use to figure out what is using up electricity in your home. Some appliances and electronics use electricity even when you're not using them. The device just plugs into the wall, and you plug your electrical appliance or electronic gadget into the device. It then tells you how much kWh (kilowatt hours) of electricity is being used! *(I did a quick check, and you can find these at your local Radio Shack.)*

There are numerous simple tricks you can use to lower your gas and electric bills. Most of them are covered on the pages that follow. By following Ron's advice, and utilizing the tips that follow, some people have saved as much as $1,800 per year on utilities!

## HVAC repairman reveals how to turn $500 into $5,000.00 of utility savings (R018)

Bob Coleman is an HVAC repairman. And he hates to see people throw money away on gas and electric bills. Especially when they can do simple steps to stop the meters from running wild.

Like Bob says, *"You wouldn't drive down the street throwing $20 bills out the window, would you?"* Yet, this is exactly what people do when they don't take Bob's simple and cheap advice to save hundreds each season and often a thousand or more in each year!

Below is Bob's plan to turn a $500 investment into $5,000 of utility savings.

**Here's exactly what you can do to slow down your utility meters.**

1. **DIY Window Shields (Radiant Barriers).** This may sound strange, but it can save you a bundle. Take some poster board and cut it to size to fit your windows. Sandwich some aluminum foil in between the

two pieces of poster board. Tape or glue it together, and then make some handles out of furnace tape to easily place and remove this energy shield from the window. This easy DIY heat shield can save you a lot of money in the summer time, especially when used on the South and West facing windows. Windows are usually the biggest bleeder of energy in most homes.

2. **Radiant Barriers in Your Attic.** According to the U.S. Department of Energy: "Radiant barriers are more effective in hot climates than where it is cool, especially when cooling air ducts are located in the attic. Some studies show that **radiant barriers can reduce cooling costs substantially** when used in a warm, sunny climate. The reduced heat gain may even allow for a smaller air conditioning system saving even more money."

3. **Programmable Thermostat.** This money-saver was already mentioned but is worth repeating. A $50 investment here can be $300 or $400 per year in savings!

4. **Fans.** In the winter, ceiling fans can help circulate warm air that usually rises, so you can lower your energy costs. In the summer, set the thermostat at a slightly warmer temperature and use fans around the house. Remember to reverse the direction of the blades from summer to winter. Not only do ceiling fans save on your energy bill, their decorative touch adds a classy feeling.

**Just add up all the ways a ceiling fan helps you save.**

- Less wear and tear on your heating and air conditioning system which means you'll spend less to maintain it.
- Lower heating bills in the Winter.
- Lower cooling bills in the Summer.
- You can expect to save between $500 to $1000 per year.

If taking steps like these gives you even a modest $800 in savings per year, the results over the long haul will really start to add up.

Just look at the graph based on savings numbers from the U.S. Department of Energy:

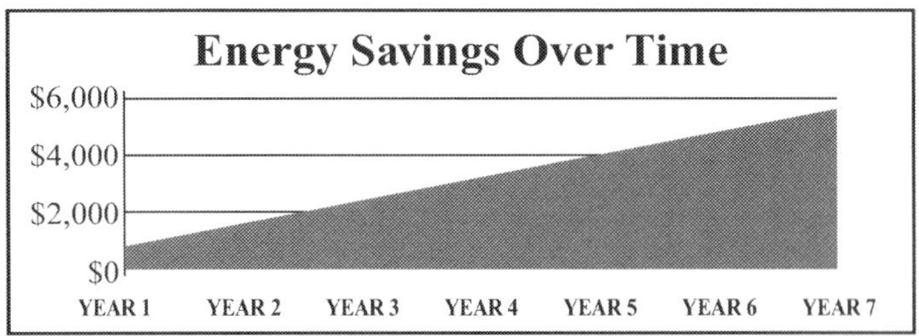


## The dirty thief in your attic which is stealing up to $900 per year from you (R090)

The worst thing you can have in your attic is *nothing*. Empty space with no purpose or plan is a thief that steals from millions of Americans without them knowing about it. If your attic has just plain insulation or worse, nothing—then consider taking these steps to root out the dirty thief:

- Use **spray foam insulation** for a quick, easy, and effective fix.
- Install **radiant barriers**.
- Install thermostatically controlled **ventilation fans**.

Any one of these steps could save you a bundle. Combine them, and the savings just multiply.

*The thing to understand about these low-cost steps is that some companies charge consumers as much as $15,000 to do "energy efficiency improvements" that amount to little more than what was mentioned above. Watch out for companies selling energy-efficiency improvements on the radio, internet, and door to door. Often times there are pushy sales presentations, high-pressure tactics, and of course empty promises. Don't accept their inflated numbers or buy into their inflated pricing.* ***Do it yourself instead, and save a bunch of money!***

## How to legally "slow down" gas and electric meters and save thousands (R065)

We've all been there. You endure a sweltering summer or hunker down for a frigid winter and then you check your mail and **can't believe how big the bill is.** And worse, you have to scramble to be able to pay it on time.

**Well there's a lot you can do to control energy costs** and many things you can do yourself or with the help of a handyman. Whatever you do, **beware** of companies charging large sums to do what will be covered in this report.

You may have heard a radio advertisement for something called *Eagle Shield*. The company claims to use "NASA technology" to help you save thousands on your utility bills.

But what Eagle Shield does is charge consumers a fee to make their home more energy-efficient. And you can do almost everything their 'experts' do (and when you need help) a handyman in your town can fill in the rest.

When you take action for each of the proven energy saving techniques we'll cover in a moment, you can **save thousands in energy costs**.

One of the simplest techniques involves installing a radiant barrier (available from Home Depot) in your attic. Some companies charge up to $5,600.00 for this, while individuals often do it themselves with the help of a local handyman for as little as $1,500.00!

Then add the big do-it-yourself savings to all the energy costs you'll save for years to come.

Now, go down this list and make a plan to **implement each of these techniques and you'll see your electric meter slow down** before your eyes as you put cash in your pocket.

- Regular professional tune-ups. Once a year is usually enough.
- **Programmable thermostat.**
- Adjust the thermostat when you're going to be away for extended periods.
- **Attic insulation. (Save up to $100 per year.[4])**
- Spray foam insulation around windows and doors, and in other gaps.
- **Attic radiant barriers.**
- Attic ventilation.
- **Ceiling fans, and circulating attic fans.**
- Room air circulation fans.
- **Turn your thermostat down 15 degrees during sleeping hours.**
- Insulate your ductwork.
- **Radiant Barriers for windows.**
- Monitor appliance energy usage.
- **Swap out older appliances for newer energy efficient models. (An old fridge, for example, can cost over $300 per year more to operate than a new one!)**

[1]Source: Bankrate.com

- Install and use an attic fan or "whole house fan" during temperate weather to delay the use of your air conditioning unit.
- **Close off unused or barely used rooms, and block the vents for those rooms.**
- Avoid blocking return air vents with furniture, shelves, etc.
- **Use energy saving light bulbs. (Savings of up to $50 per year* for 15 light bulbs.)**
- Use an energy-star compliant A/C unit. (Save an average of 15% per year over standard A/C.*)
- **In summer, avoid using appliances that will heat up the house. (Grill outside instead of using the stove. Air dry laundry instead of using the clothes dryer.)**

Personally, I saved as much as $1,500 most years with these techniques alone. That's $125 a month in found money. Money you can invest or use to start your own business.

(*) Source: Energy.gov

## How to receive up to $6,500.00 in benefits to weatherize your home (R026)

According to the U.S. government, as many **as 30 million Americans qualify for a program providing "Weatherization Assistance"**. And many of them don't realize they qualify.

The average price tag on the weatherization services received is $6,500. That's $6,500 FREE... to make your home more energy efficient, and to save you even more money!

**Here's where to go** to find out if you qualify:

http://www1.eere.energy.gov/wip/wap_apply.html

If you qualify and you don't utilize this valuable program, you could be leaving hundreds or even thousands of dollars on the table. Don't miss out. Find out if you qualify today!

## How to get $750 in rebates towards new household appliances (R059)

While we're on the subject of energy-efficiency, I have one more tip to share that I learned from Ron the energy consultant.

There is one **special website you can visit to find out about rebates, discounts, tax breaks, and other energy-related incentives that are available to you in your state**. Some of them are state programs, others are special rebates offered by utility companies.

"I've sent homeowners to the site that used it to find as much as $750 in rebates for energy-efficient appliances," said Ron.

The programs available vary by state, and are subject to change. To search for programs in your state, visit: http://www.dsireusa.org

## A new way to watch your favorite television shows and save up to $600 per year (R028)

You can give yourself a break on entertainment costs by applying some simple math to your TV watching habits.

Here's an example:

- 90% of the shows that Amanda watches are on network television. She watches a total of 10 shows regularly, and one of them is on HBO.
- Amanda pays $65 per month for cable TV with a DVR
- Is it worth it for Amanda to pay $780 to watch a single show? (Probably not.)

**Here's how Amanda fixed the situation and now saves a lot of money:**

- She bought a stand-alone DVR for $250 that would record her shows on network television.
- She decided to buy or rent the DVDs of each season of her HBO show (about $40) when they become available each year.
- She cancelled her cable service.

The first year Amanda **saved $530.00**. Each year after that she **saves $740.00**!

**"But what if the reception in my area isn't good?"**

There are still things you can do.

If you have high speed internet, consider subscriptions to Hulu and Netflix. The two subscriptions will cost a total of about $15 as of this writing, and you can get most of the shows you get on network TV, many cable TV shows, and a large selection of movies.

Paying $15 for Netflix/Hulu versus $60 or more for cable service can still save you hundreds of dollars a year versus cable service. . There is even a handy box called "Roku" that you can use for seamless access to these online services through your television. As of this writing the "Roku" box costs around $89.

***"But I really want to keep my cable!"***

Then do the math on your premium movie channel usage. How much extra are you paying for HBO, Showtime, and other premium movie channels? Consider cutting back, and buying or renting the DVDs to keep up with your shows. You'll save a lot of money in the long run!

BONUS SAVINGS: Your cable or satellite TV box is the **third largest energy hog in your home** after your air conditioning and heating system. In fact, your cable box is sucking power all night while you are fast asleep. Dump it and help pay for your Internet TV subscriptions with the energy savings.

## The $10,000.00 coffee secret Starbucks (and cafes) don't want you to know (R038)

Here's something that keeps the stockholders of Starbucks rolling in dough while you count pennies to deposit.

For starters, let's talk about the cost of those fancy coffee drinks. They often cost in the $3 to $5 range. At $4 average per cup, just one fancy coffee drink every day, 5 days a week, for a year (minus 2 weeks for vacation and most people drink-up then too), you will spend about $1,000 just for coffee in a single year!

Add it up over time. 5 years = $5,000!

**How about you start pocketing all that cash.**

Instead of pulling up again and again at Starbucks, do the following.

High priced coffee consists of espresso and milk. Some add chocolate or other flavorings, but the core ingredients are espresso and milk.

A latte is espresso, filled up to the top with milk. Mocha usually is the same thing, with Chocolate added.

Next time you roll into Starbucks, just order a shot of espresso in a to-go cup, and use the milk and chocolate at the self-serve bar to make your own expensive coffee, for **HALF THE PRICE**!

Here is what to say when ordering…

…"I'll have 2 shots over ice with room for cream."

(Then head to the condiment counter for some milk.)

We could also add…

…"I'll have a large Americano with room for cream."

(Again, head to the condiment counter and add what you want.)

If you were paying $1,000 a year before to grab your daily java fix, then doing this will save you about $500 per year ($41.67 per month).

**Make Starbucks At Home**

Did you know the fancy coffee sold at places like Starbucks isn't necessarily the best coffee you can get? To add to their bottom line, you are often drinking a very acidic and usually pesticide-ridden, mass produced bean.

A bag of some of the best organic coffee you'll find will cost about $15 even at Whole Foods, and buying just two of those bags a month, you'll still be saving lots of money while consuming a much better blend!

**But I like espressos and lattes!**

Then make it at home with these three things:

- A Bialetti Stovetop Espresso Maker
- An Aerolatte Milk Frother
- A Copco eco-friendly to-go coffee cup

You can get them ALL for around $50 bucks, the equivalent of 10 trips to Starbucks.

With these three tools, and buying the best organic coffee available, you can make some of the best coffee you've ever enjoyed.

**And not only will you save big time, you're consuming a much healthier, organically produced product.**

Think about it: you'll pocket over $600 a year, while eliminating the pesticides from your coffee… you've got yourself a real life-and-money-saver!

Don't think organic coffee is a big deal?

Think again. Coffee is the most toxic crop in the world, making the pesticides on the fruit that you insist on washing look like a health tonic. If you are concerned enough to wash your fruits and veggies, then you should pay close attention to the coffee you drink!

If you want to get the scoop on healthy coffee, do a search for "HealthyRoast®", U.S. patent #6,723,368 and #8,357,419

You'll be amazed at the high quality, organic, great tasting coffee drinks that you can make at home. It just takes a little effort, and you'll be healthier while saving $40 or more a month!

**And what about your time?**

From the moment you pull into the parking lot to the time you leave every cafe, let's just say it takes you 15 minutes per day, 5 days a week to feed your coffee cravings.

That's 60 hours a year just for grabbing coffee. A work week and a half!

If you're spending $1,000 and 60 hours each year just for mediocre coffee that could ultimately have negative effects on your health, you need to think long and hard about what you are doing.

A good friend of mine used to spend $2000 per year going to Starbucks every day and sometimes twice a day. On top of that, add in the time wasted and gas to drive back and forth.

I kept telling him "you need to get an espresso machine! Do you realize in 10 years an espresso machine would put an easy 20 grand in your pocket?" He thought for a minute and a few weeks later a brand-new $600 Breville espresso machine arrived at his house.

And if you like how your coffee tastes with the $79 espresso machines many people have, well you haven't tasted coffee like my friend can make at home now. Even though the high-end machine costs $600, it was paid for in 3 months by avoiding Starbucks!

## How to permanently reduce your water bill by over $200.00 every year (R043)

You can save up to $200 on your water bill every year by changing a single, simple device. Install a water-saving shower head in place of your standard one and watch the savings come in. It's better for the planet, too.

And don't forget about installing a programmable thermostat. Just $50 (or $100 for a really nice one) can save you $300 or more per year on heating and cooling.

## How to make your washing machine give you over $100.00 a year (R046)

A lot of people don't know that they can **save as much as $75 a year by using cold water in their washing machine instead of warm water**. Remember, that hot water costs money to heat and to keep heated. The less of it you can use, the more money you will save. It will also prevent your clothes from wearing out and the colors from fading prematurely.

You can also **save money on hot water** by making sure your hot water heater is well **insulated**. There are special insulating wraps that you can purchase for hot water heaters. These help the water heaters retain the heat and not run as much just to keep the hot water hot.

## The secret to saving up to 50% on quality chicken, steaks and fish (R033)

Will a steak that is approaching the expiration taste as good as a steak that has 10 days to go? The answer is *yes*. They taste the same. But as steaks, chicken, fish, and other high quality meats approach the expiration dates, stores commonly mark them down to as much as 50% off. That means you can get the same great cut of meat for half the price, by simply timing your purchase right!

Here's how one grocery guru and stay-at-home mom does it:

*"I just watch for the bargain stickers on meat to see when it's on sale. The big thing that I think people miss is the date on the meat is "use or freeze by". I almost always FREEZE. In other words, I purchase the meat a day or two before it expires for about half price, and then I freeze it and use it whenever I am ready to cook it. It's one of the cheapest ways I have found to get quality meats, poultry, and seafood."*

*- Pauline Parker, St. Paul MN*

"If the best things in life are free, we have too many of the worst things."

## Three sneaky (but legal) techniques to wear top brand fashions for up to 70% off (R058)

Clothing expenses can really add up. Many families spend $1,000 or more per year on clothes. If you can cut your clothing budget, the savings could be substantial. Here are some ways that others have drastically reduced the money spent on clothes.

**50% Off Your Favorites**

If you purchase your winter clothes in the spring—when winter has passed—**you can get a steep discount… as much as 50%**. If you buy your summer clothes at the beginning of winter, you can get the same great discount.

**Helpful Hint:** The key to this and to the other methods mentioned below is consistency. You need to have a system, and work that system year after year. Decide when and where you will shop to get the best discounts, and do it without fail. If you systematically use this approach, it can have a substantial positive impact on your finances.

**90% Off High End Shirts**

I once had a friend who always dressed nice. He always wore Eddie Bauer or Structure clothes—or pricey but high quality brands. I used to think he had some secret source of money that funded his expensive clothing habits. He didn't work at a high paying job. He didn't get a big inheritance that I knew of. *But his clothes were always so nice!*

Well, one day he let me in on his secret. We were driving by a local thrift store when he whipped into the parking lot and got out of the car, saying "Sorry, this will only take a sec." We went in, and he quickly scoured the shirts and pants. "Aha!" He had found what he was looking for. We went to the cash register and he paid.

**His total cost was $4. The shirt was an Eddie Bauer button-up that probably cost around $40 new.** And the thing is… the shirt looked like it was new. You couldn't tell it had been used at all by looking at it.

After that we got to talking, and my friend told me that he made regular trips to all of the thrift stores in towns. "But I have rules," he said, "I don't buy anything at a thrift store that costs less than $30 new." In other words, he only bought the very best name brand items he could find, and he bought them at a huge discount—90% that day and sometimes even more.

With this simple strategy, he dressed nicely for prices substantially below retail. His dress shirts would usually cost less than a t-shirt from Wal Mart!

**50%-75% Name Brand Clothes**

Another thrifty shopper told me that she buys name-brand dress shirts for her husband at 50% to 75% the normal prices by **shopping at stores that specialize in damaged or flawed clothing**. There are stores like TJ Maxx, believe it or not, that sell nothing but clothing that for one reason or another can't be sold in a regular department store.

Some clothes have simple issues like missing buttons. This woman just buys them up and sews on a button herself. Other clothes may have tags that are torn off, or with other minor defects that don't affect the look or usability of the piece of clothing.

Her one piece of advice, for those of us who want to try it:

*"Just make sure you look over things well. A piece of clothing could have more than one flaw. As long as you* ***take your time, you can walk out with hundreds of dollars in quality clothing for just pennies on the dollar****."*

**Example of Possible Savings:** If you buy 10 $50 shirts each year for $500, and start buying those shirts for $5 each instead, you'd be saving $450 per year—just on shirts. Applying these tactics across the board could add up to thousands in just a couple of years.

## How to get paid up to $50 to eat locally grown produce (R053)

There is a **special program for low income seniors** that can give you up to $50 per year for the purchase of fresh, locally grown produce.

It's called the "Senior Farmers' Market Nutrition Program". It's a federal government program that gives grant money to states that is then passed on to seniors in the form of coupons for up to $50 worth of food at local farmers' markets and roadside stands.

According to the SFMNP:

*"In 2012, benefits were available to 885,116 low-income seniors from 19,882 farmers at 3,988 farmers' markets as well as 3,075 roadside stands and 154 community supported agriculture programs."*

**How to Check Eligibility and Apply:**

To apply for this benefit, you'll need to contact the state agency that administers the program in your state:

http://www.fns.usda.gov/sites/default/files/SeniorFarmersMarketcontacts.pdf

## The clever (but nice) way to eat at your favorite restaurants for up to 50% off (R079)

There are a variety of excellent ways to save money at restaurants. Not all money-saving strategies are created equal, however. In our research we learned that certain online operations that sell "50% off" coupons are mistreating and otherwise hurting the restaurants you know and love.

According to one restaurant owner:

*"I can't believe how some of these companies operate. They were selling coupons to my restaurant that I never authorized... and they never sent me a dime! I had to either give away food for free or not honor the fraudulent coupons."*

Obviously, this is something you want to avoid. So here we have a list of safe, "nice", restaurant-friendly ways to save big when you eat out.

It may be surprising that the best source of restaurant coupons is usually NOT the internet. Sources that are good and trustworthy include:

- The **"Entertainment Book"** - This resource provides a number of coupons for local and regional areas around the country. Save on dining out, rental cars, hotels, and more. The Entertainment Book often features "buy one, get one" deals at restaurants.
- **Coupon books sold by local schools and charities** - Some schools even sell the Entertainment Book (above) as a fundraiser. Others sell discount cards and coupon books to local restaurants. These are often great deals such as "50% off" or "buy one get one".
- **Valpak and Money Mailer** - These are similar options that both offer great deals. Usually the coupons come in the mail, and include coupons to restaurants and other local businesses. If you do not currently receive either Val Pak or Money Mailers, go to www.valpak.com and www.moneymailers.com to find out what's available in your area.

Here's another under-utilized option:

**Rewards!** Sign up for the rewards programs, clubs, email lists, Facebook fan pages, and mailing and cell phone text lists of your favorite restaurants. Many major restaurant chains have these programs, as do many smaller local restaurants. Some give you free food on your birthday (Red Robin*, Baskin Robins*, and more). Others give you free food for every 5 or 10 times you eat there, and/or give you a discount that you can use every time you eat.

Whether you eat at P.F. Changs, Wolfgang Pucks, or your local burger joint... find out if they have an email list or rewards program (or similar) that you can sign up for—and reap the benefits.

* As of this writing.

## The secret to booking your dream cruise for up to 75% OFF (R084)

A guy I once knew named Jarrod was always taking vacations—seemingly on a whim. I used to think, "I could never travel that much." Jarrod had been a travel agent years ago, and I thought surely he had some special connections that allowed him to travel cheaply. That's what I thought, that is, until one day when Jarrod told me his secret.

As it turns out, Jarrod was taking advantage of the types of bargains that most people hear about but never know how to find. He told me a powerful secret that I never knew previously—that some **airlines will give you better rates on the phone** than you can get online. Like hotel front desk clerks, phone representatives at airlines are often authorized to give you better deals. All you have to do is ask.

According to Jarrod:

"Most people don't realize that the person at the hotel front desk is usually authorized to offer them better rates in order to sell a room... especially if you walk in last minute!"

And of course, always remember **the magic words** we mentioned in an earlier report;

*"Is that the best you can do for me today?"*

So the first key to Jarrod's travel strategy was the phone. He also told me another secret…

*"If you can travel at the last minute, you can usually get much better deals. Cruise lines almost always have un-booked space that they want to sell—and it usually goes cheap. Hotels do the same thing."*

So the second key to Jarrod's travel strategy was to do everything at the last minute! He used a variety of websites to accomplish this:

- http://www.hotwire.com
- http://www.priceline.com
- http://www.bid4vacations.com
- http://www.luxurylink.com
- http://www.connectedtraveler.com
- http://www.inntopia.com
- http://www.travelclearinghouse.com

He did say that if you plan on flying, it is usually cheaper to book in advance. But if you can be flexible on *when you actually travel*, he said just **wait for the great deals to come up** and *then* buy your tickets. Airline travel on Wed., Thur. and Sat. will usually get you a better rate because they are in the least demand by the business traveler, where the airlines can sell full fare.

So Jarrod's steps are:

1. Use the phone, ask for better deals.
2. Do last minute bookings or flexible-schedule bookings when you can.

Then sit and watch the prices fall.

## The truth about Government seized and surplus cars, homes and merchandise (R093)

Everyday various Government entities sell surplus cars, homes and merchandise for pennies on the dollar. A lot of folks pick up some fantastic deals on stuff they would otherwise pay full retail for. While others **scoop up various items and then flip them for huge profits.**

I'm sure you've seen the ads: "Police auction! Government seized cars!" However, many are come-ons for scam artists taking advantage of simple information you don't know.

Here's the **truth** about buying surplus and seized merchandise from the Government.

There are multiple websites used by police departments, sheriffs, and other municipal agencies for the purpose of auctioning off stolen, seized, and surplus goods. Here is the first one:

**http://www.propertyroom.com**

This is an auction website (not my favorite) that contracts with police and other municipal agencies around the country to auction off stolen/seized/surplus goods. It's kind of like the eBay for police and government agencies.

It works like any other auction website. You bid against other users, and if you have the winning bid you will pay shipping/handling and your bid price. **TIP:** Be sure to check the shipping prices before finalizing your bid.

**Even Better Deals on Real Estate, Cars, and More Can Be Found By Digging Deeper!**

Here's another website portal offering Government property.

- **http://www.govsales.gov**

And then there are state and local sites (even better) you can access here.

- **http://www.usa.gov/shopping/auctions/surplus.shtml**

**Snap Up Souvenirs, Books and Gifts Here.**

- https://www.usa.gov/buy-from-government

**And Don't Forget To Check Out Individual Federal Agencies Here.**

- http://www.usa.gov/shopping/byagency/byagency.shtml

You may also call **1-800-333-4636** 8am to 8pm Eastern Standard Time.

Surprisingly, some people have been able to **earn a full-time living** just buying and selling government seized and surplus merchandise. If you do your research, you too can profit by flipping Government merchandise. **RULE OF THUMB: The HARDER the website is to find the BETTER deals you will find.**

## Angry hair dresser reveals how to get your hair done for half price (R191)

In almost every city, there are schools where stylists go to learn the trade. And you can book an appointment with them and get a huge discount versus going to a salon.

Some consumers only get their hair done at the schools. Check your local phone directory for the stylist nearest you. You'll save a lot of money and get a cut supervised by a professional.

While your hair stylist has lots of experience, there are several more ways to save big money on hair care.

If you are careful and follow directions, you can **do small dye jobs at home** on your own.

Just do exactly what the directions on the product package says and you can achieve salon quality results doing it yourself.

And use less aggressive shampoos. 99% of the shampoos on the market contain Sodium Laurel Sulfate or Sodium Laureth Sulfate and these chemicals are used in labs to **denature proteins**!

For those over 30, you can extend the life of your professionally done hair job by **touching up the gray roots yourself.** Again, carefully follow the directions on the product and you can extend the time between visits to the salon.

And whatever products you are using, if they work, stay with them. Sometimes hair stylists will 'sell' you on a product they stock when in fact what you are using will continue to fit the bill.

**Mend your split ends.** Unless you are due on the runway for fashion week, you can deal with up to a quarter of an inch of split ends yourself. Simply cut them off yourself and save an expensive visit to the salon.

**Paul Mitchell at Wal-Mart.** Your salon will tell you that brand name products at discounters are not the real deal when in fact they are.

While the Paul Mitchell's of the world don't sell to discounters, they do sell to distributors and they in turn move the product to whomever they want.

I even bought a name brand product off **Amazon** and the entire label was in Spanish. Exactly the product I use, just diverted by an overseas distributor.

**Hold the dressing.** Did you know home remedies like olive oil can condition your hair just as well as an expensive salon treatment? Try it, you'll be amazed.

# Taxes

- ☑ **The biggest tax deduction 99% of America is missing**
- ☑ **Ex IRS Agent reveals how to reduce your chances of being audited**
- ☑ **How to find out if you are 1 of over 910,000 people owed over $763 million dollars in unclaimed tax refunds**
- ☑ **How your spouse or children can lower your taxable income by up to $15,200.00**
- ☑ **CPA Reveals: Tax loophole which lets you deduct 100% of preschool, daycare, after care (even a nanny) up to $5,000.00 each year**
- ☑ **Avoid these 27 tax reduction schemes or risk facing jail**
- ☑ ***And More!***

“

You don’t have to be smart in order to enjoy the rewards which come from working smart.

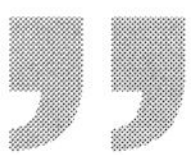

## The biggest tax deduction 99% of America is missing (R347)

What is one of the best tax savings strategies of all time?

According to accountant Roger Moler, it's "starting a business."

"*Starting a business* is one of the best ways to save on taxes if you do it right," says Roger. "Obviously, you need to have a legitimate business goal," he adds, "but the potential for **tax savings are huge** when you start to look at things from the 'tax' perspective."

Roger's strategy goes something like this:

- Start a business… usually as a sole proprietorship. Start it with the goal of making money.
- Once the business is making $25,000 to $30,000 per year, incorporate.
- Structure your pay through the business in such a way as to minimize taxes. This is typically done by paying yourself a salary (that is subject to self-employment tax) and then adding on a **profit sharing sort of bonus (which is not subject to social security tax)**.
- Once you have sufficient cash flow, start purchasing real estate, stocks, bonds, CDs, annuities, and other similar investment vehicles to build up a passive income.

But starting a business is at the heart of the whole plan. Why would starting a business help with your taxes? *Because there are a **lot of tax breaks designed just for businesses.***

Keep in mind; this is a **long term** solution. But the reality is if you are EVER going to find any kind of financial freedom, you are going to have to start thinking for the long term.

Short term thinking almost always leads to poverty.

Long term thinking almost always leads to at least a modest amount of wealth.

You'll be better off if you think for the long term. And Roger's strategy is just one example of how to do this.

## Ex IRS Agent reveals how to reduce your chances of being audited (R074)

Have you ever heard one of those stories about an Ex-IRS agent who is angry and disgruntled and fighting the system? Well, this is not one of those. Peter, an ex-IRS agent, was perfectly happy with his government job. He just left to work for a private firm for better pay. But Peter does have some **valuable tips for those of us who would like to avoid trouble with the IRS**.

As it turns out, studies done based on statistical data provide shocking facts.

There are certain things that can make you more likely to get audited. There is an element of chance—some returns are simply selected randomly—but there are things that can increase your chances of an audit.

Here are a couple of examples…

**Filing a Schedule C**

Obviously, there are instances in which you've got to file a schedule C. But doing so can increase your chances of being audited. "Avoid it if you can, but do it if you have to" is the general rule.

The trigger for increased scrutiny when it comes to Schedule C is "business expenses" when the filer does not actually have a "business".

One example is landlords and rental properties. The IRS may look closely at a loss from a rental property if your main source of income is not from rental properties. The "business" of the rental property may not be "business" enough.

Another example that can lead to extra scrutiny is when someone files a Schedule C with a **large number of expenses, and takes a standard deduction on their personal taxes**. This is a pattern that is different from the norm, and it could lead to an audit. (By using the Schedule C and taking the standard deduction, a person could defraud the IRS by essentially "double dipping" with regards to their tax deductions.)

The best advice is to only file a Schedule C if you have a legitimate, actual business. An actual business would have an actual chance of making profit, and an actual risk of loss, and would be something that you put a considerable amount of time and effort into. Otherwise the IRS may see it as a hobby or as simply a way to avoid taxes.

**Doing Your Own Taxes**

According to Peter, a self-prepared tax return is more likely to result in an audit than a professionally prepared one. Why… because **errors** on tax returns are red flags for audits. Since you probably aren't a tax expert, you are more likely to make errors.

"But my tax software guarantees against errors," you say. We wondered about this too, so we did some research. As it turns out, it is a lot harder to make a claim on that guarantee than you might think. Many users of popular tax software that attempt to get the company to "make good" find out the hard way that promises of accuracy aren't always what they seem. (Many users report that the company indicates that the error was the users fault when it was not. Also note that often updates are released AFTER the tax filing deadline. What about all of those returns filed before the deadline?)

If that isn't enough, we also found the following clip from the *Minneapolis Star Tribune* about problems with Turbo Tax in 2013:

*Citing "multiple issues with the products", the Minnesota Department of Revenue issued a crisp statement today urging tax filers to avoid using Intuit products to prepare or file their state income taxes. The products include TurboTax, Lacerte, Intuit online and ProSeries. The state warned that using the products could "jeopardize the accuracy of your return or delay your return."*

*In a conference call, the department said there were multiple issues with the software including assigning political contributions to the wrong party, failing to give an education credit for multiple dependents, incorrectly calculating property tax refunds, and a variety of other calculation errors. Some of these issues surfaced just in the past several days, according to Terri Steenblock with the Department of Revenue.*

*"The Department of Revenue is not affiliated with Intuit and we find these errors unacceptable. We expect Intuit to correct these problems immediately. If they fail to do so, the department will stop processing returns filed using Intuit," the department said.*

The bottom line on all of this tax software stuff is that you are probably better off if you don't do your own taxes. It may also be worth asking your accountant what tax software they use, so that you can be aware of any possible issues.

**Income Discrepancies**

One big "red flag" is when you have income discrepancies. Any time you receive a 1099 or a W2, the IRS also gets a copy of that. If you fail to list income from a 1099 or a W2 on your tax return, or if you mistype an amount from one of these forms, you will probably get an automated notice from the IRS that includes a bill for taxes due.

This can also happen when a 1099 or W2 is incorrect as initially issued, and a corrected one is issued later. The corrected one may not be reported or recorded properly, and this can cause a discrepancy and trigger an automated collection effort. The lesson: If you ever have to get a corrected 1099 or W2, make sure you hang on to the documentation to back it up—just in case.

**Disproportionate Charitable Donations and Other Deductions**

According to Peter, **charitable donations can come under scrutiny when they are in larger amounts than those that are typical for individuals in your tax bracket**. If you do make charitable donations, do not exaggerate the value of non-cash donations, and make sure you thoroughly document all donations. Keep that documentation with your tax records so that you can back up your claims if the need to do so arises.

According to BankRate.com, the average charitable donations compared to income may be something like the following:

*(Note: For Illustrative Purposes Only)*

| INCOME RANGE | AVERAGE DEDUCTIONS FOR DONATIONS |
|---|---|
| [illegible] | [illegible] |
| $30,000-$50,000 | $2,285 |
| [illegible] | [illegible] |
| $100,000-$200,000 | $3,857 |
| [illegible] | [illegible] |

Aside from avoiding the above and/or being extra careful and diligent with documentation, Peter offered the following tips:

- If you have realized you made a mistake on your taxes, call the IRS to let them know about it. Occasional small discrepancies (say $50 or less) can be noted and forgiven, while larger ones may require filing an amended return and paying interest and penalties. It is always better, however, if you find the problem first and get it fixed. Often people ignore the problem, hoping that the IRS will not notice. Several years later the minor issue can multiply tenfold due to penalties, interest, and of course the stress of getting a surprise tax bill in the mail.
- Be conservative when it comes to deductions. Large vehicle, travel, and meal deductions can sometimes lead to closer scrutiny. Only take these deductions if they are justified.
- Don't be afraid to take the deductions and credits that you are entitled to. **It isn't a crime to take a legitimate deduction or credit that you are legitimately entitled to. Just be prepared to back it up.**

**Some Other Audit Triggers**

1. The more money you make, the more likely you are to be audited (see table below).
2. If you make substantially more money one year than you do a previous year, it can trigger an audit. **Jumps in income—in either direction—are generally "red flags"**.

To illustrate the impact of income, consider the following table of audits compared to income:

| SIZE OF ADJUSTED GROSS INCOME | RETURNS FILED IN CALENDAR YEAR 2001 (PERCENT OF TOTAL) | EXAMINATION COVERAGE IN FISCAL YEAR 2012 (PERCENT) |
|---|---|---|
| All returns | 100.00 | 1.03 |
| None | 2.15 | 2.67 |
| $1-$25,000 | 39.92 | 1.05 |
| $25,000-$50,000 | 23.91 | 0.70 |
| $50,000-$75,000 | 13.16 | 0.64 |
| $75,000-$100,000 | 8.11 | 0.64 |
| $100,000-$200,000 | 9.77 | 0.85 |
| $200,000-$500,000 | 2.41 | 1.96 |
| $500,000-$1,000,000 | 0.38 | 3.57 |
| $1,000,000-$5,000,000 | 0.18 | 8.90 |
| $5,000,000-$10,000,000 | 0.01 | 17.94 |
| $10,000,000 or more | 0.01 | 27.37 |

(Source: http://www.irs.gov)

## How to find out if you are 1 of over 910,000 people owed over $763 million dollars in unclaimed tax refunds (R037)

Jody, a past customer, recently told us about how she used a tool over at the National Taxpayers Union (NTU.org) to discover a $1,053.00 tax refund she was owed but never received. The tax year in question was a hectic time for Jody. As a result she never received the $1,053.00 refund because of an error in her mailing address!

But think about this…

According to ABC News over **910,000 Americans are due tax refunds totaling 763 MILLION DOLLARS**! This means the average refund owed is about $838.00!

Find out if you are CURRENTLY OWED a REFUND CHECK by using the same tool Jody used. Just go to http://www.ntu.org and type "unclaimed tax refund" into the search box located in the upper right hand corner.

http://www.ntu.org

Search term "unclaimed tax refund"

## How your spouse or children can lower your taxable income by up to $15,200.00 (R019)

The most important thing when it comes to approaching taxes is best explained by telling the story of Jim Roberts. Jim is a family man who (as of this writing) makes $125,000 per year and is raising 6 kids. He lives in a 5 bedroom house with his wife and kids, and works hard to provide for his family.

Jim pays taxes. But unlike many tax payers, Jim does not habitually pay more taxes than he is legally required to. Here's how Jim explains it:

*"A lot of **people are paying a lot of extra taxes because they have not taken the time to do actual TAX PLANNING**. By having a plan and approach for taxes, you are almost guaranteed to SAVE MONEY because you will be thinking about all of the things that other people aren't thinking about."*

How does Jim do it?

First of all, you should understand that what Jim does is 100% legal. Our tax system, which was only 4 pages in 1913 and now totals over 74,000 pages, is designed with a complex system of deductions, exemptions, and credits. These deductions, exemptions, and credits are there to use—*legally*—for those who qualify for them.

Jim's strategy can be broken down into four main tax saving buckets. We'll talk about each of them now.

**Strategy #1: Lower taxable income.**

There are numerous ways to lower your taxable income. There are deductions for everything from donations to medical expenses to school expenses… and of course we can't forget *business expenses*.

Jim utilizes all of the deductions that he can legally utilize to lower his taxes. He keeps close track of business expenses, medical expenses, and any other expenses likely to result in a tax deduction.

Then there are deductions for saving for retirement or health care expenses.

And every year there are new deductions, with some only available for a number of years like during the recent Great Recession.

The whole goal and strategy here is to LOWER your taxable income so that you pay taxes on less.

**Strategy #2: Take advantage of tax credits.**

Whenever there is a tax credit that Jim can legally qualify for, he goes the extra mile to track the associated expenses and activities so that he can claim the credit. Some people don't do this because they think it will be too much work, or they don't think it will be worth it. Meanwhile, Jim puts in perhaps two or three hours of effort per year to qualify for whatever tax credits he can. *Is it worth it?* Jim certainly thinks so:

*"Some years I've made $1,000 per hour in tax savings for the work I have done making sure my ducks are in a row for tax credits. It's definitely worth it!"*

Now unless you have a team of CPAs on the payroll, how do you keep up with the ever changing tax credit landscape? Simple, just look at each line of your tax forms. Compare last year's forms with the current forms to spot new credits. And when you see a credit you don't understand or feel you may qualify for, simply search the IRS website to read the 'rules' for taking the credit.

**Strategy #3: Take advantage of tax-free and tax-deferred savings and retirement options.**

There are retirement and savings accounts that qualify for special tax treatment. When used wisely, these accounts can be used to lower your taxable income (see #1 above) and save for important events in the future. Some can even be used as a vehicle to let your funds grow tax free. Whether it is Coverdell education savings accounts or ROTH and SEP IRAs, the options available are generally well worth the trouble for those in the right situation.

The real goal of strategy #3 is tax deferred or tax free **growth**. Earning interest is great. It is better if you can earn interest and either not pay taxes at all on those earnings, or defer the payment of taxes until later.

**Strategy #4: Start a business and pay for as many expenses as you legally can with pre-tax dollars of the business.**

Anyone who doesn't own a business should start one on the side, according to Jim. And they should employ their kids. Most people are going to give money to their kids anyways. Why not do it with pre-tax dollars that the business earns? Pay your kids a wage to work in the business (note: subject to IRS guidelines), and they'll get the money they want and need, you'll have lower taxable income, and your kids will learn about how to work and earn money.

The key to this strategy, according to Jim, is making your business part of the "pie" with regard to the money you make. It's a paycheck that you can take with you from job to job, that will always be there. It can always be calculated in as part of your income… and money you'd be giving your children, can come "right off" of it and lower your taxable income.

Another great point about starting a side business is, with deductions you may very well 'lose money' during the start-up year. You'll have costs for a computer and software, office supplies, cell phone, Internet, mileage on your car and the home office deduction.

The start-up year's 'loss' will lessen your tax burden.

That's it. That is the sum of Jim's 4-point strategy for lowering taxes and making the most of the U.S. tax system.

It starts with simple awareness: **many people pay too much in taxes because they simply do not know better**. Others are afraid of the government and of the IRS, but the reality is - taking tax deductions and credits that you are legally permitted to take does not make you a "target" and—in the event you ever do get audited—it will not hurt your case. If anything your increased awareness of the tax system and the laws that govern it will help you should you ever face such a situation.

So remember the four part tax strategy:

1. Lower taxable income.

2. Utilize tax credits.

3. Utilize tax-deferred and tax-free growth.

4. Start a business.

Now let's get to the topic in the title. How can your children and spouse lower your taxable income legally? It's quite simple really, if you have followed the above 4 steps. Because step 5 would then be to put your kids and/or spouse to work in your business, and put them on your payroll.

## CPA Reveals: Tax loophole which lets you deduct 100% of preschool, daycare, after care (even a nanny) up to $5,000.00 each year (R044)

One powerful tax tool for those with children in daycare or with other qualified "dependent care" expenses is a **Flexible Spending Account**, or FSA. Using an FSA, an individual or working couple can use up to $5,000 in pre-tax dollars for dependent care expenses such as daycare costs.

The funds for flexible spending accounts are deducted from your paycheck and are not subject to payroll taxes. This means that if you have, for example, $5,000 per year in daycare expenses (not at all uncommon), you can pay for those expenses with up to $5,000 of pre-tax money using an FSA.

There are flexible spending accounts for several purposes. The one you want for daycare costs and the like is known as a **"dependent care FSA"**.

Dependent Care FSAs can be used for:

- Child care costs for children under age 13
- Care for a child (of any age) who is mentally or physically incapable of caring for him or herself
- "Adult daycare" expenses for **senior citizen dependents** who live with you

Withdrawals from FSAs are most commonly made using a special debit card for the FSA account, similar to what is commonly used with an HSA (a health savings account).

**There is one catch to FSAs.** Unused funds exceeding $500 will be **lost** if you don't use them. This is better than it used to be. Prior to Obamacare, ALL unused funds left in the account at the end of the year would be lost. With the current laws, you are now allowed to carry over up to $500 in unused funds.

### How the Numbers Play Out

What exactly is the tax impact of a dependent c are FSA? If you use the maximum $5,000 in dependent care expenses through the FSA, then you essentially get that $5,000 **tax free**. If you are in a 28% tax bracket, this is like putting $1,400 of cash in your pocket. (The "adjusted cost" of the daycare expenses, then, would be $3,600 instead of $5,000!)

It's a *big deal* for those with kids in daycare.

### What if Your Employer Doesn't Offer A Dependent Care FSA?

The second option, for those whose employers don't offer a Dependent Care FSA, is to utilize the **dependent care deduction**. This is not as powerful as the FSA option, but it is better than nothing. Your total deduction is up to 35% of the total paid for dependent care—depending on your tax bracket (lower income earners get higher deductions). Many people could knock as much as $1,000 off their tax bill with this deduction.

### How to get it:

In order to get this deduction, you will have to get statements from the preschool or daycare that detail the amounts paid for the year, and include the business information and tax ID of the daycare or preschool. It is recommended that you seek help from a qualified tax professional in order to most effectively utilize this and other deductions.

## Avoid these 27 tax reduction schemes or risk facing jail (R346)

One of the most dangerous tax scams out there is so serious, it could land you in jail. Yet more people are sucked into it on a daily basis. Just ask Wesley Snipes… who went to jail for tax evasion because of his "tax protestor" related actions.

A quick search on Google or YouTube will reveal a seemingly large selection of people touting various claims that all boil down to an effort to get out of paying federal income taxes.

While the excuses might be creative, they are far from credible. While supposed "former IRS employees" may claim that the income tax system is illegal, the courts seem to disagree… by clearly saying that it is instead *avoiding* the income tax system that is, in fact, illegal.

If you listen to the tax protestors' argument, you may think they made some good points, but nothing they say is rooted in law.

These scams continue to swell to such a large degree that the IRS felt compelled to put out a document "The Truth About Frivolous Tax Arguments", where the IRS lists and provides rebuttals for the following common tax protestor arguments:

- Filing a tax return is voluntary
- Payment of federal income tax is voluntary
- Taxpayers can reduce their federal income tax liability by filing a "zero return"
- The IRS must prepare federal tax returns for a person who fails to file
- Compliance with an administrative summons issued by the IRS is voluntary
- Wages, Tips, and other compensation received for personal services are not income
- Only foreign-source income is taxable
- Federal reserve notes are not income
- Military retirement pay is not income
- The taxpayer is not a "citizen" of the united states and is therefore not subject to taxes
- The "United States" consists only of the District of Columbia, Federal territories, and Federal enclaves

- The taxpayer is not a "person" as defined by the IRS code, thus is not subject to income taxes
- The only employees subject to federal income tax are employees of the federal government
- Tax payers can refuse to pay income taxes on religious or moral grounds
- Federal income taxes constitute a "taking" of property without due process of law, in violation of the fifth amendment
- Taxpayers do not have to file returns or provide financial information because of the protection against self-incrimination found in the fifth amendment
- Compelled compliance with the federal income tax law is a form of servitude in violation of the 13th amendment
- The federal income tax laws are unconstitutional because the 16th amendment to the U.S. constitution was not properly ratified
- The 16th amendment does not authorize a direct non-apportioned federal income tax on U.S. citizens
- The IRS is not an agency of the United States
- Taxpayers are not required to file a federal income tax return because the instructions and regulations associated with the form 1040 do not display an OMB control number as required by the Paperwork Reduction Act.
- African Americans can claim a special tax credit as reparations for slavery and other oppressive treatment
- Taxpayers are entitled to a refund of the Social Security taxes paid over their lifetime
- An "un-taxing" package or trust provides a way of permanently avoiding the obligation to file federal income tax returns and pay federal income taxes
- A "corporation sole" can be established and used for the purpose of avoiding federal income taxes
- Taxpayers who did not purchase and use fuel for an off-highway business can claim the fuels tax credit
- A Form 1099-OID can be used as a debt payment option, or the form or a purported financial instrument may be used to obtain money from the treasury

Believe it or not, there is more to the list. If you'd like to read the IRS rebuttals and see what else is on the list, you can do so by visiting the IRS website at IRS.gov.

**The bottom line is that any argument that ends in "therefore I am not subject to income taxes", or "therefore I do not have to file a tax return" is doomed to fail, and will very possibly result in big fines or jail time and in some cases, both.**

## The costliest tax mistake 99% of America is making (R338)

According to accountant and tax specialist Corbin Fritz, there is one mistake that most tax payers make on their taxes… and it is costing us millions. It happens year after year, and most people either don't know they are making it or think—wrongly—that it is not a big enough issue to worry about.

Here's the costliest tax mistake you'll ever make. It's simple. Most people simply do not put enough EFFORT into PLANNING their tax STRATEGY. In fact, most people do not even have a tax strategy. The bottom line is that for those who put the *effort* into saving on taxes, the payoff can be huge.

*Why bother?* **Listen:** they say two things are unavoidable in life… taxes and death. But that's not entirely true. By some estimates as many as 70% of American families are paying **more than they are legally required to** in taxes. Taxes are unavoidable, but there is a good chance you may be part of the 70% who could legally avoid paying at least a portion of what you currently pay. And again, we're not talking about "tax evasion" here. We're talking about legal tax deductions and strategies to reduce taxes that can pay off hugely in the long run.

Because taxes are one of the biggest expenses you will have in your life. Even with a modest income, you could pay *millions* in taxes over your lifetime. So the lifetime savings to be realized in simply TRYING and implementing a sensible tax strategy could be huge. (We're talking tens of thousands or even hundreds of thousands of dollars.)

Here are just a few examples of ways in which you can improve your tax strategy and savc big money:

1. Maximize charitable donations. Itemize deductions and create a system to regularly donate and recycle clothes, toys, electronics, cell phones, etc. If you own stocks and sell at a loss, be sure to claim the loss on your taxes. If you have investments that have gained, you can give the stocks or bonds to charity and claim the higher (gained) amount as a deduction even though you paid less. Remember—deduction amounts are "fair market value" which, in the case of stocks, is the value of the stock on the day that you donate it.
2. Research Tax Credits to take Maximum Advantage. With the Internet, it's easy to stay abreast of all the tax credits that come and go every year. This may mean getting tax credits for "green" energy-related home improvements, taking a tax credit for college education or even for saving.
3. Deduct the cost of Moving. If you relocate for a new job at least 50 miles away, then you may be able to save big by deducting your moving costs—including deductions for miles driven as well as costs for looking for the job. Check the current tax laws for the current numbers of allowable deductions. (Note: as of this writing you do not have to itemize deductions to take advantage of this.)
4. Teachers - Keep track of expenses. If you're a teacher or teacher's aide, you can deduct up to $250 of your own out of pocket expenses related to the classroom, even if you do not itemize deductions.
5. Use special accounts to the maximum. Make the most of FSA (flexible spending accounts), HSAs (health savings accounts), Coverdell savings accounts, and childcare reimbursement accounts, and other special tax-advantaged accounts. Many of these accounts allow you to use pre-tax dollars for various expenses, which enables you to effectively save 25% to 30% on those expenses, depending on your tax bracket.
6. If you're married, file tax returns jointly. Check with your accountant to be sure, but in most cases married people will save money by filing jointly. Filing jointly will

allow you to take advantage of certain tax credits that you won't be able to if you are filing separately. (Example: The lifetime learning credit, mentioned earlier, and more.)

7. Take full advantage of Roth IRAs and SEP IRAs. Using IRAs to the maximum means that you're putting as much money away as you can… and you're not paying taxes on that money! You keep your money. You lower your tax bill. It's win-win. And Roth IRAs have the added benefit of allowing you to withdraw money tax free (conditions apply). This means you can pay for college and more with Roth IRA funds—i.e. *tax free money*.

8. Make the most of medical problems. Medical bills can show up big and if you itemize, you can deduct them. Keep track of all expenses related to your health, from doctor bills to medically necessary home improvements. These burdensome expenses could save you money down the road, as many qualify as deductions. The key is to keep meticulous records, and talk to your accountant about how to best maximize your savings. Note that portions of health insurance premiums (long term care insurance, regular insurance) are deductible in many cases as well as your contribution to your Health Savings Account.

9. Utilize the home office deduction. A lot of people shy away from this or just don't understand it. But taking the home office deduction for your legitimate business can save you a lot of money in the long run. Now the IRS has simplified the deduction allowing you a set amount per square foot. Compare that amount versus the percentage of your home used for business, as well as utilities, Internet, etc.

10. Take advantage of Section 179 for Business Vehicles If you own a business, and use a vehicle in the operation of your business, then a Section 179 deduction the year you purchase your vehicle—even if you finance the vehicle—could save you a BUNDLE of money. How to manage this deduction is detailed in the next report.

## How to get the IRS to pay up to $10,000.00 towards your next truck or SUV (R348)

***WARNING:*** *Tax law is subject to change, and the tax laws covered in this document are no exception. Please check with the IRS and your qualified tax advisor for the latest information on your options related to this report.*

It's true.

If you qualify there is a special government program **which can pay up to $10,000.00 towards the cost of your next truck or SUV.** I know it sounds too good to be true but everything I am about to share can be backed up by actually referring to the **IRS tax code.** So let's start with a little history lesson...

**In 1913 the tax code was around 400 pages. Today it has swelled to over 74,000 pages.** Why so many? Because multinational corporations and their lobbyists spend millions of dollars every year to get special **tax deductions** and **credits** written into the code which will benefit their business. As a result, within those pages are deductions and credits not just for rich corporations, but also, for *you*.

The deduction I am about to share with you is what I believe to be one of the **greatest tax deductions in America for the average business owner.** Because this tax deduction can allow you to purchase your next truck or SUV and **have the IRS pay up to $10,000 of its costs.**

The sad part is, because the tax code has become so many pages, many tax professionals when asked about this deduction will actually tell you it does not exist! Let me share a story to get my point across.

**"How One Letter Sold $1,100,000.00 Worth of Trucks and SUVs."**

I had a conversation with a friend working in an automotive dealership and he was complaining about how hard it was to sell trucks and SUVs because of the economy. I told him there was a way he could sell millions of dollars' worth of vehicles **by making his potential customers aware of the simple tax deduction being discussed here.**

I explained by educating his customers who own businesses they could purchase a vehicle and expense the entire purchase the first year through this special tax deduction, the dealerships' sales would likely increase when consumers took advantage of the deduction. And increase they did!

The dealership mailed one letter explaining the tax deduction to his customers and the phones began ringing off the hook. Of course, many of the customers called their accountants and most of them had *no clue about this deduction buried in the tax code*.

In fact, one man called up my friend at the car dealership and wanted to argue with him saying that he was going to turn him into the IRS for tax fraud! *Can you imagine?* My friend said "before you do that, why don't you stop by the dealership so I can give you a copy of the law from the IRS website, okay?"

The man agreed. **Two weeks later he bought two large trucks costing over $80,000.** He also fired his accountant for giving him bad advice.

If you have a business with annual revenues of over $25,000 you may find yourself angry with your accountant for *not* pointing out this deduction. **Becasuse you can not only use it for certain vehicles, but for many other capital expense you need to run your business**.

**IRS SECTION 179**

The big deduction is in **IRS section 179**. It's a powerful tool in the hands of the right business owner, and it could save you thousands and even TENS OF THOUSANDS of dollars.

**Here's what the IRS website says:**

*"You can elect to recover all or part of the cost of certain qualifying property, up to a limit, by deducting it in the year you place the property in service. This is the section 179 deduction. You can elect the section 179 deduction instead of recovering the cost by taking depreciation deductions over the lifetime of the property."*

**The "big deal" here is that you can deduct the full purchase price of qualifying purchases all in the first year** you put the purchased equipment (or software) into service. Instead of depreciating the equipment over time (you can get the deduction all at once).

What makes this even more powerful is that it **applies to FINANCED purchases.**

And unlike some so-called tax "loopholes", this one isn't going to land anyone behind bars. The IRS offers clear instructions on their website for section 179 deductions. **It's a perfectly legal and legitimate way to save "big" money.**

But in order to use it, you have to qualify.

To qualify your business must purchase or finance less than $2,000,000 of qualifying equipment. (This is a general guideline, check with the IRS or your tax advisor for current requirements.) Also, the amount you deduct using section 179 is limited to the amount of your business's taxable income.

In order to qualify for section 179, **purchases must be for business use**, must be in the required limits, and must meet other qualifications as defined by the IRS. This means it must be tangible personal property or qualified real property, off the shelf software, or one of a variety of certain other types of property.

**Here's How You Can Deduct the Cost of a Car, Truck or SUV**

For more details on section 179 qualifications, visit:

http://www.irs.gov/publications/p946/ch02.html

Now let's talk about how exactly the **section 179** deduction can help you purchase your next truck or SUV and have the IRS foot up to $10,000 of the bill.

First of all, the tax savings you get with section 179 will depend on your tax bracket. In a 40% tax bracket, $100,000 worth of section 179 qualified expenses equates to **$40,000 in tax savings.**

In essence, this lowers the cost of the equipment purchased by 40%.

Let's say you purchase a vehicle for business use.

The vehicle costs $35,000.

You deduct the full cost of the vehicle this year using the **section 179** deduction.

So if you are in a 40% tax bracket the vehicle will cost $21,000 after it is "written off" as deduction in the first year.

*Would you rather pay $35,000 for that vehicle or $21,000?*

Using the **section 179** deduction puts more cash in your pocket and helps you by getting the IRS to help with your business purchases by giving you a FIRST YEAR deduction.

As you can see, if you aren't taking advantage of the **section 179** deduction and you qualify to do so, you are missing out!

**Conclusion**

The section 179 deduction is a big tax break available to small businesses that many entrepreneurs (and accountants) simply don't know about. **Remember, you should never depend on your accountant for 100% of your tax strategies.** Why? Because they are too busy running their own business to stay on top of every way you can save. They have hundreds of clients in dozens of different industries. There is no way they can help you optimize the tax code for your benefit. To do that, you need a tax attorney or strategist as well as your own motivation to keep up on the laws.

To find out what a **section 179** deduction could do for your business; check out the IRS website at: www.IRS.gov

Also, be sure to check with a qualified tax advisor about **Section 179**.

## Accountant Reveals the Painful Truth about the Mortgage Tax Deduction That Many Homeowners Miss (R400)

How many times have we all heard the saying *"If you're renting a home, you're throwing your money away?"* We've heard that statement from homeless people to PhD's. The funny thing is, you never hear any of them back up the claim with the numbers.

Of course, the group of people who is probably the most guilty of this is realtors. After all, realtors want you to believe you're throwing your money away if you're renting, so you'll be more motivated to buy a home. When was the last time a realtor ever said it "wasn't" a great time to buy?

But unlike realtors, numbers never lie. So in this article, we'll actually crunch the numbers on renting versus buying so you can see in TRUTH which is a better deal.

And who better to help us crunch the numbers than an actual Accountant who's done over 14,000 tax returns?

Remember, buying a home is the biggest investment you will most likely ever make in your life. So, before reading we want you to keep these points in mind:

1. There is a time to "rent" and there is a time to "buy" our goal is to give you an accountants perspective so you can make a solid decision based on facts and not emotions.
2. As of this writing, in order to "write off" your mortgage interest against your taxable income you must "itemize" your tax deductions. This means your mortgage interest must amount to MORE than your itemized deduction to benefit you in the short term.
3. When you "buy" a home you are in one sense buying the "right" to benefit from the homes appreciation but... with the opportunity of appreciation comes the OBLIGATION of potential depreciation.
4. There are many additional costs on when owning many people fail to factor in because they never had to pay them when renting. These include, but are not limited to: Property Taxes, Homeowners Insurance and Maintenance (which can be from $4,000 to $6,000 per year on a $200,000 home).
5. The Cost to Sell: the biggest mistake we see new homeowners fail to factor in is the cost of selling. Remember, 90% of the time, the seller pays all realtor commissions and closing costs. These can run 10% so even if your $200,000 home goes up 10% in 2 to 4 year and you have to sell because of a job relocation or being laid off, your $20,000 gain will go back to realtor commissions and closing costs when you sell.

**Here is a TRUE story told by an accountant...**

Sitting in my office during the 2011 tax season, filing tax returns for 2010, were new clients. In July a real estate agent sold them a home with two stories - one story <u>before</u> the sale and another after.

The first story the real estate agent told them was, "You'll pay about $6,900 of interest and about $2,040 in real estate taxes. That's an $8,940 tax write off and it's a great time to buy, but if you keep renting you're just throwing you're money away."

To help my clients afford the monthly mortgage payments, the real estate agent advised the couple to lower their withholding by $110 per month, which they did.

This married couple had never before owned a home or filed a long tax form. They were very excited about all the tax deductions they would get for owning a home.

However, according to the IRS, in 2010 64.4% of all tax payers could not itemize their deductions on a Schedule "A" but had to take the standard deduction on their tax returns.

Unfortunately for our new homeowners, even if they had actually paid the full $6,800 of interest and full real estate taxes in 2010, which they did not, in 2010 their itemized deductions were not greater than the standard deduction of $11,400.

When I added up their medical deductions, other state taxes, charitable contributions, and miscellaneous deductions their total still did not exceed the $11,400 standard deduction.

**They received no new tax benefits from home ownership.**

They did not even qualify for the $8,000 First Time Home Buyer Tax Credit because they signed the binding purchase contract after the deadline of April 30, 2010.

The <u>second</u> story the real estate agent told the couple was, "Owning a home is better than renting because you'll build equity in your home.

Again, when you're renting you're throwing your money away."

My name is Brian A. Regalbuto, CEO of Proactive Tax Planning Services. During my career of 26 years as a tax professional, I have seen this happen <u>many</u> times and I have personally prepared over 14,000 tax returns during my career.

I always try to teach my clients, "If you spend one dollar ($1.00) just to get a tax write-off and the government sends you back twenty-five cents ($0.25) you are still throwing away seventy-five cents ($0.75)!"

During the above interview, I also found out my clients planned on moving in five years because of their jobs. That is not unusual. According to the National Association of Realtors®, most people move every five to seven years. Given these facts, let us do an analysis to see if it is truly better for a median couple to buy or rent who will move in five years.

The following case study will be based on information obtained from the recently released *American Housing Survey for the United States: 2009* (AHSUS), the National Association of Realtors® Historical Sale Price Data Table, and the U.S. Census Bureau FactFinder2 web site.

When one does an analysis, one must make some assumptions. In other words we must predict the future. If I were any good at predicting future numbers; I would have won the Mega Millions Lottery by now, and I would not have to work.

These are the assumptions we will use in this case study:

1. Purchase price of home $170,000[5]
2. Home Owners use FHA 3.5% Down Program
3. Loan $164,050 for 30 years at 5.00% which includes the 0.55% FHA Insurance
4. The median real estate tax for an owner-occupied home is $10 per year per $1,000 of value[6] - $1,700 ([170,000/1,000] x 10 = 1,700).
5. Median sale price declined by 9.42% from December 2010 to February 2012[7] (That median home lost $16,000 and is now worth $154,000.)
6. Sales price in 2015 - $170,000 (I have no idea what the value of the median home will be by 2015. Let us be optimistic, and assume the value will go back up to what it was in 2010.)
7. Use average costs to purchase or sell a home in the US
8. Monthly maintenance cost $29[9]
9. They have $16,000 cash to buy a home.
10. 2010 median monthly rent was $855[10]

Table One calculates the cost of buying the median home in 2010. The total cost is $15,725.

Table 1 - Move in Cost of Owning a Home

| **Move In Costs** | | |
|---|---|---|
| Purchase Price | 170,000 | $ Costs |
| Down Payment | 3.50% | 5,950 |
| Lender Points | 1.00% | 1,641 |
| FHA Fee | 2.25% | 3,825 |
| Other Closing Costs | 2.50% | 4,250 |
| **Total Purchase Costs** | | 15,666 |

---

[5]Median Owner-Occupied home Value - AHSUS Table 3-14

[6]Median Owner-Occupied Annual Taxes Paid Per $1,000 Value - AHUS Table 3-13

[7]National Association of Realtors® Historical Sale Price Data Table

[8]National Association of Realtors web site

[9]Median routine Maintenance in Last Year - AHSUS Table 3-13

[10]The U.S. Census Bureau FactFinder2 web site

Table Two calculates the monthly cost of homeownership of a median home in 2010.

Table 2 - Monthly Costs of Owning a Home[11]

| Monthly Costs | |
|---|---|
| Mortgage (PI & FHAI) | 881 |
| Real Estate Taxes | 142 |
| Major Repair Bills | 29 |
| **Total Monthly** | 1,051 |

Note: The median monthly rent is $855. Thus, it costs $196 more a month to own then rent. ($1,052 – 855 = $196)

Table Three compares the home owners' mortgage interest and real estate tax deductions against the standard deduction. Note that the interest deduction is going down while the standard deduction is going up. As you build equity by paying back the loan the interest amount goes down.

The standard deduction is adjusted each year for inflation.

That is why it goes up each year.

If the home owners cannot itemize their deduction before they own a home then it is likely they will not get the full benefits of the tax deductions. In this case the home owners cannot itemize.

Table 3 - Home Owner's Tax Savings[12]

**Owner Tax Savings**

| Yr | Interest | RE Tax | Total Ded | Stand Ded | Tax Savings |
|---|---|---|---|---|---|
| 1 | 8,148 | 1,700 | 9,848 | 11400 | None |
| 2 | 8,024 | 1,700 | 9,724 | 11600 | None |
| 3 | 7,894 | 1,700 | 9,594 | 11700 | None |
| 4 | 7,757 | 1,700 | 9,457 | 11800 | None |
| 5 | 7,613 | 1,700 | 9,313 | 11900 | None |

Table 4 – Sale of Median Home in 2015 - Results

**Getting Investment Back**

| **Sale of Real Estate** | | | | **Total** |
|---|---|---|---|---|
| **Sales Price** | | | **170,000** | |
| Loan Payoff | | | (150,645) | |
| **Equity Build Up** | | | 19,355 | 19,355 |
| Less cost of Sales | | | | |
| Real Estate Comm. | 6.00% | 10,200 | | |
| Closing Costs | 4.00% | 6,800 | | |
| Total Closing Costs | | | 7,000 | (17,000) |
| | | | | |
| Net Gain/(Loss) from sale | | | 2,355 | |
| Additional Tax Savings | | none | | 0 |
| Return of Purchase Costs | | | | (15,666) |
| Net Effect of Home Ownership | | | | (13,311) |

Table Four above tells us the final results. In this economy the home owner was under water by the end of the first year. According to National Association of Realtors® Historical Sale Price Data Table, the home lost $16,000 of value and is now worth $154,000. To regain just its lost value, that home must appreciate over 10.38% in two years.

When you carefully review Table Four you see that the home owner had a net equity build-up of only $2,355 after you subtract the cost of sale. Their equity buildup was less than 1.5% over five years. After you figure in the cost to purchase the home, the home owner has a total out of pocket loss of $13,311.

Of course the home owner would not sell under these conditions. They would 1) rent the property, or 2) walk away.

[12]Interest and Principal - Mortgage Calculator on Internet

Table Five shows how much the property would have to sell for just to break even.

Table 5 – Sales Price to Breakeven

**Getting Investment Back**

| **Sale of Real Estate** | | | | **Total** |
|---|---|---|---|---|
| **Sales Price** | | | **184,856** | |
| Loan Payoff | | | (150,645) | |
| **Equity Build Up** | | | 34,211 | 34,211 |
| Less cost of Sales | | | | |
| Real Estate Comm. | 6.00% | 11,091 | | |
| Closing Costs | 4.00% | 7,394 | | |
| Total Closing Costs | | 18,486 | 7,000 | (18,486) |
| | | | | |
| Net Gain/(Loss) from sale | | | | 15,725 |
| Additional Tax Savings | | none | | 0 |
| Return of Purchase Costs | | | | (15,725) |
| Net Effect of Home Ownership | | | | 0 |

To breakeven, the home would have to appreciate over 20.04% during the next two years. In other words, the home would have to appreciate by more than $30,856 in two years and sell for $184,856. *How likely is that in the current economy?*

Conclusion:

1. Mortgage Deduction may or may not be helpful. It varies for each person. There were no tax advantages in this example.
2. Equity buildup only happens in the short run when the property values are going up, not down.
3. The home owners in this example threw away $26,775. It is better to rent than own when you are going to live in a home short term. In this case study, if the home owners rented, they would have saved $196 per month or $11,760 over five years. Add this savings of $11,760 to the $16,000 they started with and at the end of five years they would have had $27,760 plus interest earnings on that money.
4. Buying a home is a good investment for the long term. Once you have the mortgage paid off at the end of 30 years, you have a good retirement program. You never have to worry that your rent payments will go up.

The real estate agent in this story was using rough rules of thumbs to give tax advice to my clients. This unfortunate couple may have felt as though the real estate agent had hit their thumbs with a hammer. Moral of the story, never use rough rules of thumb. Before you buy a home, talk to a tax professional first to truly determine the tax effects of home ownership in your circumstance. You never want to throw away money.

# REAL ESTATE AND MORTGAGES

- ☑ **The scariest secret you need to know about Home Owner Associations which 99% miss**
- ☑ **The 5 most common ways your realtor can cost you $15,000.00 or more**
- ☑ **Eight secrets you need to know BEFORE signing up for a reverse mortgage**
- ☑ **Deadly secret you must know if you don't have a will or trust**
- ☑ **The biggest mistake you DON'T want to make with your homeowners insurance**
- ☑ **Did you take out an FHA mortgage between 1983 and 2004? You may be due a mortgage insurance refund. Over $514 million is sitting unclaimed**
- ☑ **Your best source for reliable FREE help to stop foreclosure**
- ☑ ***And More***

“

There is no greater
motivation than *Love*.
To do what you *Love*.
To provide for those you *Love*.
To be loved by those you *Love*.

## The scariest secret you need to know about HOAs which 99% miss (R199)

Homeowners associations are, to some, the mafia of real estate. They are notorious for a wide array of problems, from embezzlement by leadership to outright abuse and harassment of homeowners.

The board members of home owners associations have no training to do what they do, are usually not well-versed in contract and real estate law, and have been known to abuse their place of power to carry out personal vendettas. There have been numerous cases of homeowners paying fines demanded of them by their HOA, only to have more fines and late fees stack up because the HOA failed to properly record the payment.

We have given the advice before, and will give it again, that if you can choose to buy a home that is NOT under the oppressive weight of a homeowners association, then that is what you should do. The fees of the homeowners associations usually far outweigh the purported "benefits".

And yes, there will be some who say their HOA boards are reasonable. Their fees are reasonable. They've never had a problem. But what happens when the board changes? What happens when they make a neighbor angry, and that neighbor retaliates through the HOA? We can choose to look the other way, but it won't change the fact that this very thing happens all the time in association neighborhoods.

So even if you know all of this… and you still choose to live in an HOA neighborhood, you could be putting yourself at serious risk. Here is the pattern of HOA behavior that you might not know about—and that **could cost you big time**:

1. Homeowner gets fined for some small offense. Sometimes it happens when the homeowner has already gotten the "offense" cleared with the HOA.
2. Homeowner either fights fees or pays them and the fees fail to get recorded properly by the HOA.
3. The fees stack up quickly (being as much as $50 per day—sometimes more), and soon the HOA places a lien on the home.
4. The HOA forecloses, taking the home away from the homeowner. In fact, in 2014 in hard hit housing markets in Florida, homeowners are being forced to sell at underwater prices because the builder wants to convert to more lucrative apartment rentals.

If you can't accept the above pattern, then you are in denial… because this exact thing happens repeatedly in the United States of America… where we have "constitutional rights". **When you are a member of an HOA, you give up many of your rights.** And since the board (and/or manager) of the HOA may act quite unprofessionally and not know what they are doing, you may lose rights that the HOA has no real legal right to take from you.

What types of small offenses can **you lose your home over** in an HOA neighborhood? Here are a few examples:

- Late HOA dues due to being overseas in the military.
- The wrong color of house
- The wrong types of flowers
- Too many flowers
- Cars that don't look fancy enough parked in your driveway
- Overdue HOA fees
- The wrong fence height
- The wrong type of fence

- Allowing kids to play outside
- Any non-violation that you fail to win in court over when an HOA board member misinterprets (or ignores) the rules

So your home could be at risk, as it turns out, over something quite small. People have been fined by Homeowners Associations for things that, as it turned out, were not actually violations of the Homeowners Association rules. Fail to pay those fines, and guess what? **You could lose your home… or face a lengthy court battle to (possibly) keep it.**

What makes it worse is that the issues are often personal. Many people who live in "nightmare" HOA neighborhoods fear retaliation by the homeowners association for speaking out. This means you could lose your home for no other reason—*in reality*—than because some neighbor or HOA board member doesn't like you.

*Why all the negativity? Aren't we being a little hard on those good ol' HOAs?*

Maybe it's perfectly reasonable to ban children from playing outside (Source: WFTV, Florida), or to send a man to jail because he can't afford to sod his lawn (Source: St. Petersburg Times)?

Or consider this story of a woman who was threatened with foreclosure over a dispute involving initially small fines that she claims to have **paid**:

*"It started in 2009 when [Nancy] Ruedeman's Homeowners Association slapped her with two $25 fines for not removing the grass in the cracks of her driveway.*

*Nancy says she paid the fine, but her HOA said she didn't. That's when the fees started racking up. "Not only was I getting a $25-a-month late fee every other week, I was also getting $35 collection fees," recalled Ruedeman.*

*In the months to follow, the 50-year-old homeowner says things really got ugly. "The grass in the cracks was one of many frivolous violation charges that they sent me notices on."*

*Ruedeman says she got hit with fines for not painting the trim on her house and for bald spots in her lawn. She was inundated with registered letters seeking payment. The HOA then demanded that she pay for attorney fees.*

*When the fines and fees finally reached more than $1500, her HOA placed a lien on her home and threatened to foreclose. "It makes me upset to think I worked hard my whole life and in an instant, over something as frivolous as grass growing in the crack of the driveway, the HOA can take your home and just throw you on the street," said Ruedeman."*

*(Source: CBS News, Dallas Texas)*

Here's the bottom line of HOAs:

- In most cases, the **cost outweighs the value** in our opinion.
- In almost all cases, even a good HOA is capable of becoming a bad one. You can't predict which yours will be.
- Until the laws are changed to regulate and restrict HOAs and to protect consumers from their many questionable, unfair, and even illegal practices, your best bet is to stay far away from HOAs.

## The 5 most common ways your realtor can cost you $15,000.00 or more (R066)

The thing to understand about working with a realtor is that every $10,000 they drop the price of your home only costs them about $150. Research has shown that Realtors who sell their *own* homes sell them for higher prices. On average, the Realtor selling his or her own home takes 10 days longer to sell it and gets

$10,000 more for the home. This tendency can be extremely costly to you (the homeowner) because for the Realtor—who will do anything to sell your home fast—who will no doubt operate slightly differently than if they were selling their own home—it isn't going to cost them $10,000 or $15,000 to sell to an early lowball bidder. But it may **cost you** that.

So what should you look for in a realtor, then…and what are the other ways even a "nice" realtor can cost you?

**1. A Smile and A License Do Not Count as Qualifications.** One mistake people make when using a real estate agent to help them find a home is that they often go into it blind. They go with the choice that they "feel good about". This usually equates to a licensed real estate professional with a nice smile who makes the person feel warm and fuzzy. (You'd be surprised how many people choose a realtor of the opposite sex, in part, based on *attractiveness*.)

But when it comes to who can SELL your home and get you the most money and do it the fastest…those things just don't matter. The smile, good looks and warm fuzzies - none of it matters. And chances are it will cost you. That smile might mean "I like to please". It could mean they like to please others as well like other real estate agents (buyer's agents) and the buyers. Sometimes in sales, you have to be tough. Warm and fuzzy does not equal tough. This is one area where leaning in the direction of the warm and fuzzy feeling could cost you.

**2. Nice Does Not Equal Innocent.** When someone has a nice demeanor, people tend to let their guards down. Whether you're selling your home or looking to buy a home, letting your guard down in this way can really cost you. Some "nice" real estate "pros" have been known to use that implied trust against you, by only showing you the higher priced listings with the better commissions.

**Another trick** that has been used: delaying the MLS listing so that the realtor can show the home to their existing "buyer" clients. That way the realtor can collect both sides of the commission coin. (The commission is usually split between the buyer's and seller's agents.)

**3. That Nice Realtor At The Open House** It may surprise you to hear that **an open house is actually not very effective** when it comes to actually selling a home. *Want to know what open houses are good for?* They are an excellent way for a nice realtor to collect leads.

**4. Nice sometimes means pushover and that can cost you.** A truly nice realtor is often, as we said above, nice to everyone—not just you. They are less likely to fight for a higher or lower price in your favor. Worse yet, they may be lazy and simply prefer a quick transaction over drawing out and potentially losing the sale.

**5. Uncle George may be nice, too. Don't use him as your real estate agent.** A lot of people lose a lot of money by choosing less qualified and less experienced friends and family over more qualified/experienced agents they don't know personally.

Other things you should watch out for include the following:

- **"Part time" real estate agents.** Part-time sometimes means undedicated and/or unsuccessful. This isn't always the case. Just beware, and be choosey.

• **Free Appraisals.** One seemingly underhanded tactic for getting new customers is for a realtor to offer a "free appraisal" to a potential seller or even to a "for sell by owner" seller. **The trick?** They appraise high, giving you the impression that the high figure is what they'll be able to get for your home. In one example, the home was "appraised" by the realtor at $120,000, was listed on the market at $112,000, and eventually sold for—drum rolls please—a whopping $84,000.

• **Super Producers.** Some of the highest producing real estate folks get that way by being picky about the properties they choose to sell. To put it bluntly, they go for the *easy* ones. If your property isn't an easy one, you get ignored and/or forgotten.

**So what should you do?**

You may be wondering what all this means. Should you avoid a Realtor? Not necessarily. Sometimes a FSBO (For sale by owner) is warranted, other times it is not. You've got to think smart and make the right choice for yourself. What's the market like for the house you're selling? Are there buyers likely able and willing to buy in a FSBO deal? These are just examples of things to consider.

# Eight secrets you need to know BEFORE signing up for a reverse mortgage (R030)

A reverse mortgage is a loan based on the equity on your home. Your home may or may not be paid off when signing up for a reverse mortgage. It is similar to a home equity loan with one major exception:

You make NO PAYMENTS on the loan as long as you live in the home. When you move, sell your home, or die, the loan must be paid off. Usually this happens when the home is sold, either before or after the death of the owner.

Reverse mortgages usually have higher interest rates than a comparable home equity loan and often have numerous fees attached to them.

For some, a reverse mortgage may sound like a great idea to use the equity in their home in their golden years. But reverse mortgages aren't without their pitfalls. Here are eight things that you absolutely must know before you sign up for one:

**Secret #1 - Payout Options**

Reverse mortgages have 3 payout options:

1. A line of credit
2. A monthly payout
3. A lump sum payment

The option that you choose matters a lot. Perhaps one of the most commonly chosen options is the "lump sum" payout option, and in many cases that is the worst option to choose. With the lump sum payout method:

- People end up blowing the money irresponsibly and are back where they started
- People borrow more money than they actually need, and end up paying more interest than they actually need to
- The money runs out before the person expects it to
- The amount that will need to be paid back when you die may be larger than it would have been using the other methods

The line of credit and monthly payout options are often better because both represent a more controlled use of the loan. They reduce the risk of frivolous spending and poor financial decisions because of the "windfall" effect.

### Secret #2 - You put your home at risk

Like any other loan secured by your home, a reverse mortgage requires that you maintain insurance on the home and that you pay the property taxes. If you fail to do either of these things, the lender for the reverse mortgage can **foreclose** on your home. This can happen even if your home was paid off before you signed up for the reverse mortgage. (Granted, if you fail to pay your taxes you are putting your home at risk anyways. Even failing to insure your home puts your home at risk by not protecting you in case of a catastrophic loss.)

### Secret #3 - Your kids might not like it

Maybe this isn't a big secret. But your kids may be the first to complain about you signing up for a reverse mortgage. *Why?* Sometimes kids want to keep the house in the family after you die. Or maybe they plan to sell it and keep the proceeds as their inheritance. In either case, a reverse mortgage may put a damper on those plans. Obviously, you've got to look out for yourself first—and if a reverse mortgage is right for you, then your kids will find a way to live with it.

There are other ways you can provide an inheritance or enable your kids to purchase the home after you die, such as by purchasing a life insurance policy on yourself with your children as the beneficiaries. An alternative: if your kids want to preserve their inheritance, it may make sense for them to help out with your expenses now so that you can avoid a reverse mortgage. (Always go through the numbers carefully to figure out what is best!)

### Secret #4 - It could affect your benefits

According to some sources, the pile of cash that you get out of a lump sum reverse mortgage deal may be **counted amongst your assets when applying for government programs** such as Medicaid. (Check with your financial advisor for the latest on this!)

### Secret #5 - You could be forced to sell the home before you are ready to

According to various reports by watchdog organizations, as many as 60% of reverse mortgages are paid off for reasons other than the homeowner dying. You have to actually be living in the home, and if you are not, the loan must be repaid.

An example: imagine that you suffer a serious injury and have to go into a care facility to recover for a year. The loan may have to be repaid at that point, even if you are planning on moving back into the home. That could mean that you'll be forced to sell your home in order to pay back the loan.

### Secret #6 - The interest can be downright shocking

The interest charges on a reverse mortgage are added to the loan each day that you have it. This can lead to balances that are *downright shocking*. According to one state attorney general[1], <u>a $200,000 loan may turn into a $400,000 loan in as little as 10 years</u>.

### Secret #7 - The longer you wait the better

While (as of this writing) you can get a reverse mortgage as early as age 62, that may not be the best move. <u>The longer you wait, the better loan you can normally get, the less interest you will pay, and the less likely it is that you'll outlive the proceeds</u>.

### Secret #8 - Scams and horror stories abound

There are numerous scams where a salesperson will attempt to get an elderly person to pay for an expensive product with a reverse mortgage. These include attempts to get someone to purchase long term care insurance, annuities, or various investment products with proceeds from a reverse mortgage.

<u>Taking out a reverse mortgage in order to buy long-term care insurance, an annuity, or to make</u>

an investment is almost always a bad idea, because reverse mortgages are simply too costly for such a scheme to make good financial sense. **The numbers just don't work.**

Take, for example, the New York woman who took out a $275,000 reverse mortgage for which she now owes over $1,000,000.[2] According to the *Seattle Times*, her mortgage featured:

*"A reverse mortgage with a base interest rate of 9.95 percent, plus a 50 percent share for the lender of increases in value of the house after closing, plus an additional 2 percent "maturity fee" to sweeten the payout even more and on top of that, there's a $33,000 mandatory purchase of an annuity by the homeowner that is added to the principal balance and incurs compounding interest while lessening the lender's future payments to the homeowner."*

And then there are those times where seemingly legitimate reverse mortgages go horribly wrong.

In one such case, an elderly woman faced foreclosure by Wells Fargo because her husband died after the couple had taken out a reverse mortgage on the home. When the last surviving borrower on a reverse mortgage dies, the loan becomes "due" immediately. That's what happened in this nightmare case—a possibility that should have been explained, or that the loan should have been structured so as to avoid—when Wells Fargo came knocking to kick her out of her own home after her husband died.

**What can you do about it?**

Here's the number one thing you can do if you're thinking about a reverse mortgage: educate yourself first. Don't believe the loan officers and the sales pitches. Don't sign up with someone who shows up at your door. Do some research of your own and see what can go wrong. Learn what the current trends are and what scams are common in the industry.

And what is the best, #1 most important step you can take? Don't sign up in the first place if you can avoid it. Some financial "tools" are especially prone to problems and abuse. This is one of them.

(1) Minnesota state attorney general's office

(2) Source: *Seattle Times*

## Deadly secret you must know if you don't have a will or trust (R085)

Probate is the name given to the legal process through which the courts determine the validity of a will. It is a process feared by many—at least those with assets—and perhaps for good reason. The probate process can be full of problems and pitfalls, and it's best to avoid the nasty stuff if at all possible.

**"Probate Horror Stories…"**

One family told a story of losing over $200,000 due to the probate process. Another woman said: "My mother died of cancer at 46 years old without a living trust. Probate went on for over ten years and was never terminated. In yet another case, a family paid over $4 million in legal fees before issues related to probate were resolved.

Probate horror stories abound. But the question is…*how can you avoid a probate horror story of your own?*

**It starts with "trust"…**

We'll start with the big one. A trust is a tool for being very specific about how your money is dispersed after you're gone.

Without a trust, the inheritance of your heirs could be tied up in probate for a year or more, and could be subject to **probate fees of up to 5%** of the value of your estate.[2] Some people think that having a will avoids all that, but this isn't the case. Probate is the process through which the *validity* of the will is determined. So even if there is a will, you won't avoid probate unless you have **properly** set up a trust.

**But without a will…**

With that said, **both a will and a trust** are important for protecting your heirs and making sure your wishes are carried out. Here are a few things you should know:

- Without a will, established laws will decide who gets what. This usually means that your surviving spouse will get half of the inheritance, and surviving children and/or grandchildren will get the other half. This isn't always the desired scenario. (Usually it is not, in fact.)
- Without a will, you cannot leave assets to charity.
- Without a will, your minor children could fall into the "wrong" hands. A will is the best (and only) place to say who will be the guardian of your children if you die before they come of age.
- Without a will, you will have no say in who gets to control the inheritance of your minor children. Another thing a will often does is appoint a trustee for children. This is the person who will take care of the money until they are old enough to receive their inheritance, and it is an important choice for you to make in advance.

A will is an important part of estate planning. But as we've already mentioned, it isn't the whole picture.

**Back to trust!**

A trust is an important estate planning tool that should be considered by many Americans. Here's what you should know:

- Without a trust, your heirs will have to endure the probate process. This means that there could be substantial delay in getting their inheritance, regardless of what is in your will. The **probate fees will also reduce the inheritance** available to your heirs.
- Without a trust, the likelihood that heirs will squander their inheritance is greater. A trust enables the disbursement of funds in installments instead of a lump sum, and this is a decision that can be made by you… not the person receiving the inheritance (as is the default scenario with most life insurance).
- Without a trust, options for disbursement are limited. A trust enables flexible payment of inheritance funds for things like education and the care of minor dependents.
- For wealthier Americans, trusts provide a way to **reduce or avoid estate taxes**.
- Without a trust, the likelihood of conflict among family members may be greater. A trust gives you more control over how certain assets are divided up. Specific assets can be given to named beneficiaries in a detailed, clearly spelled out manner.

For most people, the first line of defense in estate planning is the will. For many, however, setting up a trust for certain purposes may be advisable.

(1) heritagelivingtrust.com

(2) estateplanningandtaxlawyer.com

(3) Nolo.com

## The biggest mistake you DON'T want to make with your homeowners insurance (R072)

Some people have made mistakes with their homeowners insurance that have **cost them anywhere from $300 per year, to thousands of dollars in unpaid or underpaid claims**.

Here's how not to be one of them. Read the following carefully:

**Failure to research policies.**

One common problem is that people fail to research the policy and/or company they are being offered.

**Here's a trap many fall into:**

It has become commonplace in recent years for Insurance companies that traditionally offer one particular line of insurance (such as auto insurance) to offer a second line of Insurance (such as home insurance) to their customers. What is *implied* in the associated advertising is that the insurance being sold is offered by the same company, is of the same quality, and will be at an advantageous rate because of the existing relationship with the company.

However, this isn't always the case.

For example, both Geico and Progressive do not directly offer home insurance. Instead, they sell the insurance products of other companies to their customers. While in theory this may seem like a great idea, consumers have encountered some problems. Often the experience with the claims department of the third-party insurer is not of the quality that the consumer would expect. Billing issues and discrepancies are also common complaints. Consumers go into these insurance agreements expecting an experience like that they've had with their normal insurance company, and often come out sorely disappointed.

And the big problem is **if you fail to do your homework (to read the fine print, and to research the companies and policies involved)**, you may end up a victim, regretting (in hindsight) your decision to "bundle" your insurance products.

**Forgetting About It**

Another very common mistake that people make with their homeowners insurance is that they forget about it. Often the insurance is paid for through an escrow service, so the payments are included with the house payment. While convenient, it can also have an "out of sight, out of mind" effect.

**Bottom line: don't forget to shop around, and don't forget to watch your homeowner's insurance for sneaky rate increases.**

**Making Unnecessary Claims**

Claims, whether they are approved and paid or not, can negatively affect both your insurance rates and your ability to get insurance. Even when an insurance company says that a small claim (such as one of those common claims for windshield repair) won't hurt your insurance rates, it may not be entirely true. **The truth is - a claim of any kind, in any amount, may affect your rates with other insurers or other insurance products.**

How can this be? It is facilitated by what is known as the C.L.U.E. database. The C.L.U.E. database is what insurance companies use to report and check claims history. **According to reports, even a simple phone call to your insurance agent to ASK about a claim may be recorded in the C.L.U.E. database!**

*So what else is on your C.L.U.E. report?*

Here's what the LexisNexis Website says about the C.L.U.E. product:

"LexisNexis® C.L.U.E.® Property reports contain up to seven years of personal property claims matching the search criteria submitted by the inquiring insurance company. Data provided in C.L.U.E. reports includes policy information, such as name, date of birth and policy number, and claim information, such as date of loss, type of loss and amounts paid."

There is, of course, more to it than that. Here's an F.A.Q. for the C.L.U.E. database, for your convenience *(Source: oci.wi.gov):*

**What is C.L.U.E.?**

C.L.U.E. (Comprehensive Loss Underwriting Exchange) is a claims history database generated by LexisNexis® that enables insurance companies to access consumer claims information when they are underwriting or rating an insurance policy.

**Who has access to C.L.U.E.?**

Insurance companies that contribute loss data to C.L.U.E. can withdraw information from the exchange. In addition, some insurance agents, with the authority of the company they represent, can withdraw data.

**How do insurers use C.L.U.E. reports?**

C.L.U.E. reports are used almost exclusively to **underwrite and rate new policies**. Most insurers renewing existing policies do not access C.L.U.E. reports at renewal, largely because they already have loss histories for these properties in their own database.

**What information is included in a C.L.U.E. report?**

It includes policy information such as name, date of birth, and policy number, claim information such as date of loss, type of loss and amounts paid, and a description of the property covered. For homeowner's coverage, the report includes the property address, and for auto coverage, it includes specific vehicle information.

**Is there any other information besides loss history in the database?**

Only policy information including loss history is stored in the database. No other sources of data, such as credit reports, criminal records, civil lawsuits, or legal judgments are incorporated into C.L.U.E. reports.

**How long is loss history kept in the C.L.U.E. database?**

The database contains up to 7 years of personal property claims history.

**Who contributes to the C.L.U.E. database?**

Only insurance companies that subscribe to C.L.U.E. can submit loss data and access C.L.U.E. reports. Consumers can access C.L.U.E. reports on themselves and their own properties.

Some companies choose not to subscribe to C.L.U.E. <u>Losses filed with nonparticipating companies will not appear on a C.L.U.E. report</u>.

**Why are insurance companies allowed to obtain a copy of my loss history report?**

Under the federal Fair Credit Reporting Act, LexisNexis® is allowed to produce a C.L.U.E. report for the following insurance-related purposes:

- When the consumer reporting agency has reason to believe a person or company intends to use the information in connection with the underwriting of a consumer's insurance policy. This includes situations where the consumer asks for an insurance quote or applies for insurance.
- When the request for the C.L.U.E. report is initiated by and at the request of the insurance company or agent.

**Can I order a C.L.U.E. report on property I want to purchase?**

No. Under the federal Fair Credit Reporting Act, C.L.U.E. reports can be accessed only by the owner, insurer, or lender for the property. <u>However, you can request that the current owner of the property order a C.L.U.E. report</u>.

**How can I obtain a copy of my C.L.U.E. report?**

Under the federal Fair Credit Reporting Act you can request a copy of your C.L.U.E. report from LexisNexis® toll free at 1-866-312-8076 or by visiting https://personalreports.lexisnexis.com.

**How can I correct erroneous information on my C.L.U.E. report?**

If you discover an error on your C.L.U.E. report, an invalid claim report, or an incorrect loss payment, for instance, you can contact LexisNexis® directly and report the problem. LexisNexis® will then contact the insurance company on your behalf, ask for clarification on the matter, and notify you of the results within 30 days. If you feel an item in the C.L.U.E. report deserves an explanation, you can submit a personal statement, which LexisNexis® will add to all future C.L.U.E. reports.

**Can insurers add notes to a consumer's C.L.U.E. file?**

<u>Only consumers can add notations</u> to their individual C.L.U.E. reports. For instance, if a dog bite claim occurs and the homeowner gets rid of the dog, the consumer can add this notation to the C.L.U.E report for the property. Insurance companies are not allowed to add notations to the database.

**Can C.L.U.E. reports distinguish between an inquiry and a claim?**

The distinction between an inquiry and a claim is an important one. An inquiry is generally regarded as a call by a consumer to a company representative or agent to discuss terms of coverage including the extent of coverage on a specific loss.

C.L.U.E. reports indicate losses by type. Consumers contacting their company or their agent to discuss an actual loss might be considered reporting a claim, even if the company does not end up making a claim payment. This is because when a loss occurs, the policy requires the company to take specific actions within specified time frames. Consumers should be specific as to whether they are filing a claim or only making an inquiry.

For instance, a consumer may contact his/her agent to report an event, such as a broken water pipe and to determine the extent of coverage in order to decide whether or not to go forward with the claims process with the company. A consumer discussing this situation generally may be making an inquiry but if discussing an actual loss may be making a claim. The insurer might not indemnify the consumer for this loss for a variety of reasons: the amount of damage may be below the deductible, the consumer may decide to pay for the damage, or there may be no coverage for such a loss under the terms of the policy.

If the consumer filed an actual claim and the insurer made no loss payment on this claim, this information would be recorded by the company and may appear on a C.L.U.E. report.

<u>Many insurers are working on ways to inform their policyholders about the important distinction between a claim and an inquiry</u>.

**Can an insurance company use loss history from the prior owner of a home in determining my eligibility to get insurance on the home?**

If a company can show a relationship between the prior owner's loss and the probability of a future loss to the home, they may use the information. There are no laws that specifically govern the use of the prior owner's loss history in determining your eligibility for coverage.

**Can the insurance company report claims to the C.L.U.E database that are closed without payment?**

If those claims were reported to the company

as a claim (not merely an inquiry about possible coverage) and subsequently denied, it would not be considered contrary to current law to report the claim to C.L.U.E.

C.L.U.E. has instructed insurers not to report inquiries about possible coverage.

There is another claims database that keeps claims history and has a larger focus on auto insurers. As of this writing over 900 insurers report claims history to the ISO "A-PLUS" database. The company claims to have over 90% of the market share for automobile claims reporting.

To order a copy of your ISO A-PLUS report, call 1-800-627-3487.

*(SOURCE: http://www.verisk.com, http://www.iso.com)*

## FHA mortgage between 1983 and 2004? You may be due a refund (R014)

This is one of those areas in which a lot of people are owed money and don't know it. There are so-called businesses that revolve around finding this money for people. People who call themselves "tracers" try to track down people who are owed refunds, and help them get it—for a share of the money of course. The thing is, you can get the refund on your own without paying anyone any part of the money owed you.

Here's what HUD says[1] about who may be owed money…

**Premium Refund:** You may be eligible for a refund of a portion of the insurance premium if you:

- acquired your loan after September 1, 1983
- paid an up-front mortgage insurance premium at closing and
- did not default on your mortgage payments.

Review your settlement papers or check with your mortgage company to determine if you paid an up-front premium.

**Distributive Share:** You may be eligible for a share of any excess earnings from the Mutual Mortgage Insurance Fund if you:

- originated your loan before September 1, 1983
- paid on your loan for more than seven years and
- had your FHA insurance terminated before November 5, 1990.

It is very easy to find out if you are owed money. You can just visit HUD's website at: http://www.hud.gov/offices/hsg/comp/refunds/

Complete the form with your name or part of your name to search.

While you're there, you can also read their information about tracers, which also has a link to the page where complete data for all 50 states can be downloaded to get a full list of people who are owed refunds. Check it out here:

http://www.hud.gov/offices/hsg/comp/refunds/alerts.cfm

Being a tracer is illegal in some states, so if you are contacted by someone claiming to be one make sure you check your state laws, and remember…**you do NOT have to deal with them in order to get your money**.

(1) https://entp.hud.gov/dsrs/help/fhafacts.cfm

## Your best source for reliable FREE help to stop foreclosure (R086)

One of the worst kinds of problems are those that threaten your home. A big part of owning your own home is *security*. And when financial, employment, or medical problems threaten that security it can be extremely stressful.

"I didn't know my mortgage was *that* adjustable!"

The good news is there is FREE help available from one special organization dedicated to helping homeowners avoid foreclosure and stay in their homes. It's called the Homeownership Preservation Foundation:

"The Homeownership Preservation Foundation (HPF) is a nonprofit group that helps financially challenged homeowners navigate their budget problems and, whenever possible, **help them to avoid mortgage foreclosure—and we do it free of charge."**[1]

If you are in trouble or are struggling to pay your mortgage, completely <u>FREE</u> help is just a phone call away. Here's the phone number:

1-888-995-HOPE

According to their website, 71% of the people who seek HPF help are either unemployed or underemployed, and they carry an average of $15,000 of unsecured debt. If this is you and your situation feels hopeless… it isn't. Things can get better. You can get help. So do not despair! Just call 1-888-995-HOPE and get help today.

(1) www.995hope.org

## How to quit paying for private mortgage insurance (PMI) even if you owe 80% or more on your home (R200)

If you take out a home loan and don't make at least 20% as a down payment, your lender will require you carry Private Mortgage Insurance to protect them should you default.

Your policy will typically cost anywhere from 1/2 percent to 1 percent of your mortgage and you will be required to pay it every year your loan is 80% or more of your home's value.

As soon as your equity reaches over 20%, you can write your lender and have the PMI removed.

If your home value rises or you make significant improvements to the property, your home's loan-to-value ratio will be reduced, giving you a back door to having your lender cancel the PMI.

A clever way to side-step PMI all together is to make a 'piggyback' mortgage.

In this scenario you would obtain a mortgage for 80% of the home's value. Then you make a 10% down payment and take out another loan for 10%.

If you are currently paying PMI and you've reached over 20% equity or the value of the home has increased and you have the appraisal to prove it, then you may write your lender and have PMI removed.

Below is a handy letter you can use when you want your lender to cancel PMI.

Your name
Your address
Certified mail, return receipt requested
Today's date
Your mortgage company name
Your mortgage company's address
REF: Your account number - request to immediately remove PMI
Dear (Your Mortgage Company Name):
This letter is to formally demand Private Mortgage Insurance be removed from the account number and address indicated above.
PMI is no longer required on this loan because;

a) The current amount owed/balance financed by your company is less than 80%: [state your current balance here]

b) The current appraisal on property for the loan number and address listed above is: [current appraisal goes here]

c) After subtracting the current loan balance from the recent appraisal, the balance is: [balance goes here]

d) My percentage equity in the loan number for the property listed above is: [percentage goes here]

As you can clearly see, my equity exceeds the 20% so I am no longer obligated to carry PMI.
I also request a refund of any amounts in escrow to pay for PMI that I'm no longer required to carry.
A copy of the current appraisal is attached as further proof.
Furthermore, please confirm in writing that the PMI has been eliminated.
Looking forward to hearing from you at your earliest convenience.
Sincerely,
Your signature
Your name as it appears on the loan

## Why you must understand the "Rule of 9" before buying or selling a home (R312)

Almost anywhere in the U.S., when you sell a home it will cost you about 9% including the commissions paid to the realtor, closing costs, escrow and moving expenses.

Keep in mind; these costs do not include maintenance of the property.

Because of the 'rule of 9' you are likely to be better off renting if you only plan to stay in a home for 2 years.

Even though many homeowners count on the mortgage interest deduction when factoring their return on investment, it's often not as much as they expected.

IX

Let's say you buy a home for $200,000 and sell at 24 months, using the rule of 9, your costs as outlined above will be about $18,000.

Unless your home appreciated in value by at least 9%, you will likely lose money.

Realtors will often try and convince you to lower the price so your property will move faster. But remember, for every $10,000 you lower the price, it only costs the realtor about $300 in commissions. This is because their commission is 3% of the selling price.

So if your home appreciates to $220,000, but your realtor convinces you to sell at $210,000, you'll lose about $9,000 on your investment.

Remember the "rule of 9" anytime you are looking to buy or sell a home. It can either help you make money or come back to haunt you.

“

A person who *believes* in you is a tremendous source of power.

# Cars and Car Buying

- ☑ **Ex car salesman reveals how to save up to $2,200.00 on your next car purchase**
- ☑ **Incredible "FBI Tactic" to get the truth about the reliability of any car, computer or appliance before you buy it**
- ☑ **How to get a low interest auto loan through this special program less than 1% of America knows about**
- ☑ **The biggest mistake you DON'T want to make right after getting into a car accident**
- ☑ **How to get car repairs covered even if your factory warranty has expired**
- ☑ ***And More***

“

Criticism can be a friend or enemy, depending on its motive, accuracy and *our response.*

## Ex car salesman reveals how to save up to $2,200.00 on your next car purchase (R041)

Marty Copeland used to be a car salesman. He worked at several car dealerships over his career. Now when Marty buys a car from a dealership, there is one method of negotiation that he starts with that will set the tone for the rest of the visit. It helps him to avoid a lot of the usual games, and says that he **has gotten as much as $2,200 knocked off the price of a car**—instantly—by using this simple trick.

According to Marty:

*"Part of the car dealership game is keeping prospects there as long as possible. For one, someone who walks off the lot but is still "car shopping" may end up buying from someone else. Secondly, it's part of a psychological game to wear down the prospect's defenses. You know those situations; those times when the salesman goes and talks to his manager, and it takes like 20 minutes, and he comes back with a deal for you... and then he goes back to his manager.*

*Well those so-called manager meetings really don't take 20 or 30 minutes, or even 10. It's all part of the game designed to wear you down. So I avoid that from the start. I tell them I am on a tight schedule and that I have an hour in which to buy a car if I am going to do it at all. That puts an end to a lot of the games! It also lowers the price pretty quickly."*

Next time you go to a dealership, refuse to play the game. Don't spend 4 or 5 hours there allowing them to control you and your schedule. Instead, take control and put a limit on the craziness. You'll be glad you did.

## Incredible "FBI Tactic" to get the truth about the reliability of any car, computer or appliance before you buy it (R045)

Frank Abagnale started his career as a con artist at the young age of 15. His first victim was his own father. His crimes escalated quickly to include—by the time he was 19—numerous instances of bank and check fraud along with months of impersonating an airline pilot, an attorney, and more. (As a fake commercial pilot, Abagnale reportedly rode on over 250 free flights totaling over 1,000,000 miles.) Frank was eventually caught, and served time in both foreign and U.S. prisons.

Frank's short criminal career is and was simply amazing to some. But we can learn even more from what happened after Frank cleaned up his act.

After just 5 years in federal prison, Frank was released as part of a deal with the FBI. As part of the deal, frank would give the FBI regular assistance with investigations into crimes like those he had committed. **To put it plainly, Frank was an expert at counterfeiting and check fraud... and the FBI wanted to use his expertise.** Frank continued to have a *legitimate working relationship* with the FBI for over 30 years.[1]

We can learn a big lesson from this. The FBI understands something that you should understand too if you want to get the "real" dirt on anything you plan to buy, use, or sign up for.

**"To learn the truth about anything, you must go to the REAL experts who are immersed in it."**

Frank was immersed in his life as a con artist. He knew every trick in the book. (In fact—if you believe the stories—he invented half of the tricks in the book.) So the FBI sought his help.

You can use this simple but incredible FBI tactic in your own life by going to the trenches to get the information you're looking for.

Here are some examples:

**Who should you ask about the reliability of any car?**

To start with: NOT the people who sell the car. Instead, find mechanics who have worked on a wide variety of cars. Ask the mechanics about the reliability of the car you're considering.

Another source of information: *commercial car fleets*. Any owner or manager—and most workers—in commercial car fleets will be able to tell you about the reliability and common problems associated with the cars they use. These are just ideas but hopefully you get the point: go to the people who REALLY know about the car you're considering.

**How do you know if a computer is fast and reliable?**

Again, the last person you should ask is the person trying to sell it to you. Instead, find an expert—someone immersed in computers. Again, this can be done by calling a local computer repair shop. It can also be done by asking business owners or others who have purchased or used a lot of computers. This could be a simple matter of noticing the brand of computer being used at a business, and inquiring with a worker or manager about the reliability of the computers and/or their experience with the brand/company.

**Who knows what refrigerators work best?**

A simple approach, here too, is to call multiple appliance service centers and simply ask which refrigerators break often, what the common problems are, and which brands and models you can expect to be the least error prone.

**How do you know what kind of problems you can expect with any purchase?**

When considering an online service, a purchase of a "long term use" item or anything that may involve expected or unexpected bumps and hiccups along the way, your best source of information is NOT necessarily the happy customers and users of those items.

Instead, look for people who have had trouble with the item or service in question. Look for negative reviews, delivery problems, and other issues… and most importantly: look at how those problems were solved or were not solved.

This will tell you a lot. For online services this may be a matter of visiting their help pages or forums and looking at the amount of difficulty or ease with which users are able to get help. In other cases it might mean calling the customer service number instead of the sales number, to see if the assistance you get is as good on the back end as it appears to be on the front (sales) end.

Using these and a variety of other tactics based on the FBI's method of seeking help, you can get to the bottom of almost anything!

(1) Sources: Catch Me If You Can, Frank Abagnale, ISBN 9780767905381 and WikiPedia.org

# How to get a low interest auto loan through this special program less than 1% of America knows about (R055)

If you've ever had car problems, then you know how frustrating it can be. Many Ameri cans find themselves in times where they have a unique problem: they have a job, but do not have a reliable way to get to their employment. Believe it or not, there are programs *designed* just for people in that situation.

Working Cars for Working Families is a group of organizations dedicated to getting reliable transportation at fair terms for working families.

To learn more about the available programs and to find out if you might qualify, go here:

http://www.workingcarsforworkingfamilies.org

The money saved through programs like this and others is like money given away. Any dollar you don't have to spend is like a dollar "given" to you by the universe to use for other purposes. It's the most legitimate type of "free money" out there—like so many people are looking for and need. *(Even getting a lower rate auto loan could translate into several hundred dollars in savings—"money in your pocket!")*

## The biggest mistake you DON'T want to make right after getting into a car accident (R071)

What's the #1 mistake that people make after getting in an accident? Here it is:

**"I'm sorry, it was my fault."**

What may seem like the polite thing to say and do could actually lead to more problems down the road.

For starters, by admitting fault up front you have eliminated the possibility that the police officer who works the accident will find that the other person was at fault or even partially at fault. You also **throw the door wide open for lawsuits**.

**These days you have to be careful.** There are crooks and con artists who prey on people in car "accident" situations. They will purposely cause "accidents" that appear to be your fault in order to collect insurance money—or worse—to sue you, commit extortion, or to otherwise make your life miserable.

***How can you protect yourself?***

Protecting yourself against these and other issues requires a mixture of strategy and common sense. Here are a few steps you can take:

- **Always be sure to carry adequate liability insurance.** Do not get the "state minimums", as these are rarely enough to protect your assets in the event of a lawsuit.
- **Never, EVER admit fault.** Even if you know it is your fault. Even if you feel terrible. Even if it is completely obvious that it is your fault. Do not admit fault. Let the police officer come, and let the police officer determine who is at fault. Exchange information, be cordial and polite, and let the police do their part.
- **Use video and pictures to protect yourself.** Most people carry cell phones capable of at least still images, and these days many people carry phones capable of taking HD video. Use that capability to the best of your ability to document the entire scene of the accident. This will help to protect you, especially in cases where the other driver caused the accident purposely in order to commit fraud.

## How to get car repairs covered even if your factory warranty has expired (R076)

When a rear seatbelt unexpectedly locked in the "in" position in his Honda Accord, Brian Henderson wanted to get it taken care of right away:

"It was my 7 year old daughter's seat… it was a high priority to get it fixed. We always wear our seatbelts for safety sake… and in this case, it was my kid's safety on the line. We called a couple of places, and ended up making an appointment at the dealership for the very next day. The first place we called wanted $300 just to look at it!"

Expecting a repair of no less than $300, Brian took the car to his local Honda Dealership. A mechanic and manager at the dealership looked at the broken seatbelt, and quickly determined that a new one would have to be ordered. But here's the good news:

**The repairs would be done for FREE because of the Honda warranty on the seatbelts.**

The **car was 12 years old**. Brian was the third owner—not anywhere near the original owner. And the seatbelt repair (which easily could have cost in the range of $300) was done completely free of charge thanks to a warranty that Brian didn't know existed!

In addition to saying something about Honda, this story says a lot about the value of secret or hidden warranties. The seatbelt in Brian's car was fixed quickly and easily for free. In a world full of unpleasant surprises, wouldn't we all like to get a "good" surprise like that one?

The fact is that so-called "secret" and "hidden" warranties do exist. Sometimes they are not widely known or advertised, and perhaps not the first thing you think of when something goes wrong. But they are there for those who take the time to look.

Brian also told us that when he first purchased his 2001 Honda, there had been a recall on the airbags. Brian found out about the recall through the CarFax report on the car. Those repairs were also done at the local dealership, and were also done free of charge.

What is the **best way to find out about these hidden warranties and free repairs?** The easiest way may be to go to http://recall.carfax.com/ and, after choosing the correct company, enter the VIN number of the car in question. As of this writing, this service is provided free at CarFax.com. It can also be done at many manufacturer websites (such as http://owners.honda.com/service-maintenance/recalls).

Sometimes dealerships and even local mechanics will do minor repairs or checks as a matter of goodwill.

In one example, a woman named Beth took her car to a local repair shop. The plastic splash guard on the bottom of the car was dragging on the ground. In about 3 minutes using a wrench and a couple of washers, the head mechanic at the shop had re-attached the splash guard.

He did the (admittedly minor) repair completely free of charge and told Beth, "Come back and see us sometime!" This is the kind of "goodwill" service that can lead to long term customers. In Beth's case, the splash guard repair happened about 8 years ago—and *she still uses the same mechanic today!*

## Instantly save $150 on auto insurance by calling this number (R080)

We've talked about various ways to save money, including saving money on auto insurance. I'd like to offer a quick note about a not-very-well-known, but well-established insurance company.

Amica Mutual Insurance Company has been around since 1907 and has an A++ rating from A.M. Best.

Their underwriting is partially based on credit, so **those with good credit are eligible for better rates**.

If you have not gotten a competing quote to check against what you're currently paying for insurance, then call Amica at:

1-800-242-6422

Or, visit their website at www.amica.com.

You may be wondering why you shouldn't just stick with one of the insurers that hammers you with those cute television ads constantly. According to one insurance industry expert, insurers with smaller advertising budgets are usually able to offer better rates.

The rates companies can offer are highly regulated according to what the insurance company can afford to pay in terms of claims. So the highest rated companies (i.e. A++)—those with the best financial picture—are usually the ones that can offer the best rates and still pay claims responsibly.

And every six months or annually when your policy renews and you notice an increase, stop to **check around for a better rate**.

## The irreversible mistake you don't want to make when applying for a car loan (R089)

When you walk into a car dealership looking to buy a car, one of the first things they want to do is run your credit. Many dealerships have numerous financial institutions through which they attempt to get loans. This may sound harmless, but it can create irreversible damage to your credit score if you're not careful.

I'll explain what happens, and how you can avoid it, but first let's talk about credit and car shopping.

When a car dealership or anyone else "runs" your credit report, what they are actually doing is placing what is known as an "inquiry" with one or more credit bureaus that asks for the information that's on your credit report. That inquiry—when it is connected to an offer for credit—is known as a "hard inquiry". The "hard inquiry" stays on your credit report for 2 years.

But here's the thing.

A "hard inquiry" actually hurts your credit score! Yes, you read that right. The act of applying for credit can hurt your credit. And the more of the inquiries you have, the more it hurts your credit.

But it gets **worse**.

It is common practice at car dealerships to try to get financing through 20, 30, or even 40 banks. Normally, the inquiries associated with applying for an auto loan should be coded so that the multiple inquiries are not counted against you. In other words, if everything goes like it should, all but one of the 20 to 40 inquiries should be ignored by the credit bureaus.

In practice, it doesn't always happen that way.

Sometimes due to a clerical error, lack of training, or similar reasons, all of those credit pulls from all those banks can get listed on your credit report as separate inquiries! They simply don't get coded correctly, and your credit can suffer dramatically as a result.

**How to Protect Yourself**

Unfortunately, talking to someone at the dealership isn't going to help. Most dealership employees and salespeople don't even realize that the problem exists.

One approach is to avoid dealerships that use multiple lenders, or request a specific, single lender. Then, of course, you are dependent on the dealership honoring your request.

The best line of defense against this all-too-common problem is to walk into the dealership with financing of your own. You can get approved for a loan from a bank or credit union before you visit any dealership at all, and you can avoid being a victim of the dice-roll-credit-pull game. (Be sure to read any credit release you sign carefully.)

## The best time of year to save thousands on a new car (R096)

There are a number of times when you're more likely to get a better deal when buying a car. For starters, if you can choose your shopping season, always choose winter. Cold weather, snowy weather, bad weather, all brings on special deals and incentives at car dealerships. Christmas time—or the **entire month of December**—is by far the best time of year to buy a car at a dealership.

Generally, **towards the end of a month** is better than the beginning of a month. **Weekends** are better than quiet weekdays. The **end of the day** is better than shopping at the beginning of the day.

Why are these times better than other times?

- Because these are the times that dealerships are looking at their numbers and trying to make improvements.
- These are the times you are least likely to run up against the more aggressive sales tactics
- These are the times that the dealerships and salespeople will generally be more desperate to sell cars.
- These are the times when, based on the numbers, consumers tend to get the best possible deals on cars.

## Auto technician reveals the only "device" proven to increase gas mileage (R105)

According to Mike, an auto mechanic, the vast majority of the gadgets that are touted for improving fuel economy are a complete waste of money and time:

> *"They just don't work," says Mike, "but sometimes people think they work because of the simple fact that they drive differently when they are using them. After a week or two the effect wears off because they are back to their old driving habits."*

Adding to this, Mike says that there is **ONE device that is proven to increase gas mileage** consistently, and best of all it works on the very principal of psychology that fools people into thinking their other so-called "fuel economy" devices are working. But this device actually has use beyond the fuel economy benefits.

The device, according to Mike, is a simple **fuel efficiency monitor** that plugs into the OBD-2 port of your car.

One popular brand is ScanGauge (http://www.scangauge.com/). The ScanGauge 2 can report on and reset check engine lights, and offers up to 37 digital gauges to tell you what is going on in your car as you drive. But the most simple and common use of the ScanGauge and other similar devices is to use it to monitor your mileage per gallon in real time as you drive.

> *"Using it while you drive, watching the miles-per-gallon becomes second nature... like watching your speedometer. You drive better, and your car gets better mileage."*

The devices cost from $150 to $200 in most cases, and plug into the OBD-2 port found on most modern cars.

## Six sneaky but legal ways to get out of almost any speeding ticket (R095)

Imagine one of those rare moments when you're passing someone on the highway. Suddenly you hear the sound of a siren and see flashing red lights in your rearview mirror. It's a patrol car pulling you over…

What you know and what you say (or don't say) can be the difference of hundreds of dollars out of your pocket. Not to mention points on your driving record. And your insurance costs going up.

Matt is a small town police officer who we talked to "off the record" about **how to get out of a speeding ticket**. We learned some new things from Matt, and confirmed some things that we had researched elsewhere.

Below are the **top 7 ways to get out of speeding tickets**. The first 4 methods are for avoiding a ticket in the first place—that's always your best bet.

**1.** When you are driving along, see an officer clocking, and suddenly realize you are speeding. *Wave* at the police officer as you slow down. A simple wave of the hand can do so many things! On the one hand, it says "Oops, yeah… just realized I was speeding. Sorry about that." It could be interpreted as you acknowledging the error and self-correcting. It may also be interpreted as "Hey, I know that person." The police officer might think you're a friend or someone they know, wave back, and let you be on your way.

**2.** Hold on to your credibility. Ditch the radar detector. Keep your car clean. Don't argue or make excuses. The officer's impression of you—whether subconscious or conscious—can affect the likelihood that a ticket will be issued.

**3.** Be polite, but don't make too big a deal (see the #4). A **good attitude** may be enough to get a warning instead of a ticket.

**4.** Make the incident a non-event. In other words, allow the police officer to finish with you quickly and quietly. Do not draw attention to yourself or say anything that would single you out or make you especially memorable. If you are argumentative, for example, the officer will likely remember you and will be more likely to show up for later court dates.

**5. Never admit** any wrongdoing. Some people say "I'm sorry I was speeding" right away. Sometimes the officer isn't even pulling them over for speeding! Don't shoot yourself in the foot in that manner or by admitting guilt before you even get your "day in court".

**6.** Delay the court date for as long as you can. This involves pleading "not guilty" and deferring (rescheduling) your court date as many times as possible. The longer the period between the time of the ticket and the court date, the better off you will be. Why? Because any variety of circumstances **may result in the officer not showing up**… especially for an old ticket that he or she doesn't remember issuing. And if it has been long enough, the officer who does show up may not specifically recall any details.

**7.** Use a variety of possible tactics to get the ticket dismissed in court. What is available to you will vary by location, but here are some possibilities:

- There were no speed limit signs in the vicinity of where you were pulled over.
- There were two officers present for the ticket writing, and only one present in court.
- The officer who wrote the ticket did not show up in court.
- Errors on the ticket, such as incorrect location of the incident or errors in driver's license or license plate numbers.

# College professor reveals how he gets 50 miles per gallon (R332)

Dr. Jack Martin is a professor of sustainable technology at Appalachian State University in North Carolina, who, according to an article in *Mental Floss Magazine*[1], drives as many as 124 miles on a single gallon of gas. The technique used by Dr. Martin to accomplish this is known as hypermiling, which has become a word for a set of strategies for **VERY efficient driving**.

How does the professor do it? By doing things like:

- Accelerating very slowly
- Coasting whenever possible
- Avoiding rolling the windows down or using A/C
- Driving reasonable speeds
- Avoid using brakes unnecessarily (except for what you have to, obviously)

We were intrigued by the story of Professor Martin, so we dug deeper into the hypermiling concept. We found, to our surprise, that there are whole communities of hypermilers, and even hypermiling contests.

But it isn't all fun and games. Some common hypermiling techniques are actually illegal. One such technique—shifting your car into neutral and coasting down a hill—is illegal in multiple states.

Other techniques like driving very closely behind tractor trailers to prevent drag will not only get you in trouble, they aren't exactly safe and could end in disaster.

With that said we found a number of hypermiling techniques that can actually **lead to safer and better driving**, if used correctly, and could save you substantially by increasing your fuel economy.

Here's the list.

1. **Get rid of excess weight.** Clean out your trunk, and avoid hauling junk around unnecessarily.
2. **Keep tires properly inflated.** That might sound elementary, but if you're going to go for big mileage, you need to pay attention to the basics, too.
3. **Remove unused accessories.** Cargo racks and other accessory items that are mounted to the outside of your vehicle increase drag and reduce fuel economy.
4. **Accelerate slowly, brake mindfully.** You need to learn to take off very slowly. Yes, people behind you will probably get annoyed, but <u>a lot of fuel is spent by accelerating</u> too quickly, and if you can learn to gradually increase your speed you may be surprised at the amount of fuel you save.

   Also, don't use your brakes unless you have to. Braking too much increases the chances that you'll have to use the accelerator again. <u>Allow your car to slow down naturally</u> and come to a gentle stop. If you have to break hard a lot, then you are wasting fuel on acceleration when you don't need to. (In other words, taking your foot off the gas sooner and allowing yourself to coast before stopping will save you fuel and money.)

According to the U.S. Department of energy[2]: "Aggressive driving (speeding, rapid acceleration and braking) wastes gas. **It can lower your gas mileage by 33% at highway speeds and by 5% in town**."

5. **Slow down.** The optimum speed for many cars is around 50 mph. According to the U.S. Department of Energy: "You can assume that each 5 mph you drive over 50 mph is like paying an additional $0.24 per gallon for gas." (Based on $3.48 per gallon.)
6. **Schedule your trips. Allow plenty of time.** Having to rush to an appointment is a sure way to burn fuel unnecessarily. Plan ahead. Schedule your trips. Plan your routes. If you have errands to run, plan to visit the one furthest from home first, and plan your route for the way back. And do what UPS does, it schedules so drivers avoid left turns so they save both fuel and time.
7. **Less traveled roads and lanes.** If you can, choose to take roads that aren't as busy. This will give you the room you need to apply efficient driving techniques safely. When you're traveling on a road that has a clear set of tracks where other drivers have gone, according to Dr. Martin you are better off driving slightly off center (by say, a few inches).
8. D**on't try to overpower hills.** If you allow yourself to coast down one hill and part way up the next, and give yourself *enough* gas to get up the next hill and over it (without over-doing it), you're hilly-area driving will prove to be much more efficient. (Remember to abide by local laws!)
9. **Avoid excessive idling.** Any situation where your car will sit and idle is one you should try to avoid or plan for to minimize the impact of.
10. **Anticipation.** You should always try to anticipate the actions of other drivers, sometimes referred to as *defensive driving*. If a driver is going to turn or brake quickly, adjust your own driving accordingly to minimize the impact and possible accident.
11. **Use the wind.** Whenever possible, you should aim to drive with the wind instead of against it.
12. **Monitor your fuel efficiency.** They actually have gadgets that can be installed in your car to tell you how fast you are burning fuel. One such example is called the Scan-Guage MPG Guage from ecomodder.com
13. **Hit traffic lights right.** Time traffic lights, anticipate them turning red, utilize your breaks and acceleration as little as possible—but remember to stay safe, obviously, and obey all traffic laws.
14. **Learn to cruise without cruise control.** Many drivers have a hard time keeping a steady speed. For those drivers, using cruise control may be the best way to get the most efficiency. For those who dare to be better, however, there may be other more efficient techniques. One such technique is to put the throttle in a position, and hold it there. Cruise control adjusts the throttle to maintain the same speed. Keeping the throttle in the same place, your speed may vary, but you will enjoy better mileage. You can further increase your mileage by learning to reduce the throttle when headed downhill.
15. **Drive slowly for the first few miles to allow your car to warm up.** According to expert hypermilers, driving too fast too quickly, or letting your car sit and idle to warm up are less efficient than this technique.

Now, perhaps you are thinking that this must be too good to be true. But even the U.S. government agrees that you can dramatically improve your mileage by simply driving smarter. **According to the U.S. Department of Energy, by using just a few techniques: driving sensibly; observing the speed limit; avoiding idling; removing excess weight; not hauling cargo on the roof of your car—you may be able to increase your fuel efficiency by as much as 64%.**[3]

(1) *Mental Floss*, Volume 12 Issue 1, Jan/Feb 2013

(2) Source: www.fueleconomy.gov

(3) Source: www.fueleconomy.gov

## Car Buying Secrets guaranteed to save you thousands (R341)

### Secret #1: Wrecked Cars and Dealerships

Only deal with reputable dealerships. Many smaller dealerships buy wrecked cars and fix them up to sell. This would be OK, except sometimes the quality of the workmanship is questionable. If you buy from a small dealership, make sure it is either someone you know personally or that you know exactly where the cars have come from.

### Secret #2: More Than just CarFax

Always get a CARFAX report before any used car purchase. This will tell you a lot of what you need to know…including things that might be hidden by dishonest dealers and individuals. But a Carfax report won't tell you everything. Call your mechanic and ask about common problems with the car. Search online for common problems. Many cars, for example, experience the same part failures at particular mileages. Find what those common failures are, compare to the mileage of the car, and find out if the corresponding replacement or maintenance has been done.

### Secret #3: Depreciation Costs You More Than You Think

Save money (and depreciation) by purchasing used cars over new cars. "Last year's model" demo cars and other similar deals with very low mileage are sold at many dealerships at lower prices, and some of the depreciation will have already happened. Some experts say you should purchase a 2 year old model as opposed to the latest one.

What is the true cost of depreciation?

**Consider this:** a new car loses about 10% of its value the minute it leaves the lot. It loses about another 10% each year thereafter. By the time you have owned a car 5 years, it will have lost at least 60% of its value (with the exception of a couple of models with especially good resale value).

Because of this, you should consider how long you will own the car and what the potential resale value is… this will help you to truly understand the impact of depreciation. As of this writing, the cars with the best resale values include:

- Toyota SUVs
- Toyota Pickups
- Chrysler Jeeps
- Some Hondas
- Lexus SUVs

Why does resale value matter? Because it helps to determine how much it actually costs you to drive a car.

Let's say that you purchase a barely used car for $20,000 and sell it 3 years later for $14,000. That means that it cost you a total of $6,000 (plus maintenance) to drive that car for 3 years… or around $166 per month. But remember a new car loses 10% of its value immediately.

If you bought a new car for $20,000, and sold it just one year later, you might get $16,000 out of the car. The car would cost you $4,000 to drive for that year, and would come out to about $333 per month.

The older the car, the more it will have already depreciated. There is a "sweet spot" where you can purchase a car that is fairly recent, in good shape, with good mileage, but where most of the depreciation has already happened. With these cars… especially those that retain resale value well, you could end up with an ownership cost of around $100 per month or even less in some cases.

**Secret #4: The Role That Race and Sex Play In Car Deals**

If you are a woman, take a man with you. This is not meant to be sexist or Racist. Statistics show that white/Caucasian men get quoted better prices for cars than any other group. While this may be a reflection of the sad state of our society… it is unfortunately the truth, and this knowledge can help you when buying a car.

Also realize that the prices at many dealerships are NOT set in stone, and that the salesman may quote you a price based on what they think you can or will pay rather than based on the value of the car.

**Secret #5: Strength In Numbers**

Even if you are not a woman or minority, it may pay off to bring a friend with you to act as an instant "second opinion" and as someone who can assist you when the dealer resorts to intimidation tactics.

**Secret #6: Dishonest Dealers Hate "Bluebook" Values**

Make sure you know how much a car is actually worth before you accept a price. Kelly bluebook is the best resource for this. We've actually heard stories of car salespeople getting angry when the consumer compares the prices of the car offered by the dealer to the bluebook value. Don't let an angry salesperson scare you. You have a right to know how much a car is worth and know what kind of deal you are *really* getting.

**Secret #7: Fear and Pride Are Your Top Two Enemies**

Don't be afraid to ask for a lower price, and don't be afraid to walk away if they won't give it to you.

You see, a lot of people go into a car buying experience with fear. They fear the salesperson. They fear the impression the salesperson might have of them. They don't want to look flakey or unsure of themselves, and so they try to appear and act confident. What this translates to in practice: a lot of people end up buying the wrong car!

Do not let fear and pride rule your buying experience. The top two rules:

1. NEVER be AFRAID to ask for a *BETTER PRICE.*

2. There is NO SHAME in walking away from a deal if it isn't right for YOU.

You don't have to feel afraid or feel bad. That's what many dealerships count on and prey on. Don't just try to appear confident. Be confident enough in yourself to ask for the price you want, and to walk away from the deal if they don't give it to you or if you otherwise feel you are being mistreated.

**Secret #8: Most people spend much more on cars than they need to spend.**

Keep it reasonable. Don't buy a car just for image, or just because you want a new toy. This is the attitude that puts many people in debt… and keeps them there.

Get what you **need**. It doesn't have to be a "junker". A Lexus that's a few years old is still a Lexus. Be creative, and be financially smart.

When you consider purchasing a car, ask yourself this: Is there a car that is just as reliable that costs half as much?

If you answer "yes", you need to re-examine your approach to car buying, as you may be throwing away money that you can't afford to throw away.

---

## Ex auto mechanic reveals 18 tips to save you thousands in auto repairs (R151)

Few things in life are as demoralizing as going in for a car repair or worse, being out of town, on the road and your car breaks down far from your usual mechanic.

Robert, my mechanic has 18 sure-fire tips to take the mystery and agony out of maintaining your car while you wonder if they really did anything at all.

1. **When should you avoid purchasing gas?** When a gas station is getting its supply replenished by a truck. Any gunk in the bottom of the tank will get stirred up, and guess where it ends up? In YOUR gas tank.
2. **What services do mechanics offer that are usually rip-offs?** Many so-called "tune-ups" are unnecessary services. It used to be that cars actually needed regular tune-ups to function properly. Now most cars have computers that keep everything running right, and take the place of what the "tune-up" used to do. Be skeptical of any "tune-up" service being offered, and make sure you get an itemized list of the work to be done.
3. **How often should I rotate my tires?** Rotate your tires when they show signs of uneven wear. Doing it regularly on a schedule is usually a waste of time and money.
4. **What should I do when my car won't start?** That depends on what it is doing. If the starter is engaging, then don't keep the key turned longer than say 10 seconds at a time. Doing so could damage your car. If you hear a clicking noise and nothing else, your battery may be dead or dying. If there is no sound at all and nothing happens, it may be a loose or corroded battery terminal connection. (Pepsi or Coke can be used to clean corroded terminals.) If the car "cranks" but fails to start, it may mean that your engine isn't getting fuel or that your spark plugs aren't firing.
5. **How can I keep my paint from cracking and peeling?** This is typically from repeated off-and-on exposure to the elements. You can drastically reduce the chances of cracking and peeling by giving your car a wax job on a regular basis. The most common recommendation is every 6 months, but some environments (near the ocean, frequent driving in salt/snow, rain season) may warrant waxing 3 or 4 times per year.
6. **How do I know if my car needs to be waxed?** Look at the car after it rains. If water beads up on the surface, then you're good. If not, then you are overdue for a wax job.
7. **What kind of oil should I use in my car?** Contrary to what some mechanics suggest, you should follow the recommendation in your owner's manual. For most modern cars, this will mean using SAE 5W30 oil.
8. **Is synthetic oil worth the extra cost?** If it is not a "synthetic blend", then it probably is worth it if you plan to keep the car for a long time. Synthetic oil is much better for your engine. Many "million mile club" car owners attribute their high mileage accomplishments to regular oil changes with synthetic oil.

9. **What are the most neglected maintenance items?** First, oil changes. It's amazing how many people neglect this important maintenance. Second, is the air filter. A lot of people fail to replace the air filter. A dirty air filter will reduce your miles per gallon. Third, timing belts. These can be expensive to change, so a lot of people either ignore them or put them off until they break, which results in a much more expensive repair. (I've heard horror story after horror story about this one.) Also, transmission fluid, power steering fluid and coolant should be changed every 30,000 miles.

10. **Why does my car make a squealing noise?** The most common cause of squealing noises is a loose or slipping belt. They have spray-on "belt dressing" that can be used to temporarily stop the squealing. A mechanic can also scuff pulleys lightly with sand paper to prevent slippage.

11. **How can I increase my gas mileage?** Replace your air filter regularly. Dirty air filters can result in over a 10% loss in fuel efficiency. It's also a good idea to use fuel injection cleaners as often as you change your oil. Also, drive sensibly. A lot of people waste a lot of fuel by driving like a race car driver. Drive like a grandma instead, and you'll save a bundle on gas.

12. **How can I keep door locks from wearing out prematurely?** Don't ruin your door locks with de-icers. If you must use a de-icer, lubricate the lock afterwards, as the de-icer will wash out the graphite lubricant.

13. **Should the area under the hood be cleaned?** Oil spills can corrode wires and electronic components, leading to failure. It's a good idea to have the under hood area cleaned occasionally, or at the very least clean up any oil spills. *(Tip: Automotive hand cleaner can be used to get the oil off.)*

14. **How can I find the cheapest place to get repairs?** A lot of people assume that the dealership is the most expensive place to get your car repaired. Often, this isn't true. However, some repairs, in fact, should always be handled by the dealership. Electronic or wiring problems are always best handled by the dealer. For other possible problems, you should always check with the dealer for pricing because often their price will be better. Some repairs may be covered by unknown warranties or free because of a recall or safety concern. And even without the warranties and recall repairs, the dealership will just be able to offer better prices for some services. The moral of the story is: call around, but always check the dealership too.

15. **How can I save money on air conditioner maintenance and repairs?** The first step is to keep the A/C in good shape. Running it periodically, even when you don't need it, will help with this. Make it a point to run your A/C for at least a few minutes every week. Next, some simple repairs can be done yourself for a fraction of what a mechanic would charge. In most states A/C "charge" kits are available at Wal Mart or Auto Zone so you can charge your A/C for around $40. Be sure to follow the instructions carefully. Another simple and inexpensive repair is the replacement of a leaky A/C valve. Kits to complete this repair can be found online for a decent price, and can save you substantially versus what a dealership or mechanic might charge.

16. **How can I make the most of my car's warranty?** This is a simple one that many people miss. Listen: just have a mechanic go through your care carefully to look for problems that might be covered by the warranty. It's really that simple. Getting your car a "checkup" for $100 or $200 could save you thousands in the long run as you

may find otherwise expensive repairs that will be covered by the warranty.

17. **How can I make sure my car will pass smog testing?** One of the biggest things you can do is to make sure your car is warmed up when you get the smog test done. If your car has been sitting and the test is done immediately without, say, a 20 to 30 minute warm up period, then your car will be more likely to fail the smog test. "Test only" stations are also better than stations that do tests and repairs, because the person doing the testing does not have any incentive for failing a car unfairly or dishonestly (e.g. to sell you the "necessary" repairs).
18. **How can I get the most money when selling my car?** A lot of people think taking a car to a mechanic before they sell it is a good idea. It isn't a bad idea, but the reality is that most people aren't going to pay more for a difference they can't "see". Instead, pay a little to get your car detailed when you are ready to sell it. It will look clean and well taken care of, and you're likely to get more money for it. This is especially true for more expensive cars. (The lower the price, the less impact this will have. If you have a car where the blue book value is $500, it probably won't be worth it!)

In wrapping up, let's talk about something that can be worth its weight in gold and save you a small fortune, and that is, how to find a dependable mechanic you can trust.

**Here are 4 tips to finding a reliable, cost-effective mechanic**

**ONE:** ask around. I know this sounds simple, but you would be amazed how many times people violate this cardinal rule. I had a friend whose transmission went out on his SUV. In this situation, it would have been best to have it replaced at a dealership, because if anything goes wrong, the dealership could back him up while a private shop may give him the run-a-round.

My friend spent $3000 with a mechanic and guess what? The transmission still had problems. He brought the car back three times. They kept giving him excuses. Then, things got even worse when his head gasket went out. And you know what the auto shop did? They used that as an excuse as to why the transmission wasn't working! I'm not making this up. If you know someone that can give you a good referral to a mechanic use them, otherwise stay with your dealership whose reputation is on the line.

**TWO:** check the shop with the local Better Business Bureau and the Bureau of Automotive Repair. Now, you have to be careful with the Better Business Bureau because sometimes a company can have a great rating because no unsatisfied customer filed a complaint with them. Also, the Bureau of Automotive Repair will have any complaints that may be filed against the shop mechanic.

**THREE:** look for clean shops and always get a second opinion. When the shop is filthy with junk lying everywhere, beware. It shows you they do things sloppy and what my father would call "half ass".

Second opinions are important. You never want your mechanic to feel like you'll do whatever he says. Mechanics are like anyone else, their financial and personal lives can change causing them to have unforeseen burdens. This stress will cause them to change their ethics and morals at your expense. So always get second opinions on any automotive work costing over $500.

**FOUR:** look online for reviews. Simply Google 'name of shop review' and you'll see what people are saying. Because of what I read about the quick oil change shop just blocks from me, I go out of my way to get my oil changed at the same franchise, just operated by better management.

Remember, this may seem like a bit of work, but you're talking about a working relationship you're going to have for years to come and automotive expenses add up over the decades. Plus reliable maintenance and repairs keep you from being stranded on the side of the road begging for the mercy of whomever you can find to help.

## How to get paid up to $240.00 a day for driving your car (R352)

There are several ways you can dramatically reduce the cost of driving your luxury car—or even get PAID up to $240 per day to drive it. Here's how.

**1. Rideshare Programs**

A rideshare program is a program that connects commuters so that they can share rides with one another. These programs usually involve the exchange of money as the individuals work out a monetary arrangement to share the commute costs. In practice, these programs can be extremely profitable when used correctly. "For-profit ride sharing", is a growing (and even booming) business.

Here's how it works:

Someone needs a ride, and **plugs in their location information into a ride sharing app on their smart phone**. Their ride shows up in a few minutes, and they're off to their destination.

Sarah Davis, a 56 years young grandmother who has been a ridesharing driver for a year now, says she has made $5,400 in the last year by giving occasional rides to others during her usual travel times. Many others claim to average anywhere from **$20 to $30 per hour** giving rides to others.

There is a lot of buzz around for-profit ride sharing and rightfully so. It's a big deal. It has the potential to change the way we do transportation, and have a dramatic impact on the environment and even the economy. A lot of people are doing it for a business. A lot of people are looking for rides. The future looks bright for ridesharing.

Want to get involved in ridesharing? Visit one of these three "for-profit ride sharing" websites:

- http://www.lyft.com
- http://www.uber.com
- http://www.side.cr

*(Note: The ride sharing industry is young, and regulations are being passed slowly that address various concerns related to ridesharing. So be sure to check your state laws (if applicable) regarding for-profit ridesharing.)*

**2. Get paid to advertise on your car.**

Some companies will pay you to advertise their products or services on your car. This is more common in areas with higher population densities, and your car along with your driving record will probably have to meet certain minimum requirements. (Such as a nice car and clean driving record.) Companies (http://www.wrapmatch.com) will pay as much as **$400 (sometimes more) per month** for you to put their ads on your car. If you're interested in going down this path, search the internet for "on car advertising" or "car wrap ads" to learn more.

**3. Advertise your own product or service on your car.**

If you have your own product or service, this one is a no-brainer. Simply get a special magnet advertisement made for your own product or service. If you drive 1,000 miles per month and 5 people see the sign for every mile you drive, that means you'll get 5,000 views per month promoting your product or service. That's 60,000 views per year! On a $45 dollar product, if just 120 people in 60,000 buy as a result of the ad, you would earn $5,400 per year—$450 per month—just for driving your car!

One local woman—Lisa Knight—**runs her dog walking business entirely off her on-car advertising**. According to Lisa: "My business started with just a couple of clients I knew. I went to their houses daily in my car to walk their dogs, and thought it would be a good idea to put a sign on my car. Since then, my <u>business has grown leaps and bounds</u>, and I have to turn people away!"

One "Auto Dent Removal" company has had similar success. John Gooding, the owner, says that "I spent $100 to get 3 magnetic signs for my cars. It has been, by far, the best advertising money I ever spent." Joanie, the manager of a carpet and upholstery cleaning store had similar things to say. She said they get a steady flow of business from their on-car advertising phone numbers and websites.

One key to this approach is to make the ad short and simple. It needs to be something that someone can read and register in seconds. Example:

**"Paintless Dent Removal"**

**DentRemovalExpert.com**

**1-800-555-5555**

# Debt & Credit Tactics

- ☑ **Credit Card Secret: How to get a low introductory rate extended**
- ☑ **Financial Planner reveals the guaranteed way to turn $3 a day into $50,000.00 with your mortgage**
- ☑ **Five secrets every married person should know before signing any credit application**
- ☑ **12 insider programs to get your student loan payments reduced or even forgiven**
- ☑ **Credit Expert reveals how to build $50,000.00 in business credit in only 150 days**
- ☑ **How to use introductory rates to put cash in your pocket**
- ☑ ***And More***

Yes, things happen
for a reason.
But, you get to
*decide* the reason.

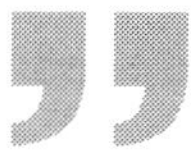

## Credit Card Secret: How to get a low introductory rate extended (R067)

This strategy helps you extend those low introductory rates so you can pay off debts faster.

If you have applied for a new credit card with an introductory offer but were turned down, you will still get an inquiry on your credit report. However, other creditors will not KNOW that you were denied credit… only that you applied. After 60 or so days, it will be clear that you did not get the credit. But if you **act quickly**, you can bluff your way to a better deal with your current creditor, for example by getting them to extend your introductory rate.

After you are denied, **tell the current creditor that you have a better offer** and are going to transfer the debt if they can't help you extend your introductory rate for you.

Getting an intro rate extended can be worth a lot. A lot of people are shocked when their interest rates go up and suddenly they are paying $70 per month in interest where they had been paying ZERO. The savings on this can really add up… even to $700 or $800 (or more) over a year.

Try it, you'll be surprised at how easy this strategy works.

## Financial Planner reveals how to turn $3 a day into $50,000.00 with your mortgage (R025)

Did you know there's a guaranteed way to turn $3 a day into $50,000 if you have a mortgage, and your credit score doesn't matter?

What would $50,000 mean to you? How would $50,000 change your life?

And what about later in life when you are nearing retirement? Would $50,000 matter then?

If you are like most folks, $50K is real money and if you can find a way to grab it, you will. Well, by utilizing as little as $3 a day can add up to a whopping $50,000 savings.

**Did you know 99% of America does NOT know how much interest they are paying for their mortgage?**

I challenge you. Ask anyone the total amount of interest they will pay after paying off their mortgage (whether in seven years or 30 years) and most won't be able to tell you.

The same is true with credit cards. And this ignorance is why the bankers live lavishly while others clip coupons. Ask yourself, how much interest did you pay last year? Even last month!

The fact is, most people don't keep up with how much interest they are paying. They just struggle to crack their monthly nut, keep their head above water and hope their clunker of a car rolls for at least another year.

Mortgage interest is **front loaded**. For as much as the first 20 years of having a mortgage, **over half** of the payment goes towards **interest**. For the first 7 to 10 years, 75% to 80% of your payment goes towards interest. As you can imagine, these numbers (which most people ignore) can really start to add up:

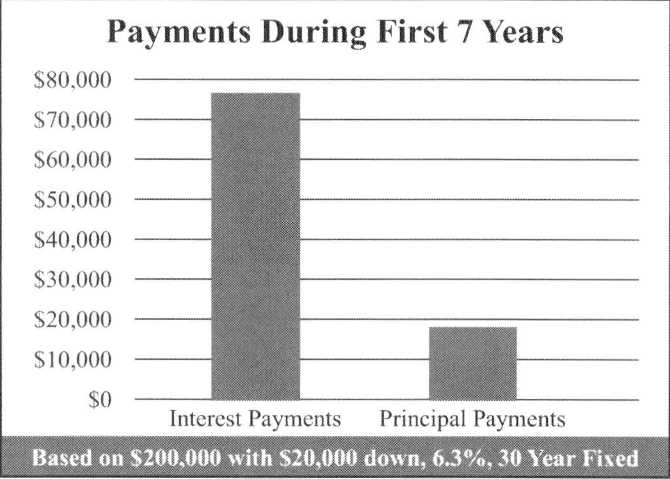


But here's the thing. All that interest is based on the amount of remaining *principal*. If you can lower the principal, even by a seemingly insignificant amount, it can have a dramatic impact on the amount of interest you pay over the term

So answer this one simple question: **is $100 per month worth $50,000.00?**

Can you spare $100 per month if it was GUARANTEED to turn into $50,000.00 with zero risk? You can easily do it by using one of two simple strategies to lower the principal on your mortgage.

**Real Cash Secrets: Savings Strategy 1**

Strategy 1 is very simple and the most powerful.

1. Pay an extra $100 per month towards your mortgage.
2. Be sure to indicate that the extra payment is to go towards PRINCIPAL.
3. Because you are reducing the amount of principal on which you are paying interest, you can knock tens of thousands off the total interest over the life of the loan.

Here's how the numbers play out:

**On a $200,000 mortgage…**

| PAYMENT | TOTAL INTEREST PAID | SAVINGS |
|---|---|---|
| Normal Payment | $245,657.00 | 0.00 |
| Normal Payment + 100 | $192,501.00 | $53,156.00 |

On a $200,000 mortgage at 6.3% interest you would normally pay a total of $445,657.00 for your home ($245,657.00 in interest). By adding an extra $100 per month to your mortgage payment as an "extra principal payment", you will lower the amount of interest you pay over the course of the loan to $192,501. **That's a total savings of $53,156.00 with only $3 a day! Imagine if you did $5? Here's how that would look.**

**On a $200,000 mortgage…**

| PAYMENT | TOTAL INTEREST PAID | SAVINGS |
|---|---|---|
| Normal Payment | $245,657.00 | 0.00 |
| Normal Payment + 150 | $174,454.00 | $71,230.00 |

It's best to use this strategy when you have extra money to put towards your mortgage, have steady income, and are relatively certain you won't be moving in the next few years.

But what if you are afraid to tie up all that money in your home? What if you'd rather keep your money out of your home for a while, "just in case"? Then apply strategy #2.

**Real Cash Secrets Savings Strategy 2**

If you can spare an extra $100 per month but are hesitant to put the money directly towards your mortgage right now, consider this strategy as a viable money-saving alternative. By doing so you could save up to $35,000 on mortgage interest and turn your $100 into $35,000! Here's how it works:

1. Put your extra principal payment of $100 each month into CDs, a high yield savings account, or similar investment tool.

2. Save up for 10 years, and make a lump sum principal payment at that time. By then you can probably be relatively sure that you won't be moving or need the money soon.
3. **By making the lump sum principal payment at the 10 year mark and no later**, you can knock a big chunk off the mortgage interest you'll pay.

Here's how the magic of interest works for you.

On a $200,000 mortgage at 6.3% you would normally pay $245,660 in interest alone. When you save $100 per month in a savings account for 10 years, you keep your money and add interest to it. At 6% interest, $100 per month saved over 10 years ends up being $16,569.87.

**$100 Per Month at 6% Interest...**

| YEAR | TOTAL VALUE |
|---|---|
| 1 | $1,339.72 |
| 2 | $2,655.91 |
| 3 | $4,053.28 |
| 4 | $5,536.83 |
| 5 | $7,111.89 |
| 6 | $8,784.09 |
| 7 | $10,559.43 |
| 8 | $12,444.27 |
| 9 | $14,445.36 |
| **10** | **$16,569.87** |

When you make a lump sum principal payment for that amount, at that time, towards your mortgage, the interest you pay in the end will be approximately $210,000 instead of $245,660. You will have turned your $100 into $35,000!

This strategy is perfect when you want to hang onto your money as long as you can, "just in case" you need it. If you think you might move in the next few years or your job situation is unpredictable, this is a safe and worthwhile method to save you a ton of money but still allow you to hang on to your cash as a backup as long as you need to.

**BONUS TIP: Two Quick and Easy Ways to Come Up with $100 per Month!**

If you're wondering about how you might come up with an extra $100 per month to put towards your mortgage, I've got two quick strategies that will apply to many if not most people reading this.

Strategy #1: Make your own coffee (or tea, or latte, etc.) at home. Many people don't even think about the fact that they spend $4, $5, or $6 per day at Starbuck or the local coffee shop—and they don't realize that if they only saved that money and made their own (better) coffee they could turn $100 into $50,000 in mortgage savings!

Strategy #2: Raise your insurance deductibles. Many people will be able to come up with $100 per month extra by just adjusting their home and auto insurance policies. Some also adjust their tax withholding on their paycheck and take a smaller refund each tax season, after all you can make more investing what you have now versus giving the government a free loan for a year.

Either strategy can help to get you what you need—and then some—to implement what you've just learned in this report.

**The key to using your mortgage to turn $100 into $35,000.00 or even $50,000.00 is your ability to think "long term".**

**You've got to think ahead! Look at it as a gift from the "current" you to the "future" you. Do you think you can benefit from not throwing away that $50,000.00 in interest?**

**You better believe you can. And you will if you take the simple steps needed to make these strategies work. And they will!**

This is the easiest, simplest most risk-free guaranteed way to turn $100 into $50,000.00 you'll ever find. It's almost like going to a horse race and knowing in advance which horse is going to win!

## Five secrets married people should know before signing a credit application (R088)

**Secret #1:** What you may not know about credit is that there is LEGAL discrimination taking place against women in the credit world on a daily basis.

*How?*

**Consider this:** women, on average, make less money than their male counterparts. Credit, in part, is based on the amount of money you earn.

In other words, women will have less credit opportunities out of the gate because the credit system discriminates against them (All this while the Federal Equal Credit Opportunity Act says that creditors can't deny consumers access to credit because of their sex).

**But here's the good news:** there are still strategies women can use to help themselves in the credit world. If you're a woman, you only need a little KNOWLEDGE to build on in order to have the POWER to navigate the credit system successfully.

**Secret #2:** For women, "joint" credit often translates to "no" credit.

Joint credit with your husband, based on his income, might seem to make sense for a stay-at-home mom.

But there is a big problem with this.

If you get divorced down the road (50% + marriages end in divorce), you will have ZERO credit once your credit is separated from your husband's.

Another problem is, if you run into financial troubles, your husband's credit could suffer.

Married women should build credit of their own, entirely separate from their husband's. This will provide **extra protection** for you by giving you a "fall back" credit file… even if you stay married for the rest of your life.

**Secret #3:** You can leverage your spouse's excellent credit in order to build credit of your own.

Through the use of joint accounts and/or authorized user accounts, you can build your credit profile enough to qualify for credit of your own. Then you can even cancel your joint accounts but still be on your way to building a healthy credit file

**Secret #4:** If you are a couple about to get married and each of you already has excellent credit, then it is usually best to keep your credit SEPARATE .

*Why?* Because many times one spouse will damage the other's credit, and this will just fuel the fire of conflict and hurt your relationship. (Not to mention ruin your credit.)

Some credit accounts may have to be joint credit accounts, such as a mortgage where both incomes are required to qualify. That's okay, but keep everything else separate as much as possible.

**Secret #5:** Even if you don't already have strong credit, married couples are much better off if they will take the time and effort to build **solid individual (not-joint) credit reports**.

By building individual credit, married people will have two credit files to use when they need them. On the contrary, those who put all of their "credit eggs" in one basket by doing everything jointly will be represented in the credit system by only one credit file.

As a couple, **you want two strong credit files** instead of one because it gives you OPTIONS in the event you run into financial problems. One spouse's credit could be completely ruined, and you would still be able to operate as a couple by getting car loans, rentals, and filling other credit-dependent needs.

Think of it this way: it's better to have two boats at your disposal than for both people to depend on the same boat. If one runs into trouble and you're sharing your "credit" boat, then you're both sunk.

Obviously you're not going to plan on having financial problems, or even marital problems… but the old saying holds true: **"Expect the best, but plan for the worst."**

## 12 insider programs to get your student loan payments reduced or forgiven (R052)

There are two programs that can *eventually* get your federal student loans forgiven. They are the "Pay as you earn" program and the "Income-Based Repayment" (IBR) program.

With the first program (for federal student loans taken out after October 2007), your debt can be forgiven after 20 years of on time payments. With the second (for older federal student loans), your debt can be forgiven after 25 years of on time payments.

Both programs put a limit on the amount that your student loan payments can be as a percentage of your income. What this means in practice is that you could pay for 20 years on your student loans at a reduced rate, and then the loan could be forgiven.

**10 More Ways to Get Your Student Loans Forgiven… (From the Fight Debt and Win Coaching Program)**

Student loans don't go away easily, and it can be quite harmful to your credit (not to mention your financial and professional life) if you default on them.

**"But I can't take early retirement - I haven't paid off my student loan yet."**

However, there are several ways provided by the government that **you can get a student loan CANCELED**. We're going to cover them today.

**1. Military Service**

If you have served in the military you may be able to cancel all or part of your student loans. According to the U.S. Department of Education website, if you received a National Defense Student Loan you may be able to receive partial cancellation of your loan for your service in the armed forces.

If you served a year in a "hostile fire" area, you may also qualify for partial loan cancellation.

**2. Teaching in a school serving low income families**

If you are a full time teacher in a school that serves students in low income families you may qualify for cancellation of all or part of your Stafford Loan or Perkins Loan. As of this writing, Stafford loan cancellation requires 5 years of full time teaching in schools serving low income families.

**3. Special Education Teachers**

If you teach children with disabilities you may qualify for cancellation of your Perkins Loan.

**4. Teachers in fields where there are shortages.**

If you teach in a field where there is a shortage of qualified teachers, you may qualify for loan cancellation. This varies by state and by what the state determines to be areas of shortages.

**5. Disability**

If you have become "totally and permanently" disabled, you may qualify for cancellation of your loans based on your disability.

If you are a veteran and you've been deemed "unemployable" as a result of a condition related to your military service, you may qualify for loan cancellation.

**6. False Certification**

If the school falsely certified your eligibility for a loan, the loan can be canceled.

There are several possibilities that could apply here. Basically, any misrepresentation on the part of the school regarding your ELGIBILITY FOR THE LOAN, in order to get you the loan, can give you the right to have the loan canceled.

Many schools are quite aggressive about getting students in the door with whatever "package" of loans required, and shortcuts are often taken in that process.

According to the U.S. Department of education website, loans canceled for this reason will not have any more payments owed, and **any payments already made will be refunded**, and any related adverse credit history will be deleted.

**7. School Closing**

If the school you were attending closed while you were in attendance, you may qualify for loan cancellation.

**8. Identity Theft**

If the loans were fraudulent because of identity theft your loans can be canceled based on the fraud.

**9. Forged Signature**

If your signature was forged on documents related to the loan, you may qualify for loan cancellation if you can provide evidence of the forgery.

**10. Bankruptcy**

In most cases bankruptcy will NOT result in the discharge of your student loans.

However, if you are filing for bankruptcy and can prove that repaying the loans would cause "undue hardship", then you may be able to get the student loans canceled.

## Credit Expert reveals how to build $50,000.00 in business credit in 150 days (R017)

Imagine if you had access to $50,000 cash (in hours) with nothing but your signature? Well you can, (when you know how).

Now you want to use the money to grow a business, not buy a boat, swimming pool or redecorate your home.

The *cash* is in the form of **business credit**. This means if you make a bad business decision, you'll be in debt. But on the other hand, if you play your cards right, you could be in the chips before you know it. So let's talk about how people just like you have established $50,000 business credit in only 150 days.

**How to Fast Track Your Business to a $50K Credit Line**

Just like personal credit, there is also business credit. Except business credit, (when you know the secrets), can be obtained faster and for greater amounts.

Here's how…

Jake Patterson's 9 Step Plan for building $50,000.00 in business credit:

1. **Have (or create) a Corporate Entity like a Corporation or LLC**. You can build business credit without a corporate entity, but you can do it *much more effectively* with one… and according to Jake, it makes more sense.

2. **Have (or create) a well-established business address**. You should have a corporation or LLC with a real physical commercial address. Avoid P.O. boxes. The longer you have this address, the better.

3. **Have (or create) a well established business bank account**. If your business has an established relationship with a bank, you may be able to get your current bank to issue a corporate credit card and drastically speed up this process.

4. **Have (or get) a land line established in your corporate name**. This must be under your corporations Tax Identification Number and should be listed in 411 directory assistance as well as listed in the Yellow Pages.

5. **Establish your DUNS number using your commercial address**. You can do this by going to http://www.dnb.com and calling the phone number available on the website 1-800-526-9018.

6. **Apply for 2 trade credit accounts** with the following three websites/companies: http://www.quill.com (1-800-982-3400)) and http://deluxe.com (1-855-533-5893). Be sure to use the credit accounts, and pay them off.

7. **Get 3 more vendor credit accounts** (once the above 3 are paid off and being reported on your business credit report): http://www.officedepot.com, http://www.staples.com, http://fedex.com. Again, use them but pay them off immediately each time.

8. **Repeat the above purchases and payoffs until your Dun and Bradstreet Paydex score hits 70+.** After that, apply for a business credit card with each of the following http://www.chevron.com, http://www.enterprise.com, http://www.bankofamerica.com. You may need to rely on your personal credit to get approved.

9. **Use your accounts and continue to build your credit profile.** In short time you'll be able to apply and get approved for even more credit. But more importantly you will likely begin receiving PREAPPROVED credit card offers because of your high Paydex Score. Within 150 days from starting you can have $50,000.00 in business credit. Some have been granted over $100,000.

## How to use introductory rates to put cash in your pocket (R330)

You can save money and put cash in your pocket if you learn to use those "introductory rate" and "balance transfer" offers from credit cards wisely. Here's how.

First, understand that most balance transfer offers come with a 3% or 4% balance transfer fee. This fee equates to INTEREST. Because of this, you must include the fee in your calculations of what you will or won't save by doing a balance transfer.

For example, imagine you have one card at 8.9%. You get an offer from a second card for 4.9% for a year, with a 4% balance transfer fee. Is it worth it to switch? NO! That 4% plus the balance transfer in interest rate makes the interest rate virtually the same as what you're already paying.

Here's a simple way to look at it:

- a 3% balance transfer fee for a 1 year rate is like a 3% APR for that year.
- a 4% balance transfer fee for a 1 year rate is like a 4% APR for that year.

Occasionally there are offers—usually for new cards—that include NO balance transfer fees and a zero percent interest rate. Those are the best "prime" offers that you can get, and they are usually the ones to go after if your credit is up to the task.

But when a transfer fee is involved, you should always calculate it in, and ONLY make those transfers every once in a while—no more than once per year. Because if you transfer balances between cards with 4% transfer fees three separate times in a year, then it's like you're paying 12% for that year! The fewer transfers over a longer period of time is ideal.

So here are the offers to look out for that will yield the **most bang for your buck**:

- 0% balance transfer fee offers with 0% rate for a year or more. (Somewhat rare.)
- 2% to 4% for the life of the balance, with a 3 or 4% transfer fee. (Also rare.)
- 3% or 4% balance transfer fee with 0% interest for a year or more. The longer the better.

By doing this, you can pay off your debts at 4%, 3%, 2%, or even 0% interest… instead of 9%, 13%, or 19%. That adds up to some serious CASH in your pocket!

## A 5-Minute trick that will help you get out of debt (R329)

"Yes, two thousand dollars does seem expensive but remember, that's in today's dollars."

There has been a lot of research in the field of psychology that seems to indicate that the way we talk to ourselves—or our "self talk"—actually matters in terms of our success in life. Methods of therapy have been built around the idea of diffusing or eliminating what is referred to as self-defeating self-talk.

*What does that mean in practice?* It means that statements like "I'll never get out of debt," and "I suck at sales," actually do **hurt** us, and can turn into self-fulfilling prophecies.

**You can combat this tendency by first learning to recognize your negative self-talk, and second deliberately replacing it with more positive, reasonable, and realistic thoughts.**

Instead of saying "I will never get out of debt," argue with yourself and say: "No, never is a long time. Other people have gotten out of debt—and many were in worse situations than I am."

Then follow this up with a series of questions and thought experiments that will help you change your thinking and your attitude:

- What are 5 possible strategies I could use to become debt free in 5 years?
- What can I do to increase my income? If my first plan fails, what are some other things I can try?

Some therapists recommend keeping a "gratitude" journal for a month or two as an exercise to help you improve your thinking. *Why?* Because it will teach your brain to look for positive opportunities as opposed to negative ones. Changing your self-talk from negative assertions to positive questions may also prove helpful. One client simply asked himself—daily—the same question over and over for weeks. And then one day, the answer just came to him. Out of nowhere, he suddenly had a plan of attack that would get him out of debt faster than he ever thought possible.

## How to use your debt like a checking account to eliminate it years earlier! (R334)

In the Fight Debt and Win Coaching Program we teach about a method that we named the "deposit" method. Here's the lowdown on using this technique to help you to get out of debt MUCH faster.

Here's how it works: you use your debt like a checking account. You "deposit" your paychecks into your debt by paying the entire amount of your paychecks, minus a few key expenses, towards your credit card each month. Then, in turn, you pay all of your expenses (with the exception of those few key expenses) out of your credit card.

This does two things:

1. It lowers the amount of interest you'll pay each month on your debt.
2. It puts your extra cash flow towards your debt automatically.

Plus, it is flexible enough that if you end up needing some of the money you've put towards your debt, "taking it back out" is a simple matter of a credit card transaction.

Compare this strategy to other common ones assuming a $12,000 credit card debt:

- Paying minimum payment only - 20+ years
- Paying a fixed, larger payment - Often 3 to 5 Years
- The **Deposit Method** if you have at least $500 of disposable income each month - Less than 2 years.

The numbers speak for themselves.

## "LBF" TECHNIQUE: proven to help you pay off all your bills faster (R333)

One of the biggest obstacles to getting out of debt is a purely mental one. Being in debt can be downright depressing. Feeling trapped makes it worse. And trying—and failing—to make progress, makes it even more painful yet. That's one of the biggest reasons for using the "LBF"—or *Lowest Balance First*—technique.

The method and the reasoning are both simple and easy to understand:

1. Pick your smallest debt, and put everything you can towards paying off THAT debt as quickly as possible. That's it. Once that debt is paid off, choose the next lowest balance and pay it off.
2. This works because human beings thrive on progress. We like to know that the actions that we take are having an effect. We want to see forward movement in our financial situation when we take steps to improve it. And the LBF technique gives us that **psychological advantage** that may be the key to "keeping up the good work".

It may sound counterintuitive, especially if you have another debt that COSTS you more in terms of interest and cash flow. But tackling and CONQUERING one small debt can translate into big **mental rewards** that will catapult you on towards victory. That's the thing about getting out of debt. You can't just consider the financial costs. You've got to think about the psychological costs too.

## Four questions hold the secret to getting out of debt in half the time (R344)

For some people, "How fast can I get out of debt?" is the wrong question to be asking. As it turns out, a lot of people can actually answer that question on their own if they can answer a few other questions first. Here are four simple (but significant) questions to help you find your fastest path out of debt.

**1. What sacrifices are you willing to make?**

People hate to think about making sacrifices, but in reality if you are going to get out of debt faster than the status quo, you're going to have to make sacrifices somewhere. The speed at which you can get out of debt is directly impacted by your willingness to make sacrifices.

**2. Are you willing to relocate or move into cheaper housing?**

For some extreme debt situations, drastic measures are needed. The reality about living expenses in the United States is that they are NOT the same in all places. Some people live in more expensive areas because that's where they can get the better paying job, but the cost of living increase completely voids the benefit that they get from the higher paying job! This is a question to think seriously about if you want to be debt free as fast as possible.

**3. To what lengths are you willing to go?**

This question is really about risk: what risks are you willing and able to take. Some debt-free methods are riskier than others. It's like investing: With the higher paying investments comes more risk. So it is with the fastest debt-free methods… they include increased risk.

The biggest risk decision facing most people who want to get out of debt is whether or not they are willing to sacrifice their credit. Because here's the reality: the fastest way out of debt may mean letting your credit cards get behind just a little. Some people are comfortable with that, some aren't. However, to get interest rates lowered, balances forgiven or any special program available – being behind is a prerequisite, as many people found during the housing crisis – they could not qualify for a mortgage modification because they were current on their payments.

**4. What changes will you make to your current spending habits?**

One of the biggest barriers to becoming debt free is poor spending habits. The poor habits themselves aren't totally fatal, but the unwillingness to change them is.

For example, what if we could show you where you are literally wasting $4,000 per year? Would you jump on the opportunity to save money? Or would there be stipulations attached? *("Sure, as long as you don't cut my cable.")*

A lot of people put it off until tomorrow, banking on the fantasy that they will have a windfall, get a raise or holiday bonus, or their new business idea will bail them out. The truth is, freedom in "thinking" must start before you can be successful.

Freedom from debt starts in your mind. If you are still in the "debt" mindset, and you aren't willing to make sacrifices for your **financial freedom**, then even if you experience a windfall and win the lottery, your mental and spending habits are highly likely to land you back in debt again.

Make changes now! Don't count on the windfall or the raise or the business venture. Change your spending habits and your thinking instead if you EVER want to become debt free.

## The number one reason why people fail to get out of debt (R342)

There is one simple reason why most attempts to get out of debt fail. It's because **people fail to stick to the plan** and follow their chosen method through to the end. *It's really that simple.* Becoming debt free requires follow-through. It requires continual effort.

Most books showing people to get out of debt <u>fail to account for this</u>. The methods may be sound, but the follow-through is nil.

The first book we published about getting out of debt was also the first book to address this issue by exposing and dealing with "lack of follow-through". Still, we found more was needed. That's why the "Fight Debt and Win Coaching Program" went on to be so successful, because we combined the very best in financial education

"I asked you here, Mr.Pemberton, because I wondered why you hadn't been taking part in the spending boom?"

and debt-free methodology with the <u>SUPPORT</u> needed to help people stay the course until they were debt free.

## OVERFLOW METHOD: Why the "Overflow Method" is simple to understand and can be used to pay off almost all types of debt, such as Credit Cards, Medical Bills, Auto Loans, Student Loans, Mortgages and even HELOCS (R343)

Juan was a contractor with a thriving business spinning off healthy cash flow. Still, he had managed to get himself rather deep into debt—having just over $26,000 in credit card debt. What you may find especially shocking is that even with $1,000+ disposable income each month, Juan came to us feeling that his situation was helpless.

Debt has a strange effect on people. It can make you feel trapped, even when the way out should be crystal clear.

Juan is debt free today because of a simple and accessible method called the *overflow method*. It is one of the most common methods for becoming debt free, but some people still fail to see the power that it has for their situation.

In Juan's case, it meant putting anywhere from $1,000 to $1,600 per month EXTRA towards his credit cards. Some months he would have to take a step backwards, but even with those backward steps Juan was still completely debt free in less than 2 years.

Here's how the overflow method works:

1. Add up your expenses and income at the end of the month.
2. If your expenses were less than your income, then the difference is your positive cash flow… or "overflow".
3. Take your "overflow" and apply it to the first debt on your list.
4. Repeat these steps each month until your debt is paid off.

Pretty simple, huh? It's nothing fancy. But if you have strong cash flow, it's a great method to pay down debt. Most traditional methods of getting out of debt, and even some advanced methods, are based in some way on the overflow method.

## THE "RR" STRATEGY: Why this strategy requires no extra money to help you pay off any kind of bill faster but why you don't want to use it by itself (R345)

The "RR" strategy, or "rollover" method, is the process of "rolling" one debt payment into another. It is a simple, yet powerful strategy and can be put to work with no extra money, even with limited resources.

For example, one client had a car note that was almost paid off. It was $360 per month and he had 11 months left. He also had credit card debt of $6,000 on one card and another of about $12,000.

When his car was paid off, he used the rollover method by applying the entire $360 per month car payment towards his $6,000 credit card debt. Once that was paid off, he applied his $360 car payment AND his former $110 credit card payment towards the remaining debt of $12,000. These combined with the existing payment on the $12,000 card (about $250) to pay off his debt much faster than would have otherwise been possible making minimum payments.

Also referred to as the "snowball" method, it's one of the basic strategies for tackling any pile of debt involving multiple debts.

**The big downfall to this strategy is that it is NOT always very powerful when used alone.**

For example, a person might have numerous credit cards with long term monthly payments to reduce the dept to zero. They may not have the advantage that the client had above—of having a big car payment that was almost finished.

Unless a person takes other steps (such as using the overflow method combined with this strategy), it will be very slow going to get the first debt or two paid off and gain momentum. For this reason, it is rarely recommended to use the rollover method on its own, unless some financial and/or life constraints leave you no choice (which is rare).

## Important facts you should know if you're disabled, collecting social security and have creditors harassing you (R213)

If you or a loved one are disabled and your only income source is Social Security or disability, bill collectors have very limited options when it comes to collecting the debt from you. Why? Because Social Security and disability benefits are exempt from garnishment according to federal law.

This doesn't mean collectors won't try to get the money. A bill collector can still legally freeze the funds in a bank account and force you to prove through the courts that the money's only source is "exempt" income. Obviously it is best if you can avoid that scenario.

Luckily there is a place to get help. The legal experts at DebtCounsel.net specialize in helping protect those with Social Security and/or Disability income from bill collectors who might otherwise drag them through unnecessary financial harm and court proceedings.

There are ways to protect yourself and your income. Methods include getting checks instead of direct deposit, and sheltering money in special banks that will not honor "freeze" requests if you're a DebtCounsel.net client.

If you are on social security or disability and you are being harassed by collectors, go to http://www.DebtCounsel.net to get help. For a modest fee, they will take care of the headache of dealing with collectors and help you protect your exempt income.

---

# Collection Attorney reveals the easy and fun thing to do if a bill collector calls you (R203)

If you have fallen behind on your bills then you know how stressful it can be.

Late fees, calls from the creditor, the worry of if and how you'll be able to "pull out of it"; all these things add up, and it certainly takes its toll on you.

**And then, the collectors start calling.**

Once a debt has been referred or sold to a third party collector, you'll get a collection reported on your credit report, you'll receive multiple phone calls and letters, and you could even end up being sued by the collector.

The situation can be both stressful and difficult for anyone, and especially so for someone struggling to get control of their debt and finances.

Debt collectors can add to that stress considerably as they are often rude, pushy, and sometimes even abusive and/or aggressive.

Thankfully, you have rights under the Fair Debt Collection Practices Act (or FDCPA for short) which specifies what debt collectors can and can't do and gives consumers certain methods, rights, and remedies to keep collectors in check.

**Your Rights Regarding Phone Calls**

***Can collectors call me at my home?***

Yes, but they can't call you at a time that is known to be inconvenient to you.

**A "convenient" time is assumed to be between 8am and 9pm Monday – Friday unless you notify the debt collector otherwise.**

This means that you have the option of notifying the debt collector (either verbally or in writing) when "convenient" times are for you and what days are off limits (such as your days off of work). You can't, however, tell them that "all days" are inconvenient and off limits; for that, you would use another tool that we'll discuss below.

**Note:** that if you are represented by an attorney with regards to the debt in question, the debt collector cannot call you except under certain circumstances.

Those circumstances are:

- They don't know or can't reasonably figure

out the attorney's name and contact information.

- The attorney fails to respond to their inquiries in a reasonable timeframe
- The attorney consents to the debt collector contacting you directly

***Can they call me on my cell phone?***

Generally speaking, yes. The same rules regarding convenient times and attorney representation would apply for contact at home.

***Can they call me at work?***

Yes, unless they are told otherwise by either you or your employer.

***Can they talk to my employer?***

Yes, but ONLY once, and only if they are doing so to get or verify your location information.

Note that a debt collector calling a third party to obtain location information CANNOT openly identify themselves as a debt collector OR identify their employer unless specifically asked by the person they are calling. They also cannot say that you owe any debt.

This means that if you get a message from a co-worker saying "Joe the debt collector was calling about the money you owe him," the debt collector may very well have violated the law.

***Can they talk to my neighbors?***

They can only talk to your neighbors if they are trying to get your "location information". This means that if they know where you live and they have your phone number, they have no business talking to your neighbors. If they do, they have violated the FDCPA.

***Can they talk to my spouse?***

Generally speaking, yes. Section 805(d) of the FDCPA states that "For the purposes of this section, the term 'consumer' includes the consumer's spouse [...]"

**What if they pretend to be someone they are not?**

Debt collectors will pose as anything from **government employees** to attorneys to **your mother**.

**And I'm not kidding about the mother part...**

Once, years ago, I had a friend and roommate with some credit and debt problems.

One day when the phone rang, I answered it and a sweet, older sounding lady was on the other end.

She said:

*"Oh hi! You must be John's friend... what was your name again?"*

I answered with my name, like most people would, and she said...

*"That's right, yes he's told me about you. All good of course. Is he around? Tell him his mom's on the phone."*

So I handed the phone to my friend, thinking that I had just met his **mother**.

Later I found out it was a **debt collector**.

**Whether they are claiming to be your mother or Abe Lincoln, any debt collector who claims to be someone else is breaking the law.**

Impersonating another person or otherwise claiming to be something or someone they are not, or using lies and deception in any fashion to collect on a debt are all **illegal** activities under the **FDCPA**.

**Stopping Debt Collector Calls**

**Stopping Work Calls**

To keep debt collectors from calling you at work, you or your employer simply need to inform the debt collectors that the calls aren't allowed. This can be done verbally, or you can do it in writing.

### Stopping Third Party Calls

Once the debt collector has your contact information, they should not be contacting third parties. If they do, you can contact the debt collector and inform them that they have violated the law by contacting unauthorized third parties in connection with the alleged debt.

The letter may go something like this...

*"Dear Collector,*

*On [date] you contacted my [employer/neighbor/cousin/etc.] via [mail/phone].*

*According to the FDCPA, The only reason you can do that is to obtain location information.*

*However, as demonstrated by your letters and phone calls on [dates, can list detailed specifics], you already have my location information and had absolutely no business contacting my [neighbor/friend/relative/etc.]*

*Please cease all communications with third parties as required under the law. To be clear: all future communications regarding my account should only be made with me directly. I will keep a close eye on this and you will hear from me again should any problems arise."*

**Keep in mind that if the debt is large, a single violation isn't going to bother the debt collector terribly, and you could still be at risk for a lawsuit.**

In that case, simply putting the collector on notice and demanding that they keep all future contact with you directly should be sufficient. **Keeping track of violations like this is important**, however, and could pay off substantially in the event that you ever do get sued. *(Can you say "countersuit?")*

If the debt is small and you have solid evidence of a blatant violation, you could open up the option to pursue them legally and possibly force the DELETION of the collection from your credit report!

### Reducing Calls to Your Home

If you simply want to reduce calls to your home but not stop them completely, there are a few simple methods you can employ.

**First**, you can tell the debt collector when your off limits times are (within reason).

This can be done verbally or in writing. Try for 3 days a week, and that will give you three days of peace per week.

**Secondly**, you can screen your calls. Let calls go to your answering machine, and only pick up if it's someone you want to talk to. (Caller ID can help, but the identity of the caller may not always be clear enough from the Caller ID.) Tell all your friends that you screen calls so that they will know to say something on your answering machine to see if you pick up.

**Third**, you can use speakerphone and a simple recorder to **record calls** from collectors. At the beginning of each call, simply notify the collector that you're recording the call. They probably won't want to talk as much or as long (and maybe not at all) when you do this. If you want to lessen the chance that they'll want to talk, add that you are recording calls to submit along with your complaint to the state attorney general's office.

*(Be sure to check the laws in your state regarding the recording of phone calls!)*

**Finally**, you can reduce phone calls to your home if you have multiple collectors calling you by using the following tactic selectively (only with certain collectors).

So let's talk about...

### Stopping Collector Phone Calls To Your Home

If you want to stop the phone calls to your home completely (from either one collector or from all of them), then you'll need to use a tactic known as

**"Cease And Desist - Phone Calls Only."**

According to the FDCPA,

*"If a consumer notifies the debt collector in writing that the consumer refuses to pay a debt or that the consumer wishes the debt collector to cease further communication with the consumer, the debt collector shall not communicate further with the consumer with respect to such debt, except--*

*(1) to advise the consumer that the debt collector's further efforts are being terminated*

*(2) to notify the consumer that the debt collector or creditor may invoke specified remedies which are ordinarily invoked by such debt collector or creditor; or*

*(3) where applicable, to notify the consumer that the debt collector or creditor intends to invoke a specified remedy. If such notice from the consumer is made by mail, notification shall be complete upon receipt."*

What this means is that you can ask the debt collector to **cease communications** with you, and by law they have to do it.

**But what if you just want to stop the phone calls?**

That's where the "Cease and Desist - Phone calls only" tactic comes in.

To use this tactic, simply send the collector a letter asking them to cease **all PHONE CALLS**. (**Note:** not all communication, but all phone calls.)

The letter might go something like this:

*"Dear Collector,*

*I hereby request that you cease and desist with all PHONE CALLS in relation to the collection of the alleged debt (account number [xxxxxx]).*

*From now on please correspond by MAIL ONLY.*

*Thank You,*

*Joe Consumer"*

Once the collector receives your letter, any further phone calls received are in violation of the FDCPA.

**Why wouldn't you want to just stop ALL communication?**

For that, let's move on to the next section...

Stopping More Than Just Calls

Collection agencies use three primary tools to collect debts:

1. The **phone**

2. The **mail**

and

3. The **legal system**

By using a **"Cease and Desist ALL"** (instructing them to cease all communication with you), you **ELIMINATE** options #1 and #2 for them.

*What does that leave them with?*

**#3: The legal system.**

**On a large debt that is within the statute of limitations (or "SOL" for short), this is a dangerous move that could result in you being sued.**

The larger the balance, the more likely a "cease and desist all" will be to prompt a lawsuit.

It doesn't mean that *ALL* creditors will sue. Many won't. But you don't know which ones will and which ones won't.

On smaller debts, the chances of a lawsuit are substantially less, but it's hard to tell where the line is exactly (it varies by creditor/collector.)

**It's also important to understand that a "cease and desist all" doesn't make the debt go away.** The collector can **STILL** collect as long as they do it through the legal system.

**They can also still sell the debt to another collector, in which case the calls can and will start again.**

For this and other reasons it is usually better to leave the door open for written communication by using the *"cease and desist - phone calls only"* approach.

*(It may be better to receive mail and/or negotiate via mail with an existing collector than to end up with a new collection account with a new collection agency.)*

**Rescinding a Cease and Desist All**

In the event that you have sent a cease and desist all by mistake or otherwise need to backpedal and "remove" a cease and desist all, you can rescind it by simply sending a notice to the collector in writing that you are doing so, and you can at that point selectively re-open the door to negotiation by mail.

Generally speaking, the only reason to do this would be to open up communications for the purpose of settling the debt, or if you made a mistake in sending a "cease and desist all" when you didn't intend to (which could be easy to do if you are copying and pasting letters from the internet!)

**Sample Cease and Desist Letter**

*Dear (creditor or collector name),*

*This is a formal request for you to cease and desist all collection activities including but not limited to; phone calls, letters, faxes, emails and any and all contact with me, any members of my family, friends, co-workers or employer.*

*Sincerely,*

*[name]*

“

The only thing worse than failure is to live with the regret you *didn’t* try.

# DEBT NEGOTATION

- ☑ **credit card debt up to 900% faster**
- ☑ **How to turn weakness into strength when it comes to eliminating your debt**
- ☑ **The secret to cutting your debt payments by up to 50% overnight**
- ☑ **Use this sneaky but legal method to get medical bills reduced by as much as 50%**
- ☑ **The #1 Secret to dealing with abusive creditors and collectors**
- ☑ ***And More***

“

The *only* ideas which will work for you are the ones you put to work.

## The insider method bankers use to pay off credit card debt up to 900% faster (R024)

Have you ever wondered what bankers do when they find themselves in over their heads and need to **get out of debt fast?** You may be surprised...

This legal method some bankers have used will allow you to pay off credit card debt up to 900% faster. Before I go into detail about the method, let's review a typical situation and then I'll explain how it relates to **you** paying off credit card debt up to 900% faster.

First understand this, banks and credit card companies count on some people NOT paying their debts. It's just part of doing business.

Some customers will file for bankruptcy. Others skip out completely, while a smart number get special payment arrangements with little or no interest.

So why would a credit card company reduce your interest rate and in some cases even the principal? To understand this, imagine the following scenario:

You loan Joe $5,000 with a fixed payment of $200 per month and 10% interest. After paying for 12 months ($2400), Joe loses his job.

After Joe falls behind on the payments, you realize that he may not get another job as quickly as he needs to. Joe may have to file for bankruptcy, as other creditors are threatening to sue him. **You know at this point that if Joe files for bankruptcy, you might not get any of the remainder of the money owed to you**.

But Joe calls you to talk about his financial problems, and says he has $1,000 tucked away that he can still pay you. You agree to take that $1,000, and forgive the rest of the debt. This helps you limit the amount of your loss. The rest of the (unpaid) debt goes on your taxes as a write off. **For you, in this scenario, it makes sense to take Joe's offer for the $1,000 because you might not otherwise see another dollar.**

For the banks, the scenario is even better. When you calculate in the interest paid on credit cards, some people will have **already paid back the amount of the original loan in "actual cash" by the time they get in trouble**!

This means that anything else the bank collects is pure profit. So a bank might issue a credit card on which the consumer racks up $5,000 in debt, and then after $3,500 in payments the balance could still be $4,000. If the consumer falls behind, the bank might sell the $4,000 debt to a collector for $2,000. (Notice, they have now received MORE than the amount of the original loan.)

Now they write off the "loss", and save on their taxes. [13]

So based on these facts, some have **used a method known as "debt negotiation" to lower their balances and interest... and to pay off their debts as much as 900% faster**.

This powerful method can be summed up like this: When you are in trouble, let the bank know you are in trouble, and try to work out an arrangement that will allow you to pay at least SOME of the remaining balance. In order to use this method, the following elements are often helpful or necessary:

- The ability to make the case for your financial hardship (i.e. proof of job loss, divorces, death in family etc.)
- The willingness to fall behind on your payments if you are not *already* behind. Usually you must be 30 to 60 days behind before the bank will negotiate with you in this way. (Some banks will tell you this when you ask.)

[13]Numbers based on a $5,000 credit card debt at 18% interest with minimum payment of interest + 1% where the consumer pays only the minimum payment for approximately 2 years.

| | INTEREST RATE | DEBT AMOUNT | PAYMENT AMOUNT | MONTHLY INTEREST | TOTAL INTEREST | PAY OFF TIME |
|---|---|---|---|---|---|---|
| | 16.9% | $13,000.00 | $260.00 | $183.08 | $9,643.47 | 7 YEARS, 4 MONTHS |
| ➡ | 4.25 | $13,000.00 | $260.00 | $46.04 | $1,333.34 | 5 YEARS, 8 MONTHS |

Our table from earlier illustrates your savings when going from a 16.9% credit card interest rate to 4.25% after a few phone calls explaining your situation.

And keep in mind, some people use 'debt negotiation' to get their interest rate down to ZERO… plus a portion of the principal forgiven.

## How to turn weakness into strength when it comes to eliminating your debt (R336)

Debt negotiation is a perfect example of when you can turn weakness into strength. Consider the following scenarios which are all signs of "financial weakness":

- You've just spent a month in the hospital.
- You lost your job and have been unable to find employment.
- You had an emergency room visit that totaled $6,000 but you don't have health insurance.
- You just took a cut in pay.
- Your small business just went bankrupt.
- You are being sued and have to pay for legal defense.

Most of these scenarios would equate to some level of financial distress even weakness. Debt negotiation is one way in which to turn those weaknesses into strength. Here's how it works:

1. Your hardship or financial weakness becomes the <u>LOGIC</u> used to explain your situation and justify your request for a debt "workout".

2. What cash you do have available becomes your primary bargaining chip.

For example, you may have enough cash on hand to pay only some of your debt. How should you decide who gets the money?

The best thing a person can do in this situation is work to turn weakness into strength by *negotiating*. You can make the remaining cash you have go further towards paying off your debt, and your financial hardship (weakness) may, in the end, result in your becoming debt free (strength).

Ask yourself this simple question:

*If you had only $500 available to pay, and $1,000 in debt, would you rather pay the $500 and still have an outstanding collection for the other $500... or would you rather pay the $500 and have the creditor forgive the remainder of the debt?*

Obviously, the **better deal is getting a "settlement"** agreement and letting the creditor write off the part you don't pay.

I AM STRONG, BECAUSE I'VE BEEN WEAK.
I AM FEARLESS, BECAUSE I'VE BEEN AFRAID.
I AM WISE, BECAUSE I'VE BEEN FOOLISH.

What are other ways to turn weakness into strength?

- Use an outstanding balance as a bargaining tool to get your interest rates lowered or other concessions.
- Use your high interest rates as a reason for threatening to leave the creditor for better rates.
- Use your difficult financial situation to get permanent payment terms that are more affordable with less interest.

These are just some ideas.

By using debt negotiation to turn financial weakness into strength, many have paid off their debts much faster than would have otherwise been possible. For some, the results are drastic.

## The secret to cutting your debt payments by up to 50% overnight (R040)

There are three basic strategies to cutting your payments by as much as half in a very short time (even a few hours). Here they are.

1. Use debt elimination to reduce debt, and in turn payments.
2. Use debt negotiation to reduce debt, and in turn payments.
3. Use debt negotiation to reduce your INTEREST RATES or to negotiate on your payments directly.

Let's talk about each strategy a little bit.

**Debt Elimination for Cutting Payments**

Simply paying off a small debt can eliminate the payment associated with it, but there are other ways, too.

You can use selective debt consolidation to merge certain accounts, which often results in lower payments.

The "Deposit" method (mentioned elsewhere in this manual) can be used to effectively eliminate a payment while letting everything extra get applied to the balance.

**Debt Negotiation to Reduce Debt (And Payments)**

Lowering the amount of debt will in turn lower the amount of payments. This is when debt negotiation can be useful.

One woman was able to eliminate entire doctor bills totaling thousands by making simple, short phone calls. This strategy reduces your payments and frees up cash flow.

**Debt Negotiation to Reduce Interest Rates or to Lower Payments Directly**

Asking for lower interest rates can often result in lower payments. Plus, the payments themselves are usually negotiable. Many creditors will lower payments either temporarily or permanently if you just ask. All it takes is a phone call, and a little patience to navigate the system.

Using these simple strategies, consumers have cut their payments by as much as 50% overnight. Not bad for a few hours' work on the phone!

## Use this sneaky but legal method to get medical bills reduced by as much as 50% (R069)

Medical bills are some of the most inflated, unsubstantiated bills that consumers get saddled with. According to a report from *Time Magazine*, the rates at hospitals are often arbitrary amounts chosen by a single person and can vary greatly from place to place. One hospital may charge $100 for the same ($2 cost) hospital gown while another hospital charges only $10. In some (if not most) cases, there is simply no rhyme or reason to the charges.

Because of these facts, **medical bills must always be considered *negotiable***. They are subject to change, negotiation and should be subject to scrutiny.

You've read already in this manual and it deserves repeating here:

<u>Often, getting bills reduced is a simple matter of making a phone call to the right person</u>.

Sometimes it can be more complicated, but in the vast majority of cases (perhaps with the exceptions of some especially greedy hospital executives), negotiation of medical bills is usually very possible and perfectly reasonable.

Exactly which medical expenses are negotiable? And to what extent?

This report from Harris Poll may give some indication…

***Haggling Over Healthcare Costs Happens about as Much Today but with Better Results Compared to Three Years Ago***

*A new* Wall Street Journal *Online/Harris Interactive Health-Care Poll shows that U.S. adults are no more likely to haggle over healthcare costs with various providers today than they were three years ago. However, when they do engage in discussions about costs, they are more likely to feel that they have been successful in negotiating a lower price for health-related products and services. The survey also shows that despite this increased feeling of success, adults are less likely today than three years ago to say that if their out-of-pocket healthcare expenses increased in the next two years, they would be likely or very likely to negotiate a better price for medical bills (44% now compared to 53% in 2002).*

*Below are the results of the online survey of 2,027 U.S. adults conducted by Harris Interactive® between November 15 and 17, 2005 for* The Wall Street Journal *Online's Health Industry Edition.*

*There has been little or virtually no change in the percentage of adults who have talked with healthcare service providers to negotiate a lower price for products or services. Specifically:*

- *Thirteen percent (13%) say they have talked with a pharmacist to see if they could pay a lower price than what they had been billed, compared to 17 percent in 2002.*
- *Twelve percent (12%) say they have negotiated with a doctor, compared to 13 percent in 2002.*
- *One in ten (10%) say they have negotiated with a dentist, compared to 12 percent in 2002.*
- *Nine percent (9%) have negotiated with a hospital, compared to 10 percent in 2002.*

*This year, adults were also asked whether they have tried to negotiate a lower price with a health insurer or plan, and 13 percent report having done so.*

*While these numbers have not changed much since 2002, the percentage of adults who talked with these providers and said they were successful in negotiating a lower price, did increase significantly.*

• *Seven in 10 (70%) adults who talked with a hospital say they were successful in negotiating a lower price for their medical bills, up from 45 percent 2002.*

• *Approximately two-thirds (64%) of adults who negotiated with a dentist say they were successful, compared to 47 percent three years ago.*

• *Approximately three in five (61%) adults who negotiated with a doctor say they were successful, up from 54 percent in 2002.*

• *More than half (56%) of those who talked with a pharmacist say they were successful in negotiating a lower price, compared to 48 percent in 2002.*

*In addition, among those who tried to negotiate a lower price with a health insurer or plan, less than half (45%) say they were successful.*

*"We can see that consumers who have engaged in discussions about costs have had success in negotiating lower prices for health-related products and services," states Katherine Binns, president of the Healthcare and Public Relations Research Practice at Harris Interactive®. "This suggests that as we continue to toward a world of 'consumer-directed healthcare,' consumers may find it increasingly necessary to confront health care providers and insurers about costs, and that they will become increasingly confident in negotiating for health-related goods and services as they do in other sectors of the economy."*

***Source:***

*The Harris Poll® Dec.1, 2005, "Haggling Over Healthcare Costs Happens about as Much Today but with Better Results Compared to Three Years Ago"*

*Harris Interactive Inc. All rights reserved.*

Remember—for those who may hesitate, feel bad or strange about asking a hospital to lower their bill—most hospitals have **negotiation** calculated into their business model. It's just part of the plan! Plain and simple.

One hospital automatically gives a 90% discount to uninsured. Another gives a 30% discount immediately if you call and complain about your bill. These "discounts" and write offs are built into their business. **It's part of the game for which they write all of the rules.** (So don't feel bad for playing along.)

**What to do...**

Here are some steps you can take if you have medical bills that you think may be good candidates for negotiation.

1. Look over the bills very carefully; look for inconsistencies or numbers that don't make sense. Call the hospital and ask for clarification on every detail. Ask for details on any vague descriptions or amounts.
2. Ask the hospital if they have any "programs" that can help you to better afford your bill.
3. On a separate occasion, contact the hospital, explain that you're trying to get your debt paid off, and ask if there is anything they can do to help.
4. Finally, if you haven't gotten a reduction to date, write a letter to the hospital that spells out and documents your financial troubles, and offer them a lump sum payment to settle the bill.

## The #1 Secret to dealing with abusive creditors and collectors (R335)

Let me introduce you to Rhonda. Rhonda, at one time in her life, had everything. She had a great husband, two great kids and a nice home.

But about 9 years into her marriage, everything fell apart. Her husband left her. She lost the house. She was left with two kids requiring support, and she was desperate.

So Rhonda ended up going to work for a local collection agency. What she witnessed shocked her. It bothered her so much she had trouble sleeping and wanted nothing more than to find an "honest" way to support her kids.

Well, she eventually found a better way to make a living, and now she's speaking out about her two years as a bill collector.

Here's what she advises for dealing with abusive creditors and collectors:

The sad fact is - creditors, medical providers, and the bill collectors that collect on their behalf violate the law all the time. It's part of "business as usual.".

*What can you do about it?* The answer is simple. **The #1 secret to dealing with abusive creditors and collectors is to watch them very, very closely.** Document everything.

"Documentation" is king when it comes to winning the fight with these companies who regularly disregard the law. Here are some tips on how to get the upper hand:

- First, familiarize yourself with the Fair Credit Billing Act, the Fair Credit Reporting Act, HIPAA laws, and the Fair Debt Collection Practices Act.
- Second, document (write down, with dates and times and names) every single little detail related to your interactions with collectors, creditors, and medical providers. Keep statements. Keep letters. Keep copies of your responses and payments. Keep meticulous records on EVERYTHING.
- When you find a suspected violation of the law, highlight it in your notes along with the reference to the law violated.
- Use suspected law violations to your advantage when negotiating. You can even bring them up in complaints through the Better Business Bureau, Federal Trade Commission and the Attorney General in your state.
- The more organized your notes and documentation, the more likely you will prevail. If you end up needing to take a creditor or collector to court (which happens all the time), your notes will often prove your case.

"I'd recommend becoming a Debt Counsellor: You can make a fortune."

## Thinking about credit counseling? Think again (R152)

In 2003, when the good times were rolling, everyone could get a mortgage, Detroit was rolling cars to anyone who could sign their name and prove insurance...

...And the National Consumer Law Center, Inc., published an alarming report titled **Credit Counseling in Crisis**.

Before you contact anyone advertising 'debt

relief', read the following dirty secrets of this industry.

The **National Consumer Law Center** and the **Consumer Federation of America** spent 2 years investigating the Credit Counseling industry. When they were done. Their findings were published in a 58 page report titled **"Credit Counseling in Crisis."**

Here are the abbreviated findings of that report...

**STRIKE-ONE:**

The bulk of Credit Counseling offices are members of the National Foundation for Credit Counseling (aka the NFCC), which totals over 1,300 offices nationwide. What consumers don't know is these "member offices" **RECEIVE TWO-THIRDS OF THEIR INCOME FROM THE BANKING INDUSTRY**.

**STRIKE-TWO:**

The majority of Credit Counseling Services charge a monthly fee (even though a study has proven most will lie about it). Because of this fee, **the longer you stay in debt, the more money credit counseling will make**.

Therefore they have no incentive to help you get out of debt quickly.

**STRIKE-THREE:**

A survey of **Internal Revenue Service (IRS)** tax reports revealed alarming findings. So called "non-profit" agencies were reaping windfall profits. For example...

Credit Counselors of America reported net profits of just over **$6,000,000.00 MILLION per year**.

Cambridge Credit Counseling reported a net profit of about **$7,300,000.00 MILLION per year**.

Genus Credit Management reported profits of about **$5,600,000.00 MILLION**. They also reported paying their general manager a salary of **$394,122.00** plus benefits.

Credit Counselors of America reported compensation for its President Michael Hall of **$371,542.00** plus benefits. But that's not all...

**VERIFIED FACT:**

**President of "Non-Profit" was paid over $296.00 AN HOUR**

American Consumer Credit Counseling reported paying its president a salary of **$462,350.00** plus over **$130,000.00** in benefits. This works out to **$592,350.00** a year or **$296.18** per hour.

**"Is it any wonder the Internal Revenue Service revoked the tax exempt status of over 41 credit counseling organizations?"**

**Even the largest Consumer Credit Counseling Service in the Nation (AmeriDebt) was sued by the Federal Trade Commission (FTC) for $172,000,000.00 MILLION.**

The conclusion here is – credit counseling is designed to make money for someone else and rarely does it help consumers get out of debt. Essentially, it is an organization primarily funded by the banking industry, and operating with the banking industry's best interest at heart.

“

He who trusts all things to chance, makes a *lottery* of his life.

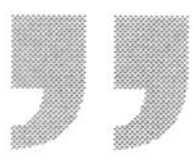

# FREE MONEY AND OTHER BENEFITS

- ☑ **Over 1 billion dollars in veterans' benefits go unclaimed each year - claim your share**
- ☑ **The secret to finding out if you qualify for thousands in free government grants or loans in under 60 minutes**
- ☑ **The secret website Americans have quietly claimed over $14.4 billion through**
- ☑ **UNCLAIMED MONEY: $58 Billion is waiting for its rightful owners with over 2 million Americans cashing in each year**
- ☑ **How to receive free financial aid to learn or improve your computer skills**
- ☑ ***And More***

We do not remember days.
We remember *moments*.

Cesare Pavese

# Over 1 billion dollars in veterans' benefits go unclaimed each year (R015)

**How a disabled World War II Veteran "lost out" on $454,000 in benefits**

My friend's father is a proud World War II veteran and he **lost out on over $454,000 worth of benefits**. Why? Because he *didn't* know he qualified... **FACT:** What you don't know CAN HURT YOU.

The good news is he's now receiving over $3,000.00 per month. Being disabled and in his 90s this is good news. But let's look into *why* he missed out on $454,000 in benefits and how this can be avoided by other Veterans.

Over **$1 billion** in veterans benefits go unclaimed each year. That's over **$83 million a month** or **$2.8 million per day!** And in most cases the Veterans who are missing out are ones who need it most (retired or disabled).

However, once you know everywhere to look, you will find there are **multiple organizations** which help Veterans claim missing benefits. However, programs are rarely advertised.

The programs a **Veteran** can qualify for vary and most will take a little research. But in many cases, the effort can pay off thousands of dollars.

Using my friend's father as an example, while living in a rundown house, he never knew to claim the benefits that were *rightfully* his.

To make matters worse, his son (my friend) was going to borrow $80,000 *against* the house in order to remodel it for easier senior living. So now a house that is mortgage free may take on a home equity loan that has to be repaid with the fixed-income of his father.

Thankfully, he learned "how to" discover different **Veteran Benefit Programs** his father was *missing out* on. Because of this, the house is now remodeled and **remains mortgage free** to make it easier for a senior in his 90's to enjoy.

Plus, this is above and beyond the original benefit money he is receiving each month.

This is just one example of what is available for veterans when **they know how to look for benefit programs** their tax dollars paid for.

Don't look for the government to start advertising all of these benefits. In fact, the **more** that is unclaimed, the *less* the government pays out. Why?

**Because the Government has no incentive to aggressively advertise these programs...**

We owe a huge debt to the soldiers who have served our country in the military. And they all deserve to know every single resource available to help them and how to both apply and receive what they are owed. *After all, they put their life on the line...*

I wish the government would spend as much on advertising this website as the lawyers do who get a piece of the action for helping vets collect.

So if you are a veteran or have a loved one or friend who is, start with the resources below.

https://www.ebenefits.va.gov/ebenefits-portal/ebenefits.portal

And while there, applications can be made for;

- **Education benefits**
- **Disability benefits**
- **VA Home loans**
- **Burial benefits**
- **Vocational rehabilitation benefits**
- **Employment benefits**
- **Life insurance and healthcare benefits**

You may also call and get answers to your questions:

- **eBenefits Questions: 1-800-983-0937**
- **Veterans Affairs: 1-800-827-1000**
- **NRD and DoD Services: 1-800-342-9647**

The site below has several FREE eBrochures to help guide you; however the site is run by a **Veterans Administration Accredited Claims Agent.**

You need to understand the terms (a.k.a. cost) before you hire any claims agent or Attorney to help you receive benefits that are rightfully yours. As in life... *read the fine print.*

**http://AmericanVeteransAid.com**

**1-877-427-8065**

An article-rich site covering everything is called **Veterans Today** and it will help you search for more information on just about every topic. Plus the site is regularly updated so you can stay current on new or *modified* programs you may be eligible for.

**http://VeteransToday.com**

There is also a special site for **disabled veterans** and at the time of this writing it has helped over 330,000 Veterans get the benefits they deserve.

**http://www.dav.org**

**1-877-426-2838**

Take your time in investigating all of the information presented in this report. If you or anyone you know is a Veteran, you will more than likely find *numerous* benefits you can claim today.

## The secret to find out if you qualify for free government grants or loans (R064)

One woman I know with an autistic child was able to complete a $30,000 kitchen remodel in her country home with the help of a government grant. How? She knew where to look, and was willing to put forth the effort necessary to get through the requirements.

Here are the four main places to look for government grants, loans, and other benefits:

**1. USA.GOV**

More precisely, http://www.usa.gov/Citizen/Topics/Benefits.shtml. This link may change, so you can always start from USA.GOV to find it if you need to.

The USA.GOV website is the hub for all things government, and it will direct you to the proper place to go for various types of assistance and government programs.

Here you'll also find links to a variety of other sites. See below for details.

**2. GOVLOANS.GOV**

The website at http://www.govloans.gov is all about federal government loans. It provides information and links for government loans on anything from business to education to loans especially for veterans.

**3. BENEFITS.GOV**

The website at http://www.benefits.gov has an excellent tool to search for and find government benefits that you might qualify for.

**4. GRANTS.GOV**

To get the real truth about federal government grants, the number one best place to go is http://www.grants.gov. You can search for and apply for grants through the site.

### A Few More Sites Worth Mentioning…

From the above websites, you may be taken to any number of additional government sites. Some examples of other great government sites with opportunities for a wide variety of benefits, grants, and loans are:

- www.rurdev.usda.gov/HSF_SFH.html — For rural housing grants and loans.
- www.ebenefits.va.gov — for veteran benefits.
- www.disability.gov — for people with disabilities.
- www.usa.gov/Topics/Seniors.shtml — help of all kinds for seniors.
- business.usa.gov and www.sba.gov — for businesses.
- www.disasterassistance.gov — for disaster victims.
- www.hud.gov — housing related assistance and related programs.
- www.eere.energy.gov/weatherization — weatherization/energy assistance.
- www.fns.usda.gov — food stamps and nutritional assistance.
- www.insurekidsnow.gov — health insurance for kids.

## The secret website Americans have quietly claimed over $37.4 billion through (R006)

Many don't know there is a website where over **9 million** Americans have received over **$37.4 billion** worth of benefits.. In fact, less than 2% of the population even knows about this website.

Now the website isn't hidden, it's just not aggressively advertised. The Gov is good at creating laws and programs but they are not aggressively advertised. After all, there is really no incentive to advertise a website promoting programs your tax dollars paid for. However...

You personally may be able to **access some of the billions in benefits** being given away.

And you are even more likely to qualify if you are a senior or disabled.

Because you're reading this manual, you are one who will be "in the know" about an organization called the *National Council on Aging, (NCOA)*. It has a website which can help you find out if you qualify for assistance with any of the following expenses:

1. Medications
2. **Food**
3. Utilities
4. **Legal**
5. Healthcare
6. **Housing**
7. In-home services
8. **Taxes**
9. Transportation
10. **Employment training**

As mentioned earlier, over $37.4 billion in assistance has been given to over 9 million Americans. That's an **average benefit of over $4155 per person**. And the number is growing!

What have you got to lose to see if you qualify?

After all, your tax dollars helped create these programs! So if you have an Internet connection, visit the website below right now. And if you don't have Internet at home, visit your local library or a friend.

**http://www.BenefitsCheckup.org**

**1-800-794-6559**

And while you are on the Internet, take the time to visit the main website for the national

Council on aging... Their website has a number of tools which can help you in a variety of ways. The website is below:

**http://NCOA.org**

**202-479-1200**

## UNCLAIMED MONEY: $58 Billion is waiting for its rightful owners (R010)

You've probably seen the ads over the years talking about things like "free money" and "unclaimed property". There have been numerous schemes in the last couple of decades designed to take advantage of people who may have unclaimed money.

**The fact is** – many people are due money from forgotten bank accounts, all types of refunds, inheritances, etc. And this report is to help you steer clear of the scammers trying to take advantage of the uninformed.

**1. Unclaimed Property And HUD Refunds**

Unclaimed property is property that is or was rightfully owned by a person or company that never made it to its rightful owner.

Examples might be life insurance payouts (to survivors/heirs), savings bonds, and other property of possible considerable monetary value. When the rightful owner of the property isn't easily found (due to things like address changes, marriage, and re-marriage), **the property goes into the state's "unclaimed property" pool where it is held for the rightful owner.**

For years there have been individuals who run ads in newspapers selling what amounted to lists of unclaimed property information and/or lists of consumers with HUD refunds due, and suggesting that people could start their own business helping people whose names appeared on these lists to be "reunited" with the money that was rightfully theirs.

This would be done for a commission, which the "tracer" or "HUD tracer" (*i.e. the person who fell for the business opportunity*) would ask for out of the refund due.

Due to a large number of complaints and considerable abuse, authorities cracked down on those selling and sharing of information related to unclaimed property, and on the practice of seeking out owners of unclaimed property for profit.

In many states it is not legal to charge a fee for helping someone else find their unclaimed property. In the cases of both HUD refunds and unclaimed property, anyone can find out if they are due on their own… and it is becoming increasingly difficult for a "tracer" or anyone attempting to earn a profit by this process to keep within the boundaries of federal and state law.

If you think you may have unclaimed property, a good place to start is **www.unclaimed.org.**

If you think you may have a HUD refund coming your way (or if you aren't sure but want to find out), go here: **www.hud.gov/offices/hsg/comp/refunds/fhafact.cfm**

**According to the *Wall Street Journal*, as much as one billion dollars in unpaid life insurance benefits may be sitting on the books of life insurance companies.** While the insurance companies might not want to let go of it, if state regulators have their way, the money will eventually end up in unclaimed property pools.

According to the *National Association of Unclaimed Property Administrators* (NAUPA), in 2006 over **$1.7 billion** (that's $1,700,000,000) in unclaimed property was returned to the rightful owners. Their website also states that there is currently over **$32 billion** ($32,000,000,000) in unclaimed property in the U.S.

The **$32,000,000,000** is spread over **117 million** different accounts.

*Could you be one of the over 117 million people with unclaimed property?*

To find out go to **www.unclaimed.org**

And even if you've checked in the past, it might pay off to check again. According to *CNN Money* from January 2013:

*"Florida's chief financial officer announced this month that the state had received **61,271 new unclaimed property accounts worth more than $25 million** as part of a settlement with insurance company AIG (AIG). The settlement is one of several reached last year with major insurers, including MetLife (MET), Prudential (PRU) and Nationwide after regulators in 20 states audited the methods they used to locate life insurance beneficiaries after a policyholder's death."*

Here are some more places you can check for possible unclaimed money:

**2. Life Insurance Policies**

- http://www.mib.com/lost_life_insurance.html

(Note: some life insurance companies also offer searches on their websites so you can find out if there is life insurance money that might be waiting for you.)

**3. FHA**

- https://entp.hud.gov/dsrs/refunds/

**4. Treasury Bonds**

- http://www.treasuryhunt.gov

**5. IRS Unclaimed Refunds**

- http://www.irs.gov/Refunds

**6. The Pension Benefit Guaranty Corporation**

- http://www.pbgc.gov/wr/trusteed/plans.html

**7. The Employee Benefits Security Administration**

- http://www.dol.gov/ebsa/

**8. Unclaimed Retirement Benefits**

- https://www.unclaimedretirementbenefits.com

**9. SEC Enforced Claims**

- http://www.sec.gov/divisions/enforce/claims.htm

**10. FDIC**

- http://www2.fdic.gov/funds/index.asp

**11. Credit Unions (Unclaimed Deposits)**

- http://www.ncua.gov/Resources/AM/Pages/UnclaimedDeposits.aspx

**12. Unpaid Foreign Claims**

- http://www.fiscal.treasury.gov/fsservices/gov/pmt/unpdforclaims/unpdforclaims_home.htm

And don't forget… **Your current state and other states you have lived.** If you moved, be sure to check the previous states you lived, which can all be done at…

- http://www.unclaimed.org

### Free Money And Gov't Grants

Although it sounds good, "apply and get free money from the Government" the **truth** is, it doesn't happen often.

If you are an individual, then you can be 99.9% certain that they are **NOT** for you.

**Government grants are most often awarded to places like universities, researchers, and non-profits.** They are usually awarded for particular types of research or particular projects, and the process of getting the grant money isn't exactly a matter of writing a letter and asking Uncle Sam for a kick-back.

**<u>Grant-writing is an art form in itself,</u>** which is why many successful non-profits have staff they pay full time to "write" grants, which simply means they complete the application process for the non-profit to be *eligible* to receive money.

There are certain circumstances in which an individual *might* qualify for a Government grant, but those are few and far between. To learn more about government grants, go to:

https://www.usa.gov/benefits-grants-loans

**Give Yourself The Gift Of...**

Alright, so let's say that you've searched the unclaimed property databases and found nothing. You don't qualify for government grants. *Where's your lucky break?*

One thing I always say is, *"Windfalls are great, but you can't build your financial future on them."*

But there is one source of so-called "free money" that a lot of people have immediate access to and do absolutely nothing with it. Want to know what it is?

**Unused gift card balances!**

According to ABC News there have been **$41 billion (that's $41,000,000,000) in unused gift cards since 2005**. That's over $100 worth of unused gift card funds for every single U.S. citizen!

I once knew a coffee shop owner who started selling gift cards in his store. When I commented on them, he told me about the company selling the gift cards had specifically said "**one of the benefits is 20% are NEVER redeemed!"** This meant that if he sold $1,000 in gift cards, $200 worth of those gift cards would just be "money in the bank" for the coffee shop... all because some people lost, forgot or just plain did not use their gift card.

So if you do nothing else today, take advantage of the one source of free money that you probably already have sitting right under your nose (or in your wallet, or your purse)... unused gift cards.

**Conclusion**

Some people have discovered thousands of dollars they didn't know they had by searching unclaimed property.

Obviously, not everyone is going to have funds due to them but (based on the numbers we've already talked about) many people do have something waiting for them in their state's unclaimed property pool.

It might be $50 or $5,000... and in either case it's probably worth looking into and going through the process of seeing if any of the money is rightfully yours.

As for "free money" in the form of government grants, as I've already said, most grants just *don't* apply to individuals. A lot of the ads you've seen are a bit misleading. With that said, I should tell you a quick story about a woman I knew who had a child with developmental disabilities.

The woman heard one of those ads and decided to look into grants and "free money" for herself. She found a special grant designed for people with disabilities. After going through the application process she was able to get a large sum of money to help with certain aspects of caring for her son. Keep in mind this woman was the exception, not the rule. Sometimes people need a lucky break, and every great once in a while they actually get it. Maybe next time it will be you...

For the rest of us, the last bit of advice I have is simple:

Make Your Own Windfalls.

*"How?"*

By making better use of the money you have.

**Did You Know That Investing Just $300 Per Month At 12% Interest Will Amount To Over $24,331.00 In Only Five Years?**

You could spend the next five years chasing after windfalls that never materialize, or put some basic learning and knowledge into practice… and with minimal effort make a $24,331 "windfall" for yourself.

# How to receive free financial aid to learn or improve your computer skills (R317)

No doubt about it, computer skills put you in demand as an employee and give you a big advantage for running your own business.

If you have trouble hooking up your printer, don't feel like you are too late to the party because there are a number of programs designed to 'school' you...

...and best of all, the **government will pay for you to learn**.

Below are programs you may have never heard of, but should investigate to see if you qualify for **educational grants or assistance**.

**"Rapid Response Services" For Laid Off Workers**

This government program helps employees in transition.

If your company has layoffs, relocates or closes all together, you may qualify for assistance designed to get you back on your feet and into the workplace as fast as possible.

Typically, the programs take place on your company's site and company time so you can start getting services and new training before you lose your job.

**The "Workforce Investment Act"**

This federal employment training program is designed to increase your employability, earnings and skills.

**Trade Adjustment Assistance**

If international trading pressures have caused you to lose your job, take a pay cut or forced your company to relocate or close, then you may be entitled to **benefits and services** allowed under the Trade Adjustment Assistance program.

Some of the main benefits you may receive include but are not limited to;

- career counseling
- training programs
- income support
- reimbursement for job search expenses
- reimbursement for relocation expenses

Plus older workers may qualify for up to **2 years compensation** to cover the difference between their old job and new, lower paying position

**Senior "Community Service Employment" Program**

This special program helps pay for you to obtain part-time employment and training in community service.

The idea of the program is, if they help pay for your training, it will allow you to develop the skills to find a full time job.

There are many other education and training programs you may be able to get involved with.

All of the programs mentioned above (and more) can be found at this website:

https://www.careeronestop.org/LocalHelp/service-locator.aspx

Then follow these links:

Home > Service Locator > Training

And remember; visit the site often because you will know as soon as new programs become available, plus enhancements to existing programs.

---

## Special Government program will give you money to make your home more energy efficient (R189)

Energy efficiency, you hear the words almost daily.

Your utility company wants to help you save by plugging gaps where you're cooling and heating escape.

Your state wants to **subsidize** certain energy efficient steps you can take to not only save on energy, but on taxes or get a rebate (even a cash grant.)

And then there are the federal programs and that is where we will start.

**Federal Tax Credits For Energy Efficiency**

Up until 2016 (and maybe beyond) you can get a tax credit of 30% off the cost of alternative energy equipment.

You can spend as much as you can afford for a solar hot water heater, solar electric panels and system, even a wind turbine - and get a **30% tax credit** off the full cost.

And if you are fortunate enough to have a second home or income producing property, the credits apply there too, as long as the property is in the U.S.

**State Tax Credits for Energy Efficiency**

Your state may also add to the incentive from the Federal government and the easiest way to find out is to check the **Database of State Incentives** for Renewable & Efficiency at their website: http://www.dsireusa.org

**Beware of the Green Scheme**

Of course, anytime the government introduces a program requiring certain conditions to be met for a rebate or tax credit, the scammers start running ads nonstop.

Below are some tips on how to avoid these fraudsters.

Don't buy more than you need. Whatever a contractor says you need, double check the claim. Over insulating your attic is often a money burner.

They mislead you with **technical mumbo jumbo** like 'R' value. R-value is simply how effective the insulation they are recommending will resist heat flow.

**Where they trick you** is by claiming their product has a high R-value, yet do not install it thick enough to achieve the stated value.

They dangle high-tech solutions, while **your best energy savings come from simple stuff**. Are your air-condition ducts sealed? Windows caulked? Weather stripping installed? Attic ventilated?

Whatever any contractor or salesman claims, **ask to see the research** proving it, because it's against the law to say a product will cut your energy consumption when in fact it won't.

**They push the biggest option.** Certainly old homes with lots of leaks need more powerful cooling and heating systems. But new homes built energy efficiently don't need these powerful systems, yet they will still try and get you to buy one.

**Figure the payback.** Unless you can pay for the new system, insulation or equipment with less than 5 years of energy savings, you probably aren't saving much if anything.

Finally, as with everything run by the government, it changes constantly and you often don't hear about programs that will help you until they have expired.

Check out http://energy.gov savings **at least once a year** to see the current tax credits and rebates available.

“

In one minute you can change your attitude. And in that minute you can change your *entire* day.

Spencer Johnson

# BANKING AND INVESTING

- ☑ **The dirty secret you should know about your retirement savings**
- ☑ **Ex bank teller reveals 4 reasons why you should never use a debit card**
- ☑ **CPA reveals how to get the government to donate up to $1,000.00 to your retirement plan**
- ☑ **TAX ATTORNEY REVEALS: How to save money and watch it multiply TAX-FREE with this special instrument everyone should be using**
- ☑ **A rare kind of CD which pays up to twice your local banks rate with no risk**
- ☑ ***And More***

There are over
100 languages in the world…
...but a smile
speaks *all* of them.

## The dirty secret you should know about retirement saving (R337)

We've all been told to pack money away into tax deferred and tax advantaged accounts for retirement. Often, though, we don't think about the impact that these deferrals will have down the road.

"Remember, we all make mistakes. We're only human. It's not our fault that they just happen to all be in our favour."

When you reach the age of 70.5, you are required under current tax law to start making "Required Minimum Withdrawals", or RMDs for short. An RMD is a minimum amount of money that you must withdraw from your tax deferred retirement account. And of course, you have to pay taxes on the money withdrawn!

Here are the problems that a lot of people don't see coming:

- RMDs sometimes result in a person going into a <u>HIGHER TAX BRACKET</u>. This means you not only pay taxes on the withdrawn funds, you also pay **more taxes** on your *other* income.
- RMDs can become **confusing** when you have several IRAs and 401Ks. The more accounts you have, the more confusing it will become because each "required minimum withdrawal" is calculated individually for each account. You can total them up and take them all out of one account if you want, but the requirements are calculated and specified per account. (Some experts recommend consolidating retirement accounts as much as possible before you are RMDs come into play.)
- RMDs can make you pay more taxes on your Social Security Income.
- RMDs can also affect other benefits, such as Medicare. (In practice, you could end up paying more money for *numerous* things because of the RMDs.)
- RMDs often hurt more when you are older. This is why some experts recommend taking some money out of accounts that would require RMDs earlier in life—starting at age 59—so that you will have less "RMD" headaches later.

*So what can you do about it?*

The best advice is to talk to your accountant and come **up with a plan *before* you need it**. This is one case where waiting until the last minute is most certainly <u>NOT</u> a good idea.

**Some general strategies include:**

- Donating money from RMDs to charitable organizations to make the RMD tax-free. (This is a loophole that congress will likely close. Please check with your accountant and current tax laws.)
- Maximizing withdrawals early in retirement to avoid the impact of RMDs as much as possible later in retirement. You could, for example, withdraw as much money as is possible without going into another tax bracket.
- Utilize tax-deferred accounts before ROTH IRAs (where the money was taxed going into the account.)

Whatever you do, don't avoid RMDs altogether. The *substantial penalties* for not taking them will most likely be worse than the tax implications of the required minimum withdrawals themselves.

## Ex bank teller reveals 4 reasons why you should never use a debit card (R007)

A lot of people don't realize that using a debit card can cost you hundreds or even thousands of dollars if you aren't careful. In one 2007 study it was reported that U.S. financial institutions lost an estimated $662,000,000 to debit card fraud.[1] *And you can lose money, too.*

Joseph Rizks didn't think using a debit card was a big deal. He made the mistake of paying with a debit card on a trip to Taco Bell. He overdrew his account by a few dollars, and the inevitable snowball effect resulted in over $350 in overdrafts and related fees.

The problem with debit cards is the transactions can happen and stack up very *quickly*. So a simple miscalculation can lead to hundreds of dollars in overdraft fees in a very short time.

Which brings us to…

**Debit card Secret #1:** Overdrafts can happen more easily, and can pile up faster than if you paid by check.

It is estimated overdraft charges have cost consumers as much as $17.5 *billion* in past years.

The "overdraft protection" problem got so out of hand that a couple of years back, congress enacted laws requiring financial institutions to make overdraft protection *optional* on debit card transactions. If you have a debit card you would be well advised to **turn overdraft protection off**.

By doing this, your transactions will simply decline, which will let you know about the problem immediately rather than racking up significant overdraft charges.

Then there's the problem of unexpected consequences of pre-authorizations. For example, if you check into a hotel they may put a "hold" on your debit card, essentially preventing you from accessing the money until the hold is lifted, sometimes weeks later.

**Debit card Secret #2:** Your money can be tied up and there may be nothing at all that you can do!

One man—R.C. Welborn—learned this the hard way. He had $80 in his checking account, and made a few small purchases (including gas) which totaled about $65. A few days later he checked his account to find that he had incurred $120 in overdraft charges. *How had his account with $80 in it gotten overdrawn with only $65 in transactions?*

Many consumers—like Mr. Welborn—have been caught by surprise by what are called "pre-authorizations", and the effects they have on account balances. A pre-authorization is a way that a merchant can make sure there is enough money in an account to cover a purchase. They are common at places like restaurants, hotels, gas stations, and car rental agencies. Many online merchants also use pre-authorizations.

The effects of a pre-authorization may not always be obvious or advertised… and it is difficult to know when and how much a pre-authorization might be placed for.

A small purchase of gas could be pre-authorized for $100 even though the actual gas purchase was, say, only $30. A hotel may pre-authorize your debit card for $500 on check-in… without mentioning it to you.

In these cases, your balances are tied up. You can't access pre-authorized money. And what is worse, if you aren't expecting it, it can lead to overdrafts and further headaches.

But the story with pre-authorizations gets worse…

**Debit card Secret #3:** A declined pre-authorization still ties up your money.

This is one that "snags" many consumers and by the time they realize what is going on, the damage is already done.

Most online merchants use a variety of verification and security measures to avoid credit card fraud. Some of those measures—such as AVS—or "address verification"—may lead to a legitimate credit card or debit card being declined when a consumer makes a mistake such as mistyping a zip code, or inputting an old address out of habit.

Here's an all-too-common scenario:

Rose wanted to make a $400 online purchase. She had $600 in her checking account. She used her debit card, but the transaction was declined. Rose realized she accidentally mistyped the zip code. She corrected the mistake, and ran the card through again. The purchase went through.

What Rose didn't realize at this time, however, is that she had just overdrawn her checking account by $200. She ended up with over $150 in additional overdraft fees before all of the dust settled.

*But why?*

Because, the first pre-authorization on Rose's card *still held the funds* even though the transaction was declined. In other words, instead of making a single $400 purchase, the effect on Roses checking account balance was, temporarily, as if she had made TWO $400 purchases!

You might be wondering: *"How can merchants do that?"*

The problem with debit cards is the transactions can happen and stack up very quickly. So a simple miscalculation can lead to hundreds of dollars in overdraft fees in a very short time.

Which brings us to…

**Debit card Secret #4:** The banks designed this system. It is not the merchants' faults.

A while back we did an interview with a particular bank teller who shared some enlightening information—the very information forming the basis of this report.

Among other things, he told us **there was a company that pitched the overdraft system to their bank, demonstrating how it could be a huge source of revenue**… all by simply offering "overdraft protection" and related services.

In fact these overdrafts were a big source of revenue. And the **banks abused it**. Transactions were ordered in such a way (highest amount drafted first) as to maximize the profit from overdrafts—profit that came directly out of your hard-earned money. The banking system was swimming in cash from overdrafts, which amounted to countless "mini loans" with astronomical interest rates.

Eventually, Congress caught on, and the laws changed a little. Banks now must give you better options with regards to handling overdrafts on your debit card. Banks obviously want you to use their so-called "overdraft protection"—*because it is insanely profitable for them.* But **overdraft protection is usually NOT so good for you**.

Now you have the option to simply let overdrawn purchases decline. Does that fix the problems? It helps, but it does not fix the issues. And it leaves many problems (that we haven't even mentioned here) untouched.

For example, having the option to opt-out of overdraft protection doesn't change the fact you have much better protection against fraudulent transactions when using a credit card.

Find the terms and conditions of your favorite cards, and read the fine print. You will soon see you're much safer using a credit card for online and other purchases than your debit card.

And even with no overdrafts, the pre-authorizations can still cause big problems for your finances. Any automatically debited amounts—which include health insurance and mortgages for some people—will be *declined*. Those merchants may charge you fees for the declined transactions.

Meanwhile, the bank will point the finger at the merchant over the pre-authorizations, when in reality—it is the **bank's policy that determines how long those pre-authorizations stay on your account**. You'll feel as though you are getting the runaround. The merchant will be powerless to act. And the bank will pretend to be.

If it's too late and you find yourself and your money stuck, do this: insist—or even demand—your bank issue a temporary credit to cover the authorization. This isn't something you can do all the time… but as a one-time fix in a crisis, if your bank's customer service is up to par, this will usually get you through what could otherwise be a very problematic cash flow issue.

You may be wondering if there's a solution to the "debit card" problem. Here it is:

Use a credit card instead of a debit card. The rules are Visa/MasterCard rules not EFT rules, and you're using the bank's money instead of your own. (Guess which one is easier to get back in a fraud case?)

(1)Source: PULSE EFT Association

# CPA reveals how to get $1,000.00 "donated" to your retirement plan (R029)

Have you heard of the Retirement Saver's Credit?

It's yet another beneficial program that most people know nothing about.

**Here's How It Works**

An individual's earnings at the time of this writing can't exceed $30,000, $45,000 for head of household and $60,000 for married couples.

If you meet the criteria above and contribute to an IRA or 401K, you are eligible for a tax refund as much as $1,000 for individuals and $2,000 for couples.

And those income thresholds typically increase yearly as the government adjusts for inflation.

**How to Calculate Your Credit**

Here's how to calculate your credit or as we like to call it, a 401k or IRA match, because the lower your income, the higher your credit.

**Individuals** can receive:

- 50% credit for $18K or less income
- 20% credit for $18,001 to $19,500
- 10% credit for $19,501 to $30,000

**Couples** combined income must fall within the following ranges to receive the credit.

- 50% credit for $36K or less income
- 20% credit for $36,001 to $39,000
- 10% credit for $39,001 to $60,000

And any **head of household** earning below $45,000 in 2014 can obtain the sliding scale income based credits.

Remember, your contribution to your 401K or IRA gives you an automatic break in determining taxable income...

...then on top of that, if your taxable income falls within the guidelines, you essentially get a percent back as a **FREE savings match** by the government.

Also keep in mind, if other credits and deductions completely eliminate your tax liability, you cannot receive the credit as it is nonrefundable.

For the estimated 7 million taking advantage of this credit, it usually equals to a few hundred dollars per year.

(However, if your income will remain within the threshold for a number of years, a couple hundred extra each year, applied to savings will add up fast.)

## TAX ATTORNEY REVEALS: How to save money and watch it multiply TAX-FREE (R032)

A Roth IRA is a special type of IRA with which you avoid taxes on money taken out of the IRA. It differs from a traditional IRA in that you are taxed on the money as it goes in. While a lot of people think "tax deferred" is always better, this traditional wisdom may not be so smart for some. Ask yourself this question:

- Are tax rates likely to go up or to go down between now and the time you retire?

Chances are, they will go up. Unless you are taxed at an especially high rate now and expect to save a lot of money by being taxed at a lower rate in your retirement (due to lower income), a Roth IRA may be a smart move.

So what's the difference exactly between a Roth IRA and a traditional IRA? The main difference is a Roth IRA is tax-free when you take the money OUT of it. A traditional IRA is tax free when you put the money INTO it.

The **growth on funds in a Roth IRA is therefore tax free**. Let's say your money doubles in your Roth IRA between now and the time you retire. How much tax will you have to pay on those earnings? Zero. $0.00. (Unless, of course, tax laws change.)

Some experts recommend using a combination of tools to balance out your tax strategy and account for the fact that you don't know what your income, tax laws, or other variables will do over the next 20, 30, or 40 years. But a Roth IRA deserves a good look because of its simplicity and the advantage of tax-free growth.

**Tax Free Growth Example**

| | |
|---|---|
| Interest Rate | 3% |
| Annual Contribution | $1,000.00 |
| Years | 20 |
| Balance after 20 Years | $27,397.92 |
| Total Tax-Free Growth | $7,397.92 |

(Note, another type of IRA worth mentioning if you have a small business or are self-employed is a SEP IRA. See http://www.irs.gov for details.)

## A rare kind of CD which pays up to twice your local banks rate (R075)

Seniors and careful savers have every right to tread lightly in the stock and bond market.

But with interest rates on savings accounts being horribly low and Certificates of Deposits not much better, where can you invest at a good rate and be sure you'll get your principal back plus interest?

Even more important, is your investment insured?

Well there's something called a **'brokered CD,'** which is a certificate of deposit banks give to brokerage firms at a discount.

If you have an account at one of the brokerage firms, such as Charles Schwab and others, you can buy a CD from them and **get almost double the interest you can from a bank**!

Best of all, your deposit becomes an obligation of the bank issuing the CD, not the brokerage firm selling it - so **you are covered by FDIC insurance up to $250,000**.

There are other advantages too…

The CD can be traded on the secondary — market through your brokerage account.

And you can spread your risk among a number of banks, so no one bank is issuing a CD of more than the max insurable amount, $250,000 - yet you can still control all of them from a single brokerage account.

If you are a senior and wish to leave one of these CDs to your heirs, they can **cash in immediately without fear of penalty** upon your passing.

So if you want a **safe investment** that gives you higher returns than your savings account or a bank CD, check with your stock broker about investing in a brokered CD.

## 4 dirty secrets you should know before investing in gold or silver (R356)

According to Charles Munger, Warren Buffet's long time right hand man, in a CNBC interview - "civilized people don't buy gold, they invest in productive businesses."

The disdain of the golden metal is also echoed by debt guru Dave Ramsey who said on his website, "It sucks. Gold is a horrible investment. It's speculating in precious metals, and you're going to lose your butt when you play with gold. The deal with gold is really simple. Gold has a 70-year track record of 4.2% returns. That's about the rate of inflation. It's awful."

While doomsday proponents claim you can use gold as currency after civilization fails, the facts are basic commodities such as food and water will have more value.

Gold, just like paper money, is only worth what people are willing to give for it.

Still you'll see advertisements from 'dealers' promising you coins and bullion you can buy for 'investment' but what they don't tell you is that they drastically mark-up their inventory to pay for their marketing. Often you can get a better deal at a pawn shop.

And bullion dealers actually count on the uninformed to keep them in business.

Did you know the dealer you click to buy from online may have 'shorted' bullion to protect them in case of a price collapse? Not the kind of activity you'd like to see for an investment advertised as 'safe.'

Many people worry about the government buying precious metals because they have been led to believe the transaction is 'private'. And it is… *when they buy it*. But when they **sell** it the dealer reports it to the Feds.

The Gold Confiscation Act of 1933 has many dealers advertising 'rare and collectible' coins as protection from any new government confiscation laws, but unless you own a coin dated before 1933 it isn't considered 'rare.'

As the world economy wobbles back and forth (as has always been the case) precious metal dealers will pop up offering 'protection' when your safest bet may be to avoid bullion and coins altogether. Unless you are an expert in rare coins where you can project appreciation (just like stamps or any other collectible), it's best to invest in something *other than gold*.

If Warren Buffet doesn't think gold is a good investment, what chance do you think you have?

## How a banker teaches his kids to "automatically" save money with zero effort (R130)

One of the first things you want to teach your children is the old adage, "a penny saved is a penny earned."

Many people go through life not saving and they pay more for everything as a result of having to borrow money, much less being able to invest so they can receive the passive income necessary to creating wealth.

Even though you preach to your children about 'saving money', being children it's easier said than done.

So what do you do?

**Create "automatic" deductions.**

If your children receive an allowance, automatically deduct 10% and put it in a savings account.

If your children are enterprising and mow yards, deliver papers, wash cars - anything to generate income, help them automatically set aside 10% into a "don't touch" account.

Teenagers who receive a paycheck from part time work or a summer job are easier to manage, because you can insist that 3% of their pay be automatically deducted by their employer and placed into a savings account.

When the money is automatically deducted, the temptation to spend it goes away.

And when the **account accumulates and compounds with interest**, your children will be imprinted with a valuable lesson that will put them on firm footing the rest of their life for building real wealth.

## Five secrets to finding the highest interest rates (R094)

*Where can you find Certificate of Deposit rates over twice the national average?*

Before you walk into your local bank and plunk down a large sum for a Certificate of Deposit, take some time to look at all the alternatives.

To find the best interest rates for CDs and savings accounts, follow these steps:

1. Shop around locally *first*. Many people use their "normal" bank for CD purchases, and miss out on better deals offered by other local banks and credit unions. Shop around in your local area, particularly with **smaller banks and credit unions**. This will give you a good comparison of the competitive rates available.

2. Shop **nationally**. Understand the national averages and how local banks compare. Don't be afraid to purchase CDs from FDIC insured banks in other states. Websites you can utilize in your search include:

- bankrate.com
- imoneynet.com
- http://exithub.com/banxcorp/

3. Consider **Brokered CDs**. A Brokered CD is simply a bank CD that is purchased and re-sold by a broker, who can help you spread money between many banks so you stay under the $250,000 FDIC insured ceiling. Brokered CDs traditionally provide higher returns, but you have to watch out for fees charged by the broker. Brokered CDs are especially powerful if you have a large sum of money to put away and you want to spread it out between many banks.

4. Consider **alternative savings and investment vehicles**. There are many options for investing you may not be aware of. Some can be less risky than the stock market. Others have a philanthropic element.

   **Local credit unions** are a good start. "Internet" banks such as Capital One 360 (Formerly ING Direct) and Emigrant Direct are other good examples.

   Another new and exciting option is known as **peer to peer lending or peer to peer investing**. Websites like Prosper.com and LendingClub.com enable investors to earn returns of up to 10% on peer to peer loans. Risk can be spread out by contributing small amounts to several loan requests, reducing the chances that you will experience a loss. If you have the time to put in the necessary due diligence and to educate yourself about peer to peer loans and the platforms that enable them, this could be a powerful and fruitful path to take.

5. **"Offshore"** banking is something many people have heard about, but may not fully understand. If you ask the average person about offshore banking, you may get answers ranging from mafia connections to IRS regulations, to "big business" and "rich people".

   Offshore banking is also **perfectly legal** as long as you fulfill the disclosure requirements of the U.S. Government. (You must report all income worldwide… even from offshore accounts, and you must complete required disclosure forms annually.) For some people the red tape associated with offshore banking is a deterrent. Still, offshore banks may offer products and rates not available locally that can be an attractive option for savvy savers

**The Effect of Double Returns over Time (Based on around $100/month being saved.)**

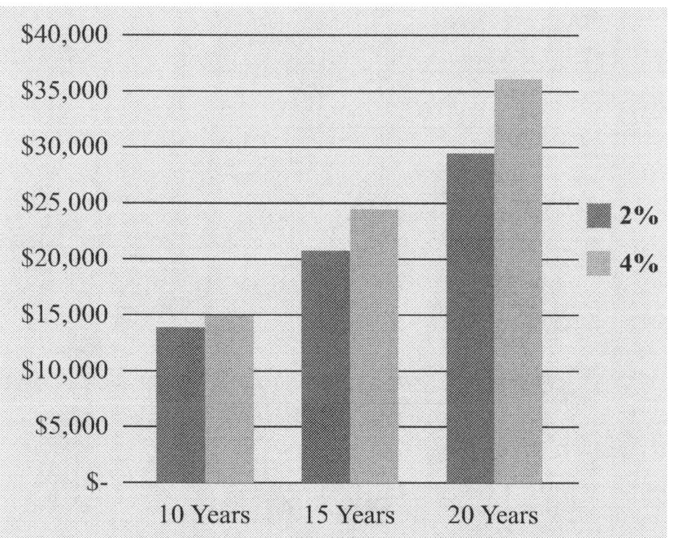


## What web based money management services don't want you to know (R087)

Here's the #1 "secret" web-based money management services don't want you to know:

Many of these companies are running what amounts to a hugely profitable and **legal *scam***.

Here's how it works:

1. You hand over your life's savings to the company to "manage" your money and investments.
2. The company—not an individual at the company—uses software to automate the investment of your funds.
3. You get duped, in most cases, because you feel like you've put your money into the hands of a competent money manager, when in fact you've put your money into the hands of a fully automated process with a customer service call center and perhaps email support.

It's often referred to as "web-based money management", and the **performance track record is less than stellar**. Compare the returns of these automated services to those of a truly skilled professional money manager, and you'll quickly see a gulf of difference between the two.

What makes it worse is that the so-called "reviews" posted online for these services are often **fake** and/or purchased, so even consumers who do a reasonable amount of "due diligence" may be duped into using one of these services.

You may wonder why these services even exist. Here's why: because they are *extremely profitable* for the companies that run them! This is because people all over the U.S. put their life's savings into these programs without knowing the real story behind them. Buyer beware!

**What can you do?**

If you don't have a lot of money to pack away, consider using traditional investment and/or savings vehicles. If you have a large sum of money that you want to have handled by a professional money manager, find a "real" professional money manager (i.e. a human being) with a proven track record.

## Two crazy secrets about Social Security (R340)

To begin with, we should be clear: Social Security is not a savings plan. The money you put in is not put into an account used to fund your retirement later. Instead the money put in today is used to fund today's retirees. In other words, if you're retired right now it is not your dollars providing your social security payments… it is those of your children and grandchildren.

And it is because of changing demographics (i.e. more 'boomers' retiring and less young people paying in) that many people believe the social security system must change or die.

**Crazy Secret #1: As a savings plan, Social Security is about as "bad as it gets"**

You will pay a lot of money into Social Security over your life, and you should understand it is one of the poorest savings plans you can use in terms of the benefits you will get from it.

For example, according to one estimate, a couple paying in just over $700,000 in their lifetime will get back about $950,000 in Social Security and Medicare benefits. Paying in that same amount of money to an interest earning account with an average APY of 2% would yield a savings with interest of over $1.2 million.

Your money will go much further if you invest long term for *yourself*. The benefits of saving and investing your own money will far outpace—dollar for dollar—any benefits you receive as a result of having paid into social security.

**Crazy Secret #2: If you subtract MEDICARE, Social Security pays out LESS than it takes in.**

According to *Time Magazine*: "People retiring today will be among the first generation of workers to pay more in Social Security taxes than they receive in benefits over the course of their lives."

So if we're sticking with the "savings plan" analogy, Social Security no longer even qualifies as a savings plan. It's a money pit and *bad investment* for Americans.

Add to this the fact that as of 2010 it is paying out more in checks than it takes in through taxes, and you have a system not only likely to fail, but virtually guaranteed to do so.

**What can you do about it?**

The best thing that you can do to protect yourself and your loved ones from the pending disaster(s) related to social security is to plan on funding your own retirement. Here's an example of what's possible if you save an average of $500 per month:

**Retirement Savings at the Rate of $6,000 per Year**

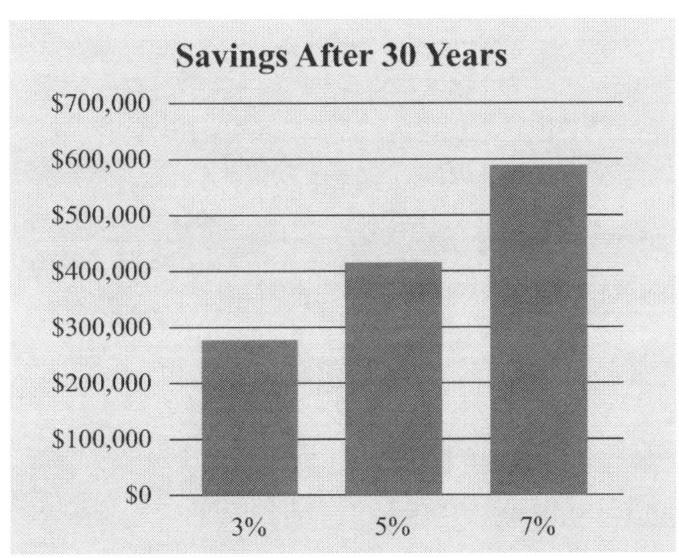

## History has proven this day is the single best day to sell your stocks (R097)

According to a study cited in the *Journal of Economics and Finance*, Volume 25, number 2, 2001, based on research of stocks from 1973 to 1997, the best stock returns are on Wednesday, while Monday was the lowest. The most volatile day is Friday. One could infer from this study that it's best to buy stocks on Monday and sell them on Wednesday.

On the other hand, in a book titled 'Stock Market Rules', the author claims the market tends to drop on Mondays and Fridays, based on the 37 year period from 1953 to 1989.

The data in these studies seem to mirror what investor Thomas Bulkowski, (author of 30 books about chart patterns and whose stock trading acumen allowed him to retire at 36) found by examining more recent data from 2000 to 2001. Bulkowski concludes, the best day to buy is Monday and **the best day to sell is Wednesday or Friday**.

So if there are historical "best days" to buy and sell, are there also good months?

According to a chart on the website Investopedia.com where the S&P 500 average monthly returns are shown from 1926 to 2004, the best month to buy is September while the best months to sell are December, July and January.

If you've been involved in stock trading or watch any of the financial news programs, you've probably heard of the 'January effect' brought on by investors doing year-end tax loss selling in December. The market then (typically) returns with both fists at the beginning of January.

As you've read, there are historical best days and months to buy and sell, however, you are not encouraged to get involved in what Warren Buffet calls "a fool's game" of trying to time the market.

It is best to keep the information handy for your own investing purposes and utilize it when appropriate, but remember the more you buy and sell, the more commissions you pay, thus giving you another hurdle to overcome in achieving a profitable return on investment.

## How to get the business start-up capital you need without a bank (R211)

Do you have an idea for a new product or business? Today more and more entrepreneurs and even some established professionals are turning to 'crowd funding', websites where micro investments from thousands, even hundreds of thousands of people can capitalize your new project or new business idea.

In the spring of 2014, '60s rock icon Neil Young funded a music player promising to design and build a prototype of what he bills will allow music fans to hear high definition music the way the musicians hear it when they record in the studio. His campaign on Kickstarter.com raised over $6 million to fund the project.

A product called the "coolest cooler" combined an ice chest, blender, bluetooth speaker and all the necessities for the coolest picnic or tail gate party. In 30 days they raised almost $2 million.

People who pledge to these projects typically get something in return, like in the case of the 'coolest cooler', those who pledged $165 received the cooler as a gift, saving almost 40% over if they waited to buy it retail.

According to *Forbes*, the top 10 crowd funding websites include:

- Kickstarter.com
- Indiegogo.com
- Crowdfunder.com

- RocketHub.com
- Crowdrise.com
- Somolend.com
- appbackr.com
- AngelList.com
- Quirky.com

Now, you may ask: why these sites all have seemed to arrive at the same time, while the Internet has been around for decades?

They are the outgrowth of the Jobs Act, which loosened the laws for entrepreneurs to raise money.

In addition to these sites, entrepreneurs are now directly contacting potential investors with prospectuses, where they were barred before the Jobs Act.

So if you have a business idea and want to raise money to set the wheels in motion, Forbes also offers in a January 2014 article, "Crowdfunding Secrets: 7 Tips For Kickstarter Success."

Number 1 (as simple as it may seem) is to "solve a real problem."

In the case of Neil Young's music player, it solves the problem of digital music sounding as if you are underwater. It's one of the reasons music purists have propelled resurgence in vinyl record sales in an overall declining music recording business, because vinyl sounds better than compact disks or the music you can download to your smartphone.

Second is preparing. If you go for funding you need to have a working prototype, manufacturing and distribution set up in advance. Potential investors want to see you have better than average chances of succeeding.

Third is having some skin in the game, either through your development process, product testing or using your own funds during the start-up phase.

Fourth is to set a realistic funding goal, because when potential backers see you are attracting lots of investors and are likely to reach your goal, the 'crowd effect' kicks in because everyone loves a winner.

Fifth, your presentation is everything. You need to clearly show you are solving a problem, have the team in place to make your business work and engage with potential backers so they like you and want to get involved.

In fact, the video presentation may be the most vital part of your crowd funding project. With this in mind, here are some tips for making a highly persuasive video.

As in all marketing, you've got to focus on the prospect - what do they want and can you translate those wants and needs into a compelling reason to make your project worth donating to?

You'll need to sell yourself. If they don't believe in YOU, they won't believe you can do what you say you will.

Don't talk 'corporate'; instead speak like you are talking to a friend, telling him or her about your great idea.

You must demonstrate your product or service so potential backers can visualize your idea coming to fruition.

And if you want to come off as really 'together', hire a production company to make your video look head and shoulders above all the ones filmed on a smart phone.

You want to project your 'story' as credible and tell it in such a way your potential backers can make an emotional connection.

Sixth, the feedback you get from backers can help you hone your product or service to better deliver on its promise. So it's not all about the money, it's about making your project a success by giving the market something it's demanding.

Seventh, when you launch you are conducting a campaign and it will take a lot of focus. You'll need a large email list and social media following to tap as soon as you go 'live' on any of the funding networks. Without an initial rush of funding, others will think your project has no merit and won't want to be on the 'bleeding edge.'

Still, the crowd funding arena is littered with lots of 'busts.' Entrepreneurs either set their funding goal too high, so they didn't meet it and all the money was returned to investors. Or the funding idea isn't 'viral' enough to get passed around the Internet.

Entrepreneurs who are lazy and don't prepare and follow through rarely raise a dime.

And remember, raising money shouldn't be the primary goal, it should be to get the all important feedback from the market by having them voting with their money as well as opinions, many of which you can incorporate into a better product or service.

Even though some projects have raised millions, the most popular funding level is about $20, so focus on delivering real value to that investor and piling it on for everyone who gives significantly more.

In the case of the 'coolest cooler' the inventor promised to come and personally bartend a party to any investor who gave at high levels.

Still, entrepreneurs who do everything right, the preparation, the well thought out product, the excellent story telling video and the pre-launch buzz... may find they come up short reaching the funding goal, meaning all the money raised will be returned to investors.

In this case, you want to have an 'angel' investor standing by. If your goal was to raise $10,000 by a certain deadline and as it approaches you are $500 short, have someone ready to step in to meet the shortfall.

Crowd funding is an excellent way for you to jump start your business or product idea, but like everything else in life, you'll get out what you put into it.

# Protecting Yourself

- ☑ **Computer genius explains the mistake people make with their computer passwords**
- ☑ **Divorce Attorney reveals the 6 things you must do the minute you think you might be getting a divorce**
- ☑ **Computer technician reveals the secret to avoiding 99% of computer viruses**
- ☑ **The first thing you MUST do in order to safeguard a winning lottery ticket**
- ☑ **Computer hacker explains how to eliminate 99.9% of all junk email**

“

Confidence comes
from one thing,
work and dedication.

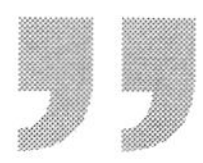

# Computer genius explains the mistake people make with their computer passwords (R073)

What is the biggest mistake people make with their passwords? **"Writing them down,"** says computer genius and software developer Ron Lampy. "Most passwords are stolen because someone has the password written down either on a piece of paper or in a file on their computer, even smartphone." This may account for the fact most identity theft is done by someone you know.

Another common mistake people make is using passwords easily guessed. Ron gave the example of "Lampy1" for a "bad password" that he should not use. Other common but poor passwords[1]:

(In order of rank.)

1. 123456
2. password
3. 12345678
4. qwerty
5. abc123
6. 123456789
7. 111111
8. 1234567
9. iloveyou
10. adobe123
11. 123123
12. admin
13. 1234567890
14. letmein
15. photoshop
16. 1234
17. monkey
18. shadow
19. sunshine
20. 12345
21. password1
22. princess
23. azerty
24. trustno1
25. 000000

So what can we do to protect our passwords? According to Ron and a number of other experts, it's best to have a **system for organizing and remembering** them in your head. Don't use actual words or common passwords like those above. Also don't use sequences of numbers or characters that are easily guessable (such as qwerty … which is the first 5 letters of the top row of the computer keyboard).

One example of a way to make your passwords more secure is called the **sentence system**.

Using this system, you think of a sentence or phrase that will be easy for you to remember but hard for others to guess. An example:

"When I was 7 years old I weighed 50 pounds."

Next, you combine the letters and numbers in

that phrase, using the first letter of each word.

WIw7yoIw50p

To take it a step further, you can replace particular letters or numbers with characters that are similar. For example, an S or a 5 might be replaced with a $. An e ("E") might be replaced with a "3". The letter I or L could become the number one ("1") or even a pipe character ("|"). Like this:

W|w7y0|w$0p

If you want to have different passwords for different websites, you can expand on this idea by including part of the domain name with your password, using the same replacement rules. Like this:

fac3b00kW|w7yo|w$0p

If you use a system such as this, you will <u>never have to write your passwords down, and they will be much more secure</u>.

(1) Source: CBS News

## Divorce Attorney reveals the 6 things you must do the minute you think you might be getting a divorce (R195)

1. Even though you'll need an attorney to

handle your divorce, you'll also probably need a counselor to guide you through this emotional time (especially if children are involved).

2. You need to quietly take inventory of <u>all</u> property, whether it's owned separately or you and your spouse own together.

3. Get together a list of accounts with cash and liquid assets, because your attorney can protect these during the divorce proceedings, otherwise they can be easily raided by an unhappy spouse.

4. You'll also need a detailed list of your debt and balances on charge accounts.

5. As soon as you file for divorce, cancel all joint credit cards and other charge accounts. Many credit card companies will issue new cards in a single person's name, providing your credit hasn't suffered leading up to the divorce.

6. List everything you want to ask your attorney so you can prevent your emotional state from continually calling the attorney (who bills by the hour).

Now, here are some **things you DON'T want to do**.

Don't try to **hide money or move money from accounts** without specific direction to do so from your attorney.

**Don't agree to ANYTHING** with your spouse without having your attorney review to ensure your rights are being protected.

Don't agree to any settlement until you have obtained **a release from joint liabilities**. The debt needs to be either settled or re-financed under separate names; otherwise your ex could clobber you in the future by sticking you with the full liability.

Divorces are rarely a cake walk. Take your time to deal with the essentials outlined in this report and get outside help to guide you to nonemotional review of the facts, and then proceed as your attorney advises.

## Computer technician reveals the secret to avoiding 99% of computer viruses (R320)

Computer viruses and hackers are as common as a mugger in a big city.

When you buy a new computer or download a free version of popular software like Adobe Acrobat, you will likely get a free trial period from a number of the better known anti-virus software manufacturers.

Then there are many free versions.

The free anti-virus software I use is **MicroSoft Essentials**. Once installed it updates automatically for the latest threats, scans your system at regular intervals and warns you if an incoming email has been compromised.

Still hackers are always one step ahead and lurking to infect your computer.

After installing anti-virus software, here are the **other precautions to take**.

Make sure you download all the **software updates** for the programs you use. That's easy enough these days because the software auto updates and many times these contain "patches" to thwart known hacker holes.

Only install software from people and companies you trust. If you are using the latest operating system you'll likely be asked "do you trust" before any software automatically installs. If you don't know them, click NO especially for any software that started installing automatically.

**Avoid file sharing software.** This is typically used for friends to exchange movies, songs and software. Anything that has been passed from computer to computer could easily be infected.

**Don't open emails from people you don't know.** We've all seen them, the "you've won" type emails or one that looks like a shipping company saying they tried to deliver a package. Just clicking to open can infect your computer. Hit the delete key instead.

**Don't click on ads** unless it is a company you know. Often ads will entice you to 'click and see if you've won' and that action will install a bug on your computer.

**Don't stick a thumb drive** into your computer unless you are absolutely sure it doesn't contain a virus. You might be at a coffee house reading your favorite blog and an acquaintance offers to share something with you by inserting the thumb drive in your computer. This can allow a virus to automatically launch and wreak havoc in your computer.

Steer clear of **questionable websites**. You may think you've cheated a musician out of song royalties by going to a site and stealing a copy of a song, but that download is typically loaded with viruses.

Check your **firewall settings** by going to your control panel and making sure they are turned on. And if your home or office has a **wireless router**, make sure the firewall settings are set there too.

Use a **complicated password** for all of your websites and computers. This will block many auto-hacking programs.

On top of everything mentioned here, you've also got to worry about your **smart phone** being vulnerable to attacks.

When using a public network, make sure to note if it is secured or not and keep your Bluetooth turned off unless you are actively using it.

Also, use Firefox or Chrome browsers instead of Internet Explorer, which has historically been a bigger target for viruses and hackers.

Finally, simply remember the old adage...

...if it's too good to be true, it probably is.

Free stuff isn't free if your identity has been stolen as a result.

## The first thing you MUST do in order to safeguard a winning lottery ticket (R070)

Before we talk about safeguarding a winning ticket, let's talk about the fact that you might not want to buy the ticket in the first place.

**If you are having any kind of financial problems whatsoever, the last thing you should be doing is playing the lottery.**

From a purely financial and social perspective, playing—and *winning*—the lottery is a bad idea for many people, especially those with financial problems.

Why? Because playing the lottery often creates more financial problems. Many people, especially those prone to financial trouble, are not equipped to handle millions of dollars. They are also usually surprised by the social fallout associated with winning the lottery. Just like the old song[1] says, "Once you get back on your feet again, everybody wants to be your long lost friend."

According to many past lotto winners, *scammers and con artists come out of the woodwork and stop at nothing to get at your cash.* Sounds like a great life, doesn't it?

Don't take my word for it. Here are some words of wisdom (and regret) from real past lottery winners[2]:

*"I was much happier when I was broke."*

*-William Post III, Winner of $16.2 million*

*"It's brought me nothing but unhappiness. It's ruined my life."*

*-Callie Rogers, Winner of £1.9 million (about $3 million U.S. dollars)*

*"I haven't got two pennies to rub together and that's the way I like it. I find it easier to live off £42 dole than a million."*

*-Michael Carroll, Winner of £9.7 million (about $15.5 million U.S. dollars)*

*"Winning the lottery is the worst thing that ever happened to me."*

*-Billie Bob Harrell, Jr., Winner of $31 million*

Here are the facts about playing the lottery:

- There is a certain mental wiring that changes as you learn how to build wealth and handle your money. This mental wiring is developed as you slowly improve your financial situation. Many people who win the lottery do not have that mental wiring. Their brains are simply not prepared for it, and instead of handling the money correctly their "rewards circuits" of their brain get hijacked by their lottery winnings, leading to stupid decisions and ruined lives.

- Even those who handle their money correctly are at risk. In the *Time.com* article providing the source for the quotes above, there are several stories of murder and betrayal that were far outside of the control of the person who won the money.
- Your chances of winning are almost nil. It makes no financial sense to play, and if you "need" to win then you probably shouldn't be playing it anyways.

**The fact is that you are much better off learning to handle your own finances and improve your own financial situation without the windfall of the lottery or even an inheritance. If you can gain financial intelligence on your own and use that to build wealth for yourself, you will be much happier and more successful in the long run.**

Now, with all the warnings made… let's talk about how you should safeguard the winning lottery ticket if you do decide to play, and you actually beat the overwhelming odds and win.

### Protecting Yourself If You Win the Lottery

The very first bit of advice is to tell absolutely nobody you have won the lottery. Some would say tell nobody but your immediate family. But that might include your parents, and your kids… and in that case telling your immediate family is a bad idea. Tell as few people as possible. Perhaps yourself, and ONE other person if you have a spouse that you believe can handle the information. (If we're being honest, not everyone can.)

You may find it easiest to pretend as if you haven't won the lottery. Do not think that your problems are over, at least… but instead brace yourself for a whole new set of problems.

Once you've got your mouth and your mental game under control, you need to **sign the back of the lottery ticket. Make photocopies (in private) of the front and back of the ticket**. Some experts also advise to type a "certificate of authenticity" that you then sign and have notarized, but this would require telling yet another person.

Make sure you understand the correct procedure for claiming your winnings, and follow it precisely.

Here are some other tips to help protect yourself:

- Do not start blowing money and showering people with gifts. This almost always backfires. Don't do it.
- Get an unlisted phone number. This will help to protect your privacy. You could even ditch the land line altogether and stick with a prepaid cell phone for the ultimate privacy.
- Get a security system for your home. This will help you sleep better at night, and further protect you.
- Take your time to **carefully** plan out how to deal with the money and the impact it will have on your life.
- Don't quit your day job. Or at least, make sure you keep employment somewhere. If you hate your job, sure… it's good to find another. But if you quit working altogether, you may end up depressed, bored, and suicidal (or simply dead) like some past lotto winners. It's important to **stay active and keep doing meaningful things** in your life. And as much as we might claim we "hate work", the fact is having a regular job or business where we work day in and day out is good for us.

(1) Nobody Knows You When you're Down and Out (1929), Jimmie Cox/Bessie Smith

(2) Source: *Time Magazine*

## Computer hacker explains how to eliminate 99% of all junk email (R158)

What can you learn from a junk-food-eating, video-game-playing, 16 year old computer hacker? The answer may shock you.

When a hacker attacks a website, they use a variety of techniques to try to "break in". It's often a challenge to keep them out because every website is attacked every 12 seconds.

One 16 year old hacker—we'll call him "Joe"—let us into his world, and showed how to prevent hacking AND even spam. As it turns out, it's a very simple concept called white listing.

"It's a matter of simple math," says Joe, It can be virtually impossible to keep a spam list or black list for a website. It makes more sense to keep track of the websites known to be good. We want to recognize the good guys, and keep out all the rest."

So how do you accomplish this?

Start a white list. This can be done in a variety of ways, but one simple method is to set up a filter that sends anyone who is in your address book to a "known" folder, and puts everything else in the bulk or spam folder. You'll still want to check the bulk/spam folder periodically, and it will require some work on your part to keep your filter updated if you opt in to email lists or frequently give out your email address.

If you want to eliminate spam, malicious emails and junk mail, this is **the method** to use.

# Work Related

- ☑ **The 4 dirty MLM / Network Marketing secrets you probably don't know**
- ☑ **64 year old Millionaire reveals unique way to find your dream job and get the employer to call you for it**
- ☑ **Executive recruiter reveals the secret to asking for a raise and getting it**
- ☑ **Three things you must do before even thinking about starting a business**
- ☑ **The two types of income you must have to create long term wealth**
- ☑ **$4,000.00 per month from home as an employment recruiter**
- ☑ **$2,000.00 per month visiting garage sales 2 days a week**
- ☑ ***And More!***

“

WORK: Doing your best is *easy* when you’re doing something you enjoy.

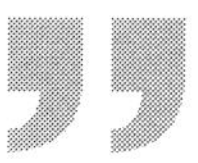

## The 4 dirty MLM / Network Marketing secrets you probably don't know (R350)

*"Just because 1 million people do something does not mean it is a good thing."*

WARNING: what I'm about to share less than 1% of business opportunity seekers are aware of. In fact, the reality is so damaging, few people are able to accept it. *Especially if you think multilevel or network marketing is a good thing.* Listen closely, in business and in life...

**"Your decisions are only as good as your information. This means the best decision based upon bad information, is *still* a bad decision."**

For some, this report will be one of the most important in the entire **"REAL CASH SECRETS"** manual. Because learning to avoid a bad opportunity (in some cases) can be just as important as picking a *winning one*.

To most people what I am about to say will come as a shock. But please, take the time to analyze the **FACTS**. Everything I am presenting is based upon **20 YEARS of DATA and RESEARCH** provided by the *Consumer Awareness Institute*. Financial experts have scrutinized this information. If you wish to challenge *any* of the material, be my guest. I will list their website at the end (truth is often a brutal teacher).

For the sake of space and to make this report as concise as possible, I have broken the argument against MLM/Network Marketing into four parts. Believe me, this is all it takes. Because a dollar saved is a dollar earned. Therefore avoiding a bad opportunity automatically **MAKES YOU MONEY.** So let's get started...

"What if five robbers were robbing for you and they each recruited five more robbers to rob for you?"

Millions of people desire to earn a second income working from home. The vast majority do **NOT** have the skills to create a business from scratch (nor do they want to take the time to *develop* these skills). This is understandable.

Therefore, multilevel or network marketing can **SOUND** attractive. *Very attractive.*

After all, you *don't* have to find a product, create a product, or even come up with a system to sell it, because the multilevel or network marketing company has done all that for you. All you have to do is work "the system" *right?*

While this scenario sounds great, it presents many problems which **negatively affect your odds of success.** Almost no one understands these problems and even *fewer* ever discuss them. Why? Because the excitement of Network Marketing has a phenomenal power of "blinding" people to facts and figures... After all *"if the dream is big enough the facts don't count."*

**DIRTY SECRET #1: Abysmal success rates**

This is one of the biggest secrets of all. Ask anyone trying to recruit you into their multilevel or network marketing program to show you **STATISTICAL DATA** of what percentage of distributors are actually earning a profit. You will find your request likely lands on deaf ears.

In the event it doesn't, you will find something just as disheartening. And that is, the dismal success rate of network marketing opportunities. **In fact, analysis of the top 12 multilevel marketing companies in the United States shows the average success rate is just 0.3%.**

Since the success rate of conventional business is about 50% based upon data from various sources (*i.e. Small Business Administration, US Census, Bureau of Labor Statistics and Venture Capitalists*).

This means by avoiding Network Marketing you instantly **INCREASE** your odds of success by over 200%. Think about that. **Just by avoiding network marketing and choosing a different business your odds of success increase 200 TIMES!**

And remember, this information is based upon data **provided by the top 12 multilevel marketing companies** in the United States. These are the **FACTS** based on **THEIR OWN NUMBERS**. *With this said, your chances of realizing a profit playing blackjack or poker are far better!* A great way to get this point across is using a hypothetical story if you got cancer.

Imagine you have cancer and statistics show you have a 50% chance of surviving by doing chemotherapy treatments? However, one of your neighbors pitches you a new "alternative" therapy which involves eating *raw apricot pits* three times a day. And, this therapy has been researched at *Bemidji State University* in *Minnesota*.

But guess what? While it may be "natural" compared to chemotherapy, the survival rate is only 0.3%. So now the question is...

Which therapy would **YOU** choose?

**DIRTY SECRET #2: A non-exclusive product with an unprotected territory sold to an endless number of people as an unlimited opportunity.**

One of the biggest secrets in business if you want to make a lot of money quickly and easily is this: have an exclusive product with a protected territory with limited competition and an unlimited market. Even if you could only have two of these four things your odds of success are *drastically* increased.

For example, if you found yourself in New Orleans Louisiana after Hurricane Katrina, which would have more value? Thousands of dollars in gold? Or, hundreds of cases of ice cold beer? The answer is simple. The beer would be worth **MORE** in cash or barter. And this is why having an exclusive product with limited competition can be so profitable.

Think about Microsoft every time you turn on your computer. Think about the gas, electric or cable company every time you pay the bill. Or, think about your favorite food products from the store. All these are examples of things you spend money on which have *limited* competition.

One of the biggest problems with network marketing is you're entering a marketplace promoting a product which is 100% non-exclusive (*meaning anyone anywhere can sign up to sell it and become your instant competitor*). Furthermore, you're taking this product and attempting to sell it in an unprotected territory. This means even more competition. But it gets worse...

Because you're recruiting others who are each allowed to recruit an endless number of reps to promote as well... each one of them outside of your down line or payline **becomes a direct competitor working against you.** This is a recipe for a lot of people working for free or next to nothing (*the reality of most network marketing programs*).

Imagine if every business in your town recruited its' customers to get into the **same business** they're in? Pretty soon there would be so much competition there would be no profit left. But what if the products were **OVERPRICED** to begin with?

**DIRTY SECRET #3:**
**Overpriced products with overhyped claims.**

One of the reasons success rates in network marketing are so low is because of the products. **Specifically, the pricing of them. Studies have shown (on average) products sold via Network Marketing cost 500% to 600% MORE than their store-bought counterparts.** Add this to the non-exclusivity, an unprotected territory and you have a product which is extremely hard to sell. Even at the "wholesale" level.

This is why over 99% of all multilevel marketed product sales are driven by non-retail methods and internal consumption by distributors. In other words, almost all the distributors are just buying from themselves.

If you're looking to start a business and "be your own best customer" than network marketing is a great way to do it. The problem is not so much distributors recruiting others to become distributors who buy from themselves, but the fact **almost no one is buying the products at retail.** In other words, 99% of people get recruited as distributors and purchase the overpriced products "wholesale".

Again, nearly 99% of all sales generated by multilevel marketing companies are at the "wholesale" level. Retail sales are almost nonexistent. Let's face it. In network marketing "wholesale" means retail. This is why in recent years the term **"PRODUCT BASED PYRAMID SCHEME"** has been used to define network marketing opportunities.

**DIRTY SECRET #4:**
**Deceptive compensation plans.**

Probably the most entertaining part of multilevel or network marketing is the fact 99% of the people who are pushing an opportunity are **unable to completely explain the company's compensation plan by which they are paid.** To compare, can you imagine walking into a restaurant where no one knows how much they are being paid?

Network marketing companies have incredibly deceptive compensation plans for a reason: because it's a *clever* and *effective* way to **steal from the distributor force.** It's almost like buying a five dollar bill for four dollars. Let me explain...

Almost every multilevel or network marketing company in the United States does **not** pay commissions on actual dollars of products sold. Instead, they assign what's known as a "Point Value" (PV) or "Commission Value" (CV) to each product. In many cases, when someone orders $100 worth of products, the actual point value or commission value may only be $50 to $80 which you are paid commissions on.

In other words, you could build a giant down line which is purchasing $100,000 worth of products each month, *but the company will only be paying you commissions on $75,000 or $80,000 AFTER your down lines purchases are converted to PV or CV (point value or commission value).* Again, this is just the tip of the iceberg as we are limited in space for this report. One of the dirtiest parts of the network marketing industry is that which falls under the topic of "breakage".

Breakage occurs a number of ways but the result is the same; you end up **not** being paid on volume generated within your down line because you did not "qualify" to earn commissions through deceptive means. The topic of deception within multilevel or network marketing is one which an *entire* book could be done upon.

But I think you know enough at this point to avoid it like the plague.

In its current state, network marketing (a.k.a. Multi Level Marketing or MLM) is a *flawed business model* which should be eradicated from the face of the earth. The mantra of ***Citizens Against Network Marketing*** (aka C.A.N.M.).

*Special thanks to Dr. Jon M. Taylor of the Consumer Awareness Institute for donating content and time for this report. If you wish to research more or save a friend or family member from Multi Level/Network Marketing, you may visit his site at:* ***http://mlm-thetruth.com***

## 64 year old Millionaire reveals unique way to find your dream job and get the employer to call you for it (R057)

John Rojas is 64 years old and has made his millions by owning his share of successful businesses. During his reign, he's hired and fired dozens of people.

But he has a powerful secret on the best way to land your dream job.

According to John, every employer has at least one employee they are not happy with. And this is where the opportunity is. You can leverage this fact to land your dream job by **working the typical job seeking process in reverse**.

Here's what to do…

"Advertising yourself and your skills directly to the employer… even if they have not posted an opening."

*How do you do it?*

"By using one of the most powerful advertising methods out there," says John.

John is talking, of course, about DIRECT MAIL.

Here's how the method works:

1. Do not use your resume. Don't send it. Don't offer it.
2. **Send a letter** to the business telling them about what you can do for their business as an employee. Provide your contact details. **Pitch** your reliability, your skills, your integrity… and any benefits the company will experience when they hire you.

   The goal here is to **sell yourself**—and the idea of hiring you. You want to come across as someone who is committed, invested, and determined. Be as professional as possible, and write from the perspective of "what's in it for them." You need to think from the business owner's perspective, and what you have to offer that others don't. There is a lot of power in approaching work as a way to help the business owner solve problems. If you come at it from that angle, you'll be ahead of the pack.

"ANY OTHER REASON YOU WANT THIS JOB BESIDES BEING QUOTE: 'DEEP, DEEP, UNBELIEVABLY FREAKIN' DEEP, IN DEBT'?"

## Executive recruiter reveals the secret to asking for a raise and getting it (R327)

Many times when people are considering ways to increase their income or make extra money, they forget about one of the most logical and simplest places to start: *their existing job*.

Jack Warner has been an executive recruiter for over 19 years, headhunting corporate and CEO talent for some of the biggest names in the business. His fees average 20% of the placements first year's compensation. This means an executive placement for a $125,000 executive earns Jack and his firm a cool $25,000 commission. With happy clients paying fees like this it's not hard for Jack to earn up to $400,000 per year with most of his business coming from referrals. Jack reminds us he spent half a lifetime building his reputation.

"I NEED ANOTHER RAISE SO I CAN PAY FOR THE CAR I BOUGHT TO CELEBRATE MY LAST RAISE."

Here's his advice on asking for a raise and actually GET it…

*"People don't always think about raises when they are new hires. But that's when the planning should start. Even before they are hired."*

*"For example, some companies have very mechanical pay structures. If you're at the company X number of years, you are going to be making X more than you were making when you started. These limitations are hard to get around. So to give yourself the most flexibility, it is best to* ***start with a company where employees are more likely to be rewarded according to the value they bring to the table****."*

*"But even in the worst-case-scenario, following just a few simple steps can lead to surprising results."*

Jack says that the employees who get the most raises (and the biggest ones) are usually employees who do one or more (and usually more) of these things:

**1. Act like an owner.**

*"This is the number one principal to being valued as an employee. You must start by valuing the company in the same way that an owner would."*

Employees who act like owners are personally invested in the profitability of the company. This doesn't mean they have invested *money* per-se. But it means that they *act* like they have.

When an employee acts like an owner and sees money being wasted, they point it out. They question it. They offer solutions for saving money or for better use of the funds.

When an employee who acts like an owner has information that would be helpful to the company, they try to get it to the right person.

*"Acting like you care about the profitability of the company is one clear way to act like an owner.* ***Prize employees are often those who go the extra mile.*** *They may 'sell' the company's services even though they are not in the sales department. They contribute marketing and sales ideas, product improvement ideas, and more."*

**2. Always Act With Integrity**

This probably seems like a no-brainer, but a lot of perfectly honest people still fail this test. How?

*"A lot of people don't know how to handle it when they make mistakes on the job. Many resort to hiding things, blaming others, or pretending to be oblivious to the problem until someone finds out and they are forced to admit the mistake."*

*"The best way to handle mistakes is to admit them as quickly as possible and as directly as possible to the most appropriate person in the chain of command. Often people make huge mistakes that may have otherwise gotten them fired, but since they proactively sought out management to alert them to their own error, their jobs were spared.*

Serious errors on the job shouldn't be hidden, according to Jack. They should be communicated to the right people as quickly as possible, preferably with a **solution already in the works**, and a plan for preventing future recurrences.

Handling problems this way will help demonstrate your personal investment in the company, and will further set you apart from the crowd.

**3. Demonstrate Excellent Work Ethic**

Working hard when you're at work is one key to proving your worth. Make your time count.

*"Avoid long talks at the water cooler, excessive breaks, and similar activities. They give the impression that you don't value company time."*

This should be common sense. But a lot of people want to show up at work, do as little as possible, and still make it home with a fat paycheck (not the way to get ahead).

**4. Build Appropriate Relationships**

Build relationships with people in the company from the very bottom to the very top.

*"You can always tell when a person is just trying to brown-nose their way to the top. They treat management like royalty, and step on everyone else."*

*"On the flip side, the person who truly cares about the company cares about the employees of the company, too."*

According to Jack, it's **common for management to ask coworkers and subordinates about you when it comes time for performance reviews**, promotions, and raises. His advice: *don't give anyone anything bad to say.* While you might make temporary gains by stepping on others, you'll make the most long term gain by developing deep roots in quality professional relationships.

**5. Know your own value.**

While you don't want to come across as full of yourself or pushy about "what you are worth", you should still keep track as if it matters (because it does).

*"Make notes of ways in which you have saved the company money and other accomplishments such as increased efficiency or other gains. These will help you when it is time to talk about money and merit."*

**6. Know When and How to Ask**

*"Most people ask for raises at the wrong times and in the wrong manner," says Jack. "Knowing when and how to go about it is just as important as knowing why you deserve it."*

So how should you go about asking for a raise?

First, you've got to wait for the right time. If the company only gives raises at reviews, then wait for your review. If there isn't an annual review policy, you may have more flexibility, but you still have to choose the right time.

Don't chase down your boss as she's heading out the door. Don't bring it up in meetings scheduled for other purposes. Instead, schedule a time in advance with the appropriate person to discuss your performance on the job.

Once you get the timing right, you must also ask in the right manner.

"In the meeting with the supervisor, the thing to understand is - **this is a sales presentation**. You are selling your own worth to the company. Like any sales presentation, you should prepare for it in advance."

The best preparation is to have written documentation of why exactly you deserve a raise. This is where you will outline all of your accomplishments, where you have saved or made the company money, projects you've contributed to, and other highlights.

Focus on things that are **unique to you**—that set you apart from the crowd.

Also, it is best to know how much people in your position and industry make on average. Don't go in expecting or asking for ridiculous amounts. Do your research first to make sure you understand the common limits of your position. (You may be able to surpass those limits, but don't expect miracles right away.)

**7. Handle rejection with dignity.**

*"Many people who are initially turned down for raises are granted the raise they asked for shortly thereafter."*

Many others make the mistake of acting with embarrassment, anger, or other emotional outbursts that serve no purpose but to reinforce the manager's decision to not grant the raise. If, on the other hand, you handle yourself with dignity and act in a respectful and gracious manner, the manager will be more likely to reconsider your pitch later after they have had time to think about it. Other times, the "higher ups" will get wind of your request, and grant you the raise. But negative overreactions will disqualify you for such opportunities.

"If you can't get by on your present salary, Slocum, I suggest your wife get a second job."

## Three things you must do before even thinking about starting a business (R328)

There are three indispensable steps to starting a business. These steps could not only help would-be business owners to avoid unnecessary expenses and wasted effort, but they can help make sure that a business has the best chances of success from the start.

Here they are:

**1. TEST MARKET THE PRODUCT.**

You must test market the product or service you plan to sell. Some people do this by simply running ads and measuring the response based on clicks, phone calls, mail back return pieces, etc. The exact method isn't as important as the lessons you learn from it.

If you can't generate leads for the product before you've launched the business, chances are you won't be able to do it afterwards either. And test marketing the product can give you important information that might help to shape the product or sales and marketing plan. You might find you "missed the mark" on your idea in terms of what the market wants, and then you'll have the opportunity to correct your course before investing in a start-up.

**2. You must develop a business plan.**

A business plan is extremely important... especially if you are thinking of starting into a new business venture where there are many unknowns. *Why?* Because if you take the time and put forth the effort to create a real business plan, it means you will have projected "profit and loss" statements, and have an idea (ahead of time) what the "breakeven point" will be.

Your business plan will clarify the costs and potential profits associated with your business idea... and you can reasonably analyze the risks before you put any further effort (or money) into starting the business. This helps you save a ton of time and money when you can't verify on paper the ideas that are unlikely to work, or you'll require more capital to reach critical mass.

You might think you can start a business with, say, $1,000 ... but when you go through the business plan you will realize that it will really be about $10,000 of money put in before you start to turn a profit. This valuable projection on return on investment will help you make smart decisions in advance.

**3. Before you do anything else, start selling.**

After you have developed your business plan and confirmed that the concept is sustainable, it is time to start selling. Notice that I didn't say "get everything put together and perfect". I didn't even say "develop your product". If at all possible, sell your product or service before you are ready to.

You want to confirm your plan will work. Again, this can prevent a lot of wasted time and money. Don't wait for everything to be perfect. Start selling as soon as you possibly can, and then grow from there once you know that you can actually sell your product.

*How can you sell without an already developed product?* Here are some ideas:

- Pre-release sales
- Sell a product like yours someone else will wholesale to you
- Sell a "no frills" version of the product—the minimal required product—until the "refined version" is ready.

## The two types of income you must have to create long term wealth (R331)

If you want to achieve real wealth, you'll need two types of income.

The first is typically what everyone working has, it's called active income. You work, you get paid. If you own a business and it does well, you get paid and can pull a bonus.

Whatever you can save from working (or the extra cash your business throws off) **should be invested** and now you have your money working for you – passive income.

Roger, a CPA, says that in order to build "real" long term wealth, a person can do it much faster if they have **both "active" and "passive" income**.

But before you can invest, you need to save money or have extra money from business activities which you can put to work.

Then you take this money and invest it. Below are some of the ways people like you **created the all-important "passive" income stream**.

- Rental income from property you buy
- Investment gains from stocks, bonds or plain old savings accounts
- Royalties on book or music sales – it's easier than you think to publish a book or write a song today with the Internet delivering an instant audience.

Here's a list of places you can sell your product on the Internet.

- www.clickbank.com
- www.amazon.com
- www.itunes.com

- Dividends from stocks – a lot of people don't know you can get your stock dividends paid in stock, so as your investment gains each year, so do the amount of shares you own. Another good thing about stocks is you can borrow against them without selling them. The interest you pay is deductible, yet you don't have to sell the stocks and trigger taxes.
- Interest from private investor loans that you make. And today you can even make micro loans online using a growing number of websites that match borrowers with people with money to lend. One example is www.prosper.com.
- Interest from CDs, Bonds, etc.
- Income from Annuities

**If you are not saving, you can't put money to work.** So saving or getting into a a business that makes you extra money is your first goal in order to accumulate enough cash to start receiving passive income.

But even if you don't have a dime saved today, have you considered sharing your experience with others in a book? You can become a publisher and author on Amazon literally overnight.

In fact, an elementary school teacher wrote a book detailing school lesson plans for a certain grade level and charging only $9, the book sold 100,000 copies on Amazon. That's almost a million dollars! A windfall she can invest for massive passive income.

Here's another example, one man wrote a book based on his experience in the videogame business of all things. Although he has a full-time job, the commissions from his book continue to come in at the rate of $5,000-$9,000 per year and he is now in his fifth year of earning royalties from this book.

While writing a book or creating a song are both inexpensive ways to generate cash, you

may also want to consider going into a side business that will pay you over and over again.

First, pick something that is within your capital budget. If you can only risk losing under $2000 per year, then that's all you should be investing into your business start-up.

And typically you don't want to go into debt to fund passive income unless you can make enough to service the debt and generate income at the same time. Do be careful because debt crushes businesses and individuals every day.

**The secret to being successful is to pick a business opportunity you know something about and feel passionate to learn even more.**

Although the restaurant business has one of the highest failure rates of any startup, I have a friend who has successfully launched three restaurants and all are still making money today.

Why? Because he knows the restaurant business from top to bottom. Although he is an engineer by trade, he put himself through college by working in restaurants! Who knew he'd end up being in the restaurant business when he was older? But because of his **insider knowledge**, all three restaurants are giving him a passive income as they pretty much run themselves.

So as soon as you finish reading this, make a list of what you know that people would pay for in a book. Any 'how-to' will always have buyers.

## $4,000.00 per month from home as an employment recruiter (R360)

If you like communicating and have the fortitude to get a lot of "no's", especially during the critical first start up year, then you may want to consider becoming an executive recruiter, currently a $10 billion dollar industry in the U.S. alone.

Why would a company use an executive recruiter? Because they are having trouble filling a position and will pay a hefty fee for you to solve their problem with a quality hire.

You'll need to join a number of professional organizations where you can constantly network and when you land clients, you want to retain them year after year so you fill more positions.

Most executive recruiters are retained to fill the needs of companies for middle managers and professionals. Very few operate in the rarified space of placing CEOs.

So why can't a company simply hire people on their own through their HR department? You don't have to have worked in any corporation very long to know most cultures operate with "eyes wide shut."

It's your job to know the marketplace as well as their particular corporate culture and screen candidates who will produce the best fit.

To make a good living as an executive recruiter, you'll need to possess the following skills and abilities.

You must be **enthusiastic**, like you are touting a political candidate.

You must be **patient**, because some of the highest commissions you'll earn are the result of a lengthy screening and then interview process.

You must **think creatively** and help companies try something new, especially since their corporate culture will rarely spot an 'out of the box' opportunity.

You must be **resourceful** as you'll need to tap this skill again and again as you side-step corporate gatekeepers and doomsayers.

You'll need to focus on a **niche**, such as technology, legal, financial, etc. Your accumulated insider knowledge will help everyone win, especially you financially.

You'll need to be **objective**. Both companies and candidates will postulate more than face reality. It's your job to make a true connection, not fulfill an out of reach dream.

You'll need to be a good **juggler**, balancing numerous assignments at once, because deals fall through all the time for no fault of your own.

You'll need good **negotiation** skills so you can be the conduit between the company and the new hire.

If these traits sound like you, then you may be ready to jump into this financially and personally rewarding field. Here are 5 tips to speed your success along the way.

1. Be a gumshoe. Investigate and get to know everything about the company you want to find talent for. If you become known as someone who can place candidates well, you'll get a lot of repeat business.
2. Over deliver - don't just fill a position, find a candidate who will be an impact player and raise the level of your client's corporate effectiveness.
3. Mine data. Know everything about the market, the skills involved, where your client's industry is heading, and what you can do to help your client stay on the forefront.
4. Treat talent like they are the only pearl in the ocean. Through numerous touches, regular feedback and being very personable, you'll become known as the quality recruiter and gain many referrals.
5. Service after the sale - don't stop after your candidate has accepted the position.

Help them during the transition process, the move, and track their progress with the client company so you become known as hands-on.

To win big at the executive recruiting game, cultivate the image of being an influencer and this reputation will serve you well as long as you continue in this lucrative profession.

## $2,000.00 per month visiting garage sales 2 days a week (R359)

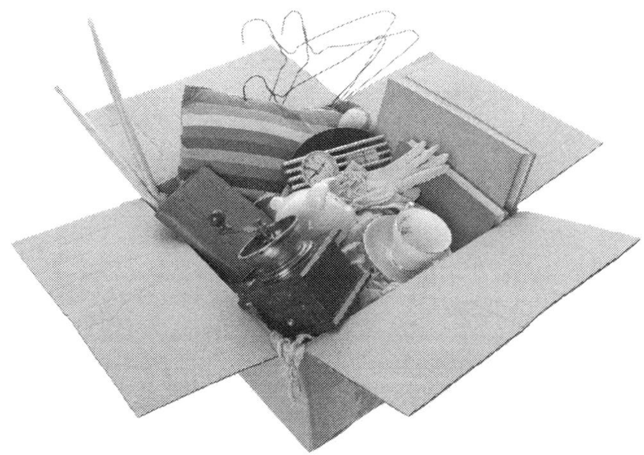

Everyday someone is unloading bargain gold and silver at a garage sale, flea market, yard sale and even thrift stores.

Most of the time the seller simply doesn't know the actual value and just wants to raise some cash, so you can find some really terrific buys.

If you want to turn a couple of hours a week into a nice side business buying gold and silver from the public, follow these tips.

First, know and understand purity marks. Often the seller doesn't and that is how you pick up a steal for pennies on the dollar.

Silverware, candle holders and out of fashion jewelry are the most coveted items at garage sales. And often you can "bundle" everything you want into a lump sum price, enticing the seller to go along for one large transaction. (One "key" item is silverware sets. Many can be purchased for $500.00 and then sold for as much as $2,000!)

Stories abound about people buying a gold necklace for a couple bucks where the gold content alone is worth hundreds. Or scooping up old fashioned' pendants for $5 dollars with the precious metal plus diamonds being worth thousands. Even the silver in a single sterling fork can be worth $25 dollars.

Often the stuff you buy will be dirty or tarnished and the seller will not believe it has any value at all.

Remember, you'll likely have competition so arrive early to grab the good stuff before it gets picked over.

And do your homework, such as visiting websites like www.925-1000.com, an online encyclopedia of silver marks and hallmarks.

Keep your poker face, because you will find gold worth thousands going for a few dollars and you don't want to give off a 'tell' that you've hit the mother load.

Finally, line up buyers, whether it's a pawn shop in your area or gold and silver dealer. Collectible items can be resold on eBay.

By knowing what you are doing and applying a little time each weekend, you can easily hit 8-10 garage sales and find wonderful deals and don't forget to stop by the thrift shop on the way home to see if they've added any new items to their display you can purchase for cheap.

## How to earn $18,000.00 per year cooking from home part-time (R358)

Do you love to cook? How much would you love to GET PAID to cook at home? With this amazing business - YOU CAN! Julie Setzer earns nearly $1,600.00 per month working only part-time from home cooking healthy meals.

While Julie cooks for busy two income households or single heads of households who want something nutritious to heat and serve (without spending hours in the kitchen) other home cooking pros are targeting special occasion cakes and pies, elaborately decorated for the memorable event.

Still others work for the elderly even delivering the home cooked meals.

There are as many opportunities for getting clients for your home cooking business as there are people in your town, especially with more people focusing on healthy eating instead of grabbing fast food.

You can easily launch this business with very little money. Simply create a small menu to start and put the word out.

You can advertise your services on Craigslist, in classified ads and flyers at high traffic community locations like your church, supermarket, or Laundromat. And don't be surprised if you see potential clients advertising for a cook like you.

You can even 'test market' your idea with just a handful of clients and if you feel like you can expand this into a nice income, jump over to your city or county website to see the laws concerning food preparation in your area.

Many have started with just a few customers and those clients in turn 'advertise' the product by sharing with family and friends and the next thing you know you have a steady business bringing reliable income month after month.

To make your business sustainable, you need to earn 40% profit from all of your ingredients, even down to a teaspoon of flour.

In a January 2014 article in *Forbes* magazine, it reports California legalized selling food made at home and this new law instantly created more than 1,000 new local businesses.

Home cooks are not only preparing food for busy families and singles, but they are also creating special products like breads sold at a handful of retail stores.

How much can you expect to earn? It depends on how big you want to grow and keep in mind, in some states there is a cap on how much you can cook from home until you are forced to rent a commercial kitchen (so check your state's regulations).

According to the website GoodFinancialCents.com, offering reviews of home based businesses, someone baking from home can expect to make a median income of $23,450 and that goes up for personal chefs offering healthy prepared meals, even one complying with dietary or allergy demands. And a full blown catering operation can earn even more preparing for special events like weddings.

If you are interested in turning your chef talents into a part time income or even replacing your full-time income with a cooking business, pick a niche, target a market, handle those first few clients like gold and watch your business take off.

People have to eat and many don't have time to cook or (in the case of the elderly and disabled) may not have the ability to go to the grocery store.

Then there are the specialized areas such as cakes, jams, breads and parties.

Add it all up; it's a huge market with a low barrier to entry and good income potential.

## 5 steps to making $500.00 per week selling "Electronic" Real Estate (R357)

We've all heard stories of Internet entrepreneurs cashing-in big for their foresight.

One was Marc Ostrofsky, who in 1995 as many people were still getting their first email address, bought the domain name www.Business.com for what then was the unheard of amount of $150,000.

Four years later as the dot com craze was topping out, he sold it to a venture capital group for a whopping $7.5 million, a Guinness world record at the time.

Fast forward to today, and are there any opportunities left for you, especially if you have no technical skills?

The answer is "yes" as the Internet is one giant "cyber real estate" market and people are buying and selling websites every day.

What can you do now?

The answer is simple. What do you know and more important, what are you passionate about?

Some people blog about financial topics and make as much as $30,000 a month from advertising on their widely followed website.

On the other hand, a husband / wife team in their 70's have a popular website about cooking recipes and they enjoy a comfortable retirement while staying active in their golden years.

Still others simply erect websites and then immediately sell them.

Some of the opportunities are to create a website on a popular topic and then sell it to an entrepreneur who owns other websites in the same niche or has the marketing skills to grow the Internet traffic so it becomes more valuable.

And don't think you've missed out because all the good Internet addresses are taken because today a domain name like Business.com won't command such a high price.

Why?

Because changes in the way search engines display results (especially the leader—Google) place more emphasis on the content of the website versus the domain name.

On the other hand, people still make good money reviewing products and services by including it in a domain name, however that is a tricky subject and if you erect a website such as ToyotaCarReviews.com, you can expect to hear from their lawyers.

Today the websites creating income for entrepreneurs all have the same thing in common, relevant content.

Several years ago, Ebola.com was practically worthless. Today because of the high amount of traffic because of news reports, the site is estimated to be worth $46,624, according to WorthOfWeb.com.

Appraisal websites like WorthOfWeb.com look at keywords and traffic and advertising to estimate how much a website is worth.

As you can see from visiting Ebola.com, it is a very simple site with a few articles. That's it.

But because so many web searches are being done for keyword "ebola" and many searchers simply typing in ebola.com, this simple website is now worth almost $50,000.00.

And that is if the site is sold. The owner may very well continue to mint money by turning his hefty and growing web traffic into advertising dollars.

Ad revenue is one of the ways you can make money with your website.

You've no doubt noticed advertising on just about every website you visit, unless the site was made for a company offering something directly for sale, but still they use advertising to drive traffic to their site.

The second biggest way you make money with a website is with an email list.

Let's go back to the couple in their 70s that have the recipe website. They will give website visitors some free recipes and other information for joining their mailing list.

Then the website owner sends a "newsletter" and inside is links to products and services they receive an affiliate commission from.

Here's how it works. In any given month, say around Thanksgiving, the website emails a newsletter about holiday recipes. And maybe they "review" some type of cooking utensil their readers can 'click' a link and order.

Every time someone orders, the newsletter list owner earns a commission. A rule of thumb is, each name on a mailing list is worth $1 a month, so if you have a list of 5,000 names you can expect to earn $5,000 a month from products and services you review in your newsletter.

Others actually create their own products. Using the recipe website again as an example, the owner could write an e-book on "9 Yummy Recipes for Leftover Turkey" and as soon as they email their list, a certain percentage will order.

Many Internet entrepreneurs literally email their list and watch their bank account start filling with cash hours after they hit the send button.

Still other Internet entrepreneurs do well creating websites and then immediately selling them.

In fact, there is a website especially for buying and selling web properties. Check it out at www.flippa.com and you'll see prices for a wide variety of websites.

Just like you see people on TV shows buying and flipping houses, you can do the same with Internet real estate.

If you want to get involved in flipping websites, your first order of business is to research the potential for the site's target market or niche.

Do you have insider knowledge of some trending search term or does your life experience allow you to create a website with valuable information?

If so, how much traffic is available, meaning how many people search for the keywords you will target. The easy way to find out is to get a Google gmail account (for free) and then use their search tool to see how many people are looking for information in the niche, including all the various permutations of the keywords.

Once you've found a high demand niche, you utilize an easy-to-use online publishing platform, WordPress, to launch your site.

WordPress allows you to create and post articles and upload pictures. It also has a variety of themes, many for free, so you can give your website a custom look.

If you really want to customize your site or have no interest in getting involved in the technical side at all, you can outsource that task on places like Elance.com for very reasonable rates.

Next you would create your content for the site.

Even if your website has no current traffic, other Internet entrepreneurs will buy the ready-made site and use their skills to bring visitors.

Many entrepreneurs create authorship "brands" by using a pen name and also getting social media accounts under that pen name. Then when they go to sell the website it also comes with the Internet "brand" including the social media accounts.

Back to the recipe website as an example, they also have a Facebook account to attract visitors to the website who are interested in cooking.

The best thing about Internet marketing is you can do it from home and any business you can operate without the cost of a vehicle, office rent and other overhead often turns out to be a dream lifestyle for people willing to put in the time, effort and a little bit of money to get started.

---

## $48,000.00 per year working from home. Startup cost: $850 (R361)

There's a big demand from almost 80% of Americans and it's currently going unfulfilled – It is a legitimate ways to get out of debt. And anyone, including you, can jump in as a Debt Consultant.

It's easy to become a debt consultant, working from home with low overhead and regular income potential from $480.00 to $5,760.00 per month.

Even though the headlines say the economy is recovering, consumers are still in debt and most are clueless on how to become debt free.

During the economic downturn, many unscrupulous operators took advantage of consumers drowning with crushing credit card debt or underwater mortgages...

...which means they are more likely to deal with someone in their community than a toll-free number to nowhere.

But how can you become a debt consultant?

It all starts with having the right information, and more important - the step-by-step plan to make it happen.

You can get everything you need in Zodiac Publishing's "Fight Debt and Win" Coaching Program.

Here's how it works.

You run lead-generating classified ads in your town and get your phone to ring with consumers desperate to get out of debt.

You'll then ask prospects a series of qualifying questions. As many as 8 out of 10 will qualify as a client for you.

You then offer a 12 month consulting program for $480 and after the first couple of phone calls; you'll need very little time to monitor their progress thereafter.

After they pay your $480 fee, you'll use a tested "audit process" to help your clients discover an extra $3,500 to $8,500 in 'found' money.

This is the best selling point because immediately after their audit, they will be armed with the road map for getting 8 to 16 times return on the $480 fee invested with you.

On top of that, you outline several, workable debt elimination solutions, based on their current situation - any of which can speed their getting out of debt as much as 90% faster than if they continued where they are.

From then on, you'll simply follow-up by phone or email and as their debts grow smaller, you are likely to get their friends and family as new clients.

The market for people hungry to get out of debt is HUGE!

Consider this, 64% of Americans don't have $1,000 in extra cash on hand. Most are living from check to check and just one job interruption, medical expense or car repair and they are in deep trouble.

So how much can you expect to make as a Debt Consultant?

Just one new client a month helps you pocket $5,760 per year. Ratchet that up to one new client a week, and you'll bank $2000 a month...

...earning a whopping $48 per hour for your efforts.

Your services are a BARGAIN compared to the unfair fees charged by the credit counseling industry, which by the way is owned by the BANKS!

Do the math. Almost 8 out of 10 Americans are in debt and to pay off their credit cards will take decades, unless you show them the proven shortcuts.

And you'll be an expert because in the Fight Debt and Win Coaching Program, there are 978 pages of insider secrets to help you become a debt elimination expert in almost no time.

Potential clients will love what you'll do for them and that will unleash a windfall of referrals, giving you a high paying second income or allowing you to kiss the corporate world goodbye forever!

**Find out now how you can launch your very own debt consultation business fast; call today 775-298-4700.**

“

True security depends not so much upon what you have, but upon *how much* you can do without.

# HEALTH

- ☑ **Natural alternative to Viagra proven to work which 99% of men don't know about**
- ☑ **The truth about natural breast enhancement methods**
- ☑ **500 year old Asian dental secret reverses gum disease while whitening your teeth**
- ☑ **New breakthrough ends sleep apnea without a CPAP machine**
- ☑ **Scientific study reveals a "new way" to make your wife less cranky**
- ☑ **The truth about natural penis enlargement methods**
- ☑ **Natural ingredient clinically proven to clean your arteries for .50 cents a day**
- ☑ ***And More!***

"

The path to long range goals is paved with *short range* objectives.

# Natural alternative to Viagra proven to work which 99% of men don't know about (R012)

There are several herbal supplement products known to promote healthy male performance that may be better tolerated by some men than their prescription counterparts. Many have been the subject of scientific research and are scientifically proven to work.

For example, in a double blind study by the American Journal of Urology[1], **Korean Ginseng** was shown to be an effective alternative treatment for erectile dysfunction. The men in the study were given Korean Ginseng 3 times per day over a period of 3 weeks.

There are some other "alternatives" that have received considerable attention:

- Tongat Ali
- Yohimbe Bark Extract
- Horny Goat Weed
- Tribulus
- MACA
- L-Arginine and L-Citruline

These herbs, or supplements that offer a combination of them, have been shown to improve the symptoms of Erectile Dysfunction (aka ED) in some (but not all) men. As with any supplement, it is important to review it with your doctor and make sure that it will not interfere with any medications you are currently taking. Also, do research on the side effects of any herbs in formulated supplement products, and on any individual herbal supplements that you choose to take.

This is important, as herbs can have side effects just like prescription medications. (L-Arginine, for example, is known to suppress the immune system with continued use even at typical dosages. It is still a powerful and useful supplement for certain conditions—but you should discuss its immune system effects with your doctor before taking it.)

On the plus side, some herbs are very powerful—some have even been developed into prescription medications. Yohimbe, for example, is available in purified form as a prescription drug in the U.S. for the treatment of erectile dysfunction. (Note, Yohimbe is also a supplement that one should be very careful with. Always check with your doctor before taking herbs or supplements!)

**On a side note:** Remember that problems with sexual function can also be routed in conscious and unconscious emotional issues. Don't overlook the possible emotional components if you or someone you love experiences problems of this sort. For reference and information that might be helpful, research the work of Dr. John Sarno, Dr. David Schechter, and Dr. Howard Schubiner. (Some of which is mentioned elsewhere in this manual.)

(1)http://www.jurology.com/article/S0022-5347%2805%2964298-X/abstract

## The truth about natural breast enhancement methods (R339)

Ladies, are there any legitimate ways for you to increase your breast size without going to the plastic surgeon?

Here's what our investigative journalists uncovered.

**FACT** - Women can help boost the size and firmness of their breasts with exercise. From chest presses with weights to push-ups, regular strength training will improve your breasts, maybe not a cup size, but they will be perkier as you get better muscle tone.

**FACT** - Poor posture will make your breasts look smaller. If you have a slump or slouch, practice yoga and other exercises designed to rebuild your posture and see the difference in the mirror.

**FACT** - A known side effect of hormone based birth control pills is breast growth. But you are not encouraged to take them ONLY for larger breasts.

**FACT** - Middle aged women prescribed estrogen to relieve menopause symptoms often experience some breast enlargement. Unless your doctor prescribes estrogen, you should not begin taking it, especially with the goal of breast growth.

Same is true with progesterone, another female sex hormone often prescribed in conjunction with estrogen. You may experience mild breast enlargement, but you should never take it for this reason only.

If your doctor prescribes an antidepressant known as a selective serotonin reuptake inhibitor (SSRI), they have been known to enlarge the breast but as with the other medications mentioned above, you should never take them only for bigger breasts.

According to Dr. Adriane Fugh-Berman, professor of complementary and alternative medicine at the Georgetown University School of Medicine...

..."The use of bust-enhancing supplements should be discouraged because of lack of evidence for efficacy and long-term safety concerns."

Miracle breast enlargement pills are based on centuries-old folk remedies whose main ingredients include fenugreek and fennel.

But there's never been a study on the safety of taking large amounts of these herbs.

Breast massage has also been hailed to increase breast size. However, avoid buying special costly gadgets or creams promising results as science cannot be called upon to verify any of the claims.

Many women experiment with a wide variety of do-it-yourself breast enhancing methods and they report them on a website: http://www.breastnexus.com

However, before blindly accepting anything you read on an Internet message board, do some research yourself - especially if you are considering buying a supplement where the long term use has not been scientifically studied OR if you plan on buying any "device" or cream promising more than they can verifiably deliver.

Then there is a website devoted to "adult nursing relationships" (A.K.A. ANR). Some women report increased breast size of up to 2 cup sizes by regularly and consistently being engaged in such a relationship.

Here's the website: http://www.landmilkhoney.com

Finally, a Miami Doctor has developed "an implant-free fat transfer breast augmentation technique." And Dr. Roger Khouri sells his technique to other physicians around the U.S.

You can view his site and read about "Natural Breast Augmentation with Fat Transfer"—including impressive before and after photos showing increases of up to 2 cup sizes—here:

http://www.miamibreastcenter.com/augmentation/natural-fat-transfer

In conclusion, women who want to enhance their breasts and do not have the money for a plastic surgeon, may want to carefully consider some of the natural techniques available for a slight or more noticeable size boost.

The facts, ideas and websites presented in this article are for research and you would be well advised to thoroughly consider your options before trying any of the suggestions, no matter how enticing the 'before and after' pictures appear.

## 500 year old Asian dental secret reverses gum disease while whitening your teeth (R354)

Have you heard of "oil pulling" for dental health?

Although the term was coined in the 1990's by Ayurvedic practitioners, its traditional use dates back thousands of years in Asia.

Essentially, one swishes an oil (sesame seed is believed to be the best) in the mouth for 5 to 20 minutes, then spits it out and rinses with water.

The process is done to "pull" bacteria from your mouth and gums and discharge them when you expel the oil.

As with most folk remedies, the scientific community says there have been little studies to support these claims, yet as with most natural health advice, studies often are not funded because Big Pharma can't patent something occurring naturally in nature.

**The Facts:**

In a report published in the US National Library of Medicine National Institutes of Health, a double blind study of 20 age-matched boys found **"the oil pulling therapy showed a reduction in the plaque index, modified gingival scores, and total colony count of aerobic microorganisms in the plaque of adolescents with plaque-induced gingivitis."**

So exactly how does oil pulling work?

According to *WebMD,* "Most microorganisms inhabiting the mouth consist of a single cell. Cells are covered with a lipid, or fatty membrane, which is the cell's skin. **When these cells come into contact with oil (a fat) they naturally adhere to each other."**

So basically you "pull" the bacteria from your teeth and gums by swishing about and then after you spit out the oil, the bacteria stuck to it goes away.

Verified reviews on Amazon for the book *Oil Pulling Therapy: Detoxifying and Healing the Body Through Oral Cleansing*, overwhelmingly endorse the practice with people stating:

"After only two weeks of the described therapy, completed twice a day exactly as recommended for twenty minutes each time, I have experienced profound physical changes that are measurable."

"I have followed the guidelines and have bright white teeth."

"I am religiously following the advice on oil pulling. My nodules shrank in size. Thank God."

"I've been oil pulling for a month now, and I immediately saw an improvement in my oral health!"

Many people are reporting fresher breath, whiter teeth and even reversal of gum disease.

While "Dynasty Sesame Seed Oil" from Japan is often used by most "oil pullers", others use coconut oil because as *WebMD* states, "while you can get the same bacteria-fighting benefits with sesame or sunflower oil, coconut oil has the added benefit of lauric acid, which is well-known for its anti-microbial agents."

In no way is oil pulling recommended as a substitute to good oral health including brushing after every meal, flossing regularly and rinsing with mouthwash.

However, those who have introduced the therapy into their daily routine by oil pulling once a day, are reporting improved oral benefits as well as whiter teeth because of a reduction in oral bacteria.

## New breakthrough ends sleep apnea without a CPAP machine (R355)

Sleep apnea obstructs airflow during sleep and left untreated, can reduce life expectancy because of the increased risks of having a heart attack or stroke.

More than 18 million Americans suffer from sleep apnea and many do not receive treatment.

According to *WebMD*, the common symptoms of sleep apnea are:

- experiencing a dry or sore throat upon wakening
- heavy snoring
- being awakened by gasping for breath
- inability for continuous, restful sleep
- headaches in the morning
- all the symptoms of not getting enough sleep such as moodiness, poor memory, being tired throughout the day and a loss of sex drive.

The condition can disturb sleep so much that sufferers nod off during work or worse, while driving.

Some sufferers stop breathing as many as 100 times during the night, depriving the body and brain of vital oxygen.

In addition to all the problems previously mentioned, left untreated sleep apnea can cause:

- a spike in blood pressure,
- development of diabetes,
- onset of depression,
- Attention deficit Hyperactivity Disorder.

Those who do seek treatment are often put on Continuous Positive Airway Pressure (CPAP) machines, but this is not without problems.

According to the Mayo Clinic, CPAP machine issues include:

- wrong sized mask,
- patients have trouble getting used to using the machine,
- problems having air forced into your nose and throat,
- developing a dry or stuffy nose,
- not being able to relax while wearing the mask,
- air releasing into eyes causing dryness as well as skin irritation around the face,
- having a hard time falling to sleep,
- not being able to put up with the noise.

Fortunately, there is a breakthrough alternative to the bulky, uncomfortable CPAPs and it lies with a dental solution.

It's called an **Oral Airway Dilator (OAD)**. These devices looks similar to the mouth guard athletes wear.

They work by moving your jaw slightly forward or placing just enough pressure on your tongue to keep it from sliding back - both opening your airway and providing relief from sleep apnea.

The custom fitted mouth guards are much easier to wear than CPAPs and much easier to carry when traveling.

If you wish to consult a dentist on this easy-to-use alternative to CPAP, then make sure the practice is a member of either the "Academy of Clinical Sleep Disorders Disciplines" or the "American Academy of Dental Sleep Medicine", insuring they have the training to properly deal with sleep apnea.

## Scientific study reveals a "new way" to make your wife less cranky (R051)

Men listen up – if you've been married for a while or are in a committed relationship, chances are you've dealt with more than your fair share of what we will politely refer to as 'moodiness.'

And if you are lucky enough to never have experienced such a situation, just wait until the menopause years where your lady will probably suffer from aches, hot flashes, trouble sleeping and a roller coaster of emotions.

Fortunately, thanks to the results of a **Middle Eastern study**, you have a way out.

It's not a massage, but more important, an **aromatherapy massage**.

What's aromatherapy?

It's the use of aromatic plant extracts and oils, most often applied during a massage or bath.

What does it do?

It enhances the massage by igniting chemicals in the brain responsible for pleasure, specifically serotonin and dopamine.

Here's what the study found.

Women with similar menopausal symptoms were divided into three groups for study.

Group 1, (the control), received no massage therapy and naturally, reported no relief from menopausal symptoms.

Group 2, received massages with standard oil and 1 in 7 women experienced relief from menopausal symptoms.

Group 3, got massages with aromatic oil and nearly 1 in 2 **reported relief from menopausal symptoms!**

So men, as soon as you finish reading this, schedule your lady an aromatic massage at the nearest quality spa. (Or, even better, do it yourself!)

You'll BOTH be glad you did.

## The truth about natural penis enlargement methods (R353)

The Internet is full of penis enlargement offers based on everything from pills to pumps. But the scientific facts do not support any of the claims.

No U.S. based medical facility will perform a "penis enlargement" operation and in the countries where such an operation can be performed, complications are often cited, with further surgery required or outright disfigurement.

According to the Mayo Clinic's website, *"Most of the techniques you see advertised are ineffective, and some can damage your penis."*

Still men feeling inadequate are tempted to try the following as reported on the Mayo Clinic website;

**Pills and creams** - "None of these products have been proven to work, and some may be harmful."

**Pumps** - "A vacuum pump can make a penis look larger temporarily. But using one too often or too long can damage elastic tissue in the penis, leading to less firm erections."

**Jelqing** - "A hand-over-hand motion to push blood from the base to the head of your penis. Although this technique appears safer than other methods, there's no scientific proof it works, and it can lead to scar formation, pain and disfigurement."

**Stretching** - "Stretching involves attaching a stretcher or extender device to the penis to exert traction. A few small studies have reported length increases of half an inch to almost an inch (about 1 to 2 centimeters) with these devices. However, the studies are not high quality. More rigorous research is needed to establish safety and effectiveness."

Still, men being men, the Internet is full of discussion boards where various methods are "reported" on a regular basis.

You can check out:

http://ThundersPlace.org

and

http://MattersOfSize.com

and

http://PeGym.com

Finally, many in the scientific community believe the surge (no pun intended) in Internet traffic for penis enlargement is due to the feeling of inadequacy developed by men who spend too much time with Internet porn.

Once a therapist or doctor advises a male that his size is average and produces studies where "size" is more important to men than women, many men abandon their enlargement quests.

## Natural ingredient clinically proven to clean your arteries for .50 cents a day (R036)

According to Dr. Louis J. Ignarro, who—along with his colleagues—was awarded the Nobel Prize[1] for his research on **Nitric Oxide**, (the gas known as "NO" for Nitric Oxide) could hold the key to preventing and even reversing heart disease.

**Nitric oxide** has since been referred to as the "atom" of the cardiovascular system. It's a tiny molecule with a **huge value for human life and longevity.** *So how can you get it?*

Here's the thing:

Nitric Oxide is a *gas*. You *can't* take it in pill form. Instead, you have to give the body the raw materials it needs to *make* Nitric Oxide. Usually our bodies make enough, but in today's world of fast food diets and sedentary lifestyles, it is highly possible that an average individual will **NOT** produce enough.

According to Dr. Ignarro, the body uses **Arginine** and (to a lesser degree) **Citrulline** to make nitric oxide. And you can *increase* nitric oxide levels by supplementing with these two ingredients. **Dr. Ignarro claims that such supplementation can prevent and even reverse heart disease.**[2]

The effects of arginine, citrulline, and the nitric oxide they help the body create, can be experienced (for men) in the *"Viagra-like ef-*

*fects"* of these popular supplements. What is more, if the supplements are used correctly, the long term health benefits could far outweigh any short term reward. One 80 year old man reported a **3% reduction** in blockage in *just 9 months*, and an **additional 5%** reduction in the *9 months* that followed.

And the best part of all about arginine and citruline is the *price*. As far as supplements go, these can be found for relatively cheap. A 30 day supply at typical dosages (500 to 1000 mg) can be purchased for $15 or less at many health food stores and online supplement retailers.

(1) Source: http://www.nobelprize.org/nobel_prizes/medicine/laureates/1998/ignarro-bio.html

(2) NO More Heart Disease: How Nitric Oxide Can Prevent—Even Reverse—Heart Disease and Strokes by Louis Ignarro, ISBN:0312335822

## Pharmaceutical companies receive $200 million to provide you with FREE medication (R022)

Did you know there are hundreds of programs available that can help you with your prescription drug costs? Listen up, because you may be missing out.

There is a place called the Partnership for Prescription Assistance that acts as a "single point of access" for over 450 different medication assistance programs. According to their website, over 200 of the programs are offered directly by pharmaceutical companies.

Their goal? It's simple: to help you get your prescription medications for free, or nearly free.

Here's a snippet from their website written by a guy named Bobby Campbell, who suffered a heart attack and went to the Partnership for Prescription Assistance for help with the medication costs that followed:

*"After my heart attack, I was unable to work full-time and therefore did not have prescription medicine coverage. But, I needed my heart and blood pressure medications so that I would not have another heart attack. The Partnership for Prescription Assistance helped me to get signed up for various drug company programs and now I receive four of my life-saving medicines for free, which saves my family about $275.00 a month. Therefore, the Partnership for Prescription Assistance has been a real life-saver for my family and for me."*

Why do the drug companies have these programs? Because the government gives them money to do it! There is no need to feel like you're getting something for nothing or like you're somehow abusing the system here—the reality is that this is a benefit that you've paid for with your tax dollars.

If you have high-cost prescription drugs and need help, go to http://www.pparx.org to find out if you qualify. You can also call them at 1-888-477-2669.

***Warning:*** *Some companies do the exact same thing that this organization does, but charge you for it. Don't fall for one of those scams! Protect yourself, and use only PPARX.ORG.*

## Doctor reveals 38% of men over 45 have male menopause. Are you one of them? (R021)

Male menopause, known as 'andropause' does a real number on men, usually between the ages of 40 all the way up until their late 70's.

The cause is simply a decline in androgen (testosterone) hence the name andropause.

What's troubling, is, left untreated; andropause can shorten a man's lifespan.

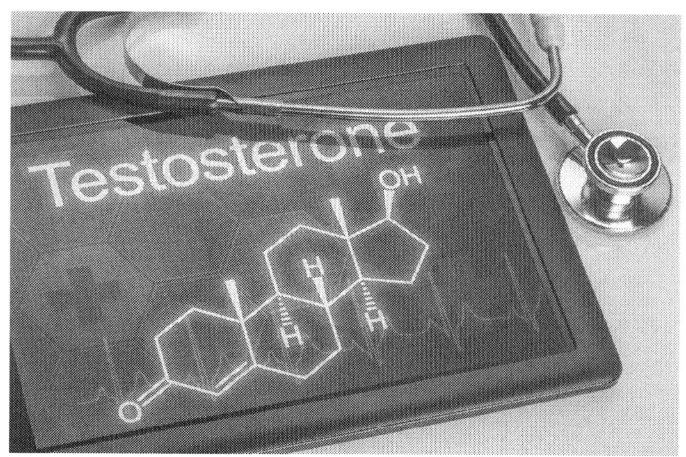


**Know The Symptoms**

The most easily recognizable symptoms are feeling tired all the time, low sex drive and when you are in the mood, your erection is softer, trouble sleeping, expanding love handles around your belly, trouble concentrating and unexplained changes in mood.

But before you rush out for 'low T' therapy, you must consult with your physician because "replacing testosterone may worsen prostate cancer" as well as come with other unwanted side effects, according to *WebMD*.

Still, leaving low testosterone untreated will increase your risk of diabetes, high cholesterol and body fat. For older men, bone fractures become a concern.

So if you feel you are experiencing any of the symptoms, you would be well advised to get checked by your physician and consider testosterone therapy. Currently a blood test is the only way to diagnose andropause… and generally it takes multiple blood tests over time because testosterone levels generally vary from day to day. It also may not hurt to get a second opinion as there are some variations in the "reference ranges" used to determine a deficiency. (What actually constitutes a deficiency in older men is not yet known.)

**All-Natural Alternatives**

There are a number of natural alternatives you may want to consider for raising your testosterone.

Are you getting enough vitamin D? The *European Journal of Endocrinology* published a study linking 'low T' to vitamin D deficiency.

In addition to vitamin supplements, make sure your diet includes fish like salmon, tuna and sardines. These are rich in vitamin D, omega-3's and packed with protein.

And while shopping the seafood aisle, consider oysters. They are rich in zinc and known to help men suffering from 'low T.'

If you've ever traveled near any oyster producing regions of the U.S., you've certainly seen the bumper stickers and signs proclaiming "eat oysters, love longer!"

Shellfish are also good sources of zinc where just a couple ounce serving will give you almost half of the daily zinc you need to stay healthy.

Since 'low t' can lead to bone problems, you are also encouraged to drink milk, especially the low-fat kind. You'll get both vitamin D and calcium for bone health.

And you can load up on vitamin D for breakfast with egg yolks. Although they've received a bad rap from the fat avoidance dieticians, the truth is, egg yolks have the **type of cholesterol that can boost testosterone**.

In fact, breakfast is the perfect time to get your vitamin D when you drink orange juice and enjoy certain grains.

Now, men love hearing they can increase their testosterone by eating more beef. So get your grill on, but eat smart, choosing lean cuts and don't eat beef daily.

Even better, get ground beef and make a big pot of chili. The **kidney beans you use have the plant protein proven to promote heart health**, as well as add even more of the vitamin D and zinc you need for contending with 'low T.'

If you stop at the local BBQ place to enjoy beef, be sure to order the baked beans too, as they are just as healthy as kidney beans. Same goes for white and black beans.

Wellness guru Dr. Mercola, suggests men suffering from 'low T' consider the following.

**Lose weight,** because overweight men typically have higher occurrences of low testosterone.

For exercise, **short intense exercises** will boost testosterone while aerobics or routine exercises have shown to have no effect.

Personally, I take a fitness break every evening to watch the 6 o'clock news and during the broadcast, I go through a series of highly intensive exercises that really get my metabolism roaring while building muscles.

And several of my exercises use hand weights because strength training also increases testosterone levels.

In today's modern society, the commutes, the offices, boring meetings, goofy bosses and just trying to get through the airport - all add to your **stress levels**, which can block the effects of testosterone.

Take a short meditation break during the day or stretch, especially yoga. Otherwise, stress will wreck your life in more ways than one.

**Get off the sugar!** Sugar cravings can be a side effect of stress. You feel bad, tired and then reach for some sugary snack that raises your insulin level, another factor contributing to low testosterone.

To fight those hunger moments, keep a bag of almonds, cashews or walnuts handy. You'll be getting your omega-3's, but not the junk carbs.

Nuts also contain healthy fats, as well as avocados - all essential for optimum testosterone production.

In addition to managing your diet to combat low T, you may want to consider supplements.

The Maca plant from Peru, comes in powders, extracts and capsules and has been known to increase testosterone, while blocking estrogen production. **Maca is a common ingredient in most over-the-counter supplements promising to boost testosterone.**

If you think for a second you could be suffering from low T, have your physician verify.

Then consider the diet and exercise changes mentioned in this report as well as supplementing your diet with natural testosterone boosters.

**Find A Doctor Who Understands The Latest Developments**

Before you start taking any 'low T' drugs, make sure you carefully understand all the possible side effects.

Something that bugs me as I'm doing my high intensity exercises during the 6 o'clock news is a commercial for 'low T' and only a few seconds of the ad are about the product while the rest of the commercial is lawyer talk to minimize the pharmaceutical company's exposure to lawsuits.

Look carefully at your diet, add some high intensity exercises and take your vitamins before going on any drug.

According to Russ Scala at the institute of Nutritional Medicine & Cardiovascular Health...

...you must get testosterone the right way and you've got to monitor blood work. If you order stuff on the Internet and don't monitor your blood composition, you can **cause a heart attack**.

Before you take testosterone, interview the doctor and ask...

...how long have you been doing testosterone therapy?

...are you on it (and those over 40 should probably be, so if he isn't on it, why is he prescribing it?),

...what pharmacy are you using?

...what is your treatment protocol?

...and ask if you can talk to some patients already on the therapy.

Russ advises that even though testosterone has been vilified in the press, it is improving the quality of life for the elderly, especially those with early signs of dementia.

**Mistakes To Avoid**

Nelson Vergel author of *Testosterone: A Man's guide* lists the top 10 errors men make when using testosterone replacement therapy.

Top of the list is using **black market** sources from the Internet or someone you met at the gym.

**Next is not looking at all the options**, which go hand in hand with the 3rd biggest error - **not using the right dose**.

And even if you've lucked upon the option that is right for you and you are taking the optimum dose, **going on and off testosterone** is a big mistake.

If you are taking **medications**, some doctors may blame testosterone for increases in cholesterol and other blood problems, when in fact it's your medication.

Then there are **side effects**. If you don't know what to expect, you can't manage it.

Also, don't be afraid to **switch doctors**. As the population ages with a baby boomer retiring every 6 seconds, testosterone therapy is becoming more prevalent and many doctors are not staying up to date on the latest research.

Finally, if you are on doctor supervised testosterone therapy - **follow the directions** because you can only be treated within the context that you are doing what the doctor ordered.

Based on all the research our editors have done, the **best advice** we can give is two expert books on the subject. 1.) *"Testosterone: A Man's Guide"* by **Nelson Vergel**, BsChE, MBA. And, 2.) *"Testosterone for Life"* by **Abraham Morgentaler**, M.D.

Ref: Dietary intake and supplementation: Effects on testosterone. (n.d.). University of Texas at Austin.

## Pharmacy insider reveals scary facts you need to know BEFORE ordering from any online pharmacy (R115)

With a baby boomer turning 60 every six seconds in the U.S. and being projected to enjoy the longest life span in American history...

...the pharmaceutical industry is serving a larger clientele and will have them refilling scripts for years.

To save money, many have turned to online pharmacies.

Before you start doing business with an online pharmacy, you need to read these startling facts.

There are **only three ways an online pharmacy can sell you a drug cheaper** than you can get at your local pharmacy.

1. The online pharmacy has lower operating costs than physical pharmacies and they pass the savings on to you.
2. You are ordering from another country that has a 'cap' on drug costs, (like Canada), so yes the same drug in the U.S. costs more.
3. **You are being scammed.**

And even if you are getting a real drug, sometimes the online pharmacy will have incomplete labeling, the wrong dosage, be a generic or you receive a completely different drug than you ordered.

Just like any business and profession, there are good and bad operators and then there are those who operate totally illegally.

Now, there is no law that keeps you from ordering a prescription drug from another country. But there are laws against illegal online pharmacies.

Not long ago, the Food and Drug Administration shut down 1,975 U.S. based websites selling drugs illegally.

**And in 2011 Google settled with the FDA for $500 million for running ads for illegal Canadian online pharmacies** (and many of the 'pharmacies' were NOT in Canada).

So at best, the online pharmacy business is akin to the patent medicines hawked at Wild West shows.

You certainly don't want to get caught up in anything deemed illegal and here's where you can get in big trouble.

**Ordering a controlled substance without a prescription** is against the law, even though the online pharmacy will sell it to you.

If you import prescriptions, you must give your physicians contact info to customs.

Finally, some try and use drugs that are allowed in other countries but have not been approved by the FDA. Again, this is breaking the law.

What you CAN do is **order from a U.S. online pharmacy certified by the National Association of Boards of Pharmacy**, but their application requires a fee.

**LegitScript** also recognizes pharmacies complying with the law and safe practices.

And while you can safely order from Canadian pharmacies, many are nothing more than **shady operators in other countries masquerading as a "Canadian" pharmacy**.

But before you jump online, certain you can save a bundle on your next prescription, be warned that recently the National Association of Boards of Pharmacy conducted a study suggesting that over **96% of online pharmacies do not comply with U.S. law**.

**Viagra** is the most common fraudulently filled prescription, meaning you are not getting Viagra.

And the FDA has estimated that as much as **40% of Mexican pharmaceuticals are simply counterfeit**.

If you venture online to save money, **follow these guidelines**.

**Look for certified pharmacies** (those with the NABP or Legit Script logo) and double check whatever the website says by visiting the National Association of Boards of Pharmacy (NABP) website to see indeed the online pharmacy is actually certified.

Don't buy from any website that does not require a prescription or offers to write one for you.

Double check the **privacy policy** of the website. The last thing you want after placing an order is to have your email address shared with thousands of shady operators.

Don't order from a website that doesn't share their physical address and the name and number of the pharmacist filling the prescription.

And if you can't call to verify the pharmacist's license, run like hell. If it's a U.S. based pharmacy, you can easily verify the license online by visiting www.nabp.net

Begin your search for a legitimate online pharmacy by visiting these websites and only doing business with whom they recommend.

http://www.nabp.net/programs/consumer-protection/buying-medicine-online/recommended-sites http://www.legitscript.com/pharmacies

For Canadian pharmacies go here;

http://www.cipa.com

**FACT:** you can save on prescription drug costs by ordering from online pharmacies, as long as you are receiving the drug your doctor prescribed, in the dosage you need.

Legitimate online U.S. based pharmacies with lower overhead can help you save money as well as **real** Canadian online pharmacies. But before you order, follow the instructions in this report to verify everything, otherwise you could be wasting money or worse, gambling with your health.

## The cholesterol myth your doctor will never tell you (R127)

The misinformation about cholesterol has many people avoiding foods they should not, while taking medications they could get off of, if they only knew the facts about managing their diet.

Everyone believes high cholesterol leads to a higher chance of suffering a heart attack. Nothing could be further from the truth.

**In a Harvard study, they found 8 out of 10 heart attacks were caused by high risk factors such as smoking, too much booze, being overweight, having a junk food diet and a lack of exercise – not cholesterol.**

To make matters more confusing, people are being led to believe there is 'good' and 'bad' cholesterol. The 'bad' they say is the LDL cholesterol.

But it can come in several forms and the one that penetrates your artery walls can cause heart disease.

If you are confused, ask your doctor for a **complete test to measure all the types of LDL cholesterol** so you'll know if you have a subset that needs to be dealt with.

A lot of people assume if their cholesterol is very low, they are o.k. But if a type of your LDL is high, you are living dangerously and the test described above will help your doctor identify your risk.

Another big issue is many people on meds like Lipitor are encouraged to take them because they have high cholesterol and the fact is you do, if you have the type of LDL described in the above paragraphs.

But **if you have the LDL cholesterol that is non-threatening, you don't need to be on drugs at all.**

Contrary to what the last several generations have been taught to believe, **you don't need to avoid meat and eggs**. Neither will increase your chances of having a heart attack. And there have been 21 studies on this one subject indicating that saturated fat does not cause heart problems.

As you know, the same generations who were told to reduce intake of steak and eggs were also encouraged to boost their carbohydrate intake, instead of fat.

And as you can see from everyone's expanding waistline, **increases in carbs, especially the refined ones, can cause a whole host of problems**.

All the packaged 'fat free' stuff you see at the grocery is simply **filling you with sugar that increases your triglycerides, a big risk factor for heart trouble**.

The takeaway from this report is, **if you want lower cholesterol**, especially the type that can cause a heart attack or stroke, focus on a healthy diet, avoid refined and processed foods in any form, have an exercise routine and if you smoke, stop.

## Better sleep, improved memory and no restless leg syndrome (R134)

Sleep problems can come at any age and often occur more frequently in older adults.

Some of the main causes of problems sleeping as we age include but are not limited to:

**Habits that interfere with sleep**, such as not having a regular time you go to bed, or drinking alcohol before bedtime that metabolizes into sugar and jars you awake.

Then there are **medical issues**, such as menopause, pain caused by arthritis and a wide range of health conditions.

**Certain medications** can interfere with sleep and if you are on them, check with your doctor about possible side effects.

**Not getting enough exercise** can prolong the time it takes you to feel sleepy. You don't have to get a gym membership though. Simply working in the garden, mowing the lawn or taking a nice long walk will do.

**Stress** can keep you awake at night, so if you are coping with a significant life change, deal with it by getting a set routine to take your mind off it, until the anxiety passes. You are probably better off exercising, doing meditation or yoga than going on meds to deal with stress.

Older adults can also suffer from **restless leg syndrome and sleep apnea**.

You can deal with all of these situations by **developing better habits in the daytime** that will help you sleep better.

1. **Be active.** If you don't have anything to do, volunteer to do something. Pick up a hobby or work for a charity. Do something to engage your mind and body, and you'll find you sleep much better.

If you frequently feel **depressed**, talk to someone. It doesn't have to be a professional. It can be anyone to take your mind off of what is bothering you.

That's why **volunteer work helps you cope better**. And you can also simply commit to **learn something new** like a computer skill or another language and this will get you active with others.

2. **Regular exercise** is the key to getting a good night's sleep. Again, you don't need to join a gym or order a gizmo from the Home Shopping Network. You can simply walk. And bring along your Smartphone and headset and listen to music as you walk. This gives you a double benefit of exercise and a mood lift.
3. Now, we all love our coffee. But drinking it late in the day instead of breakfast can keep you awake. Enjoy your coffee fix in the morning and in the afternoon **drink green tea (low in caffeine yet high in antioxidants)**.
4. **And if you drink alcohol, avoid the night cap** because consumption close to bedtime will always wake you up a couple of hours later as it moves through your bloodstream and is converted to sugar.

You can also **plan for a better night's sleep**.

A. **Too much artificial light** actually suppresses your sleepy hormone, melatonin. So turn off the lights, TV and computer and read for an hour or so to easily fall asleep.

And we all love our Smartphone and tablets, but these devices can interfere with your melatonin production too. Again, read a book under a lamp.

B. **Don't keep a clock within view**, otherwise you'll clock watch instead of going to dreamland.

**C.** As best you can, **go to bed and wake up at the same time** every day. And if you get sleepy earlier, by all means go to bed.

**D.** If you don't like reading before bed, then try taking a **warm bath and listening to music and just relax**.

**E.** **Steer clear of sleeping pills.** They are not a substitute for good sleep and healthy habits and over time, the pills can actually create insomnia.

Finally, if you've tried everything in this report and still have sleep problems, you would be well advised to get a medical evaluation.

## Three foods and compounds clinically proven to improve your memory (R121)

Do you like to enjoy a big ice cream sundae? Who doesn't?

Have you ever noticed how you feel after eating something like that or any junk food?

Sometimes it's hard to concentrate, focus and remember things after you indulge in 'naughty' consumption.

What is happening to you is brain drain. When your brain is clicking on all cylinders, it **demands twice as much energy** than other cells in your body.

So as the old adage goes, you are what you eat!

And eating the right things not only helps maintain, but even improve your memory - and helps you **grow brain cells**.

The following list includes nutritional guidelines proven to boost your brain to operate at peak performance.

Top of the list is fruits and veggies. Yep, just like your mother said.

Fruits and vegetables are loaded with antioxidants you need to protect your brain from free radicals.

Some of the very best of the bunch are;

**Blueberries** have been linked to lower your chances of developing Alzheimer's as well as slows the decline in memory that plagues so many older people.

**Spinach** is not only good for your muscles (thank you Popeye), but also helps you focus better.

**Apple.** An apple a day still works to this day because it's antioxidant-rich and can help reverse memory decline.

**Omega-3s.** Then there are the omega-3s which help your brain concentrate better and focus more sharply.

Get your Omega-3s from **wild caught fish and walnuts**.

After you get on a balanced diet, you'll start to notice less 'foggy' moments. And you can minimize them even more still with **supplements**.

**Ginkgo** boosts the circulation to your brain, helping you have more mental clarity.

**CoQ10** is an enzyme that decreases with age, so if you are a senior, take it for more mental energy.

Finally, a simple but sometimes hard to accomplish brain repairer is to **limit your calorie intake.**

Cutting your calorie intake by 30% and eating nutrient rich foods has proven in studies to **significantly boost verbal memory scores** for the elderly.

Remember, what you eat can either help your memory and brain function or accelerate its decline.

## The clinically proven way to train your metabolism to increase fat burning 24 hrs a day (R031)

A lot of people try a lot of diet pills and other fads to improve their health and lose weight. Sometimes, in our search for the best "cure" for our problem, we neglect some of the basics that can go a long way.

There are three simple keys to weight loss that are clinically proven to train your metabolism to burn more fat and calories. Don't try another fad diet until you've applied these simple tricks.

**Vital Key #1: Exercise**

It's no secret that exercise will help most people lose weight. But when is the best time to do it? According to experts, if you want to lose weight and boost your metabolism you should exercise at a moderate level in the early morning. Don't overdo it. Remember, moderation. And do it first thing in the morning. (A 30 to 60 minute walk first thing in the morning on an empty stomach is ideal.)

**Vital Key #2: Sleep.**

The next key, is simply, to make sure you are getting the right amount of sleep. This means that you do not want to get too much sleep, and you do not want to get too little sleep. Either can lead to weight gain. The most common is too little.

People who are short on sleep end up eating (usually carbs) because they feel tired and need energy. Their metabolism is lower because they are sleep deprived. Sleep deprivation also decreases the amount of leptin in your body. Leptin is a hormone that tells your body to stop eating. The net result when you are short on sleep: slower metabolism and increased eating.[1]

As one PhD put it:

> *"It's not so much that if you sleep, you will lose weight, but if you are sleep-deprived, meaning that you are not getting enough minutes of sleep or good quality sleep, your metabolism will not function properly."*

The lesson? Don't short yourself on sleep. Get enough. 7 to 9 hours is far better than 4 to 5. For those who are habitually sleep deprived, many will find that they lose weight by simply getting more sleep.

(1) Source: Web MD

**Vital Key #3: Timing.**

Tanya used to weigh over 300 pounds. She was always the first to admit that her heredity seemed to work against her when it came to losing weight. She came from a family of big people. But even Tanya found that this third key to weight loss opened doors for her that she did not know existed.

> *"My doctor told me that we should try taking baby steps. He said eventually he wanted me to start walking 15 minutes a day, but there were other steps I could take first. He told me to stop eating after dinner each night—or for at least 3 hours before bedtime. I always used to snack at night. I would be in the kitchen at 11:00 PM, making myself sandwiches, eating half a bag of chips, or indulging in ice cream. I would easily eat an entire meal's worth of calories—and do it all just 30 minutes before my normal bedtime."*

So the first step Tanya took was to change this one simple eating habit—which was more a matter of timing than anything else. She could continue to eat what she wanted. She just had to refrain from doing it at bedtime.

> *"At first it was hard. I went to bed with an empty achy feeling like I was really hungry. My body was used to the habit. But it was time to kick the habit."*

Over the next 12 months Tanya lost 30 pounds, by changing nothing but this one simple factor in her eating habits.

Don't expect to lose 50 pounds in 30 days using this strategy. In fact, you should avoid attempts to lose large amounts of weight quickly altogether. The best way to make weight loss stick is to do it in a slow and natural manner. This will allow your metabolism to adjust naturally as your body changes, and will make weight-gain rebounds (common with fad diets) much less likely.

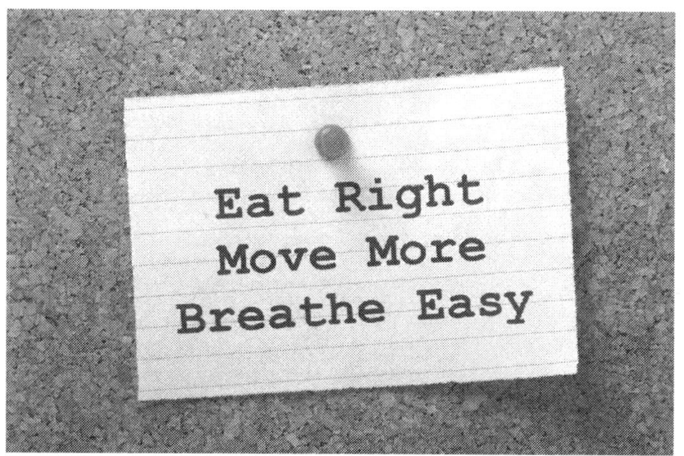


## Angry doctor reveals how to save up to 80% on popular medications (R047)

The Costco pharmacy is typically one of the most competitively priced for prescription drugs. Here's one example of how to make those prescription dollars go even further—whether you use Costco or another pharmacy.

June, a woman who lived through the great depression, has a knack for stretching a dollar. Her house is filled with signs of money-saving innovation… ideas that make every dollar count; making every purchase last as long as possible. One such idea can be found on the counter by June's collection of medications. Next to her pill bottles, she has a straight-edged razor blade.

Being someone who spends a lot of money on medications, June understands how costly prescriptions can be. So here's what she does:

1. June first makes all medication purchases with a "rewards" credit card that she pays off each month. Her card allows her to choose "bonus" cash back categories, and because of that she gets 3% back on all of her medication purchases.
2. Next, for medications where it is possible to do so, June has her doctor prescribe bigger doses than she actually needs. If she needs to take 25mg, her doctor prescribes 100mg tablets. She takes the tablets home, and cuts them into 4ths with a razor blade. She gets a 4 month's supply instead of a one month supply.

We've heard of other doctors doing this for patients, some will, some won't. And the pricing at some pharmacies makes it where the cost increases enough to offset the benefit. The key is to shop around and find out what pharmacy has the best price, and make sure that the price doesn't go up substantially for the larger dose tablets.

And of course, you have to get your medication in tablet form in order to do this. It won't work with capsules.

| Example Savings with Viagra | | |
|---|---|---|
| DOSAGE | NUMBER OF PILLS | PRICE |
| 50 MG | 10 | $327.51 |
| 100 MG | 5 | $168.44 |
| Savings Using This Method: | | $159.07 |

## Natural diabetes treatment proven to reduce blood sugar 31.9% in the first 30 days (R048)

There are a number of herbal remedies showing promise in the treatment and prevention of diabetes and associated symptoms. The problem is that the "supplement" industry as a whole is heavy on claims but super-light on *proof*.

One such remedy receiving considerable support in clinical research is known as "Banaba", or by its scientific name: Lagerstroemia speciosa L. Banaba is a species of crepe myrtle found in the Philippines. For hundreds of years the leaves from the tree have been used to make medicine.

The primary active constituent in Banaba is believed to be corosolic acid, though there is evidence other compounds in the extract may also help. The most popular supplement form is known as GlucoTrim, available in a high-potency soft-gel form.

*Just how effective might Banaba be?* Consider the following from Pub Med[1]:

*"The antidiabetic activity of a Banaba extract standardized to 1% corosolic acid in a soft gel capsule formulation has been examined. Ten type 2 diabetic subjects were given 32 mg or 48 mg of the product (0.32 and 0.48 mg corosolic acid, resp.) daily for 2 weeks. A 30% decrease in blood glucose levels was reported after the 2 weeks. It is not clear whether the observed effect was due to corosolic acid, the tannin components or a combination thereof."*

One user reported starting Banaba after receiving a high blood sugar report from her doctor. Within weeks of starting the extract, the blood sugar normalized plus she had lost weight.

Stories like this—offering a lot of anecdotal evidence—are quite common. Most people experience **drops in blood sugar between 10% and 30%**. And the benefits appear to increase over time. Some people have reported a 70% reduction in blood sugar over the course of several months.

(**NOTES:** There is a patented version of the product known as "Glucotrim" - believed to have better absorption making it more effective. It's available from SwansonVitamins.com and other supplement retailers. Supplement is most effective when combined with a low glycemic diet.)

(1) http://www.ncbi.nlm.nih.gov/pmc/articles/PMC3468018/

## Secret company keeps a "medical" credit report on you! Here's how to get a copy (R054)

There is a type of "medical" credit bureau few people know about. It's called the MIB Group, formerly the Medical Information Bureau. This company keeps track of medical information on certain individuals, and shares the information with its member companies. It's like a credit bureau for your health, and as such it is subject to the laws of the Fair Credit Reporting Act (FCRA).

Here's the thing to understand about the MIB Group:

It <u>only</u> exists as a tool for *insurance companies*.

It is owned by the roughly 500 member insurance companies in the U.S. and Canada. Known as a "data exchange", the insurance companies share information about applicants for the benefit of the group of insurers.

Specifically, the MIB Group tends to the underwriting needs of **life and health insurance companies**. From their website:

*"MIB's Underwriting Services are used exclusively by MIB's member life and health insurance companies to assess an individual's risk*

*and eligibility during the underwriting of life, health, disability income, critical illness, and long-term care insurance policies."*

What this means - if you are not going to apply for life insurance or health insurance, your MIB report (if you have one) may not matter much at all. According to the company's website, **you will not have an MIB report at all "unless you have applied for individually underwritten life or health insurance in the last seven years."**[1]

To find out if you have an MIB report—and to find out what is on it if you do—call the MIB Group at 1-866-692-6901. You can also visit their website at http://www.mib.com.

(1) Source: www.mib.com

## New type of identity theft which threatens to rob you of more than your credit (R349)

There is a new and growing threat in the world of identity theft that could hurt much more than your credit score. In typical cases of identity theft, the thief opens fraudulent credit accounts or otherwise uses the victim's credit for their own benefit. With the "new" identity theft—which I predict will eventually be more common than credit-based identity theft—the consequences of the crime could be life threatening. Welcome to the world of **medical identity theft…**

In the credit world, records are kept of your financial activities. In the medical world, records are kept of your health-related activities, illnesses, and doctor's office visits. Are you allergic to a certain drug? Chances are it will be in your healthcare records—commonly referred to as your "medical history". These records are there, first and foremost, for your safety.

But what happens when an identity thief obtains care under your name? In today's world of high-cost healthcare, today's "medical identity theft" is an all-too-real danger. Here's how it works:

- An identity thief uses phishing, theft, or other techniques to obtain your medical plan information and necessary identity details.
- The identity thief uses this information to obtain medical care posing as you.
- You get "EOB" (explanation of benefits) statements from your insurance carrier, and maybe even medical bills, for the care obtained by the identity thief.
- You get stuck with the bill and incorrect information attached to your medical history, which could be life threatening or otherwise hurt your ability to get the care and services you need.

Think about it. The ID thief could have cancer, AIDs, or any number of other life threatening conditions preventing you from getting life insurance or other benefits if the thief's health issues show up in your medical history.

Furthermore, because the **treatment they receive will be shown as your own treatment**, a doctor could make a decision down the road based on "your" medical history and inadvertently include the history of the identity thief.

If the doctor makes the "wrong" decision based on this incorrect information, the results could be devastating. And if your medical plan has benefit limits, those limits could quickly be exhausted by the fraudulent use of your plan benefits.

The most damaging and dangerous form of medical ID theft is referred to as "medical impersonation", and there are steps you can take that will help prevent it. The three biggest things you can do are:

1. **Protect Your Plan Information.** Never, EVER share your insurance card or medical plan information with anyone except the doctor's offices and hospitals you intend to do business.
2. **Never** provide medical information to unknown or unverified parties over the phone or internet. (Don't provide plan details for "health surveys" or similar telemarketing schemes.)
3. Be skeptical of any service or unexpected free benefit requiring you to disclose your medical plan information. Some of these schemes can be elaborate, such as "free health screenings" where you are asked for your plan information as part of a seemingly routine set of questions.

Next, you need to know how to detect possible medical identity theft as fast as possible. Here are the things you should do:

1. Always review the "Explanation of Benefits" statements from your insurance provider. These statements are notoriously confusing and hard to decipher, but they should still be reviewed. If you get an "EOB" statement and do not remember getting care, then follow the steps below ("What to Do If You Think You're a Victim…") immediately.
2. Know the doctors, nurses, hospitals, and other medical facilities you use. Know when you have visited. If possible, know the names of the people you deal with. *Why?* Because this will make it easier to detect problems, as any name that you **don't** recognize will be a red flag. Because if they know you and someone comes to the same facility *impersonating* you, the fraud could be prevented.
3. Review your "regular" credit reports as well as your MIB report regularly, and look for possible fraudulent activity.

**What to Do If You Think You're a Victim of Medical Identity Theft**

If you think you may be a victim of medical identity theft, here are the steps you should take:

1. Notify your insurer by phone immediately.
2. File a police report.
3. Place a fraud alert on your consumer credit reports.
4. Send copies of the police report with a letter to your insurance provider, healthcare providers, and the 3 major credit bureaus.
5. Contact any possibly affected medical providers (including those the thief used to commit fraud) and attempt to have your medical records corrected. You may need copies of your police report and other evidence of the crime.
6. Review your "MIB" file to verify that no fraudulent medical history has been connected to it. (Note: this is generally unlikely as MIB files apply only to insurance transactions, but if you have been a victim of medical identity theft you should continue to check your MIB file for up to a couple of years to verify that the fraud has not affected it or "spread".)
7. Continue to review your consumer credit files with the major credit bureaus to watch for fraudulent medical collections or other accounts, and dispute any accounts as they come up.

## What disability insurers don't want you to know (R078)

If you become disabled and tap Social Security for benefits, your payout is usually a small percentage of your earnings.

So many people look to their group disability coverage, if their employer provides it or they obtain disability insurance through an association typically having something to do with their profession or they buy coverage themselves on the open market.

Regardless of where you get coverage, you need to understand that the way the law is written, the **insurers have the upper hand**, and starting with the fact that you cannot receive punitive damages for employer-sponsored policies should the disability insurer mistreat you.

The absence of punitive damages means most lawyers won't even talk with you, and the insurers know you are unlikely to pursue them on your own.

**Here's how group disability insurers sidestep paying you.**

If you can work in your current occupation, but not your current job - you get zero. What does this mean?

Let's say you are a bartender in a historic landmark building with high ceilings where part of your job is to climb a ladder each day and 'turn' the wine.

So now you are injured and can no longer climb the ladder. But the insurance company will say **you can still work in 'your occupation'** and you must obtain a job where you simply serve drinks.

**You won't receive the benefits you thought you would.**

How do they do that? Simple. They **deduct** your Social Security, any state benefits, worker's comp, pension payments, retirement distributions and in some grave cases the settlement you received as a result of your disability.

What's worse, they can even deduct eligible Social Security benefits even if you don't claim them!

Is your job making you a little nuts or getting on your nerves? Well you had better get better in 2 years or less because that is all the insurer will cover - even if your doctor says you can't return to work.

And even if you are totally disabled, it must be from working in an occupation for you to receive benefits beyond 2 years.

So let's say you drive a bus and lose both legs in an accident, the insurer will say you could go work as a ticket taker at a toll booth or some other occupation not requiring mobility.

**The self-employed have a different set of, hurdles designed to deny your claim or wear you out so you stop asking.**

You may be asked for many years of tax returns. And you'll have to create a **monthly** profit and loss statement, something most self-employed don't have.

So you either need to start feeling better fast or get bogged down in over-burdening paperwork requests designed to deny your claim.

And then there is the **'capable of working in any profession'** escape clause. So if you spent 30 years as a master electrician and cannot do that job, the insurer will contend there are other jobs you can do, like become a fast food worker.

One **big trap** the self employed fall into is waiting to make a claim. Certainly if you provide your own income and become disabled, you are scrambling daily just to deal with everything.

The insurer will say your not filing an immediate claim taints their ability to investigate and will deny you. Read the fine print on your window to file claims because if you don't, they don't care if you can lift your head - they won't pay.

The take away from this report is - most people won't receive the amount they believe they will should they become disabled (and many won't get a penny.)

## The "non-surgical" back pain solution proven to work (R100)

"If you have back pain, don't get surgery."

That's what Chuck Wilson says. His doctor recommended back surgery (which is, by the way, one of the most over-performed and often unnecessary surgeries) for his painful back problems, and Chuck took the bait. According to Chuck, he is much worse off now than he was before…

"I can barely move now. I'm always stiff. I always feel just a little out of whack. And I'm stuck with it for the rest of my life."

For most ailments, surgery should be seen as a last resort. Of all the patients of various surgeries, those who have undergone back surgery are the most likely to warn others of the problems associated with it. "Wait and see if you can find a solution without it" is common advice.

One study found that as many as 80% of back injury patients have muscular injuries which are difficult to diagnose… and many of those end up getting surgeries they don't need to fix structural problems that either don't exist or aren't the real cause of their pain.[1]

Luckily, there are non-surgical back pain solutions clinically proven to work. Let's talk about them now…

**Stretches and Exercise**

The value of basic stretching and exercise cannot be emphasized enough. Most people who have back pain who take up a regular exercise regimen designed to heal and strengthen their back **show a reduction in pain of 50%** or more.

The key to helping your back out (and your hips), is strengthening your "core" muscle groups. This means you should focus on exercises and stretches targeting your back, sides, and stomach.

The most common exercises effective for reducing or eliminating back pain are:

- Laying flat on the floor with knees bent at a 45 degree angle, and pressing your lower back to the floor.
- Working from the same position above, with your lower back pressed to the floor; gently pull one knee at a time up towards your chest.
- The same as above can be done standing up, often in a door frame to provide stability.
- Lay on your stomach with your legs out straight behind you. Lift one leg at a time off the ground a few inches and hold. Repeat.
- Lay on your stomach with your legs straight behind you. With your face down, raise your arms a few inches above the ground, and hold.
- Roll up a towel and place it on the floor. Lie down with the towel lining your spine. Then try to squeeze the towel between your shoulder blades, and hold.
- In a "push-up" like position, with your legs straight and your feet on the ground, balance on one hand with your arm outstretched. Switch and repeat with other arm.
- Balance on one leg, and put the other leg up on a stool or chair. Carefully and gently lean forward until you feel stretching in your back and leg muscles.

Many of the exercises mentioned above, and more specifically designed exercises to target areas of pain, can be found in a book titled *Somatics, reawakening the mind's control of movement, flexibility and health* – by Thomas Hanna.

### TENS Units and Muscle Stimulators

Another powerful method of back pain relief is the use of TENS units and muscle stimulators.

These units work by sending electrical impulses into the muscles of your back. They are portable; battery powered, and for many people, provide substantial relief after the very first use.

One user of a TENS unit reported:

*"Before I started using it, I could barely walk. Barely sit. I slept poorly because every movement I made—even in my sleep—involved a lot of pain. After the first use, I still had some pain but could walk a little easier and didn't feel as tight. After two days of use, my back pain was substantially better and I was back to sleeping like a baby at night."*

TENS units can be found for $30 to $50 (and up) online and in most drug stores. Some units are more expensive, but the cost may not be justified. Many less expensive units perform just as well. Pay attention to the cost of replacement pads and cables, as those are the things most likely to need replacement occasionally. For $50 or less you should be able to get a convenient, portable, battery powered unit that will be sufficient for most needs.

TENS units and exercises are common and effective non-surgical back treatments, but there is one more highly effective method that may surprise you…

### The Dr. Sarno "Mind Body" Method

Dr. Sarno begin treating back pain in the 1970s at the Rusk Institute in the New York University Medical Center, where he was head of the outpatient department.

In treating hundreds and thousands of patients for back pain with the conventional approach, Dr. Sarno became frustrated by the lack of results. Why? Because his results were the same as everyone else's, a large percentage of patients never got better..

At this point, Dr. Sarno began asking questions and doing his own research. He knew there had to be more to back pain than just physical abnormalities or what shows up on an x-ray or scan. He started to notice patterns in people's pain. Not just back pain, but pain in the shoulder, hips, knees and many other types of physical body pain.

One interesting study published in 1994 in the *New England Journal of Medicine* reports MRIs being performed on 98 people with no history of back pain. Yet the researchers, led by Maureen Jensen, discovered 64% of people had various physical abnormalities on their MRI.

Some subjects had bulging disks, herniations and so on, yet, no pain. Dr. Sarno realized this was information most doctors were unaware of.

The key was the stress was NOT conscious but rather unconscious, primarily unconscious anger buried in the nervous system.

This is where it gets tricky. Because while Dr. Sarno's success rate is about 90%, the downside is about 80% of people are unwilling to accept the diagnosis. In other words, they are unable to accept that their pain is not physical, but rooted in their unconscious emotions.

**What are the links between unconscious emotions and back pain?**

**The link is buried emotions, primarily unconscious anger**, having a negative impact upon the autonomic nervous system. This creates a mild oxygen deprivation in muscles ligaments or tendons which in turn creates physical pain and many other symptoms.

The autonomic nervous system runs your body on "autopilot", from your heart beating to your lungs breathing to your eyes blinking. But it also runs unconscious responses.

For example, if you get anxious and your palms sweat, it's your autonomic nervous system working. If you get nervous with a police car driving behind you and your heart rate increases, again, that's your "autonomic" nervous system.

There are a number of health issues from muscle and tendon pain to chronic fatigue, fibromyalgia, acid reflux, irritable bowel syndrome and migraine headaches - which are all caused by what Dr. Sarno refers to as tension myositis syndrome or tension mind-body syndrome (TMS).

The theory is the body creates symptoms as a distraction to keep the buried emotions from coming into the conscious. Or in other words, having unconscious emotions come to the surface and be experienced in the conscious realm. The symptoms are a distraction created by the body.

**What are the steps that you should take to relieve back pain if you suspect it is caused by unconscious emotions?**

Well thousands of people over the years have improved their health and wellbeing just by reading one or all of Dr. Sarno's books. Because his concepts are difficult to accept, patients who read the book several times seem to benefit the most.

The bottom line of his books is this. Make a list of all the pressures you have in your life and review your list ten to 15 min. twice a day. What happens in this process - is you will start to get deeper and add issues to the list and they are the pressures which are buried in your unconscious.

This practice helps you to become consciously aware of the unconscious negative emotions. When you combine this process along with accepting that your pain is 100% emotionally-based and 0% physical, your body no longer needs to create the distraction by creating physical symptoms in the form of pain.

Crazy as it sounds, **it does work**! I know because I read his book and applied what I learned to overcome my back pain.

The most shocking part is buried negative emotions creating physical ailments can also be traced to many other problems beyond back pain. I highly suggest starting with Dr. Sarno's book "The Mind-Body Prescription". Then move on to his book "Healing Back Pain". And finally, the last book "The Divided Mind".

(1) Source: www.bottomlinepublications.com

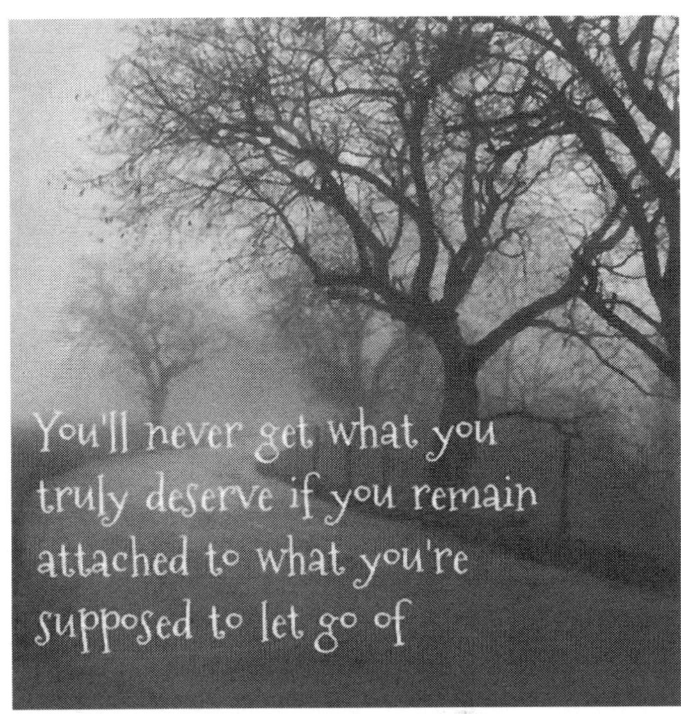


## The best beverage for avoiding kidney stones (R101)

Doctors have always advised drinking lots of liquids to prevent kidney stones.

About 1 out of 5 men and 1 out of 10 women endure kidney stones at least once in their lifetime.

Surprisingly, there are beverages other than water that clinical studies show effective for preventing kidney stones.

In a study first published in the *Clinical Journal of the American Society of Nephrology*, conducted by the department of internal medicine at Catholic University of the Sacred Heart in Rome, Italy...

...they reported results from analyzing the dietary habits of almost two hundred thousand who participated for 8 years during the course of 3 studies.

Top of the results in the category of beverages for **lowering the incidence of kidney stones was beer, followed by wine**. Yes, beer.

**Coffee** was almost as effective as beer and wine, while **orange juice** and **tea** were next.

Coming as no surprise for increasing the risk of kidney stones are consumption of sodas sweetened with **sugar** and then **fruit punch**.

So if you want to significantly **lower your risk** of developing kidney stones...

...drink orange juice with your breakfast,

...enjoy your morning coffee,

...take afternoon tea,

...and sip in moderation a glass of wine or beer in the evening.

But most of all, **avoid the sugary drinks**, especially sodas and fruit punch or 'blends' masquerading as fruit juice. And please don't consume anything containing "high fructose corn syrup."

## Three minerals many are over-dosing on are proven to cause memory loss (R103)

There are three minerals[1] in many of the foods you eat and the vitamins/supplements you take which could lead to memory loss and even Alzheimer's. According to numerous studies, these minerals:

- Are present at higher concentrations in Alzheimer's patients.
- Can impair brain function in otherwise healthy adults.

*What are they?*

First up we have **iron**. Iron is in many multi-vitamins. Many foods are also fortified with iron (example: breakfast cereals). Many more foods are naturally high in iron, such as:

- meats
- poultry
- seafood
- beans and peas
- eggs
- nuts and seeds

Most people get enough iron from the regular diet. Adding more iron vitamins/supplements —and even from food—is bad news for your brain. In one study, people with more iron in their blood performed poorly on cognitive tests compared to those with lower/normal amounts. In another study, high levels of iron in the blood were linked to the development of Alzheimer's.

Next, we have **zinc** which has been linked to improving the immune system, skin health, and proper sexual function. Like iron, excess zinc has been linked to Alzheimer's disease. **Also like iron, excess zinc intake typically occurs through the use of supplements and multi-vitamins** containing zinc. You can also get too much zinc from eating foods fortified with zinc (cereals) or foods naturally high in zinc, such as red meat, poultry, oysters, whole grains, and milk products.

And finally, there is **copper**. Many supplements containing zinc also have copper, because supplementing zinc can actually cause a copper deficiency. Like zinc and iron, most diets deliver the minimum daily allowance (even more) of zinc.

Foods high in copper include oysters, shellfish, whole grains, beans, nuts, potatoes, dark leafy greens, cocoa, and black pepper. While copper is healthy in proper amounts—promoting proper enzyme function, heart health, and bone strength—too much copper may have adverse effects. In one study, those with the best mental function and the least problems with long term and short term memory were those with the least copper in their blood. In other studies excessive copper has been linked to impaired mental function.

Together, these three minerals comprise the **"deadly 3"** for your brain. They promote free radicals and lead to impaired brain function. In short, excessive supplementation of these minerals is bad for your brain.

*"But aren't vitamins and supplements supposed to be good for you?"*

Yes. They are *supposed* to be. But in the world of nutrition you need to review all the facts before you simply start taking stuff. Keep reading to learn more about…

(1) Source: http://pcrm.org

## RESEARCH REVEALS: long term use of this vitamin increases cancer risk (R118)

Americans spend over $14 *billion* on non-vitamin, non-mineral supplements each year.[1] Over one third of the U.S. population over the

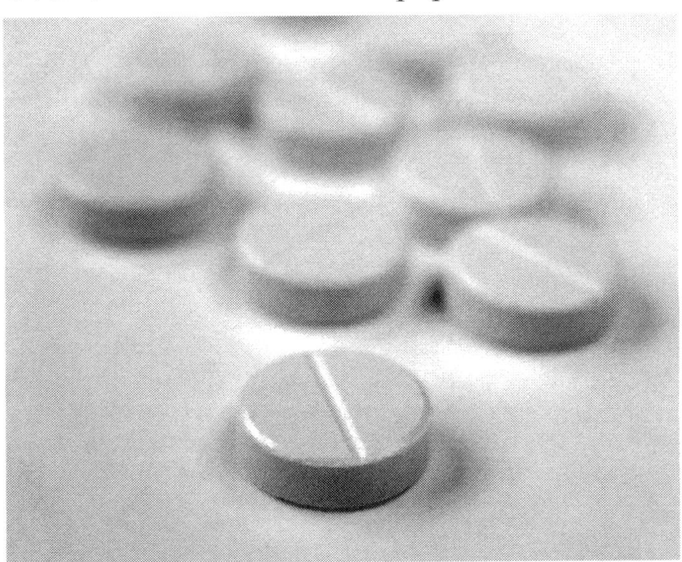

age of one takes a regular multivitamin/mineral supplement.[2] Unfortunately, according to sources, the people who are most likely to take these supplements are the people who need them the least.[3] Regarding multi-vitamin use, the National Institute of Health states that:

*"Several studies have found that MVM users tend to have higher micronutrient intakes from their diet than nonusers. Ironically, the populations at highest risk of nutritional inadequacy who might benefit the most from MVMs are the least likely to take them."*

*So just what are the effects of vitamin and supplement use for those who do take them?*

The answer may surprise you.

In numerous studies, vitamins and supplements have been shown to have little or no effect on longevity and long-term overall health.

For example one study published in the Journal of the National Cancer Institute found that vitamin E supplements can double a man's prostate cancer risk if man has low levels of selenium.

Other studies covering commonly touted "brain" supplements, such as including Vitamins E, C, the B vitamins, omega-3 fatty acids, and multivitamins showed no improvement in cognitive function whatsoever in persons with mild to moderate dementia. From the Annals of Internal Medicine:

*"Evidence involving tens of thousands of people randomly assigned in many clinical trials shows that β-carotene, vitamin E, and possibly high doses of vitamin A supplements increase mortality and that other antioxidants, folic acid and B vitamins, and multivitamin supplements have no clear benefit."*

In case you missed it, the conclusion here was - **"multivitamin supplements have no clear benefit"**. Worse, supplementation with some vitamins actually may *increase* mortality.[4]

**An important note—before you banish vitamins from your diet:** Some have criticized the authors who reached the above conclusion, in part because they didn't address certain valid uses of vitamin and mineral supplements, and failed to consider certain large studies that actually support their use.

One example of when supplements might be beneficial is when prescribed for certain acute conditions or for well-established preventative reasons. Pregnant women, for example, should take pre-natal vitamins which have been established to prevent various birth defects. Doctors may prescribe Vitamin C or other vitamins to treat a wide variety of conditions… and in many such cases the vitamins are a more effective and safer treatment than their drug-based counterparts.

*(With that said, it still stands true that the people who are most likely to use (and to be able to afford) vitamins and supplements for "general nutrition" and "well being" purposes are also the people who are least likely to need them.)*

**What can you do?**

The best advice is to review your vitamins and dosages with your doctor. Don't expect your doctor to be up on the latest research for every vitamin, however. Come prepared with the information on studies and related concerns.

(1) Source: http://nccam.nih.gov/news/2009/073009.htm

(2) Source: http://ods.od.nih.gov/factsheets/MVMS-Health-Professional/

(3) Source: http://www.ncbi.nlm.nih.govpubmed/17209206

(4) Source: http://annals.org/article.aspx?articleID=1789253

## The "non-vegetarian" diet clinically proven to reverse brain tumors and cancer (R104)

When Alex and Susan Rider's newborn baby had his first seizure, they were petrified. The boy was born with several serious problems, including a severe seizure disorder. Once the seizures started, they seemed relentless. Thirty to forty seizures a day were not uncommon. When Alex and Susan took their baby to see a specialist, the Doctor put the infant on what is known as the *Ketogenic Diet*.

In the eyes of Alex and Susan Rider, the Ketogenic diet saved their little boy's life. He is growing and thriving now, with comparably very few seizures, and the Ketogenic diet is what made it happen.

What is a Ketogenic diet? In short, it is a diet very high in fat and very low in carbohydrates. It's typically used to treat severe seizure disorders, but shows considerable promise in the fight against cancer.

In one study, a restricted calorie ketogenic diet was shown to have **anti-tumor** effects in mice and humans with malignant brain tumors.[1] Other studies support this by pointing to low-or-no carbohydrate intake as a potential way of fighting other deadly cancers.[2]

This goes against the most common western dietary advice, and might lend some credence to the "low carb" craze. Study after study has shown **calorie restriction lengthens lifespans** in animals. Combine this with the studies about the high fat ketogenic diet, and one might start to seriously question American dietary habits. Could this be why cancer seems to run rampant in the U.S., considering the high carb, high sugar diets most Americans consume?

The ketogenic diet may be a vital piece of the puzzle for fighting cancer and other diseases. Evidence of its usefulness against a variety of cancers abounds. In the future, the traditional guidelines we have followed for dietary baselines (such as the food pyramid) could very well be turned on their heads by these and similar findings.

(For more information, see the book Cancer as a Metabolic Disease by Thomas Seyfried, and Ketogenic Diets by John Freeman, MD.)

(1) http://www.ncbi.nlm.nih.gov/pubmed/17313687/

(2) http://www.ncbi.nlm.nih.gov/pubmed/17999389/

# The truth about cell phones and cancer (R109)

Way back in 2000, Margaret Thatcher's chief science advisor warned the Royal College of Physicians to suggest teenagers not use cell phones.

The issue is cancer caused by radiation and the latency period can be decades, so we've yet to really find out the full effect of cell phone radiation because the widest proliferation of handheld phones is just a couple of decades old.

Let me ask you, have you EVER read the fine print in the manual that comes with your cell phone?

Android phones suggest keeping the phone several centimeters from the stomach of pregnant women or teenagers. And the iPhone warns you to not put it in your pocket where I often put mine!

**Recently the World Health Organization carefully looked at all the studies available at the time and put cell phones in the same cancer-causing category as pesticides and heavy metals!**

Dr. Devra Davis, author of the book Disconnect, says "cell phone radiation weakens membranes everywhere."

Now where did the word 'radiation' come from, aren't cell phones radio signals? Dr. Davis adds, "a cell phone is a 2-way microwave radio."

### Fight For Your Right To Party

Do you remember when the Beastie Boys exploded on the music scene almost 30 years ago with their break out hit, "You've got to fight for your right to party"?

Well a couple of years ago one of the cofounders succumbed to a gland cancer of his left cheek. And there has been a steep increase in this type of cancer since 2001, in fact the biggest increase in the last 30 years!

Are the cancer incubation periods for the radiation damage just now showing up?

With 40% of U.S. homes ditching their landline in favor of a cell phone, one would have to wonder if 20-30 years from now will there be an explosion in the cancer rate because of self-inflicted exposure to radiation?

Fortunately, today people text more than they talk or use various social apps to keep in touch with friends and family, including old school email.

So if you are not talking, are you safe? Not necessarily. Even if you are not using your cell phone, it is sending a 'ping' to towers to say "I'm here." And that is an electromagnetic transmission.

### How Low Can You Go

If you are planning on having children or you want to one day be a proud grandparent, listen up.

There have been numerous studies linking the electromagnetic radiation to low sperm count.

Studies have been done in labs and others were done at male fertility clinics.

On top of that, this electromagnetic radiation can possibly alter your DNA, according to Dr. Martin Blank, PhD - one of the top experts in this field in the U.S.

You can read more about radiation and your DNA in the International Journal of Radiation Biology, April 2011.

Furthermore, the cell phone industry researched usage in 13 countries and concluded there is a 40% increase in brain cancer after only 1,640 hours of cell phone use.

Some teenagers surpass that many hours of use in a single year, much less a lifetime!

**Take These Precautions**

So what can you do to protect yourself while enjoying the convenience of your Smartphone which is becoming more like a personal computer every new product release?

Top of the list is - get a Bluetooth **headset** or use the wired **headphones** that come with most models, the same ones you listen to music on.

However, Andrew Goldsworthy BSc PhD of the Imperial College London says any pulsed radio frequency can be dangerous and Bluetooth uses pulsed radio frequency, exposing you to radiation, just not as much as having the cell phone to your ear.

And you may not be safer using the wired headset because it is believed the 'wire' works as an antenna, transmitting the radiation.

Still, Bluetooth will greatly reduce the amount of radiation you are exposed to from cell phone use, but your concern would then need to be where you carry your cell phone so you are not exposing your internal organs.

Next, keep abreast of all innovations in the cell phone market to limit your exposure to radiation.

So what can you do to protect yourself?

According to Dr. Frank Lipman, who bills himself as "The Voice of Sustainable Wellness," there are a number of ways to protect yourself against electromagnetic radiation.

**Use your speakerphone** and keep the phone about 12 inches from your body.

If you must keep your phone near all day, try positioning the antenna facing away from your body.

And many people don't realize, if you are **in a poor area of reception, your cell phone actually gives off more radiation** than when you see 'full bars' on your signal indicator.

You would be advised to **text more** than talking and again, hold the phone at least 12 inches from your body.

Whenever possible, use a landline and remember cordless phones also emit radiation.

Finally, whenever possible, turn off your Bluetooth and wi-fi 'connectivity' on your cell phone when not in use because even while idle, both will emit 'pings' which contain electromagnetic transmissions.

A post on the Mayo Clinic's website says, "After evaluating several studies on the possibility of a connection between cellphones and glioma and a noncancerous brain tumor known as acoustic neuroma, members of the International Agency for Research on Cancer — part of the World Health Organization — agreed that there's limited evidence that cell phone radiation is a cancer-causing agent (carcinogenic). **As a result, the group classified radiofrequency electromagnetic fields as possibly carcinogenic to people**."

However, the article does point out there is often a lag time for increased cancer rates and the determination of a new cancer-causing agent, as was the case with tobacco.

If you would like to know the radiation levels of your cell phone, the Federal Communications Commission maintains a database where you can check your phone's levels.

Just visit http://www.fcc.gov/oet/ea/fccid

Basically, the FCC does not approve any phone for sale in the U.S. if it exceeds the prescribed safe SAR (specific absorption rate) or the rate your body tissue absorbs radiation during a call assumed to last for 30 minutes.

The bottom line is, your cell phone does emit electromagnetic radiation and the more you use it, the higher your exposure and risk of developing health issues.

## 9 out of 10 cat and dog owners are poisoning their pets by not knowing this (R362)

*The New York Times* recently reported about "jerky treats" making pets sick. In fact, since 2006, more than 3,600 pets became ill and 580 died, after consuming a "jerky" made and marketed for pets.

According to the book entitled *Buyer Beware: The Crimes, Lies and Truth about Pet Food,* the pet food industry is "the only food industry given FDA permission to violate federal food safety law."

A quick Internet search using the keywords "the truth about pet food" uncovers numerous websites all with a common theme...

...most commercially produced pet food includes waste ingredients you would never feed your pet (if you knew about them).

So there is little wonder reports like *The New York Times* article keep surfacing or worse, the Chinese pet food poisoning in recent years.

Even if this report reviewed every pet food on the market today, the same baseline would apply:

1. Cheap pet food has lots of nasty stuff and you are gambling your pet's health.
2. Quality pet food is expensive, sometimes out of the financial reach of the average pet owner.

So what do you do? Continue feeding your pet the cheap stuff and hope for the best?

The facts are, diseases in pets are on the rise, just as diabetes, cancer and other problems keep increasing in the human population **as a result of "processed" food**.

Well there is some good news, according to Dr. Laurie Coger who operates the website www.thewholisticvet.com - feeding your pet raw food is actually cheaper.

Dr. Coger advises pet owners to buy human food in bulk and freeze it. She claims her pet food (fit for humans) costs between $1 to $1.50 per pound, as compared to $3 and up for 'quality' pet food.

What Dr. Coger does is buy in bulk and take advantage of sales and stocks her freezer with **chicken legs, duck necks, turkey hearts and livers**.

Plus the Dr. says feeding her pets a raw diet means less vet bills for things such as ear infections or gastrointestinal problems. And **saving just 2 vet visits per year can easily put an extra $100 - $200 in your pocket**.

So remember, cheap pet food should be avoided because it contains waste products causing illnesses, thus increasing your trips to the vet.

Quality pet food can cost as much as 3 times more than following Dr. Coger's advice of buying raw food in bulk and freezing it until needed.

What to do: Other than cooking extra for dinner and feeding it to your pet, the bulk buying and freezing of raw food is the most cost effective and healthiest alternative for pet owners. If this isn't practical for one reason or another, the next best bet is a high quality pet food.

## How to spot the early onset of Alzheimer's and the first thing to do if diagnosed (R106)

Anyone who has had a loved one suffer from Alzheimer's disease knows it is extremely sad and scary. There is no cure for Alzheimer's disease, but there are steps anyone can take to delay the onset of the worst of symptoms when the disease is detected.

In "early onset" of Alzheimer's—the victim of the disease starts showing symptoms in their 30s, 40s, or 50s. In very rare cases, early onset Alzheimer's is hereditary. In most cases, however, an exact cause has not been identified.

Luckily there has been a great deal of research on Alzheimer's patients and promising treatments.

### How to Spot the Early Onset of Alzheimer's

As of this writing there is no single test to detect Alzheimer's, though a possible candidate for quick and easy testing in the form of a nasal spray and exam is being developed. (This test, once in use, will detect certain harmful proteins often found in the nasal cavities of Alzheimer's patients.) Until this testing procedure is proven and available to the public, we have to rely on our vigilance and to detect the onset of the disease.

Here are the signs to look for:

#### 1. Memory Loss

Note that this isn't the run-of-the-mill "I forgot where I put my keys". Forgetfulness is normal and increases with age.

The type of memory loss to be concerned about are like **forgetting information immediately after being told**—needing to ask for the information repeatedly, heavy reliance on sticky notes and other memory aids, and forgetting various information normally not forgotten—especially recently learned information. (One relative of an Alzheimer's victim reported buying the victim flowers, and having to repeatedly remind the person who the flowers were for.) They may also misplace things—often in unusual spots—then have difficulty retracing their steps to find the missing item.

#### 2. Problems doing routine planning and activities

Another common sign of the onset of Alzheimer's is **trouble with planning events or following scheduled activities**. A person experiencing this symptom might have trouble scheduling plans for the future or handling money or managing numbers. They may have difficulty following any given list of instructions.

#### 3. Trouble with familiar tasks

A person experiencing the early onset of Alzheimer's may not be able to complete or comprehend once-familiar tasks, like balancing their checkbook or managing money, They may also struggle to drive or perform familiar tasks due to an upset in their perception or understanding of visual/spatial information.

#### 4. Trouble joining or following conversations, or with other speech-related tasks

Those experiencing the onset of Alzheimer's tend to repeat themselves in conversations. In some cases, the person may become confused and frustrated at not knowing what to say or how to say it. Unfortunately those experiencing the symptoms of Alzheimer's are **less likely to say "no" to telemarketers and salespeople**. They may end up buying everyday stuff in strange amounts or making purchases they don't need.

**5. Withdrawal**

Social symptoms similar to those often associated with depression are common in Alzheimer's patients. The person may stop attending favorite gatherings and even avoid social situations all together.

**6. Changes In Mood**

Alzheimer's victims often feel depressed or anxious even to the point of having anxiety attacks or becoming fearful. They may also experience episodes such as misplacing things, then becoming suspicious of others—thinking friends or relatives are stealing from them.

**7. Personality Changes or Other Alarming Changes**

Sharp personality changes or other changes that one would consider out of the ordinary and alarming should be cause for concern, especially if accompanied by any of the other warning signs we've covered. A person who was once kind and gentle may develop a bad temper or have other serious emotional disturbances.

**What to Do If You or a Loved One Are Diagnosed**

The most important thing you can do is take steps to be as healthy as possible. This might be diet changes, adding vitamins and supplements, or similar steps. Research has brought forth evidence that certain vitamins and supplements could be beneficial to victims of Alzheimer's.

Another treatment showing promise for those with early symptoms of Alzheimer's is known as "HBO" therapy, or "Hyperbaric oxygen therapy". Hyperbaric oxygen therapy uses a pressurized room or special chamber in which you typically sit or lay while breathing pure oxygen. According to studies, Hyperbaric Oxygen Therapy combined with Ginko Biloba—or either therapy administered separately—has shown some promise as possible way to improve cognitive function and play a "protective role" in the brain.

(Source: http://informahealthcare.com/doi/abs/10.3109/00207454.2012.690797, http://informahealthcare.com/doi/abs/10.3109/02699052.2010.504525)

## Amazing: Man cures 15 year prostate problem without drugs, diet or surgery (R107)

Tim Parks, a writer and professor, suffered from prostate issues for nearly 20 years.[1] To cure his symptoms and get better he tried everything from vitamins and herbs to changes in diet and nasty drugs laden with side effects. Sadly, nothing worked. His friend Carlo, a urologist, suggested surgery as a last resort. To avoid going under the knife, Tim began searching for an alternative.

During his research, he came across a book called "A Headache in the Pelvis" by David Wise and Rodney Anderson. Rather than focusing on physical symptoms, the book honed in on emotional distress for addressing tension in the body.

At first, Tim thought the book was nothing but a scam to promote the authors high-priced services at their Stanford clinic. But as he read the book with an open mind, he began the concept they were describing. Tension lodged in the body, very much fit the profile of not only Tim's personality, but could be the cause of his prostate issues.

Tim's journey was not easy, nor without frustration. But compared with surgery, it was a clearly better alternative. What Tim discovered was he was an incredibly tense individual. In fact, he was so wound up, he was not even aware of the turmoil in his body at an unconscious level.

It took time, but within just a couple weeks he noticed the symptoms subsiding. This proved he could get completely well if he stayed consistent with the program. In due time, he completely healed himself 100% of his prostate issues, with no changes in diet, no vitamins, no herbs and most important, no drugs.

The entire story is outlined in his book called "Teach Us to Sit Still - A Skeptics Search for Health and Healing". I can't remember the last time I read a 330 page book in three days, but that's exactly what happened when I began reading Tim Parks story. (And I don't even have prostate issues. I was just fascinated by the mind-body connection.)

You're probably wondering exactly what Mr. Parks did to reverse his prostate symptoms. The answer is both simple and complicated. Essentially all he did was work a little bit each day, less than an hour, to relieve the unconscious tension within his body. Once the unconscious tension was resolved, the symptoms went away. Although it sounds simple, there's more to it…

Trying to learn this process in one evening would be like trying to learn how to swim in one day. However, with consistent effort, and both the books previously mentioned, many people have been able to completely reverse their prostate symptoms and boost their well-being.

When you consider the side effects of prostate drugs and the low success rate of prostate surgery (not to mention the sacrifice) I would hardly call reading two books to get better, much of a gamble.

Either way, if you have prostate issues, I doubt you'll find either of the books boring.

(1)Source: Teach us To Sit Still, Timothy Parks

## 6 proven secrets to reduce anxiety (R092)

One fact of life is that we have *limited* time here on earth. Health issues, mental struggles, diseases, and illness can rob us of our precious time and perhaps worse—*take our focus away* from the things that matter in life. Anxiety is one of those things. It is one of those things that can rob you of your enjoyment of life—often needlessly—and yet some people spend their whole lives fighting it, feeling trapped, or feeling like an alien living in their own home.

If you struggle with anxiety, then this section is for you. Anxiety is usually either circumstantial and temporary, or generalized and chronic. Regardless of your particular case, the information provided here may give you some much needed relief.

The first key to getting better is understanding the fact that different remedies will be better fit for different causes. If you can determine the cause, finding the remedy should be easier. If you seem to have generalized anxiety and do not know the cause, experimentation may help you find a "cure" (and perhaps, give you clues as to the cause).

*(**Note:** Be sure to rule out medical causes of your anxiety troubles. Heart problems and thyroid problems can both produce anxiety-like symptoms.)*

As with any problem, there are multiple approaches to the anxiety problem. We'll break up the possible remedies by the approach:

1. Things you do.
2. Things you don't do.
3. Substances you take.
4. Substances you avoid the intake of.
5. Things you eat.
6. Things you avoid eating.

Let's get started with…

**Things You Do**

There are numerous steps that can be taken to reduce anxiety and even prevent anxiety attacks. Two of the most effective methods for systematically reducing and controlling anxiety are:

- Cognitive Behavioral Therapy (CBT), and…
- Acceptance and Commitment Therapy (ACT)

Now, right now you might be thinking things like:

*"But I don't need a therapist!"*

or…

*"I'm not going to spend that kind of money!"*

But listen… you can't rule out these methods based on cost or the stigma of therapy. And here's why:

You can do these at home, by yourself, for a fraction of the cost of "traditional" therapy. Studies have shown that for many real life cases the books describing these therapies do just as well as sessions with a therapist or drug treatments!

Visit your favorite bookstore, and look for a book on CBT or ACT. You'll usually find them in the Psychology or Self Help sections. If you're still doubtful, then do me a favor and prove me wrong. Learn about the methods, try them for a while, and if they don't help then I want to hear about it. (So far, we've gotten nothing but great reports.)

Aside from those two specific and useful strategies, there are other things that can be done.

For example, breath control and deep breathing are both extremely valuable for anxiety reduction. Try the following exercise:

- Breathe very slowly in, and then out, and count each in/out sequence as one breath. When you have done 1, think to yourself "one". When you have done 2, think to yourself "two", and so on.
- Continue this pattern all the way up to 60.
- Inevitably, at some point you will realize that you have become distracted and are no longer counting or breathing properly. If that happens don't get upset. Just reset, and breathe, and start over again from "one".
- Continue this until you successfully reach 60 without going off into the clouds.
- As you get better at it, you can progress from 60 to 70, and eventually on up to 100.

This simple exercise will teach you to breathe and to slow down. You'll have to sit in silence for some time, which for many can actually be a cause of anxiety… but with this exercise, the deep breathing offsets that and helps you to be more centered and controlled. In the end, the net result is **less anxiety**.

Another thing that you can do: *exercise*.

Expending energy and exercising is good for your nervous system along with everything else. A 30 minute period of vigorous exercise each day is enough to help balance your mental, emotional, and physical well-being.

Spending energy on an activity you love can also help reduce anxiety. And some hobbies can pay off more than others. Drummers, for example, have been shown to have lower overall cortisol levels than most people. (Cortisol is the stress hormone… the more of it you have, the worse shape you are in terms of anxiety, stress, and depression. Generally speaking, anything you can do to lower your cortisol levels is a good thing.)

You could also try **journaling** to reduce anxiety. Writing down the things on your mind can go a long way towards protecting you from the stress associated with them. One simple approach to journaling is to write daily lists of all of the things weighing on you and/or hanging over your head. Again, just getting them out on paper can be extremely valuable. (Note: Handwritten journals are recommended over typed or computer based journals.)

Another thing you can do is to <u>make sure you are getting proper sleep</u>. Sleeplessness and fatigue can cause anxiety, and your body will handle stress better overall if you are well rested.

The final thing you can do may sound counterproductive, but it has strong empirical support in the field of psychology.

Here it is:

<u>Purposely</u> expose yourself to the types of situations that cause you anxiety. Some methods would have you do it all at once in a flood, and others would have you start small and build up. Either method has merit and could work for you. Sometimes our tendency to avoid discomfort actually adds to it in the long run. Purposeful, controlled exposure is designed to reverse this trend.

Now let's move on to things you don't do…

**Things You Don't Do**

There are a number of things you shouldn't do with regards to your struggles with anxiety. Some may be surprising.

*What should you <u>not</u> do?*

Your typical list might include things like not going to crowded places or not watching certain types of TV shows. If those things are on your list, then you're already off on the wrong foot. Here's why:

The #1 rule for overcoming anxiety is to <u>not</u> avoid activities which you would normally do. One of the biggest mistakes people make is avoiding activities. Do crowds make you anxious? Don't avoid them. Remember that anxiety itself won't kill you, and while you might feel like you're having a heart attack, the truth is that you are not. It's time to take back your life. And that starts with taking back the activities that anxiety has stolen from you.

While you shouldn't avoid activities for the sake of avoiding anxiety, you should not necessarily do every activity that is offered to you. Here's the best rule I can give about this (I'll explain it in a moment):

Don't do things that you <u>don't want</u> to do. And don't over commit.

Another way of saying this is: "Learn to say NO."

In some research, a common thread among many anxiety suffers is a tendency to want to please others. Because of this desire to please others, many anxiety sufferers say "yes" far more than they should, and find that they have a hard time saying "no."

*How do you know if you could benefit from saying "no" more often?*

One method is to keep track of the activities you do in a week. For each activity, write "me" or "them" beside it. If you find that there are very few activities with the "me" label—leaving an overwhelming majority for "them—then you may have a problem with saying "yes" more than you should.

*How do you fix it if you find you say "yes" too much?*

Some experts recommend keeping track of the number of times you say yes each week versus the number of times you say no. One way to do this: buy a cheap click-counter from ebay, and carry it with you. Click it for every time you say "yes" to a request or activity. Doing this, you will teach yourself to be more aware of the instances in which you have a *choice* to say yes or no. Once you are aware of the opportunities, you can start to exercise your option to say "no" more often.

Another thing that you should NOT do is *lie*. Lying, believe it or not, can actually add a significant amount of stress and anxiety to your life. The act of lying itself increases the levels of stress hormones in your body, which will be counterproductive if you are aiming to be free from anxiety.

**Substances You Take**

Now it's time to talk about things like drugs and supplements. The drug companies would like you to believe that your best options are through their chemical substances. While there may be situations that warrant the use of prescriptions for anxiety, much of the time that is NOT the case.

There are several herbal alternatives that are proven to reduce anxiety, that are not habit-forming, and that are generally safe when taken with care.

Here are the most promising natural anxiety formulas:

- **B Vitamins**

Start with the basics. B Vitamins can help with nervous sytem health, and should be considered a first step to curbing problems related to anxiety and stress. A simple b-complex vitamin is a good place to start.

- **Magnesium**

Some anxiety suffers have been found to have low levels of magnesium. Other studies have found that magnesium has a calming effect. Taking a magnesium supplement daily, or even eating foods high in magnesium on a regular basis, can help to curb anxiety.

- **GABA**

Once I met with a man named Jeremy who had suffered from severe panic attacks. He told me stories of having attacks when he was driving, and almost wrecking his car. He genuinely thought he was having a heart attack at times. His anxiety/panic attacks were debilitating to say the least. They not only prevented him from enjoying many of his favorite activities, but also hurt his income and his work life.

*What finally ended his struggle?* GABA. GABA stands for Gamma-Aminobutyric Acid. He said when he started taking a regular regimen of GABA, his debilitating panic attacks ceased. Indeed, when I talked to Jeremy, he showed no signs of anxiety or discomfort. In fact, I had been around him in a professional setting for a couple of years before having our "anxiety" discussion and I had always thought of him as quite calm and collected.

As it turns out, there does seem to be some scientific support for GABA as an anxiety fighter. There are several forms that show varying degrees of promise. One such form is known as Picamilon, which combines GABA with niacin. In this form, the supplement is able to cross the blood-brain barrier and, in theory, have a greater clinical effect.

- **L-Theanine**

L-Theanine is found in green tea, can be taken in capsule form, and has been studied for its effects on stress, anxiety, and other ailments. According to research, L-Theanine promotes alpha-waves in the brain1 and shows promise in reducing stress and anxiety.

According to one user of L-Theanine that we spoke with, taking 200mg per day seemed to drastically reduce the level of stress during a particularly difficult time in her life. We've also heard reports of doctors prescribing L-Theanine for people going through stressful times.

Another user reported using L-Theanine combined with 5-HTP to successfully combat depression.

- **Holy Basil/Tulsi**

Tulsi is an East Indian cousin to basil. It can be purchased in capsule form, and can also be used in tea preparations. It has been used for things like controlling blood sugar, lowering stress levels, and reducing the negative effects of cortisol.

*One thing to keep in mind about supplements is this: some supplements are more fit to address anxiety for certain causes, and everyone's body is different. If you choose to use supplements, do so in a methodical and controlled manner... and if one thing doesn't seem to help, try another option.*

**Substances You Avoid Intake Of**

Just as some substances can help with anxiety problems, other substances can actually hinder your progress. Here is a list of substances that may contribute to feelings of anxiety:

- Caffeine
- Guarana (supplement ingredient)
- St. John's Wart (herbal supplement)
- Green tea extract (herbal supplement, caffeine content)
- Ephedra (herbal supplement ingredient)
- Ginseng
- Asthma medications
- Blood pressure medications
- Amphetamines
- Steroids
- Antidepressants
- phenylephrine/decongestants

Some of these may be medications that you need to be on for serious conditions. Obviously, you should not stop taking an important medication because of anxiety-like symptoms associated with it. Talk to your doctor about the symptoms/side-effects that you experience, and about possible approaches (including those here) to addressing the problem.

**Things You Eat**

The first thing to note here is that you *should* eat. In our busy world, we sometimes feel inclined to skip meals. Doing so can actually lead to tenseness and shakiness—both common symptoms of anxiety. So don't skip meals.

Another key is to make sure you are getting plenty of water. Some studies indicate that even slight dehydration can negatively affect your mood, producing anxiety-like symptoms.

The other key to eating—which may sound like common sense but is often missed—is to be sure that you are getting a proper balance of nutrients in your diet. You should have plenty of veggies, fruits, protein, and a moderate amount of healthy carbohydrates.

**Things You Avoid Eating**

Some foods and food additives have been reported to cause mood swings, anxiety symptoms, trouble concentrating, and more. Things you may want to avoid include:

- Foods with artificial food dyes (coloring)
- Foods with aspartame and other artificial sweeteners
- Foods with MSG or other chemical flavor enhancers
- Foods with high fructose corn syrup

Generally speaking, avoiding processed foods can go a long way towards contributing to better physical *and* mental health. Replacing those things with healthier whole foods can make a huge difference.

**A Comprehensive Approach**

One mistake people often make when tackling a problem like depression or anxiety is attempting to address the problem by addressing only one possible cause or condition related to it. For better results, it is best to approach anxiety from a holistic perspective. Don't just use prescriptions or supplements. Don't neglect the dietary steps and the emotionally valuable ideas like journaling. In other words, for the best results you should develop a plan that includes a variety of approaches, and apply them together. (Rather than "just another pill" to take, truly healing often involves a change in lifestyle.)

This lifestyle change can extend far into the reaches of your mind, especially with an issue like anxiety. Often there are subconscious emotional issues that flare up in the form of anxiety attacks and panic attacks. They may also show themselves as various pains and ailments such as back pain, stomach problems, or other seemingly "physical" problems. It's important to dig into the possible emotional forces involved with your struggles, as well as the physical and nutritional ones, and then approach the problem from a broad perspective and with an open heart.

(1) Source: www.ncbi.nlm.nih.gov/pubmed/18296328

## Five places to get free medical help for chronic conditions (R082)

When Jeremy and Diane's little girl was diagnosed with an increasingly common childhood cancer, their world was turned upside down. The expenses to treat their daughter—even with insurance—piled up to insurmountable amounts, putting them in debt.

Fundraisers for their little girl and campaigns to raise awareness about the disease replaced the mundane activities of their once "normal" life. Through their trouble and turmoil, they found a light in the darkness through organizations existing solely to help kids who are suffering from a serious illness.

It may surprise you to know that there are **numerous organizations dedicated to helping people with certain diseases and chronic health conditions**. We all need a "light in the darkness" sometimes, and if you find yourself facing a difficult health situation, you would be well advised to check out the organizations listed below that could help you.

**American Kidney Fund**
www.kidneyfund.org

**Association of Community Cancer Centers**
www.accc-cancer.org

**CancerCare**
www.cancercare.org

**Candlelighters Childhood Cancer Foundation**
http://candle.org/

**Caring Voice Coalition, Inc.**
www.caringvoice.org

**Chai Lifeline**
www.chailifeline.org

**Chemocare.com**
www.chemocare.com/lifeduring/financial_assistance_programs_for.asp

**Good Days Organization**
http://www.mygooddays.org/

**Geriatric Services of America**
www.geriatricservices.com

**HealthWell Foundation**
www.healthwellfoundation.org

**International Oncology Network (ION)**
www.iononline.com

**Leukemia and Lymphoma Society**
www.leukemia.org

**National Children's Cancer Society**
https://www.thenccs.org

**National Organization for Rare Disorders**
www.rarediseases.org

**Needy Meds**
www.needymeds.com

**Patient Access Network Foundation (PAN)**
https://panfoundation.org

**Patient Advocate Foundation Co-Pay Relief**
www.patientadvocate.org

**Patient Services Inc. (PSI)**
http://patientservicesinc.org/

**The Center for Medicare Advocacy**
www.medicareadvocacy.org

## The amazing hangover secret of a crazy millionaire (R351)

What if there was a hangover remedy that really worked? Think of the pain and suffering

that could be avoided. Imagine all the "day after" arguments which would never ensue? But most important, envision the millions of people who could wake up after a night of partying and just be plain happier.

Even though the following remedy may sound unbelievable, I've tested it multiple times myself as well as with friends and family. The truth is, there is an amazing hangover fix which works for about 80% of the population. Before I share it with you, let me confess I have no idea how it works. I just know it works, for me and 80% of the people who try it.

Before I go into detail, let's review some well-known remedies (when combined with the granddaddy of them all) will work wonders. Obviously, the best remedy or prevention for any hangover is to simply drink in moderation (or not drink at all). But if you do…

**PRELIMINARY STRATEGY #1:** The morning of the night you know you're going to be consuming large amounts of alcohol, begin hydrating as early as possible. I drink quality filtered or distilled water. A goal to shoot for would be to drink half your body weight in ounces. In other words, if you weigh 200 pounds, shoot to drink 100 ounces of water before you begin drinking alcohol in the evening.

The reason for this is, alcohol dehydrates you. So by hydrating your body in advance, you're in essence preparing yourself for the assault created by the alcohol and your system will be far more effective in dealing with it.

**PRELIMINARY STRATEGY #2:** Alcohol has a tendency to deplete the body of B vitamins. This is one reason beer drinkers will notice less of the hangover when drinking beer which is on tap (also known as draft beer) because most bottled beer strips away vitamins in processing. Beer on tap or draft beer retains these vitamins. So in essence, draft beer has a built-in hangover helper.

**PRELIMINARY STRATEGY #3:** Pick your poison, because alcohol is a poison. However, when mixed with sugar the poisonous effect is amplified. So it's in your best interest to avoid sugary drinks especially cocktails with high amounts of sugar.

For example avoid a Screwdriver, Tequila

Sunrise, Mai Tai or any other cocktail mixed with fruit juice, soda or sugar-based liquor. Instead, stick with beer (preferably high-end microbrew on tap) wine or cocktails mixed with non-sugar beverages like soda water or mineral water etc.

**PRELIMINARY STRATEGY #4:** Since alcohol dehydrates the body, rehydrating while drinking only makes sense. An easy way to do this is to drink one glass of water while drinking each alcoholic beverage, or drink one alcoholic beverage and then drink one glass of water alternating throughout the day or evening. This makes a huge difference.

Now, let me share the amazing hangover remedy I learned from a crazy millionaire. When I first heard it, I thought it was a joke. Because being a health nut (along with working off and on as a bartender) I heard just about every hangover remedy in the book. But because the man sharing it with me was not only rich, but brilliant, I also knew, by the tone of his voice - he was serious!

The same night I heard it I intentionally drank enough to induce a hangover. This way I could put it to the test. I did what he said and guess what? NO HANGOVER! I couldn't believe it! It worked like magic.

I was so shocked I tried it again. And again, same result: NO HANGOVER! I tried it over and over. Then I began telling friends about it. Some of them were fellow bartenders (currently working as bartenders mind you). And oh, they laughed! Boy did they laugh!

But they aren't laughing anymore, because eventually, they had to try it too. And they experienced the miraculous results as well. So what is it? You'll never guess…

**A cheeseburger.**

Yes, a cheeseburger.

You simply eat a freshly cooked cheeseburger before you go to bed. Sure, you can do everything else I mentioned and it works even better.

Many people think it's the bread in the cheeseburger that makes it work. Not true and you can try for yourself with a fresh cheeseburger (protein style) adding just lettuce and the fixings, and it still works. Not quite as well. But it definitely works.

Also, when I say cheeseburger I am referring to a **gourmet cheeseburger**. The kind you would make at home or the kind you would get at a real restaurant. While the technique will work with the fast food style cheeseburger, it will not work nearly as well.

If you <u>quit drinking three hours before going to bed it works even better</u>. And it works for about 80% of the drinking population.

If you don't believe me, try it. There is an 80% chance I am right.

## Four STD's your kids can get even if they use a condom (R113)

Authorities advise everyone that the key to safe sex is to **use a condom**. What few people know is you <u>can still get sexual transmitted diseases</u>.

The fact is that even when used, **a condom can't protect you from the following STDs**.

**Herpes:** If either partner is experiencing an outbreak of **genital herpes** and has open sores, transmission is possible.

Also, any **skin cut or lesions** (anywhere) that comes into contact with body fluids can be a pathway for transmission.

And there are three <u>other diseases</u> people transmit sexually when a condom is used…

**Lice, scabies and fungal infections like ringworm!**

What you can do: if you want to be intimate with someone, you need to have certain minimal information first. Ask them when the last time was they were tested for STDs. If you don't like the answer, then request they get tested. It would not be inappropriate or over-cautious to request that they get tested for STDs and provide proof of their "clean" bill of health before having sexual relations.

## Simple steps which cured my arthritis without drugs or surgery (R206)

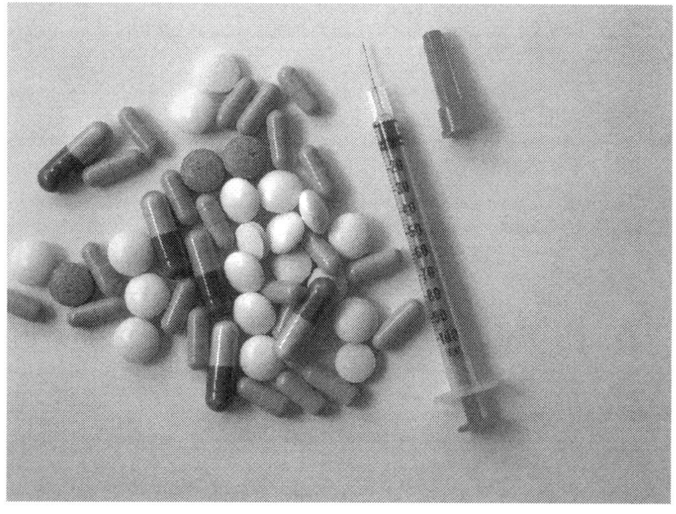

While there are more than 100 types of Arthritis, according to *WebMD*, all of them include symptoms such as pain, stiffness, swelling and inflammation.

Before you agree to begin any type of medication or worse, surgery, it's important to point out the connection to diet, stress and exercise as ways to reduce your chances of developing arthritis or minimizing it should you be diagnosed.

Many people who develop arthritis are overweight, thus applying strain to their joints, especially in the knees, hips, ankles, feet and back.

So job one to managing or minimizing arthritis is to lose weight which leads us to the second method, exercise.

Regular exercise will give you better muscle strength, a healthier heart and circulation as well as boosting bone strength.

Plus you'll just plain feel better in body and mind.

Since arthritis is basically inflammation, you would be well advised to make sure your diet contains the following nutrients.

- Omega-3 fatty acids, especially those found in fish.
- Glucosamine sulphate, to support healthy cartilage (exist in parts of certain seafood and other animal products, most often obtained through supplements).
- Chondroitin, to attract water to the cartilage for better mobility (made from animal cartilage, obtained through the use of supplements).

You can also add more non-inflammatory foods into your diet that provide essential arthritis fighting nutrients such as:

- Nuts like pecans, walnuts, hazelnuts and Brazil nuts.
- Oil rich fish.
- Low fat dairy products with calcium you need for healthy bones.
- Berries are rich in inflammation reducing antioxidants.
- Citrus fruits loaded with vitamin C also help protect you from inflammation.
- Vegetables like broccoli, garlic, onions and leeks help to protect your joints.

It is also wise to avoid inflammation promoting foods such as sugar, bread, chips, pasta, and the like.

You can also 'feel better' with a positive attitude as well as a sense of humor.

If you feel stressed out and focus on your pain, it seems to increase in intensity.

One of the earliest researchers of pain, Henry Beecher, noticed soldiers on the battlefield in World War II required more morphine than when they left the battlefield.

Just not having to face the horror of war reduced the pain, yet with the same wound while still in battle seemed to amplify the pain.

As mentioned before, exercise can lift your mood as well as relaxation techniques like yoga, stretching, meditation and even taking a moment to take deep breaths.

You may also want to supplement your diet with proteolytic enzymes known for their ability to fight inflammation as well as repair damage of your joints as you age.

Also, the herbs Boswelia and Bromelain have clinical proof they can help reduce inflammation and pain.

According to Bruce Fife—certified nutritionist and naturopathic physician as well as author of over 20 books including *The New Arthritis Cure: Eliminate Arthritis and Fibromyalgia Pain Permanently*—diet, mind/body work and nutritional supplements are the keys to a healthy immune system capable of eliminating pain and symptoms of arthritis.

And according to a study recently published in *Annals of Family Medicine*, patients with arthritic knee pain are responding well to sugar injections.

You read right, sugar injections. It's called prolotherapy and although first arriving on the scene 75 years ago, no detailed studies were done until recently.

Patients are given the 'sugar' injections in their troubled knees and after a few treatments; the pain subsides for almost a year.

It is believed to work by causing inflammation in the arthritic area, thus forcing the body to rush healing nutrients which in turn temporarily eliminates the arthritis.

Today this therapy is not covered by insurance and you can expect to pay several hundred dollars for each injection. But it does bring relief lasting many months.

Finally, before you succumb to a life of living in arthritic pain or become desperate enough to go under the knife, try the natural cures mentioned in this report because they are working for many people who maintain their weight and adhere to and supplement a non-inflammatory diet.

The path of least resistance *rarely* leads to success.

# Bonus Reports

- ☑ **The secret to "getting paid" for mailing letters**
- ☑ **\$550.00 weekly with your computer and an internet connection**
- ☑ **\$2400.00 a month working 2 days per week at garage sales**
- ☑ **How to earn up to \$115,200.00 per year as a Debt Consultant**

“

The person who does things which count, usually *does not stop* to count them.

# "The Secret to Getting Paid for Mailing Letters"

I want to share a secret with you. A secret which has allowed me to live a life most people dream about. Let me explain...

For 18 years I have awoken each day *not* by an alarm clock, but by when my body decides it's *time* to wake up. In other words, I wake up naturally.

Then, I begin my day on *my terms*. For example, I may eat breakfast, enjoy coffee and then decide I want to take a nap (and I will). It doesn't matter because (for the most part) I work when I feel like it. Which also happens to be when I am most productive.

After all, if I was your boss and I gave you a schedule and said "I don't care when you work, I just want your best work" what would you do? Obviously, you would work when you were at your best. In other words. Well rested. Not stressed. Not frustrated. Not angry. And definitely, not rushed...And that's why the secret I'm about to share is so important. **It can allow you to live *your* best life.** However, the secret may not be for you. That's my only warning. Because when I first discovered it I was 19 (and I've never been the same since). Discovering this secret gave me a dream. A dream I could live life on my terms...More importantly, it gave me energy. Energy to do the work (and press on through failures) to create a life I could love. Here's why...This secret has allowed me to enjoy a debt-free lifestyle for over 20 years. It's allowed me to drive luxury cars, live in million dollar homes and dine in fine restaurants. But most importantly, it's allowed me to "be me" and to live life on MY TERMS. **I hope the thought of YOU living life on YOUR TERMS appeals to you.** Because I do not want to waste your time...

**"What is success to you?"**

For me success was never about money or material things. Sure, I wanted to drive a nice car, live in a nice home, be debt-free and have cash in the bank. But it was more about... *what the money could do for me*. You see, money is a very emotional topic for most people. This is why there are many lies surrounding the discussion of it.

For example. We've all heard the saying "money doesn't buy happiness" right? My response to that statement would be "those people don't know where to shop." And here's why...

Money can buy a lot of things. One of my *favorite things* it can buy is TIME. Time to spend with *loved ones*. Time to spend with *family*. Time to spend *alone*. And time to *help others*.

Have you ever heard the following saying?

**"All money does is make you <u>MORE</u> of what you already are."**

I heard this saying as a kid. And years later after making lots of money I can tell you IT IS TRUE. And that's why I'm bringing it up. Because if you're already a good person, money can allow you to become an even BETTER PERSON. If you're a giving person, it can allow you to give even more.

Another saying many have heard is "To whom

much is given, much is expected." I would also relate this to the fact that wherever there is great opportunity there is also great *responsibility*. Why do I bring this up?

Because what you're about to learn is incredibly powerful. It can be used for good or evil. I hope you will use it for good… let us move on.

Have you ever wondered why some people succeed while others fail?

As someone who has enjoyed financial success, I can tell you the answer will *surprise you*. In fact, if I gave it to you right now, you would *not* be able to *get it*. Why? Because your current thinking would probably limit you from understanding it. Crazy… I know.

But this is because in order to change your life, you first have to change your thinking. I believe *Albert Einstein* said it best with this quote:

**"Our current problems cannot be solved with the same level of thinking which created them."**

I can tell you the biggest struggle I had to overcome (in order to succeed), was that of *changing* my thinking. This is because I have always found change difficult. So, if you feel like a "stubborn old mule" don't despair. Because you can succeed…

…but it will require that you *change* your thinking.

I bring this up because this report could be one of the *most powerful* in the **"Real Cash Secrets"** manual. And here's why…

You're about to learn about a medium you can use to create *massive marketing leverage*. This means you can deliver a personalized message to a mass audience rapidly. But how does this apply to generating income. Let me explain.

In order to get ahead and get rich (with limited capital) you need *two* key components. This may sound simple, but most people fail on this...

**<u>NUMBER ONE:</u>**

You need to find a problem people have which they are willing to pay you to solve. The bigger the problem and the harder to solve, the more money they will pay you.

Let me share an example. Recently, I needed a hot tub moved. Moving a hot tab is not easy and if you don't know what you're doing you can damage it. So, I had a problem. Because I wasn't going to move it myself. So what did I do?

I had to find someone to move the tub. When it came down to it. There were not a lot of options. Many of the people I called seemed flaky. Like they might not show up or, would damage the hot tub while moving.

Eventually, I settled on one individual I had contacted because he was professional and timely in all his communications. However, he charged more than anyone else. $450 as a matter of fact. The entire job (including drive time) took him just 3 hours. He had one helper.

So obviously, it's a profitable business. But not as profitable as you would think and here's why. Even if he averaged 30 hot tub moves per month (at an average of $400 per move) that's $12,000. But after fuel and labor expenses he's probably down to $8000. Not bad, but here's the issue I want you to take note of.

Because of the nature of the business. His income is limited by how many hot tubs he can move per week... per month... or per year.

Now I want you to imagine a similar business solving a similar problem BUT WITH ONE MAJOR DIFFERENCE. You *don't* have the limitations on growing this enterprise. Which brings us to the second key...

**NUMBER TWO:**

You need a market you are solving a problem for which is *scalable*. Meaning, you can go from helping 100 people a month to helping 1,000 people a month (in less than 10 months). Let me share an example...

Ever heard of *Video Professor?* I watch almost no television, but you would have to be an ostrich with your head 3 feet in the sand not to of heard of this guy. Here's his business model broken down.

**PROBLEM:**

*"Millions of Americans struggle to use their computers."*

**SOLUTION:**

*"Video Professor created multiple training videos solving this problem."*

He sells the videos primarily through 2 minute television commercials. People call up and buy one DVD. Then, the company continues to upsell or follow-up with *multiple DVDs* on different computer programs.

As a result, *Video Professor* (the man) has become "disgustingly" wealthy. Why? Because his business was scalable unlike our hot tub mover who was limited by how many hot tubs he could move…

Even if you had a PhD or a degree in psychology and were able to bill clients $150 per hour, do you see how your income would be limited by your ability to serve and help people within your market?

That's the point I want you to get *before* we move on. And in order to do that, you need to replicate yourself. This is why what I am about to share is so powerful. Because one of the most exciting ways to do that is through...

**"The written word."**

Think about it. Think about THE WORDS many billion-dollar corporations have been built on. Here are a few examples…

Think about Dominos Pizza. They came out of nowhere and grew like wildfire dominating the pizza market. And they did it with nothing but the power of words. After all, the pizza was not special.

But they weren't selling quality. They were selling *speed*. Remember the words in the advertising? Let's review them. They are simple but brilliant...

**"Fresh hot pizza delivered to your door in 30 minutes... or it's FREE!"**

Here's another one you'll remember from FedEx...

**"When it absolutely, positively has to be there OVERNIGHT!"**

Okay, so this is great for Dominos and FedEx. But what about you? How can you leverage THE POWER OF WORDS to create your own fortune? Don't worry, we will get to that. But first we have to talk about *replicating* yourself.

Whether you already have a product or service which solves a problem for people (or you need to find one) makes no difference. In order to build wealth and get ahead you need a way to *replicate* yourself to get that message out in mass.

Remember, you don't want to end up like the hot tub mover. Because your income would be limited by how many people you can help within your market...

**"And this is where the secret of getting paid to mail letters is REVEALED."**

We've all heard the term "junk mail." What you probably haven't heard are the facts about direct mail. Let me share some with you...

#1.) More political fund raising and business sales revenue was created last year with direct mail than Facebook.com and twitter combined.

**#2.) During the most recent recession, while first class mail went down, commercial direct mail for business increased.**

#3.) During the last election cycle more money was spent on direct mail than ever before in American history.

**#4.) Google.com (the search engine) sends out millions of pieces of direct mail to business owners to sell them on buying their online advertising service.**

#5.) The world's largest e-*commerce* and *Internet* retailer conference was recently sold using a 32 page direct mail piece.

**#6.) Due to abuses of text and e-mail marketing, many Americans have become *desensitized* to marketing messages sent through digital mediums.**

#7.) While more expensive than other media, nothing is more powerful than the *right* direct mail letter targeted to the *right* audience. History has proven this...

If you've read this far, then you're in for a treat. And here's why. I want you to imagine you have a product or service which solves a *major* problem for people. Now, I want you to imagine you have a direct mail letter which successfully sells your product or service. And, you have large list of people in which you can mail this letter to. *Do you know how fast you can get rich?*

Let me give you an example of just how powerful direct mail is. It's one thing to create a successful marketing message which you can use online or in digital media. But there is no other medium (other than direct mail) where you can use that message year after year and have it last as long without tiring out.

For example. What if I told you a single direct mail letter was responsible for bringing in over $2.1 billion dollars? And, that letter was mailed successfully (year after year) for over 28 straight years?

Because there is such a letter and I want to share it with you (right now). The letter is reprinted on the next page. Now remember, what you are studying here is a powerful sales message (*replicated* in a direct mail letter).

Again, this letter mailed every year for 28 years straight and brought in over $2.1 billion. Here is the letter...

# THE WALL STREET JOURNAL.

WORLD FINANCIAL CENTER, 200 LIBERTY STREET, NEW YORK, NY 10281

Dear Reader:

On a beautiful late spring afternoon, twenty-five years ago, two young men graduated from the same college.

They were very much alike, these two young men. Both had been better than average students, both were personable and -- as young college graduates are -- both were filled with ambitious dreams for the future.

Recently, these men returned to their college for their twenty-fifth reunion.

They were still very much alike. Both were happily married. Both had children. And both, it turned out, had gone to work for the same Midwestern company after graduation, and were still there.

But there was a difference. One of the men was manager of a small department of that company. The other was its president.

What made the difference

Have you ever wondered, as I have, what makes this kind of a difference in people's lives? It isn't native intelligence or talent or dedication. It isn't that one person wants success and the other doesn't.

The difference lies in what each person knows and how he or she uses that knowledge.

And that's why I'm writing to you about The Wall Street Journal. For the whole purpose of the Journal is to give its readers knowledge -- advantageous knowledge they can use in business.

(over, please)

Just recently, The Wall Street Journal made the biggest changes in it's 113-year history -- to make it easier for you to access this special knowledge. We've added color and made design improvements in every section and, as a result, today's Journal is fresher, more reader-friendly -- and more useful to you, more quickly. The day's vital stories stand out to help you select those that interest you.

### The best-read front page in America

Right now, I'm looking at page one of the Journal, the best-read front page in America. The excellent layout is unchanged, but it's a faster read. It combines all the important news of the day with in-depth reporting. Every phase of business news is covered -- business forecasts, breaking stories, politics -- stories from Washington, Moscow, Frankfurt, Tokyo -- item after item that could affect you, your job, your future.

Now, if you're jammed for time, a 10-minute scan will set you up for the day.

### An improved Wall Street Journal and "the business of life"

More than just business, the world's most trusted source of business news and information has also added Personal Journal, a major new section appearing every Tuesday through Thursday. It taps the world's largest staff of business news experts for information of personal benefit to you. Not only personal investing and personal technology, but careers, health and fitness, family, and everything about the business of life.

### The battle for the consumer

Marketplace gives you revealing insights into how consumers are thinking and spending -- and how companies are competing for market share. Plus coverage of law, media, technology, marketing, and the challenges of managing smaller companies.

### "...the best source for news...about your money"

Today's Journal is also the single best source for news and statistics about your money. In the

THE WALL STREET JOURNAL

PERSONAL JOURNAL

MARKETPLACE

MONEY & INVESTING

WEEKEND JOURNAL

The Price of Love

Money & Investing section, there are helpful charts, now even easier to grasp in color -- and three of America's most carefully scrutinized and influential investment columns -- "Abreast of the Market," "Heard on the Street," and "Your Money Matters."

So, every section, column and feature that contributes to making today's Journal the final authority in business news is right there, where it's always been -- with two major additions: A new section, Personal Journal, that's all about "the business of life"-- and design changes to make the Journal easier to use and more useful to you.

For business news, today's Journal is the only newspaper you need

And Weekend Journal wraps up the week on Fridays with wise and witty reviews of the arts and entertainment, sports, travel, country life, and fun-filled ways to spend your hard-earned free time.

No matter how many times you've seen The Wall Street Journal, I urge you to take a fresh look at today's Journal. It's the talk of the business world. For business, it's the only newspaper you need.

Your own personal subscription

Put us to the test: Subscribe for 26 weeks for only $89. (You save $38 off the newsstand price.)

Or take advantage of our better buy: 52 weeks for $175 -- and save $79! Either way, you pay nothing extra for home or office delivery every business day.

While I cannot promise you instant

success if you subscribe, I guarantee that you will find The Wall Street Journal consistently interesting, totally reliable, and always useful.

**Our guarantee to you**

Should The Wall Street Journal not measure up to your expectations, or to anything I've said, you may cancel your subscription at any time and receive a full refund for the undelivered portion.

If you feel that this is fair and reasonable, you'll want to find out promptly if The Wall Street Journal can do for you what it has done for millions of readers. So, order your subscription today and we'll start serving you immediately.

Sincerely,

Peter R. Kann, Publisher

PRK:md
Encs.

P.S. About those two college classmates I mentioned at the beginning of this letter: They graduated from college together and got started in business together. So what made their success in business different? Knowledge. Useful knowledge. And its application.

As you can see, this is no ordinary letter. This letter is a masterpiece and brought in billions for the *Wall Street Journal*. Great for them, but what about you? Let's talk about how you can harness the power of direct mail to *replicate* yourself and sell your product or service like crazy. Because this is the secret to getting paid for mailing letters...

**Remember...**
**"In the end, marketing comes down to two things: Psychology and Mathematics."**

Let's say you have a product you are selling which costs $100. Your cost to fill an order is $30 after expenses. This means you have $70 of margin within the product. In other words, it costs you $30 and you sell it for $100 leaving a $70 profit...

Now, I want you to imagine you have a direct mail letter which costs $500 per 1,000 letters to mail (or $.50 per letter). Psychologically speaking, in order to sell a $100 product through direct mail, you will need to be solving a *major* problem for the person receiving the letter.

Examples of this might be a product to improve your golf game, lose weight, build muscle, earn extra income, save money, save time, parent kids or a whole host of other ideas. But let's get back to the math...

If it costs you $500 to mail 1,000 letters and your profit margin per unit sold is $70... This means you will need to sell 7 units per every 1,000 letters mailed to break even. 7 out of 1,000 is 0.7% response. But let's say you successfully sold (on average) 18 units per every 1,000 letters mailed? This is 1.8% response. Here is how the math would work out.

1,000 letters mailed would cost $500. You generate 18 orders at $100 each which equals $1800. Fulfillment of the orders is $30 x 18 which equals $540. The mailing cost $500. Add them together and you have $1040.

But you took in $1800 in sales. The math tells us $1800 minus $1040 equals a profit of $760. Now, do the math again. A $480 profit for mailing 1,000 letters. This means...

**"You earned .76 cents for every letter mailed."**

Not bad. And remember. This is based upon you only generating 18 orders for every 1,000 thousands letters mailed. In others words...

**"982 out of every 1,000 people mailed to never bought."**

Think about that. You're not even successfully selling 2 out of every 100 people. But let's do more math. Let's say you keep reinvesting your profits back into mailing more letters. Now, let's say you are mailing 10,000 letters per month (BTW - I know a guy who mails over 100,000 letters per month).

On 10,000 letters per month you are generating 180 orders. This is $18,000 in gross revenue. Minus fulfillment costs for your orders of 180 x $30 equals $5,400. Plus your mailing costs of .50 cents per letter x 10,000 letters equals $5,000. Total expenses equal $9,400. Basic math tells us $18,000 minus $9,400 equals $7,600 per month. Again, you are earning .76 cents for every letter mailed. But...

**"Here's the most exciting part."**

If you currently have a product or service which solves a *major* problem for people, all you have to do is develop a letter and begin testing (at the end of this report I will give you resources for getting started).

If you don't have a product or service let me share a few stories with you about why this should be exciting for you...

**Advertising**
**=**
**Salesmanship Multiplied**

A well-crafted direct-mail letter can make you rich very quick. How quick? How about less than 48 months... This is because a successful direct mail letter is your own personal (replicable) remote-control selling system. It truly is, salesmanship multiplied.

**Think about it. You can have your own "well groomed" professional salesman show up and make a sales presentation for your product or service AT ANY ADDRESS IN AMERICA...**

**"...for about .50 cents."**

But the best part is once you get a letter that works, that promotion will last longer in the medium of direct mail than any other medium on the face of the earth. Do not overlook this. And here's why...

Creating a winning sales presentation is not easy. It requires a lot of testing. But when you get a winner you can ride that winner for a long time. However, in any other media (i.e. Radio, Television, Magazines, Newspapers or the Internet) a successful promotion will usually have to be "refreshed" by being recreated since the ad will tire out within 6 to 18 months...

**"But a winner in direct mail can pull orders longer than any other media."**

For example....

**"American Express had one particular direct-mail letter which mailed unchanged for 12 years and generated over $1.2 billion in new business."**

But again, let's get back to the point. If you don't have a product or service what does this mean for you? It means you need to get to work and here's why...

Forget about getting rich by hitting a homerun for a moment and listen to some of these "quick cash" life-changing stories.

## DIRECT MAIL LETTER:

**"Recruiting Network Marketing Affiliates"**

I am not a fan of network marketing (a.k.a. multilevel marketing) but I know a man who has devised a unique way of using direct mail to solve the problem of recruiting new affiliates. Here's how it works.

He is involved with an older, "no-frills" network marketing company. There's nothing exciting about it other than the fact they have a track record of providing long-term second income for folks who get involved...

**And that term "Second Income" is THE KEY.**

He latched on to the "second income" concept and developed a four-page direct-mail letter which they send to business owners across America based upon their **"SIC Code"** from yellow page databases.

If you don't know what an **SIC Code** is, it stands for **Standard Industrial Classification**. Obviously, I cannot share exactly what SIC codes he mails the letter to. But that's not the secret, because...

**"The real magic is in the letter."**

Because his letter is mailed to business owners offering them **a way to generate a long-term "second" income**. The letter does not sell anything other than responding to *learn more* about the opportunity. In most cases the letters are mailed by his distributors to addresses of business owners in their *local* communities. This is a big deal because a letter coming from a local address has much more credibility.

However, because the letters are mailed first class (instead of standard mail) they are more expensive. But his results are impressive. It costs about $80 to mail 100 letters but, they receive **up to 12 responses for every hundred letters mailed**. And about one 1 out 4 responders enroll in their program.

**"These are incredible numbers considering they are promoting a network marketing opportunity."**

But again, the real magic is in the letter. Because the letter talks to business owners about "uncertain times" and logic of taking steps to create a "second" income for security.

I should also point out the letters are mailed first class, with a postage stamp (not a meter) and are hand addressed in blue ink.

**"Because of this, I am guessing the open rate for his mailings is about 99%."**

All this because one guy decided to "solve the problem" of his affiliates not having enough new people to share their opportunity with....

## DIRECT MAIL LETTER:

### "Finds New Accounting Clients."

Another example is in the field of certified public accounting. A CPA in Santa Barbara California has developed a powerful direct-mail letter which generates new accounting clients.

When you consider the fact the average business accounting client is worth about $1,000 per year, you don't have to secure too many clients per month before the money begins to add up.

Before I get into the psychology of the letter, let's talk about who he mails the letter to. In every town and county across the United States there is a list available of what's known as *"fictitious business name"* statement filings. This is anyone doing business under a name *other* than their own. These are also known as DBAs (a.k.a. Doing Business As).

Anyway, the accountant each month secures a list of names of people who have filed or renewed a fictitious business name statement. So he is automatically mailing his letter to *every new and established business* who may be "filing" a fictitious business name statement. Now for the letter...

Money and taxes are an extremely emotional topic. And this accountant has developed a magic letter which *harnesses the power of these emotions* in order to generate appointments for business owners interested in saving money and taxes.

Basically, the letter teases you with all the ways people over pay their taxes by a lack of knowledge. By the end of the letter you are convinced how little you know about taxes. And, how much money you can save by hiring a professional (like him). Of course, the next step is to make an appointment for a *free consultation* at his office.

Without question, this is the most powerful letter I've ever received from an accountant. I am sure this letter pulls a large number of responses and many other accountants could solve their money problems if they had it. There is no doubt this letter is a goose which lays golden eggs.

Again, take note there are two components to this equation for success. *Number one* is a well-crafted direct-mail letter. *Number two* is a list of people who the letter is mailed. Pretty simple...

## DIRECT MAIL LETTER:

### "Finds New Carpet Cleaning Customers."

*"Did you know 4 out 5 homeowners are poisoning their pets and children without even knowing it?*
*This is because we now spend up to 90% of our time indoors and the E.P.A. has labeled indoor air quality as a serious concern and here's why..."*

This is the headline used for one direct mail letter sent to "new homeowners" offering them carpet cleaning services. Again, the list is very specific to *who* the letter is sent to. In every county across the United States lists are available of all the new homeowners. These consumers are prime targets for a variety of home related services.

In this case, the letter does *not* sell carpet cleaning in the normal sense. For the most part, it is a fear-based letter. Because fear is a powerful motivator and the sales argument is true. Indoor air pollution is a serious issue. In fact, the air you breathe indoors is usually more harmful than the air you breathe outdoors.

To be blunt, the letter "scares people" about the realities of indoor air pollution. Because the fact is, carpets (if not cleaned) are a breeding ground for bacteria. If you know much about indoor air quality, you understand the argument is true.

The call to action in the letter is a special discount offer for 50% off for new customers. By mailing this letter to new homeowners moving into the area I am sure the company does very well.

Again, notice the format of bringing up the problem and creating a solution. In this case dirty carpets are contaminating your indoor air and by cleaning the carpets you *solve the problem* of poisoning your pets and children...

**DIRECT MAIL LETTER:**

**"Securing a Work at Home Job."**

Dave Parsons was an average guy with mediocre computer skills who got laid off from his job and found himself in a pickle. While collecting unemployment and finding himself depressed, one day he came up with *an idea*.

He noticed more and more businesses were transitioning onto the Internet while others were ignoring it. This is where he saw an opportunity... Why not contact these businesses and...

a.) Show them the opportunity they are missing.

And,

b.) Offer them a solution to capture it by building them a website.

That night an idea was born. But how would Dave sell it? Dave's friend Michael offered to cold call businesses to sell the service. But Dave had no money to pay Michael. And because Dave didn't want to send out spam (a.k.a. junk e-mail) he came up with a crazy idea to try promoting his business with a letter through the mail.

At the time, he wasn't sure if the idea would work. But at a cost of less than 100 bucks to send out 180 letters to businesses, what did he have to lose?

Looking back, the original letter was only one page. But it got the point across. It explained to the business owner that millions of companies were getting on the Internet and they were missing out by not having a website.

The letter then offered a free consultation about how a website could improve their business for little expense. This generated phone calls from interested business owners and the rest is history.

Dave hasn't gone to work for someone else since. An entire business was successfully launched based upon nothing but *one idea* and *one direct mail letter*. Could you do the same? I am willing to bet, you can...

**"Here's what to do next...
...in 5 simple steps"**

Whether or not you currently have a product or service to market is of no consequence. Because the main equation in creating a successful direct mail letter is one of *knowledge*. You must learn the basics of direct-mail marketing.

From here you can begin creating pieces and testing. It will take time. But keep in mind, one successful letter can solve all your money problems and make you rich. Think about that...

Here's what you need to do first. Study past successful mailings. And, study the craft of writing winning direct-mail. First, whatever market you are in (i.e. health, financial, legal services etc.) you need to respond to the offers of that market and get on those lists.

I am a person who receives more junk mail than junk e-mail. If you want to hit a winner in direct mail... you need to do the same.

**Step Two:**

Step two, is to study the pieces of junk mail which are repeated again and again. You need to read at least one piece of junk mail per day. And really study it. Break down the components of the offer and the mathematics behind it. If it's asking you to call a number to enter a sweepstakes, then call the number and listen to the pitch. If it's selling an auto warranty... call and listen... you need to study and learn.

**Step Three, Four, Five:**

Steps three thru five are simple. They are books which you need to read over and over. You can get them at the library, buy them used or online. They are...

**3.) *Tested Advertising Methods* by John Caples**

**4.) *How to Make Your Advertising Make Money* by John Caples**

**5.) *The Greatest Direct Mail Sales Letters of All Time* by Richard Hodgs**

---

## "$550.00 Weekly with Your Computer and an Internet Connection."

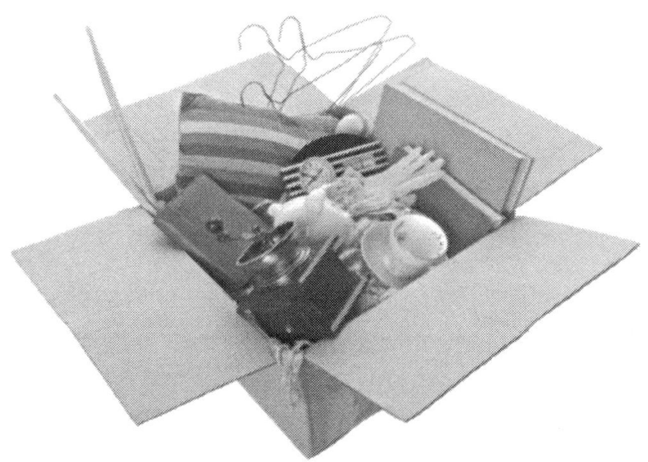

I want to share a business you can start for under $800. And, working as little as one hour a day, can earn **$550.00 to $1100.00 per week**. I know this business well, because I have experience with it. It can not only be profitable (and fun) but you will also be providing a much-needed service within your community.

To get started you need a computer and Internet connection. A cell phone is not required but *highly* recommended. If you are retired (or semi retired) you will have a big advantage in this business (you will understand why in a moment). But first, let me explain the business and provide a warning...

Though this business is fun and profitable, it is *not* glamorous. But what it can provide is *consistent* cash flow. Add this to a low start up cost and almost zero risk and you have a "part-time" winner.

**"The problem with most business opportunities..."**

Listen closely to what I'm about to say. Because if you get it, it will **save you a fortune in wasted time and money**. The number one problem in the business opportunity industry is that the market (people) have gotten increasingly lazy. What do I mean?

**For example. The majority of people buying opportunities have decided they "don't want to work" anymore. In other words, they don't want to go through the effort of being creative and coming up with an idea that creates REAL VALUE in society by solving a problem for someone. Instead, they would rather "plug-in" to a *system* to bypass all this work. But remember...**

**"Most shortcuts only shortcut you later."**

As a result, most marketers of business opportunities have responded by selling "turn-key" systems and schemes. Or what others refer to as an "automated program" attached to an "advertising" service. These are programs where the company does "all the work" and you just "pay them" to advertise so you can collect your checks. Sounds nice doesn't it?

Too bad it works for less than 1% of the participants. I do not have time today to explain all the problems with this situation, but let me be clear as to the reason why it does not work for 99%. And the main reason can be summed up in one word...

**"Competition."**

If one of these turn-key programs came out and offered you the opportunity to promote their system (and you were the only person promoting it) you *might* have an opportunity. And, you *might* make some money. Why?

Because it would be likely you would have little to no competition. Think about multi-billion dollar companies who have little competition. Part of why they are multi-billion dollar companies is because of their *lack* of competition. For example...

You probably write a check to a *cable* company every month. And, you probably write a check to a *gas* company every month. And, you probably write a check to an *electric* company every month. And, you get the idea. Now...

Take something like dentistry. How many dentists are in your community? Depending on the size, probably one to over a dozen. Now, imagine if every dentist recruited 10 patients who became dentists the following year? What would happen to the dentistry market? And, what would happen to the profitability of being a dentist? ANSWER: it would go down, down, down. Until finally, dentists at the bottom would be unable to get enough new patients to sustain a profitable living.

**"Have I made my point?"**

What's killer about this business is there is *almost* no competition. Second, it's very hard for it to get competitive **because most people are too busy chasing get rich quick schemes**. And this makes the opportunity have more *longevity* for those willing to work it. Why? Because the business has to be operated within your local community and it is impossible to outsource. All these things, add up to one thing for you...

**"Income security."**

Of course, the business I am talking about is the business of buying and selling (or flipping) merchandise. Listen, if you are retired and/or have spare time and an Internet connection along with a cell phone, this could be a god-send for you. **If you enjoy talking with people, the deck is stacked in your favor for success.** Here's why...

Like any business, there are a *few secrets* which make this opportunity extra profitable. I will share the ones I have used so you can benefit from them in a moment. But first, a quick note about buying and selling...

**First, you have to understand the opportunity of buying and selling merchandise is *not* rinky-dink. Buying and selling is a multi-BILLION dollar industry. Every day in America billions of dollars change hands through transactions of people buying and selling. Be it cars, electronics, appliances, motorcycles, fitness equipment, collectibles, antiques, furniture, firearms, sporting goods or even baby clothes.**

**"Two types of strategies to create profits."**

Buying and selling is a simple business. But it can become complicated depending upon **which strategy** you choose to go with. This is because there are two types of strategies to create profits. Both are used throughout the country (and the world for that matter). And both can be profitable. But they are very different...

**STRATEGY ONE:**
**"Buy and sell anything you can make a profit on after researching it.**

**STRATEGY TWO:**
**"Specialize. Seek out only items which you have *specialized* knowledge of that you can resell for a profit."**

Which strategy you choose will come down to your personality. For me, I was a specialist. I'll explain in a minute. But first, let's talk about strategy one. Because I know a friend who uses this strategy (quite successfully) even today.

Strategy one is where you buy and sell anything you can make a profit on after researching it. For me, I could *never* do this strategy. Because you are buying and selling so *many things* it becomes overwhelming very quickly (at least for me). Let me explain...

I've seen my friend buy **five different knick-knacks**, all of which I know nothing about. In many cases these items have a profit margin of under $25. But he will sell them. For example, he could buy a laptop for two dollars (obviously a broken laptop) but he will turn around and sell it on eBay for parts and get $40. To him, it's money in the bank. To me, it's a headache and a nightmare...

But my point is, *both* strategies can work and be successful. It comes down to your personality type. Me, I like to be *focused* and specialize.

**"Profits as a specialist."**

Don't worry, we will get into how to buy and how to sell in a moment (that's the fun part). But first, I want to talk about working as a specialist because I have experience with it. When I did this business I specialized in eight things.

**Cars**
**Motorcycles**
**4 Wheelers**
**Televisions**
**Washers**
**Dryers**
**Refrigerators**
**Furniture**

As a specialist, you can choose what you want to specialize in. But I will warn you, in this business you need to **establish specific profit margins** because everything about buying and selling *eats up your time.* In other words, hunting down stuff to buy *eats up your time*. Advertising and selling stuff *eats up your time*. And all this time has to be accounted for. Otherwise, rather than creating a profitable business, you will end up creating an expensive hobby.

For me, I had to average $25+ per hour to be happy. But what I found out very quickly (the hard way) is everything about buying and selling takes **more time than you originally planned for.** Let me explain...

When I first got in the business, I thought it was as simple as "Hey, I'll buy it for $500 and sell it for $700 and make $200. Bingo! I just made $200 in two hours!" It doesn't work that way (90% of the time anyway). Just like everything in life buying and selling turns out to be a lot more work than you originally anticipated. But like the saying goes...

**"The future belongs to those who prepare for it."**

In this business, the first thing you have to learn is *what* merchandise to specialize in. And believe me, I knew all the merchandise I specialized in. When it came to cars, I specialized in only a few which I really knew.

Same thing with motorcycles. Same thing with washers and dryers, refrigerators and even televisions. I knew what the stuff was worth and (more importantly) what I could quickly resell it for. But you want to know what blindsided me and ate up all my initial profits while learning?

**"Accounting for all the time involved in finding, buying and then reselling each item."**

Trust me. What I'm about to say will be the most important part of this report for you. Because I had to learn this the hard way by doing a lot of charity work (a.k.a. working for free). In other words, buying and selling things without making a dime. Why? Because after all my time invested there was no profit left. **It reminds me of that bumper sticker** *"If you think education is expensive, try ignorance."* Well, I was ignorant in the beginning.

The business of buying and selling is *not* capital intensive. And that's great. Because it means you can start with little capital. But what it does take a lot of, is YOUR TIME. And if you're not careful, you can end up spending a lot of time and not making a dime. Here's what I've learned the hard way to help you keep from making the same mistake...

**"Finding killer deals is easy...**
**...It's the time it takes that's the issue."**

You can drop me in almost any city in America and I can find killer deals on all sorts of items. The issue, is **the time I have to invest** to find them. And this my friend, is one of two secrets you need to understand to be successful in this business... First, you have to **study the merchandise** you are going to specialize in. You need to **know what it sells for** and **what it's worth in real dollars** if you need to sell it within one month or less... How do you do this?

You do it by studying ads in your local community. The obvious website is craigslist.org. But these days, you have to look at all the other smaller classified ad sites as well. It's simple. All you do is look at items and watch them to see how fast they sell. From this observation you can determine approximately what the items are worth based upon **how quickly they sell**.

That's the easy part. The issue is the time it takes to find the deals. I will share some tricks in a moment they can be very profitable which few people are using. But my bigger goal, is to have you not make the mistakes I did by not accounting for your time invested to find great deals. For example. I learned the hard way...

**"It takes me about four hours to find a great deal and two hours to sell it. That's six hours total."**

This means as long as I focus on deals with a minimum profit of $150 I am making $25 per hour. Don't get me wrong, there are deals where

I screw up and make no money. But there are also deals (like a Lexus IS250 I bought) where I made $1750.00 for eight hours work (that's $218.75 per hour).

But again... you have to play the averages. The average car I can flip I will earn under $1,000 profit. But cars take a lot of time. A lot of time to find and a lot of time to sell. But the biggest problem with cars is moving them. I can't drive two cars at once. And, unlike a motorcycle, I can't throw a car in the back of my truck. On the other hand, I've made **$200-$400 profit with less than 8 hours work** off televisions and refrigerators. Those are easy but the profits are smaller.

This is why I believe it **pays to be a specialist**. Because you focus in on certain merchandise like cars, motorcycles, televisions, refrigerators, washers, dryers, etc. You get to know the products well and what they can be RESOLD for. This is the first secret. But you have to figure out how much time it takes to find A GREAT DEAL. And this will vary a little bit from market to market.

But it's fun. People are selling stuff and need your money. Usually, they don't want to wait to get as much money as they can. Because in most cases they are moving and moving is a pain. And sometimes they are moving out of state and everything they are selling must go.

The fact is, all the people who are listing something for sale **need your money**, and the faster they get it, the sooner they can get on with their lives. This is why you can be a hero when you show up.

You are helping them solve a problem. And this is the foundation of every great business. But to recap, in the business of buying and selling the first key is to know your merchandise.

**"You do this by studying what the merchandise is worth by observing what it is selling for in your local market."**

This can be done by studying all the local classified ad websites (like craigslist.org and others) as well as the local papers in your area. This will give you a feel for what items are worth. But don't just be an observer. Be hands-on. This means **go out and look at items** and keep an eye on them to see what they sell for. It's no different than watching your local real estate, rental or automotive market. Now, moving on, let's talk about...

**"The two pillars of success"**

...in this business, once you've studied the merchandise you wish to specialize in, there are **<u>two</u>** pillars for success.

**NUMBER ONE:**
**"You must have a keen "reality-based" perspective of what an item's *true* 30 day RESALE VALUE is."**

**NUMBER TWO:**
**"You must have notification software to instantly "alert you" of deals in real time. The *sooner* you can respond, the *<u>more</u>* profitable you will be."**

Let's talk about number one. First, you need to know your merchandise like an expert. If you are going to buy and sell Subaru cars, then you need to know **exactly what they are reselling for in your area** based upon the condition, mileage and maintenance. Likewise, if you're going to specialize in appliances, like televisions, washers, dryers or refrigerators. You need to know the true value of what those items resell for in your market...

This is where most people's thinking becomes foggy. This is because...

**"In every transaction, between a buyer and seller, both parties establish a price in their head before they ever meet."**

And many times, this is done unconsciously. What am I talking about?

Think about it. Go back to any time you went to buy anything. Even if you had limited information about the item (maybe you only had a picture and a short phone conversation with the owner). The reality is, when you were driving over to check out the item, you established a "mental price" of **what you were willing to pay for it**. And this is my point...

In every transaction where anything is being sold, there is a **mental price established by both parties** of what the item is worth (before they even meet) When both values are *within reason*, a successful transaction can occur.

**"When both values are *unreasonable*, the only thing which will occur is RESISTANCE."**

And in this business, resistance is FUTILE. Because it costs us time and money (therefore, we must *avoid* it at all costs).

So, before you buy anything to resell for profit, you need to know exactly what the TRUE resale value is. And when I say resale value, I mean resale value based upon you need to sell it within 30 days or...

**"You will be BEHEADED in the town square!"**

Seriously. This is how you *must* approach the business in order to *avoid* wasting your time. Let's say you're going to specialize in appliances (which I highly recommend) like televisions, home gyms, refrigerators, washers and dryers.

You need to study the market closely and know *two* things. You need to know what an items TRUE 30-DAY RESALE VALUE is. But also, you need to know which items to *avoid* because of problems. For example, when it comes to washers and dryers, the older school units manufactured by Maytag are workhorses. In fact, multiple other brands are manufactured under the Maytag label because of their reliability.

However, other brands (which I won't mention) are not built the same and are notorious for having problems. If you would like to verify this information it's very easy to do using an age-old FBI tactic outlined in another part of this manual.

Here's what you do (this will take you less than 60 minutes)... Call up 10 appliance repair companies anywhere in the United States and ask them the following question :

*"When it comes to [insert name of appliance] which brands hold up better and have less problems then others?"*

Then ask the question...

**"Which models, in your professional opinion, based on your experience, are the ones to avoid?"**

If you call 10 appliance repair companies in the United States and ask this question, trust me, you'll come up with some *very conclusive data*. I know what the data is and I will not share it. *Why?*

Because I want you to *do the work* and learn it on your own. This is powerful stuff. These little details are what **make the difference** between a great profitable business and a flailing enterprise. Let's move on to pillar number two. Because this is a huge secret... one of the biggest, in fact. And that is...

**"Notification software."**

As I stated earlier, finding deals is *not* the issue in this business. The issue is **the time it takes** to find deals. The quicker you can find a deal and acquire it... The sooner you can *resell it* and earn a profit. Of course, the less time invested in these steps, the higher your **profit per hour** of your time will be. This is where...

**"Tools and technology can drastically increase your productivity."**

Let me share some real life stories to make my point and how it can help you. Here are four examples of killer deals I found. All four were found on craigslist.org but (keep in mind) there may be **LOCAL online classified sites** in your area which offer even *greater* opportunities.

I am only using craigslist.org as an example because more people identify with it. Here are the four deals I found and they all have **ONE SECRET** in common...

**"A Lexus IS250 AWD I bought for $11,500 and flipped (a.k.a. resold) within 30 days for $13,500 after putting only $250 into it for detailing."**

Profit = $1750.00
Time invested = 8 hours
**Profit for my time = $218.75 per hour**

*(So you know, deals like this are RARE but out there.)*

**"A one-year-old Whirlpool stainless steel French door refrigerator I bought for $700 and paid a mover $150 to bring to my house. Three weeks later I flipped it for $1500 because the refrigerator cost over $3150.00 new just one year prior!"**

Profit = $650.00
Time invested = 9 hours
**Profit for my time = $72.00 per hour**

*(Again, deals like this are RARE but out there.)*

**"A VitaSpa Hot Tub in excellent condition I bought for $1,000 and paid $350 to move. Another $300 for a new cover and sold it 8 weeks later for $2,200."**

Profit = $550.00
Time invested = 19 hours
**Profit for my time = $29.00 per hour**

(NOTE: I would *not* recommend flipping hot tubs unless you know the models and have a reliable mover. This deal was too good to pass up so I had to do it. Even then, it ended up burning more time than originally planned. But because it was a great deal, I still made money. Hot tubs can be a *gold mine* in certain markets but be sure to do your research.)

**"A Danby beer Kegerator (still under warranty) I bought for $250 and resold 2 weeks later for $350.00"**

Profit = $100
Time invested = 4 hours
**Profit for my time = $25.00 per hour**

(Deals like this are easy to find in most markets. However, I knew the product. Igloo, the company who makes coolers, used to sell a Kegerator through home depot, but it was poor quality. The Danby unit is superior).

Looking back, I should have tried to get $400 as a new unit was over $600 after taxes. I would have made $37.50 per hour vs. $25.00. But I don't like sitting on stuff. Too many times in the past I was greedy. The result?

I would spend months trying to sell an item. Remember, time is money and there is a balance. *The faster you can sell, the more money you make per hour but, there is a fine line on price when you are asking too much*).

**"The secret revealed."**

**Every one of the above bargains I picked up has a secret.** And the secret is this... I did not find these deals because I'm incredibly motivated. I did not find these deals because I am smart. I found these deals because I did my homework on the brands, but most importantly, I had a secret weapon. And that **secret weapon** can be summed up in two words...

**"Notification software."**

You see, the only reason I was able to find all four of these incredible deals was because **I was the first person to contact the sellers**. In other words, I had **no competition**. All of this because of one tool. And that tool is NOTIFICATION software. What is it?

Notification software is a computer program which automatically notifies you when items you are looking for become available for sale online. For example, craigslist.org has its own notification software built into the website. Although they don't advertise it and 99% of users are unaware of it. However, it is there for you and it's a huge secret which makes the business of flipping merchandise a reality.

Now, when it comes to other sites (like local classifieds sites) where a lot of opportunity exists, there are programs which in most cases are free which will alert you when the items you are looking for become available. Each software will let you set up "keywords" around the items you are looking for.

For example... You could set up searches for 8 different items (i.e. Whirlpool Refrigerator, Samsung Television etc.) and **you would be notified THE MINUTE someone posted a brand new ad selling that item**. This is a big deal and a key to the business. Because he who is first in line with no competition is an *automatic* winner. Also, this is...

**"Why being retired (or having a flexible schedule) is a MAJOR KEY to success."**

Because if you can respond faster than everyone else you are guaranteed to find more deals more often. For example, most items are listed in the evening when people are off work. When you can scout deals in the evening and contact the sellers, you are first in line and eliminate the competition. If you're at work all day... Sorry, but you are at a disadvantage. This is good news (again) if you are retired or have a flexible schedule...

**"Because you can respond faster and find better deals *more* often."**

I love this business because you help people working as a middleman. But let me explain. The people that are selling merchandise want to sell it as fast as possible. As a middleman, you buy from them right away so they sell it and get their cash faster than if you didn't exist.

On the other side, you study the merchandise and know which brands have the most resale value because of the quality. And because of this, you deal in higher-quality products so your buyers get better merchandise from you because of your education on the quality of the items. It's win-win...

Listen, in every community around the United States millions of dollars of used merchandise is bought and sold every day. And this business gives you an opportunity to cash in on the profits of this market. You are providing a valuable service for people in your community and earn a reasonable profit in return.

All you need is a computer and an Internet connection and under $800 in startup capital. Of course, a cell phone is a plus because it speeds up your communication. Though, it is not required.

**"Here's what to do next..."**

Like any real business, this business starts with education. So here's what to do next. The first thing you want to do is start educating yourself on the merchandise being sold within your local community. I know one man who specializes in farm equipment. Why? Because where he lives, this is what makes sense. In your area, things may be different. Also, choose merchandise which you are passionate about. You can start by researching the two sites below.

**http://Craigslist.org**

**http://gsalr.com/**

Keep in mind, new LOCAL classified ad websites are starting up all the time. And these new sites offer a fresh opportunity for anyone buying and selling merchandise. Remember, this is a real business and a real opportunity. Where you can take it and what you can do is up to you. The other key is to learn the reliability of what you are going to specialize in. This is where paying the small subscription fee to a research and rating service can be worth it. Sites like Consumer Reports and JD Power can be a valuable investment. Visit them below:

**http://ConsumerReports.org**

**http://JDPower.com**

## "$1,800.00 a Month Working 2 Days Per Week at Garage Sales."

Martin Jenko is entering his 16th year of full-time self-employment. In a good month he will earn as much as $6000.00. The interesting part is he only works about two days per week.

The business he's in is not only profitable, but unique. Because his success could be *duplicated* by others around the United States. In fact, a television marketing company wanted to create an infomercial about his business. They offered him a generous commission to help create an infomercial and product which could be sold on television.

At the last minute, before signing the contract, he declined. It might've been a lucrative deal. But Martin got concerned it might create *too much competition* within his local market and jeopardize his income. However...

If the thought of earning $1800 per month working two days per week at garage sales appeals to you, then get ready to discover an interesting opportunity.

I met Martin nearly 5 years ago. Because we were both self-employed, we began "talking shop" as they say. Little did I know the next few weeks would change my life. This is because Martin not only explained his business, but offered to teach it to me as long as I agreed *not* to work in his local market.

**"$4.2 million per week at garage sales."**

Every week in the United States an estimated $4.2 million changes hands at garage sales. It's an interesting statistic. But Martin doesn't *hold* garage sales. Instead, he visits them looking to buy *two* things. And this has been his "cash cow" for over 15 years. Here's how it works...

Every Saturday and Sunday Martin wakes up early, gets in his car, and drives around visiting garage sales. Naturally, when you've been visiting garage sales as long as he has, you know the neighborhoods to go. After all these years, he's got it down to a bit of a science.

Martin visits each garage sale looking for two *specific* items. Not every garage sale has them (but enough do). He then resells these items for an average 462% profit. I know you're wondering...

**"What is he buying that's so profitable to resell?"**

I will tell you. Because it's so simple you will probably scoff at the idea like I did when I first heard about it (until I spent several weekends with him visiting garage sales). So here's the deal. Martin is in the *precious metals* business.

In other words, he visits garage sales looking to buy *gold* and *silver*. And after more than 15 years in the business, he's gotten very good at it. In fact, I've seen him PROFIT as much as...

**"$1,900.00 in a single day."**

Obviously, not every day is that profitable. But I think you will be intrigued to learn about how his business works. Because it is a rare one. Also, I will explain the $1,900 day and how it came to be. But for the sake of this report (and because we are limited on time and space) let's get down to the details.

Martin buys and sells gold and silver at an average profit of about 462%. Over 90% of his gold and silver is purchased by visiting garage sales on the weekends. On rare occasion, he will make purchases from thrift stores but only if he happens to be in the area and wander in (this is rare).

**"What kind of gold and silver does Martin buy?"**

ANSWER: anything he can resell for profit! At garage sales Martin comes across about any type of gold or silver you can imagine. For example, it could be jewelry, coins, tableware, picture frames, or silverware.

Each item has its own profit potential. For example, I watched him purchase two candleholders for five dollars which had an instant profit for him of $50. But I have also seen him purchase jewelry and coins which were far more profitable.

For educational purposes (and to make this report simple) I'll focus on his biggest money maker. You see, in order to be successful doing what Martin does you need to educate yourself about gold and silver and what it's worth. This means you need to know the value of jewelry, coins, tableware, and silverware sets.

If you have a passion for this, you are in luck. Because it will blow your mind how profitable it can be if you are willing to *learn the craft* and *pound the pavement* on weekends...

**"The secret behind Martin's biggest money maker..."**

When Martin visits these garage sales he is willing to buy any type of gold or silver which he can resell for profit. Naturally, this requires learning about all the types of gold and silver which can be resold. This includes coins, jewelry, picture frames, tableware and silverware.

As you can imagine, anything else of value which he comes across while pursuing gold and silver he will also pick up at a bargain to resell for profits. This includes watches, artwork and firearms. Although he has never lost money in 15 years buying a firearm, his biggest money maker over the years is one thing...

**"Silverware Sets."**

Yes, silverware sets. The day he made $1900 he purchased a complete silverware set from a garage sale for $600. He resold that set for $2500 making him a $1900 profit. Again, this does not happen every single weekend. But it happens enough that he has continued to do business for 15 years. Real sterling silverware can be worth a fortune. For example. Depending on the pattern...

**"A single sterling silver knife could be worth up to $75.00. And an entire silverware set could be worth over $3000.00."**

You may be asking, why would someone sell a silverware set that's worth $2500 for only $600? Because people holding garage sales are usually moving. They are not concerned with trying to get as much money as possible for every item they have. They have a lot on their mind and are selling a lot of things usually. If you've ever moved, you know the feeling.

In most cases, people are *enamored* to receive hundreds of dollars for something they could care less about. Which brings me to a few secrets about Martin's business. Secrets which you need to know if you're thinking about pursuing it in your part of the country. They are...

1. You need to know **how to find** silverware sets.
2. You need to know **how to identify** what the silverware is worth.
3. You need to know **how to sell** the silverware.

It's only three steps. But like anything which is really profitable, you'd be amazed how intricate these three steps are. This is not a get rich quick scheme. This is **a real business** which requires some time and effort to develop. In the beginning, the main investment, is in that of your education. Which begins with step one...

**"How to find silverware sets."**

Believe it or not, finding a silverware set at a garage sale involves a lot more than just walking up and spotting it on the driveway. In the majority of cases, silverware sets (as well as other precious metals) are NOT sitting out in the open at garage sales. No. *It's not that easy.* It takes a little *ingenuity* to find them.

Martin has a simple process which he repeats over and over. Again, this is a process he has perfected over many years. And I would say in well over 70% of the cases where he finds precious metals, they are **NOT** sitting out open at the garage sale. Instead, he has to start friendly conversation and eventually get into the person's house. The conversation might go something like this...

As he gets out of his car and is walking up the driveway to the garage sale where all the items are spread out he will smile and (and in a friendly tone) say *"Are you still taking money today?"* And this will lead to further conversation.

Then, he will explain he is looking for silverware. If they say they don't have any, he will then ask questions about other potential metals they may have (i.e. coins or jewelry etc.). While asking these questions he's cruising around looking for anything else of value which can make his time invest in the visit profitable.

I can't tell you how many times this small conversation led us into the bedrooms and jewelry boxes of people having garage sales. The "gift of gab" goes a long way in certain businesses. And this one is no exception. On to step two...

**"How to identify what the silverware is worth."**

Of course, finding a silverware set does you no good if you're unable to identify what it is worth. A plated silverware set is worth almost nothing compared to a true *sterling silver* silverware set with the proper patterns. Solid silver and the patterns are what determine the value. If you don't know what you're doing you will not know what to offer to pay for a set. A dangerous combination.

There are a few ways to get the education you need to know what you are doing. Obviously, the best way is to get your education "hands-on." You could do this by finding someone who is a precious metals expert. You can find them by contacting what's known as a "silver matching" service. You can search "silver matching service" on the Internet. Or, go to your local library.

I would find at least three and offer to pay someone to teach you. They should be more than happy if they are smart. Why? Because ultimately you will be able to help them. You'll know why in a moment.

The point is to understand that "precious metals experts" are not hard to find. And, it is not too difficult to find someone who is willing to teach you the business for a fair price. Even $25 per hour would be a bargain to learn the trade. Remember, you're talking about a business that you can earn income from for years. Once you are confident in knowing how to spot silverware sets of value you're on to the final step...

**"How to sell the silverware."**

There are few ways to sell quality silverware sets. One is to sell to a pawn shop. This will bring the *lowest* price. The next is to sell to a smelter who will melt down the silverware set for its raw metal value. But, they only pay the *wholesale value* of the silver and not the retail. Another bad option.

To get the most money for a silverware set, you need to sell it to a "silver matching" service. The silver matching service pays based upon the *real value* of the set. This includes the value of the silver as well as the value of the pattern and artwork of the silverware by the manufacturer.

To get the most money for your silverware you will want to get at least three quotes from silver "matching" services. Again, some silverware sets are worth astounding amounts of money. A single knife can be worth from $25 to as much as $75 depending on the pattern.

But remember, silverware sets are only the "gravy" part of the business. While you are visiting garage sales (and thrift stores) you will come across a number of *other items* which can be bought and sold, in some cases, for huge profits. How huge? Here are some examples...

**"At a thrift store in Phoenix Arizona, Zach Norris, paid $5.99 for a rare diving watch which he then sold for $35,000.00"**

**"At a thrift store in Asheville, North Carolina, a man paid $.58 for a West Point jacket worn by Vince Lombardi when he was coaching football. The jacket later sold for $43,000.00"**

**"At a thrift store in Michigan, a man paid $22 for a bronze bust which was later resold for $900.00"**

**"Tips for finding garage sales."**

Believe it or not, Martin had some strategies for finding garage sales. Today, 99% of people would just go to the Internet and enter in a website like craigslist.org to find garage sales. And that's the problem...

Not that you shouldn't do that, but the best opportunities are usually *hidden*. For example, many local papers offer free ads for garage sales. This is one strategy Martin would use. But believe it or not, the bulk of what he did was drive around neighborhoods early in the morning *looking for signs*. This is because most garage sales are NOT advertised online or in the newspaper. Nope.

This is because most people when doing a garage sale just throw signs up one or two days before stating the street and time. Of course, Martin would know all the neighborhoods to drive (and you will too in time).

**"An investment in your education."**

Now, let's do some serious number crunching to break down what your time can be worth in this business. Your first investment of time will be in that of your education. You'll need to learn about different types of gold and silver and what they are worth. This way you will have the skills necessary to buy it.

Let's say this education takes 30 hours and costs you $600. This is based on finding someone (as we spoke of earlier) and paying them $20 per hour to teach you. If you received this education at a rate of five hours per week over 6 weeks it would only be $100 per week.

This is a darn good deal when you realize how much you can earn. Unless there are dozens of people scouting every garage sale in every neighborhood in your potential areas (which is extremely rare). But let's play the numbers down. Because everything is usually harder and more difficult than we originally planned. And this is where a valuable tool comes I call...

**S.I.N.A.L.O.A.**
**(Safety In Numbers And the Law Of Averages)**

One of the biggest mistakes people make in business is that of *not* knowing their numbers. A person will come across a hot product which they can sell for $500 and earn $250 in commission. *What they fail to break down is how much time and money it will take to make that sale.*

The worst case of this is in multilevel or network marketing where a person is being paid a tiny commission for selling what is usually an *overpriced* product. To make matters more difficult, there is immense competition from thousands of distributors who are all selling the SAME thing.

But in their head, the person will think "If I get two, and they get two, and they each get two. I'll have a giant down line and make a ton of money." Of course, this almost *never* happens.

And this is why SINALOA is so important. SINALOA stands for "safety in numbers and the law of averages." Let's apply SINALOA to this business...

Let's say you spent six hours a day, two days a week, for four weeks, scouting garage sales for gold and silver. This would be a total of 48 hours. And, let's say you only visited a total of 48 garage sales (that's only an average of one per hour. In dense neighborhoods, you will actually do much more). But for math sake...

Let's say out of those 48 garage sales you only found $600 worth of gold and silver items (i.e. jewelry, coins, tableware, silverware etc.). And, let's say these items would be resold at a 400% markup or $2400.00.

This would leave you a gross profit of $1800.00 before paying for automotive expenses. But let's do simple math on the $1800.00. When we divide $1800.00 by 48 hours we find...

**"You earned $37.50 per hour."**

This is pretty good spare time income for a business you can start for about 800 bucks. Also, I think we can agree these numbers are reality based. Remember, we're talking about visiting 48 garage sales in 48 hours over a period of four weeks. I've seen Martin make this much in three days. Of course, every three days in the field are not like that. But again, that's why we must remember SINALOA. Safety in numbers and the law of averages!

**ACTION STEPS:**

Here's what to do next. If you like garage sales and hunting for items of value, this opportunity may be for you. Like all great opportunities, it all begins with education. One great place you can start and learn about silverware values and get a great basic education are websites like the one below...

**www.AntiqueCupboard.com**

You can also search "silver matching service" on the internet. Remember, you want to know about gold and silver as well as other items of value. Niches to riches is a term some people use. You want to specialize. Either way, you are providing a valuable service for people. The best part... There is opportunity all over America. Because no one can monopolize every garage sale, in every city, every weekend. That's what I call a true "grassroots" business.

## "How to earn up to $115,200.00 per year as a Debt Consultant."

**"Close to half of Americans have more credit card debt than savings."**
*-CBS Money Watch*

**"More than 35 percent of Americans have debts and unpaid bills which have been reported to collection agencies."**
*- The Urban Institute*

Are you in debt or do you know someone who is struggling to pay their bills? And I don't mean a car loan or mortgage.

We're talking credit card debt with interest rates designed to keep you enslaved for decades.

Or medical debt, which often isn't even your fault. Here's an example.

Today, more Americans than ever have health insurance.

So how can they possibly end up with medical debt?

Let's say you go in for a procedure and are put to sleep. While you are out the hospital brings in some "out-of-network" providers to assist with the procedure. Later, you get a bill for the out-of-network service.

If you haven't figured it out by now, the system is rigged to against you.

The facts are, since 1979 the purchasing power of Americans has eroded every year, so the only way people could have the life they needed, whether it's to buy school clothes for their kids, take family vacations or make improvements to their homes...

...they had to turn to credit cards or the high interest loans, which today have morphed into payday loans charging interest rates so exorbitant, a banker would be put in jail if he/she tried to charge the same usury rates.

Here's another example. Several years before the Great Recession of 2008, Congress rewrote the bankruptcy laws making it harder for consumers to file.

Most consumers electing bankruptcy are being forced into Chapter 11, meaning only a percentage of their debts are forgiven, but depending on their income they are shackled to make payments to the bankruptcy trustee until they can emerge from Chapter 11 and go on with their life. Sometimes this takes years.

**"Do you know what happened after Congress rewrote the bankruptcy laws?"**

Corporations went on the biggest consumer credit expansion in history because they knew the system was "adjusted" in their favor.

You could no longer easily declare Chapter 7 bankruptcy and have all of your unsecured debts, like credit cards and medical bills erased.

Nope, they had you like shylock and you were forced to give a certain portion of your income to the bankruptcy trustee until you paid what the court determined.

But back to the main point, because the working American has continually seen purchasing power erode over the last 40 years, the ONLY way they could stay in the middle class and avoid poverty is through credit expansion.

And even though the U.S. slowly climbed out of the economic mess back in 2008, it's happening all over again.

" I NEED ANOTHER RAISE SO I CAN PAY FOR THE CAR I BOUGHT TO CELEBRATE MY LAST RAISE. "

**"Today, for the middle class to afford a car, they are turning to 10 year car loans."**

At the same time, corporations who've made out like bandits in the era of unprecedented low interest rates are quickly issuing credit cards and retail credit again (buy furniture pay no interest for 5 years) to consumers who are desperate just to put food on the table, much less drive a car or afford what their kids need for school. But...

**"What does all of this mean to you?"**

An opportunity bigger than ever... for anyone willing to advertise, answer the phone, send email and plug numbers into a spreadsheet or use a calculator. Let me explain...

**"Most consumers are desperate to rein in their debt, they just *don't* know how."**

And for those near the poverty level, their only access to loans is payday advances or pawning the title to their car - both at interest rates so outlandish; they are rarely able to catch up.

**"This is where you come in, providing a valuable service helping them as a Personal Debt Consultant."**

Surprising as it may seem, most people don't know the tricks and tips to take whatever income they have today and make it work in their favor, instead of enriching the politicians who *greased the system* so consumers slide into a hole so dark they can't see a way out.

You may believe people in debt are not good candidates to sell anything to, but when a consumer has an urgent need, they will find a way to fill it...

**"...Consider this fact."**

**If a consumer gets hit with a tax lien, they freak out and call a lawyer who advertises they help with taxes and pay $500 to $900 for the Attorney to do what the consumer could do themselves (if they knew how). Something you can teach them for a fraction of the price.**

This is just one example, here's another.

If a consumer gets in over their head with credit cards, they go into one of the 'credit counseling' places (which are primarily funded by the banking industry) and pay a fortune in monthly fees just to have someone contact the credit card companies and help... but in the end. They stay in debt even longer because credit counseling companies have **ZERO INCENTIVE** to help a person get out of debt quickly. In fact, the longer they stay in debt, the more the company makes!

**"As a Debt Consultant, you can give them everything they need to get debt free AT A FRACTION of what lawyers, credit counseling companies and loan consolidators charge."**

*The market is HUGE and not going away because "Close to half of Americans have more credit card debt than savings" and "More than 35 percent of Americans have debts and unpaid bills that have been reported to collection agencies."*

Just one little cash flow interruption like a car repair, health scare, job loss, home repair, etc. – can send them deeper into debt.

Let me ask you a question…

**"…do you think you could listen to people and plug numbers into a spreadsheet or use a calculator?"**

That's about how easy it is. You ask a client basic questions about income and obligations, and then plug them into a spreadsheet...

...and then you access debt elimination strategies, suggesting the best ones for the client's situation.

All the while you are ensuring they are following the strategies you gave them to get out of debt.

**"It's like a personal trainer... but for finances."**

It really is that simple once you know how.

*Because most consumers don't know how to get interest rates reduced, negotiate a settlement or dispute unfair charges.*

And most important of all, you can show anyone, no matter what income... even if they are on unemployment... proven, workable steps to deploy their limited capital to emerge debt free up to 85% faster.

The best part is your service is affordable. Because (in the end) it does not cost the client money. Because you help them GET OUT OF DEBT FASTER! Just one strategy (like getting an interest rate reduced) can save your client over $9,000! And they get all this in a one year program for only $480 which works out to just $40 per month. Less than a cup of coffee per day. It's a no brainer.

If you help just 10 people a month, your fees will be over $57,600 a year.

**"One new client per day and your income is $115,200.00 per year."**

That's just 20 clients a month. And remember, they are out there calling others who just rip them off.

Think of how many referrals you'll get when you deliver real debt relief results!

Now, I know the next thing you may be thinking... "How will I get these customers?"

It's as simple as advertising, passing out business cards, conducting free seminars, putting up a flyer in a high traffic location, or posting your services on a number of websites offering free consultations and education.

Now before you hide inside your piggy bank because I mentioned you will have to advertise, let me break it down on how fast, easy and (most important) cost-effective it is to get new customers.

After you develop a steady stream of customers, referrals can kick in and this can give you the profits to advertise regularly.But to develop that stream of customers you need to ask friends and family one simple question...

**..."If I could show you a guaranteed way to eliminate your debt up to 90% faster, what would you say?"**

And remember what was proven at the beginning of this report: a lot of Americans are in debt and they simply hope things will get better because they have no clue as to what to do.

One of the most powerful selling features is a demonstration, so your very first client can be YOU.

You can use the information you glean to fix your own debts and even if you are one of the lucky few Americans who don't have credit card debt, you probably still have a mortgage or a car loan.

And you'd like to pay them both off faster, right?

**"So after you apply what you've learned you can demonstrate to friends and family members how you put *yourself* on the path to financial freedom."**

Next, you can use classified ads and other easy-to-do, low cost strategies to find consumers who want to get out of debt.

You'll be doing consumers a big favor steering them away from the *debt relief industry* because it is rigged for people to stay in debt longer so the industry makes more money.

Many people are shocked when they learn the credit counseling industry receives 66% of their income from the banking industry, all rigged to keep consumers from learning the information *you'll teach them* as their personal debt consultant.

Plus most of the credit counseling industry charges a monthly fee, giving them a built in incentive for consumers to stay in debt *longer*.

Even the non-profits set up to help consumers with debt problems are really just fronts for shady operators to make a boatload of money, while the consumer continues to struggle with debt.

**"If you are skeptical about the cash-flow opportunity working as a Personal Debt Consultant let me provide you some facts..."**

Until now, people only had *five solutions* to get out of debt. And these solutions had failure rates up to 99%. But when I reveal the "flaws" with these solutions, the failure rates are no surprise. Let me explain...

**"Dirty Secrets of the Debt Relief Industry"**

There are a lot of people who *don't* want you to learn what I teach. In fact, they would love for you to quit reading - right now. All because of one thing. And that is...

**"The longer you stay in debt the <u>more</u> money they make"**

Don't forget this (it will prove priceless in a moment). Because until now, there were only five solutions to eliminate debt. You have probably seen them advertised. They are...

***1.) Consumer Credit Counseling***

***2.) Debt Consolidation Loans***

***3.) Debt Settlement Companies***

**4.) Bankruptcy Attorneys**

**5.) "How To" Books**

What I am about to share will be hard to believe. But you can <u>verify</u> it. I have nothing to hide. I have researched the <u>facts</u> and stand by them.

Here is the truth...

**"A Carson City Brothel is 100 times *more* honest than Consumer Credit Counseling"**

Prostitution is *legal* in parts of northern Nevada. And a 30 minute drive from *Incline Village* is a place you may have seen on TV...

Located in *Carson City* is the world famous

**"Moonlight Bunny Ranch"** owned by *Dennis Hof* from the **HBO Series *Cathouse***. Not only has Dennis been in the brothel business over 20 years...

...but he was invited to speak at **Oxford University** on the subject. And I don't believe *anyone* forgot his opening statement when he said...

*"Hello, and thank you for having me at the world's oldest university to discuss the world's oldest profession..."*

Regardless of what we think of legal prostitution - the fact remains...

**"Legal Prostitution is *more* honest *than Consumer Credit Counseling*"**

And here's why...

***The National Consumer Law Center and the Consumer Federation of America spent 2 years investigating the Credit Counseling industry. When they were done. Their findings were published in a 58 page report titled "Credit Counseling in Crisis."***

Here are the abbreviated findings of that report...

**<u>STRIKE-ONE:</u>**

*The bulk of Credit Counseling offices are members of the National Foundation for Credit Counseling (aka the NFCC).* Which totals over 1,300 offices nationwide. What consumers *don't* know is these "member offices" **RECEIVE <u>TWO-THIRDS</u> OF THEIR INCOME FROM THE BANKING INDUSTRY.**

**<u>STRIKE-TWO:</u>**

The majority of *Credit Counseling* Services charge a *monthly fee* (even though a study has proven most will lie about it). Because of this fee. **The longer you stay in debt, the *more* money credit counseling will make**. Therefore they have *no incentive* to help you get out of debt quickly.

**<u>STRIKE-THREE:</u>**

A survey of **Internal Revenue Service (IRS)** tax reports revealed alarming findings. So called *"non-profit"* agencies were reaping windfall profits. For example...

***Credit Counselors of America* reported net profits of just over $6,000,000.00 MILLION per year. *Cambridge Credit Counseling* reported a net profit of about $7,300,000.00 MILLION per year.**

***Genus Credit Management* reported profits of about $5,600,000.00 MILLION.** They also reported paying their general manager a salary of **$394,122.00** plus benefits. *Credit Counselors of America* reported compensation for its *President Michael Hall* of **$371,542.00** plus benefits. But that's not all...

**<u>VERIFIED FACT:</u>**

**President of "Non-Profit" was paid over $296.00 AN HOUR!**

*American Consumer Credit Counseling* reported paying its president a salary of **$462,350.00** plus over **$130,000.00** in benefits. This works out to **$592,350.00** a year or **$296.18** per hour.

**"Is it any wonder the Internal Revenue Service revoked the tax exempt status of over 41 credit counseling organizations?"**

**Even the largest Consumer Credit Counseling Service in the Nation (AmeriDebt) was sued by the Federal Trade Commission (FTC) for $172,000,000.00 MILLION.** Again, *Dennis Hofs' BunnyRanch* is *more* honest than *Credit Counseling*. But you're probably wondering...

**"What about Debt Consolidation?"**

Have you ever heard the saying "Robbing Peter to pay Paul?" It's the perfect definition for *Debt Consolidation*. Except *Consolidation* is worse and here's why...

*Debt Consolidation* is nothing more than taking on "new debt" to pay "old debt". In other words. A banker would have you *consolidate* multiple debts into one large debt. This may seem harmless. But it's financial suicide. Let me explain...

One of the keys to getting out of debt fast is this. You rarely want to apply the same strategy to *every* debt you have. Why? Because some strategies work better than others...

For example. One strategy might be great for credit cards and medical bills. While another technique is better for car loans and mortgages. As a result...

**"We use something called 'THE METHOD MATRIX' so you can determine which method is best for you in *less* than 15 minutes"**

And there are over 24 methods to choose from... but the minute you sign up for *Debt Consolidation...* you throw all 24 in the trash. But the worst part is...

...Debt consolidation *keeps you in debt longer*. For example. Let's say you have two credit cards totaling $10,000.00 at 16% interest and a medical bill for $4,000.00 at 12% interest. Your monthly payment on these is $360 a month. So it will take you about **4 YEARS** to get out of debt.

Now, a debt consolidation company says they can "help you" by "consolidating" your debts into a new loan at 11% interest... which will *lower* your monthly payment to $240 a month. And...

They say this will "save you" $120 a month. Sounds great, except there's a catch. Instead of 4 years to get out of debt, it will now take you...

**"6 YEARS and 8 Months to get out of debt"**

Can you see why banks love *Debt Consolidation*? You stay in debt longer and they make more money. Great for banks... financial suicide for you.

Debt Consolidation is nothing but taking on new debt to pay old debt. Not a smart move. But let's talk about...

**"Secrets of Debt Settlement Companies"**

If you're buried in debt. The thought of having a company "settle your debt" for you may sound appealing. Unfortunately, the *reality* is different from the advertising you see. Here are a few dirty secrets...

**<u>DIRTY SECRET #1:</u>**

**Hidden Fees**

Debt settlement companies have hidden fees which consumers rarely understand as the services are usually sold over the phone. Generally speaking, they work like this. If you have $25,000.00 in credit card debt, they will charge a settlement fee of 20% (or $5,000.00).

You will then be instructed to *quit paying* your creditors. Meanwhile, you will pay money into an escrow account "building up funds" for your settlement. This account costs about $35.00 a month or $420.00 per year.

So after one year your initial fees could be $5420.00 (or more)... and this is *before* you pay a dime of debt off. Why? Because the settlement company (or Attorney) will be paid *before* your creditors are. But more concerning is...

**DIRTY SECRET #2:**
**Lack of attention to detail**

The most troubling issue with debt settlement has to do with the lack of attention to detail. You see, debt settlement by itself can be a good way to reduce debt, but there's a catch...

Your creditors would rather hear from YOU than "some company" you've hired. Because of this fact. Many creditors enforce a policy the moment they discover you've signed up with a debt settlement company... *they automatically sue you in court.*

**DIRTY SECRET #3:**
**Tax liability on forgiven debt**

One thing debt settlement companies explain in small print is about taxes. And that is that *you will be liable for income taxes* on your forgiven debt. For example...

If your debt was settled and a total of $10,000.00 was forgiven. Then you will owe taxes on that $10,000.00 as if it were *income*. If you're in a 25% tax bracket that would be $2500.00. And remember, this is on top of *their* fees.

And if you're *not* issued a 1099 by the creditor, you are still *required* (under I.R.S. law) to claim the forgiven debt as income. Failing to do so would be...

**"NON-compliance with U.S. Tax Law"**

If you're currently able to make your monthly payments but are struggling, then debt settlement could be "one tool" in your debt elimination plan. However, there are two things you *must* know...

**(1.)** ***Your creditors want to hear from YOU - not some company.***

And,

**(2.) With our program you can get better results *without* paying fees.**

This means *more cash in your pocket* and you eliminating your debt faster. Either way, it's a more viable option than the B-Word. Which is...

**"...Bankruptcy."**

This is one option I hope you *never* explore. What upsets me is when Attorney's talk people into filing without explaining all the consequences.

I've met people who filed bankruptcy for $11,000. This is a disgrace and here's why... Many people discover the mistake of filing only *after* it's too late. There are many reasons for this. Today I will share two of them. According to a survey by the *Society for Human Resource Management...*

**"Over 50% of employers now run credit reports on job applicants"**

The days of being hired on a handshake and a look in the eye are over. Computers and automation have made sure of that.

Many professions which require licensing, bonding or a security clearance - will *not* accept an applicant who's filed bankruptcy.

I cannot tell you how many people *lose* a great job (before they start) because of a bankruptcy on their credit report.

I wish Attorneys were more honest. I think if a person is going to file bankruptcy. They should know *all* the consequences. Not just the convenient ones.

And this brings us to the fifth solution people turn to in order to eliminate debt - which is "How To" books...

**"Did you know there are now over 23,536 books on how to get out of debt?"**

Talk about overwhelming... that's a truck and trailer load. Don't get me wrong. Books are great.

But there are *two* problems with them...

**PROBLEM #1:**

**Lack of Strategies and Customization**

If you want to get out of debt *fast*. You need to use a variety of strategies customized to your situation. Because everyone is different.

And to put all these strategies into ONE BOOK would require that book to be **almost 1,000 pages** (you'll learn why in a moment). But you still would not be able to personalize that book to *your* situation. Which brings us to...

**PROBLEM #28:**

**No Follow Up Support**

Because we're all unique. Everyone has different questions when it comes to getting out of debt. And...

**"All the 'get out of debt' books in the world become worthless the minute you have a question"**

This is why 99% of people who rely on a book to get out of debt fail. Because to get out of debt fast... you need *more* than a book. You need a variety of strategies and a *support* system.

But you're probably wondering...

**"If Credit Counseling, Debt Consolidation, Debt Settlement Bankruptcy and 'How To' books are *NOT* the answer to get out of debt... then what is?"**

Again. I come back to what I said earlier **"The secret to how you can get out of debt fast comes down to two things."**

**NUMBER ONE:**

You need someone who can teach you the "inside knowledge" to get out of debt.

And...

**NUMBER TWO:**

You need someone who can help you *apply this knowledge* to your situation.

The secret to getting out of debt fast is that simple. It's also the reason why the **"Fight Debt and Win"** coaching program was designed with this in mind Because "keeping it simple" is critical.

This is because...

**"The *SAME* thinking which got you into debt cannot be used to get you out of debt."**

And this fact holds true even if your debts were *not* your fault.

For example. If you got laid off... hit by an uninsured motorist... or had a surprise medical emergency. The fact remains. As *Einstein* said...

**"Our problems cannot be solved with the *SAME* thinking which created them."**

Lack of understanding this fact is the reason *millions* of people fail to get out of debt each year. But let me be clear...

Your Debt Consultant service will be a "breath of fresh air" for indebted consumers. Why? Because you will "coach them" step by step on how to get out of debt. Remember, it's like a personal trainer but for getting out of debt.

This a REAL BUSINESS which you can start for under $800 and have the potential to earn over $115,200.00 per year. To get started you can study the various books at your local library on debt elimination. Then start your business by providing your service for free to gain a few satisfied customer stories.

On the other hand, if you would like to learn a step by step program to teach you the Debt Consultant business, then write the words **"Fight Debt and Win Info Pack"** along with $5 and your name and address and send it to:

Zodi Publishing
100 Easy St Unit 5590
Carefree AZ 85377-7133

“

Luck is
when opportunity
*meets* preparedness.

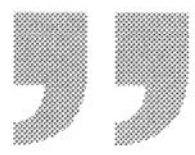

**Zodi Publishing**
*Presents...*

# Quick Cash Secrets "Newsletters" -Bundle-

## Issues 1 thru 6

- ☑ **Quickest, Easiest Way To Cook Up $3,000 Monthly Income (page 8)**
- ☑ **You'll Shine With This $1,600 A Week Easy To Do Business (page 8)**
- ☑ **What They Never Tell You About Business Opportunities (page 9)**
- ☑ **How To Turn Airport Hassles Into $40 An Hour Anytime You Want To Work And You Never Set Foot In An Airport! (page 17)**
- ☑ **Frame Up A Bundle Of Cash In Real Estate Without Ever Buying Or Selling Any Property (page 20)**
- ☑ **Lady Turns Job Loss Into Bright Income Double (page 24)**
- ☑ **Easier Than You Think To Make $25 An Hour Handing Out Samples (page 27)**
- ☑ **And much, much more!!!**

*(Details inside...)*

**Disclaimer**

This publication is designed to provide accurate and authoritative information in regard to the subject matter covered in it. It is sold with the understanding that the publisher and author are not engaged in rendering legal, accounting, or other professional service. If legal advice or other expert assistance is required, the services of a competent, professional person should be sought." (From a Declaration of Principles jointly adopted by a Committee of the American Bar Association and Committee of Publishers and Associations.) The author has attempted to provide accurate information on the subject matter covered. However, the readers are advised to conduct their own research carefully before investing time or money in any business. The author and publisher make no guarantees, warranties, or representations of any kind. Therefore, the author and publisher specifically disclaim any liability, loss, or risk, personal or otherwise, incurred as a consequence, directly or indirectly, of the content, subject matter or use and application of any of the information provided herein, or otherwise; and this publication is sold with this understanding and none other. Use of stories. In some cases stories of real customers are used but may be altered or embellished in order to facilitate the learning of a concept. These stories should be considered completely fictional though based on customer stories submitted to us. Although the sources listed in this publication are believed to be reliable, they are listed for purposes of example only and the author and publisher cannot guarantee the readers' satisfaction in dealing with any individuals and companies. Comparison shopping is always recommended.

Zodi Publishing
**Q.C.S. Newsletter**
http://ZodiPublishing.com

# Welcome to Your First Issue of the Quick Cash Secrets Newsletter

Dear Subscriber,

You know what they say... no one forgets their "first" time. And this is your *first* issue of the **"Quick Cash Secrets"** Newsletter. So let's dive in to what we are going to cover. Because our time today will go fast...



At 1:30 PM I received the phone call. The kind of call I am *tired* of receiving...
When I share the details of it, you *will* understand why. So let me explain...

If you haven't noticed lately... there are a lot of **evil people** in the world. But because of technology (and the direction the world is going) sometimes it appears there are *more* of them...

And, it seems there are *more* people to victimize because larger numbers of us are living in scarcity and fear (*thank you mainstream media and conspiracy theorists...*)

Because nothing makes you **lose** common sense *faster* than being in an emotional state of fear and desperation. Because these emotions have proven to make even the smartest people dumb (in seconds).

But let's get back to the phone call. Sherry had recently purchased the **"Quick Cash Secrets" Manual** and Audio CD's and was *very* satisfied.

She was calling because she had a few questions about the **"Fight Debt and Win"** course we offer at:

**http:/ZodiPublishing.com**

However, from the moment the call began, Sherry seemed frantic (like something was wrong...).

She was asking questions about the program (which is normal), but she was *not* in a calm state of mind. This was a concern to me...

Because anyone who is going to **INVEST MONEY** in a home study course... I want to be sure they understand *what* they are investing their money in. So...

After answering her questions (and clearing up some concerns) she mentioned "an investment" she had made which she was waiting to receive a return on.

She explained she had invested $15,000.00 with a firm, which...

**"Guaranteed her a return of $5,000.00 on her investment in only FOUR months!"**

*Think about that claim for a moment.* Making $5,000.00 from an investment of $15,000.00 in only four months? That would be a passive return of 100% annually...

This means you could invest $30,000.00 (one time) and earn $2,500.00 per month - ***FOR LIFE!***

The sad part is... the second I heard those words I *knew* she had been scammed for $15,000.00 and would never get her money back. Sadly...

**"These phone calls are happening more and more and they depress the hell out of me."**

Here's why...

Sherry, is no sprung chicken. Because not only is Sherry in retirement age (and gone through the trauma of losing family) she ***cannot*** afford to lose $15,000.00 at this point in her life. No. Not even close.

**"But I am stuck telling her the TRUTH and reality of her situation..."**

Would you like to know the truth of Sherry's situation?

Because sadly... I am not only depressed (but disgusted) to share it with you. So here it is...

The organization which *preyed* on Sherry (and her vulnerable situation) used telemarketing to con her out of **$15,000.00**. How can this happen?

It's pretty simple. The organization made Sherry *think* she was investing her money in **helping other people** and she would earn a return in the process (for her noble deed).

The reality?

She signed a contract investing her $15,000.00 in "advertising services" which are **100% non-refundable** (stated in the contract in bold print above her signature - *remember this*).

Because this means when she *disputes* the charge with her credit card company she will fail and lose her $15,000.00...

How can this happen?

Sadly... it comes down to what I call...

**The Golden Rule:**

**"He who has the checkbook... ...MAKES the rules!"**

In reality, the credit card company *should* side with Sherry because she was taken advantage of through **evil people** and telemarketing. However...

The telemarketer *"talked"* her into signing an agreement because she was *desperate*. But that's not the way the world works. Because she will dispute the charge with the credit card company and she **will** lose.
*Why?*
Because she *signed* a contract which stated...

***"All sales are final and there are NO REFUNDS."***

So the company gets to "legally" steal Sherry's $15,000.00... and this kind of thing happens everyday because...

**"When people get *desperate*... ...they tend to get stupid."**

So the next time you get depressed about losing $50.00, $100.00, $500.00, $1500.00 or $3500.00 on a business opportunity... think about *Sherry* and her loss, ok?

Because these are the depressing phone calls we keep receiving... so please... do **NOT** fall for...

**"We do it all for you guaranteed moneymaking systems, ok?"**

Before moving on... let me state the obvious. Because years ago I paid a consultant *thousands of dollars* to help me. And that was a term he used to use often...

***"Never under estimate the power of looking for the obvious..."***

Think about what I just said and how it applies to the ridiculous opportunities you might have been ripped off for in the past?

Because if someone had a *"Turnkey proven automated system"* why would they need you to invest in it?

Think about it... if they had a *postcard, letter, email, radio ad* (or auto dialer pitch) that made money... **WHY WOULD THEY NEED YOU TO INVEST IN IT?** They could just use their *own* money and keep reinvesting it. In other words, they could *"start small and grow like a snowball."*

Don't worry... we will dedicate an upcoming **"R.C.S. Bulletin"** to this. And, it will be an issue you will NOT want to miss...

## SECTION II: "Congratulations new member!"

Welcome to your first issue of the **"Quick Cash Secrets"** newsletter. Before we forget, let's get clear about the main thing. And that is...

**"THE GOAL..."**

Because the goal is simple. And that goal is to make you money on your investment in the **"Real Cash Secrets"** Club. And we take your investment *very* seriously.

Because you are not only investing your money with us, but also **your time**. So let's quickly recap...

You already received the **"Real Cash Secrets"** Manual, Audio CD's and Bonus Reports (*now printed in your manual*). And you will receive 6 issues of this newsletter.

Newsletters are normally mailed every 60 days (but may come *sooner)*. We also send out special updates and reports from time to time.

Now, before we jump into your first newsletter, let's cover some *vital* information...

...after all, we are living in a world of information *overload*. As a result (in many cases) life changing knowledge is right in front of us... and sometimes, we *fail* to grasp it. Why?

**"Because we are too busy driving the car to STOP and put gas in it."**

**"Could this be the case with you and the *'Real Cash Secrets'* Manual by chance?**

We spent 2 years and over $38,500.00 researching, writing and editing the **"Real Cash Secrets"** Manual. So if you have not read it... I suggest you do *before* reading this bulletin Because there is gold *within* those pages. Trust me on this...

## SECTION III:

**"Don't let being afraid of computers cost you thousands when their is FREE help!"**

And if you *don't* have a computer... please do **NOT** let that stop you from profitting thousands of dollars...

How do you solve this problem? Simple. Go to a library and a librarian can help you access the information you're looking for... FREE. It doesn't mean you're going to go there every day. It just means you are showing up to access some information *that* day.

Remember, your tax dollars pay for people there to help you. The beautiful part is there is usually some great folks with lots of experience (and patience) who will enjoy helping you.

The process may *seem* a bit intimidating, but don't be surprised if you find the experience fun. Because in the end "change" is never easy... but almost always - **WORTH IT.**

Bring the **"Real Cash Secrets"** manual along with you and highlight all the websites you want to visit. Someone there should be more than happy to help you. Don't worry about pecking on the keyboard one key at a time... heck, I know successful people who still type that way!

Because if you have not researched the **"Real Cash Secrets"** manual from front to back (more than once). You are missing out. And here's why...

## SECTION IV:

**"Why just ONE IDEA can solve your money problems**

Let's use deodorant for example... because **a good way to predict the future is to first study the past.** Yes... deodorant might hold the key to *your* future success.

Let me explain...

In 1888 the first deodorant was released and patented by an inventor in Philadelphia PA. It was called "mum." Yes, Mum...

But the real breakthrough came later... when in the 1940's another inventor named *Barnett Diserens* developed an ingenious method of *applying* that deodorant.

Prior to *Diserens*, applying deodorant was like rubbing wax under your arm. But Barnett looked at a **ball point pen** one day and came up with the idea of a "ROLL-ON" applicator...

**"The same applicator MILLIONS came to know as BAN 'roll-on' deodorant!"**

Between 1942 and 1957 the market for deodorant increased over **600 times** to become a **$70 MILLION** dollar market. And this was in 1940's dollars (*today we could call it a Billion!*).

The moral of the story is *two-fold.* **Not only can ONE IDEA make you rich.** But rather than "reinventing the wheel..." you can save time by applying an idea from one market to that of an *emerging* market. This was the **secret** behind the Ban "roll-on" success story...

*Barnett Diserens* applied a successful idea from one market (ball point pens) to that of an *emerging* market (deodorant) and made a fortune in the process (not to mention helped a lot of people with body odor *solve* a problem). But the real question is...

**"What IDEA is standing between you and SUCCESS?"**

Are you stumped? Good. That's why you *joined* the **"R.C.S. Club."** Not only because you are smart and seek knowledge... but because you know the value of *inside* information. And, how one idea can change your life...

## SECTION V:

**"The most life-changing income you will ever earn is NOT what you think..."**

I want you to imagine whatever your income is right now, that instead, your income is simply **DOUBLE** that amount. *Why?* Because this is the most **life-changing** income you will ever earn. Yes... you read that correctly.

And I'm willing to bet almost everything you <u>CAN'T</u> do right now (*because of a lack of funds*) you **would be able to do** if your income was only double...

*Work with me here for a minute... please.* Because so many people get caught up in making $30,000.00 a month... they <u>miss</u> the **biggest secret** to making money and changing their life. And that is...

## <u>SECTION VI</u>: "The REAL SECRET to success almost no one talks about..."

Because when I ask people about living "the life" they want... I find it's pretty simple. And it usually comes down to this:

*They want to be able to live where they want to live...*

*Do what they want to do...*

*And feel secure they aren't going to go <u>broke</u> doing it!*

Pretty simple, I'd say... and the key is this: the most life-changing money you will ever make is when your income DOUBLES. And here's why, because...

**"The real secret to success is to make enough money so the <u>only</u> problems you have are the ones money will <u>NOT</u> solve!"**

And please don't tell me buying a *Ferrari* or a mansion is a *<u>problem</u>* you have. Because that's not what we are talking about...

What we are talking about... is this. What if you could wake up tomorrow and **live where you want to live?** Vacation *when* you want to vacation? Go out to eat when you want, and... *not* worry about going <u>broke</u> doing it?

How would that make you feel?

Pretty darn good, right? And you know what...

**"I find most people can achieve this goal by simply <u>DOUBLING</u> their income!"**

Let me share a perfect example of a friend...

He's in his late 50's... like most of us, he's had his share of jobs over the years. From entry-level and sales to management and Corporate America.

He has a few different skills and is a very dedicated hard worker... willing to learn anything. And willing to "pay the price." Between his work ethic and willingness to learn he has SO MUCH going for him...

**"But there is ONE THING which (for him)... makes finding success like chasing a shadow in the night."**

And that "one thing" is this: he's too focused getting rich *quick*.

I'll never forget the day I shared a *unique* business opportunity with him (which he would be perfect for...)

And you know what his response was?

**"If I can't make $30,000.00 a month then I'm <u>NOT</u> interested!"**

I have to tell you. His response frustrated me. Because the opportunity I was sharing was something he would be perfect for. And, he was in a *perfect position* to succeed at it!

**(So you know)** the opportunity and idea I was describing was called *"Business Intelligence Services."* And the concept was both simple and brilliant. So I will share it...

How many times have you dealt with a business (online or over the phone) and because the service was SO BAD you thought to yourself...

**"If the owners of this company had any idea how screwed up their <u>service</u> was they would fix it immediately!"**

Well, that's basically what the company I was telling my friend to start would do. It would **GATHER AND RECORD INTELLIGENCE** on customer experiences (over the phone and email) and sell that intelligence to the company owners. Hence the name ***"Business Intelligence Services."***

But my point is this; my friend was so focused on $30,000.00 A MONTH, he couldn't see the **small goal** of $3,000 a month *(because it would not take much work to get 10 businesses paying $300.00 a month for the service).*

And because he would be doing all the work himself... it would be almost **ALL PROFIT** right from the get go! And this $3000.00 a month would essentially **<u>double</u>** his income! And that's when I asked him a powerful question, which was:

**"If you could be living the life you want to be living (right now) what would it be?"**

He then proceeded to tell me **<u>WHERE</u>** he would be living. **<u>HOW</u>** his house would be furnished. **<u>WHAT</u>** type of car he would be driving. And...

**<u>HOW</u>** his kitchen would be set up. **<u>WHERE</u>** he would go out to eat (and how often). As well as **<u>HOW</u>** much money he would be saving and a few things he would be doing for others (*not to mention some hobbies he wanted to indulge in.*)

**"Before we can change our lives... ...we must change our thinking"**

I then explained (in detail) how he could live this lifestyle by simply **<u>doubling</u>** his income. For example. He wanted to live in a beautiful five-bedroom home with a pool, spa and waterfall. As well as a gourmet kitchen and exceptional landscaping (*blah, blah, blah*).

So... I showed him a **$775,000** home which *met all his needs* and he could rent it for only $2850 a month...

**STOP:**

**"And think about what I just said. Because the property taxes on that home are about $800.00 a month ALONE!"**

Between him and his wife (not to mention his kids pitching in) because they are over 18 and living at home, his total living costs **AFTER** utilities would be $2000 a month.

Living in a $775,000 home for only $2,000 with utilities included? Don't forget the pool, spa and waterfall!

He also wanted to drive a new **Lexus**. So I showed him a way to *lease* a new Lexus for around $595 a month.

Normally, leasing is a *bad idea*. But I explained a way he could make it **tax deductible** *through his business* and live his dream...

Anyway, I could go on with the story, but you get *the idea*.

My point is he could "LIVE HIS DREAM" life by only **doubling** his income. The problem?

**"He failed to see it..."**

No matter how hard I tried. He failed to see it.

So... he keeps *chasing* $30,000.00 a month "get rich quick" schemes while his dream life (*easily achievable*) remains on the back burner. It's really sad. Because just one idea... just one idea could **DOUBLE** his income and allow him to live his dream.

In fact, let's talk about that...

**"The wealth building power of ONE IDEA."**

Because one of the biggest secrets of success, is this... *"The fastest way to get people to throw money at you... is to solve a problem for them."*

Think about it... most of us only part with money to have a problem solved. Because our naturally tendency (as humans) is to be LAZY.

This is why millions respond to the ad for *7-minutes abs* and *weight loss* in a bottle. Not to mention the "secret" system to **WIN THE LOTTERY** or how to stuff envelopes for $10 each. Because these offers appeal to our LAZY human nature.

In this *"R.C.S. Bulletin"* we are going to repeat a "mantra" (and I hope you are ready for it). Because here it is...

**"The truth WILL set you free but first it might piss you off if you're not ready!"**

Because the truth is... to build long-term wealth... you **WILL** have to create or do something which *serves* others... period.

Maybe it is a product? Maybe it is a service? Or maybe it's just a *different way* of doing something better? But the truth is, in order to make money (honest money)...

**"You WILL have to do something which uses your God given talents to SERVE OTHERS and that's the truth!"**

Don't get discouraged. Instead, get excited. And let me give you some reasons why. Not by giving you "false hope" and **selling you dreams** (which so many do) but by providing you something *more* valuable.

And that is... the **TRUTH**. But in the form of "ideas." Ideas which will get your mind *thinking* and *working* in a new way...

Just like Barnett Diserens... because when his breakthrough for "roll-on" deodorant hit him... I can assure you... he was **NOT** thinking about MAKING MONEY. No...

Instead, he was trying to "solve a problem." And because he LAID THE GROUNDWORK by *studying* and feeding his mind...

(NOTE: Refer to page 21 of the **"Real Cash Secrets"** Manual **Report R027)**

...he came up with the breakthrough he was seeking. And believe it or not...

...I know you might be able to do the same (and I will prove it.) How many times in your life have you had a problem... **A REAL PROBLEM** you had to solve?

And you tried and tried... stressed and fretted (all to no avail mind you!) And then... once you "backed-off" and RELAXED... forgot about it.. went for a drive... a walk.. watched a movie or played with your kids, cat or dog... or DID NOTHING and LET THINGS BE... what happened?

**"Ba-Bing..."**
**"Ba-Boom..."**
**"BINGO!"**

The "solution" came out of thin air! Maybe while in the shower? Maybe while eating? Maybe while working on something else?

But the point is... it happened when you **"disconnected"** your mind from the problem you were trying to solve. And I am here to tell you that solving the "Second Income" problem is *no different*. Nope... it's not.

Doesn't matter whether you want to earn an extra $3,000.00 a month or $30,000.00 a month (*I've done both by the way*). But my point is this...

**"The most LIFE-CHANGING money you will ever earn is when your income <u>DOUBLES</u>!"**

After that... the excitement fades *within* months. If you have had success in the past... you know WHAT I AM SAYING IS **TRUE** (because you have lived it). If not... let me explain.

Think about your life right now. If you are 50+ we both know (as far as employment) you are in the "danger zone." Why? Because the job market *shuns* you...

This is why 99 out of 100 job applicants who make the mistake of putting "dates" on their resume shoot themselves in the chest when applying for jobs. *Why?*

Because the person doing the hiring will look at those dates and *figure* out "**how old**" you are. And once that happens... we <u>both</u> know what happens...

However, if you simply *"leave off"* those dates... then you have a shot at getting an interview and "proving yourself" and your future changes. Because once you get the opportunity to "meet in person" <u>everything</u> changes.... because then you have a chance. And many times, that's what it's all about (having a chance).

## <u>SECTION VII</u>:

**"The fastest way to get people to throw money at you..."**

With the prior said... let me repeat... and I DO REPEAT... the following money making examples are <u>**NOT**</u> designed to be "*specifically*" for you. No! No! No!

But rather... provided to "help you" accomplish a **LARGER GOAL** towards your *eminent* success. Because they are designed to **FEED YOUR MIND** and get the "moneymaking machine" between your ears working. To STIMULATE IDEAS which can *lead to a major breakthrough...*

A blockbuster **"breakthrough"** of an idea which makes you feel like the first time you fell in love (with anything). Remember that? So without delay... let's begin *feeding* your mind. Because the fastest way to get people to "throw money at you" is to **SOLVE A PROBLEM** for them...

Again, you can refer to **page 21** of the "***Real Cash Secrets*" manual and Report R027**.

Believe me... it is worth reading again... because in order for your mind to really work, you need to get the ideas to SINK IN (and this takes time).

So when you read the following list of examples do <u>**NOT**</u> think about whether or not they "turn you on"... NO. Think about **THE PROBLEM** they are **SOLVING** for the customer paying money. Got it?

Ok... so here's the first example...

**"$3,400.00 a Month Cooking"**

**START UP COST: $50 to $500**

I knew a woman who would pre-cook and *freeze* healthy meals for customers. She had a menu you could pick from and everything would be placed in tupperware containers to later "thaw out" and heat up.

The food was incredible... but even more *impressive* was the price. It was reasonable. Far cheaper than eating out and tasted even better...

She had 10 clients at $680 a month. That's $6800 a month of which approximately 50% was profit. A nice business with happy customers. How do I know? Because not only was I a client, but I referred 3 friends (who became clients as well).

But the point is that she took the idea of cooking (a skill she had) and *applied it* to an <u>emerging</u> market of people wanting to **eat healthy** but were too busy (or lazy) to cook. Here's another example...

**"$1,600.00 a Week Detailing Cars"**

**START UP COST: $1,500 to $4,500**

For years Wayne was chasing the dream of "getting rich" in network marketing. After 6 years of chasing this dream (*or rainbow I should say*) he finally got smart and decided to start a "real" business. The results?

In the first 12 months he made <u>**MORE**</u> money than in **6 years** invested in network marketing. What was the business? Auto detailing... and, unlike Network Marketing, he turned a profit his <u>*first*</u> month.

What was his **secret** to getting new customers? I will tell you. He made a deal with a local gas station in a very *affluent* part of town.

He set up shop on the side of a gas station with a few tents to put the cars under. Naturally, he gave the station 20% of gross sales and used their Visa/Mastercard account to process all credit card transactions. It was brilliant. Truly brilliant...

## <u>SECTION VIII</u>:

**"THINK BIG... A dangerous myth which can keep you broke!"**

It's funny... the older I get the more I know. But, the more I <u>*don't*</u> know... For example. When I was young I read a lot of "success" books... and guess what?

Every one of them would spew the the benefits of "THINKING BIG!"

But never... did one of those books tell me about **the power of thinking small.** You see, so many people are THINKING BIG... they get stuck and stay broke. Why?

Because they are too focused on **MAKING A MILLION** when instead they should be focused on making $1,000. Yes, I said $1,000. Listen..

You have to learn how to walk before you can learn how to run, right? But you have to learn how to **C-R-A-W-L** before you learn how to walk... so here's the lesson.

If you can create a model to make $1,000... and you can than **replicate** that model... *guess what?*

You can likely get to $50,000, $100,000, $250,000, $500,000 and even $1,000,000 in most cases.

But so many are focused on **BIG MONEY** they *miss* the "gold mine" which might be laying right in front of them. Here's a quick example...

I have a friend who has a cafe and wants to increase his income. The solution (**and problem he has to solve**) is simple: his coffee SUCKS.

It really does. It's awful and he knows it. The worst part is this... he is located right across the street from a **STARBUCKS COFFEE** house!

**"Can you see the income opportunity my friend was sitting on?"**

But it get's better (or worse) we could say. Because I know a method of making **"cold brewed"** coffee.

And this method not only **reduces the acidity by 66%**... it also reduces bitter oils and fatty acids... which brings out the *true* flavor of coffee. It's incredible and over 99% of American coffee drinkers have NEVER had it!

Is there a catch? You bet there is... because cold brewing involves **"soaking"** fresh ground coffee in purified water for **24 hours** and then running it through a filter.

But trust me... the finished product is OFF THE CHARTS. Remember...

**"The coffee not only tastes better and fuller... it is also 66% *less* acidic."**

But the point is... my friend has **no interest** in pursuing it. Becaue he's too involved in chasing ***Network Marketing, Forex*** and ***Commodity Trading*** schemes.

So remember... sometimes the **secret to your success** will be not in thinking big... but in thinking small.

Because the most important money you will EVER make in launching a new enterprise... is your *first* $1,000.

**"Here is more proof how millions of people are staying stuck by THINKING BIG."**

Earlier I talked about how a big secret to success was understanding you have to do *two* things:

1.) Determine *what* your **God given talents** are and *how* you would like to SERVE OTHERS. And,

2.) **Find a problem** you can HELP PEOPLE solve so they will "throw money" at you in return.

One way millions of people stay stuck is because they do **NOT** want to do this... instead, they want to **SKIP** this step so they can "roll up their sleeves" and start making big money...

**"I am sorry... But you need to create (and/or) find a problem to solve which helps people in the process!"**

Listen... the resistance and failure to do this is responsible for ***more*** time and money lost by "opportunity seekers" than anything else!

It's the same reason why people lose MILLIONS of dollars in Network Marketing programs every year.

Because they *don't* want to create their own product or service. And they don't want to **DO THE WORK** of finding or inventing a *true* business opportunity which can create long-term wealth.

And honestly, I can't blame them... because we all like *shortcuts*. Especially when they work! The problem is that Network Marketing doesn't (... atleast 99.3% of the time).

*(NOTE: If you have not read the Network Marketing section of your* ***"Real Cash Secrets"*** *Manual please go to* ***page 173****)*

**"The problem with most Turn-Key Business Opportunities"**

Almost everyone wants a "Turn-Key" business opportunity with a guaranteed income. And why not? That kind of opportunity would be *better* than a job.

"Just tell me what to do... or give me the steps to follow and I WILL DO IT.. as long as you guarantee my success!"

Not only does it NOT exist... but it will NEVER exist. Would you like to know why?

Again, the truth will set you free... but first it might piss you off. Let me explain...

**REVEALED:**
**"Why 9 out 10 business opportunities are rip-offs."**

There is an old saying in the school of marketing which goes like this... *"People don't buy what they need... they buy what they WANT!"*

This is more true today than ever. And it's why 9 out of 10 business opportunities are rip-offs. Because it's **TRUE**. The majority of the time people buy what they want and **NOT** what they need.

For example... what people "need" in regards to earning a second income from home is simple. They need *education* and *direction* about finding a way to apply *their* personal talents and skills in order to **create value for other people** by solving a problem for them. Why?

Because this is what people in our country **PAY MONEY FOR!** And the shortest path to creating a second income is to help people solve a problem they have so they will **GIVE YOU THEIR MONEY.** It's pretty simple and logical (but people are anything *but* simple and logical).

So again, what people "need" to create a second income from home is *education*, *direction* and *motivation*.

But let's look at what people want (and buy). Because remember... most people do **NOT** buy what they need. Instead, they buy what they WANT. Remember...

**"People love to buy what they WANT more than what they NEED."**

This is why instead of buying a book called *"28 businesses you can start from home"* they will waste $299 on a program which says they can earn $5,000.00 a month stuffing envelopes for $1 each...

It's the same reason why instead of investing in the *"Real Cash Secrets" Course* and getting the **TRUTH** WHICH IS GUARANTEED TO PUT CASH IN THEIR POCKET... they will *instead* spend their money on programs which *"tell them what they want to hear."* In fact, let me give you some examples you have probably received:

**"$1497.00 a Week Mailing Postcards and You NEVER Talk to Anyone!"**

or

**"7-Time Lottery Winner Shares His Secrets with a Few Lucky Souls!"**

or

**"Don't miss out on your share of FREE Money!"**

or

**"Get paid mailing our special letters from home! Earnings up to $5,000.00 a week possible!"**

or

**"$7,000.00 a month in only 45 days! NO selling! NO MLM! No Shipping! NO KIDDING!"**

**THE FACT IS:** People will "tell you" they *want* the truth. But the reality is, most could not handle it if it landed on their kitchen table at 8am saturday morning...

You (on the other hand) are *different*. Because I know you are ready. If you were not... you never would have joined the **"R.C.S. Club"**. And the great news is... we have another 5 issues together. But since we are running out of time...

## SECTION IX:

### "Two business opportunities you might want to take a serious look at..."

Sadly, it is getting more difficult to find *legitimate* opportunities for hardworking folks to pursue, but... it's also getting harder to find well researched and written courses to TEACH YOU these opportunities.

There is so much garbage on the market today... it is disgusting. What is happening to this country? But here is a little good news...

Because today I am proud (and honored) for ***Zodi Publishing*** to endorse two opportunities.

(*I apologize upfront if you do NOT have a computer*) Because you will need to go to a local library to read about these programs. Because I am going to direct you to our website (sorry... we will work on this).

(Here we go) first up is...

### "Average $3,000.00 per deal working as a NOTE BROKER"

The "note" business has been around for hundreds of years. Here's how it works...

In any situation where someone is selling something (*a.k.a. home, land, business etc.*) and the seller takes back a note... that "note" can be sold for cash so the seller does not have to take their payments over time. Let me give you an example...

All over the Country people sell real estate *without* a mortgage company. This is done by what's known as "seller" financing. In other words, the seller will carry a "note" or mortgage so a bank does not have to.

For example... the seller will tell the buyer *"The property is $120,000. Give me $20,000 down and I'll take back A NOTE and 'carry' the other $100K" (payable over 10, 20 or 30 years)"*

In this scenario, the seller holds title to the property (but has 'a note' against the property) for $100,000.... payable over 10, 20 or 30 years.

**OPPORTUNITY ALERT:**

That "note" can be sold by the note holder (at a later date) for cash value. In other words... if the note is $100,000 payable over 30 years... they can choose to sell that note for $86,000.00 cash (for example).

In other words, a company will buy that note (at a discount) for CASH UP FRONT. Thereby, "cashing out" the holder of the note.

As a "note broker" this is where you come in...

You find people who are *holding* notes. They could be for homes, land, businesses, annuities, insurance claims (even lottery winnings).

As a "note broker" you are like a real estate agent. In other words... you _connect_ two parties into a profitable transaction and earn a commission in the process. For example...

If you brokered a $100,000 note your fee (on average) would be about 3%. This means you would help the note holder "sell" their note and earn a $3,000.00 commission in the process.

As you can imagine... the secret to success in this business is developing a strategy of finding a **"STEADY STREAM"** of note holders...

Because when you develop a steady stream of "note holders" who want their money NOW *(rather than over 10, 20 or 30 years)* your commissions can begin flowing nicely...

Of the dozens of opportunities I look at... this is "one opportunity" I have an interest in pursuing because I can see developing a profitable strategy for finding note holders. Obviously, I would use **DIRECT MAIL** to find note holders of "seller financed" mortgages.

If you want to investigate this opportunity here's what to do next. There is an excellent **HOME STUDY COURSE** which can teach you the business frome A to Z.

It's a nice **PRINTED MANUAL** and **AUDIO CD's** (shipped to your door) and it covers *everthing* you need to know to get started fast. The best part is you can learn the basics of the business in _less_ than a week.

We endorse this course and you can learn all about it the following ways. If you are on the internet simply go to:

**http://BrokeringNotes.com**

There, you will find a complete explanation of how the business and home study course works. If you have questions _AFTER_ reviewing information on the website, you may wish to call them. Their phone number is:

**1-800-349-0552**
***(please respect their time)***

This next opportunity is one I have personal experience with... and still "dabble in" from time to time. Why? Because it's fun and I still enjoy it for a variety of reasons.

You may be surprised when I tell you *what* it is... because (while not glamorous or elegant) it is a cash machine...

Not only can it be started for _less_ than $100. **It provides a solution to a problem which exists in every city in America**. And if it's something you become excited about... taking the next steps will be as easy as digging into a great meal when you are hungry. So what is this opportunity? I refer to it as...

**_AUTO_ _BROKERAGE_:**
**"The business of Real Estate ON WHEELS"**

Yes, I am talking about the business of working as an **"AUTO BROKER."**

Now, before you think "sleazy" used car salesman... let me say "I do **_NOT_** care what you think of the Auto Brokerage Business." *Why?*

Because I have done it... and I have made great money at it... and I loved almost every minute of it.

Because (next to a home) a car is the **largest purchase** most people will ever make in their life. And I like "helping people" get a great car at a good price and making a nice profit in the process (everyone wins).

Think about that...

Because working as an "Auto Broker" you are **helping people** in a major way. It's a big deal (in my opinion...)

Because you can "help people" make the *second* largest purchase of their _life_ and, you can make a **fair profit** in the process. It's win-win situation...

If you would like to find out more about the auto brokerage business, simply visit the website below:

**ZodiPublishing.com/**

## _SECTION_ _X_:
## "A movie with the _TRUTH_... and a _BOOK_ with a challenge"

America is on the edge of financial collapse. And, I.O.U.S.A. (the movie) boldly examines the exploding national debt and it's consequences.

Over 8 years President *Bush* expanded the debt **4.8 TRILLION** dollars. Then, President *Obama* grew the debt by **4.9 TRILLION** dollars... **IN HIS FIRST 38 MONTHS IN OFFICE!** *What does this mean?*

America must "mend" it's political spending, or... face an economic disaster of **epic proportions.** *Why?*

Burdened with an ever expanding Government and Military, increased international competition, overextended entitlement programs, and debts to *foreign* countries (*which are becoming impossible to honor*) American **NEEDS TO CHANGE** or face a financial meltdown.

For example... everyone talks about Americas "Social Security Problem." **THE REALITY?** Medicare is **FIVE TIMES LARGER A PROBLEM** then social security. Think about that... because that statement is **_NOT_** from me... but from the ex- accountant of the United States of America! And his name is *Mr. David Walker.*

Watch the movie my friend (even if you have to go to a library or rent it in a store.) Again, it is called...

# Welcome to Your Second Issue of the Quick Cash Secrets Newsletter

Dear Subscriber

Welcome to your second issue of the **"Quick Cash Secrets"** Newsletter... as usual, our time together will go fast. Because the goal is the same as the last issue...

**"To give you a profitable return on your time invested..."**

So let us start with something simple (yet profound) shall we? Here it is...

**"Lessons in life will be repeated until learned..."**

A few weeks ago I spent less than *10 minutes* filling out a credit card application. The best part was not that I KNEW I would be approved for the card... but that I KNEW I would earn $1,020.00 for my time (*I will explain how after I make my point...*)

Because my point is (in the past) I did not always SEE opportunities like this. THE REASON? I had to keep **repeating lessons** in life...

You see, the ability to "get paid" **$1,020.00** for filling out a credit card application was within my grasp for over 20 years... but sadly, I had to keep "repeating lessons" in life before I learned the **WISDOM I NEEDED** to be able to profit from such opportunities when they came my way. The only reason I did **NOT** see them before was because (you guessed it...)

**"I had to keep repeating the lesson before it was learned!"**

Let me explain. If you've read the entire **"Quick Cash Secrets"** manual then you know about how profitable **Credit Card Rewards Points** can be, right?

But what makes them so lucrative is when a bank gives you 50,000 to **100,000 BONUS POINTS** for signing up as a new cardholder...

Because these points are like **instant money**.. you can use them for First Class Air Travel or (like me) you can turn them into cash. In my case...

**"I received 60,000 bonus points just by signing up for a new credit card."**

To me, these points were worth $.017 cents per point. Basic math tells us 60,000 Bonus Points multiplied by $.017 cents equals $1,020.00. Imagine earning $1,020.00 for filling out a credit card application? And (if you have decent credit) **guess who could do the same thing?**

And even more exciting... there are *multiple* credit cards which give you these bonus points just for signing up. Here is a short list as an example...

**American Express Rewards**
**Chase Ultimate Rewards**
**Citi Thank You Points**
**Southwest Rewards**
**True Blue Rewards**
**Marriott Rewards**

And, guess how many "dumb me" has taken advantage of (outside of American Express) in the last 8 years? That's right...

**"ZERO!!!"**

I am a schmuck... I am ashamed and I admit it! **Because I have thrown away thousands of dollars** by not filling out credit card applications. How stupid is that? And that's my point...

I had to keep repeating the lesson in life (of ignoring the obvious) before I could **LEARN THE LESSON** and begin prospering from it. Remember....

**"Lessons in life will be repeated until learned..."**

Now, let's talk about one of the biggest problems new members of the **"R.C.S. Club"** struggle with.

Because this problem costs our members more in lost time and money... than almost anything else.

In fact, this problem is such an issue (for so many) that...

**"If I revealed the NUMBER ONE OBSTACLE stopping members from the extra income they desire THIS WOULD BE IT!"**

So what is this problem which is costing members so much? Quite simply put... it is a problem with MINDSET. Yes, mindset...

This is BY FAR the greatest problem members struggle with which is keeping them stuck.

But like any problem we wish to solve... we must FIRST acknowledge it.

And here is the issue... the vast majority of our members earn (or earned) their income by working as an employee.

**I.O.U.S.A**
(The Movie)

Have you ever wondered "why" people believe *weird* things? From Ghosts and Gods to Politics and Conspiracies... ***"The Believing Brain"*** is a book which will challenge your beliefs. If you are *not* ready for this challenge, please (do yourself a favor) pass on this one.

On the other hand (for those who are more open minded) this book may change your life and your future... and here's why.

Dr. Michael Shermer (and his team) have spent over 30 years asking the question *"How do people construct beliefs and reinforce them as truths?"*

**The answer:** will assure you are never the same. If you question that claim. Go to any bookstore and read the first 13 pages of the book (I dare you). It's called...

**"The Believing Brain"**
*How we construct beliefs and reinforce them as truths.*
**by Michael Shermer**

Let me give a warning... this book is only for those who are *open minded* because (as stated) it will **challenge** your beliefs. *But isn't that the goal of many good books?*

## SECTION XI:
## "Could business consulting create your NEXT breakthrough?"

If you *currently* own a business and would like to experience a "breakthrough" in the next 30 days... then I have an offer which you may want to consider.

My normal consulting rate is $250/hr with a 4/hr minimum. **GUARANTEE:** If after the first hour I have *not* provided you "one breakthrough" we both agree is worth $1,000 or more... you will owe NOTHING.
Yes, I said *nothing*...

Otherwise, we will work for 4 hours (or more) for only $1,000 or $250/hr. But here is the good news... as a member of the "R.C.S. Club" these fees are **reduced** by 50%.

This means you get the same guarantee but the fee is only $500 for 4 hours (*Naturally, I cannot guarantee availability. But will do my best to accomodate.*)

If you *currently* own a business and would like to experience a breakthrough in the next 30 days... learn more today by visiting http://ZodiPublishing.com

## SECTION XII:
## "The new R.C.S. Club 24hr Recorded Info line."

Donald Trump once said *"If you don't like solving problems, don't go into business..."* Boy was he right! And one of the problems we have had is helping members stay up to date with *The Good, The Great, The Bad* and *The Disgusting.*

As a result, the **"R.C.S. Club" 24 Hour Recorded Info Line** was created. This is a *24 hour* automated information system with multiple recorded options and menus.

Basically, we provide all sorts of member support on these recordings. From answering common questions to covering important topics as well as providing updates. *It is pretty cool...*

**R.C.S. Club 24hr**
**Recorded Info Line:**
**1-801-810-2020**

(**NOTE:** *Please bear with us as this system is far from finished and not free from bugs and gremlins. Be sure to call from a quiet place or put your phone on MUTE while listening.)*

## SECTION XIII:
## "The secret to turning debt into retirement income..."

If you are currently in debt, then there is a "new way" to take that debt and turn it into retirement income.

It's called the **"Fight Debt and Win"** home study course. And it will teach you how to eliminate your debt up to *24 times faster* than the average person. The best part is it takes as little as 10 minutes a day. *Sound too good to be true?*

**"What if we offered to PROVE IT by taking all the risk?"**

We didn't spend over $125,000.00 developing the **"Fight Debt and Win"** course by accident...

We spent that because we had a goal. A goal to create the greatest course in America to help you turn debt into retirement income. But how did we do it? That's the interesting part...

**Have you ever wondered what a smart banker, mortgage broker or bill collector would do if they had to get out of debt quickly?**

We both know what they would NOT do... and that's what **99% of America** is doing! Because they would do things *differently*. They would use inside knowledge and strategies (all legal of course) to eliminate their bills in record time. *How do I know this?*

Because we interviewed them... and the interviews are on **FIVE AUDIO CD's** plus the "word for word" transcripts (*which are printed in one of four manuals you will receive*). But that's only the beginning...

Listen, if you want to get out of debt in record time AND **turn debt into retirement income.** This course can show you how. Here's why...

We spent over 2 years researching every "get out of debt" program, system, strategy (and scheme) in America. *That was the beginning...*
Then we took THE BEST OF THE BEST and *flushed* the rest. What you

are left with is the **"Fight Debt and Win"** home study course. And this is why we offer an unheard of...

**"$5,000.00 Guarantee"**

The guarantee is simple. And straight forward. Order the **"Fight Debt and Win"** home study course. Study for up to 30 days. If you don't feel it can save your (or make you) atleast $5,000... return the program for a refund - no questions asked. It's that simple...

Debt payments are keeping 76% of America stuck... and this is a solution to turn that debt into income...

Once your are out of debt... all the money you have been spending on payments **NOW BECOMES YOUR MONEY - *EVERY MONTH!***

This is money you can save or use to invest in a business or just spend on yourself to enjoy life more...

Also, after acquiring the skills of eliminating debt through the **"Fight Debt and Win"** program... you may choose to earn a second income helping others get out of debt (*the same way you did!*)

It's a win-win situation. You either turn debt into retirement income or you get a refund. And the last thing to think about...

**"Where else are you guaranteed to turn $498 into $5,000.00 or your money back?"**

Sincerely,

George Bentley
*Zodi Publishing*
ZodiPublishing.com

Therefore, the majority have a tendency to **THINK LIKE EMPLOYEES** because (naturally) they have an **EMPLOYEE MINDSET.** And there is nothing wrong with this. However...

Where the problems begin is the minute they decide they want to earn extra money (on their own) by working for themselves.

Because when you set out to earn income working for yourself... you are essentially aiming to earn income **working as an entrepreneur.**

And making money as an entrepreneur means you must adopt **ENTREPRENEURIAL THINKING**. Because there is nothing worse than someone with an EMPLOYEE MINDSET trying to earn entrepreneurial income.

Listen... the sooner you start thinking like an entrepreneur... the sooner you are going to start solving problems and MAKING MONEY!

It's just that simple. And again (I cannot stress this enough!) because

**"There is nothing worse than someone with an *employee mindset* trying to earn entrepreneurial income!"**

And sadly, this is the **number one mistake** most American opportunity seekers are making!

And because this issue is **stopping so many members from achieving the success they desire...** I'm going to share a few examples *(and yes, you might think I am beating a dead horse!)* But believe me...

Even if you think you already *get this stuff* and don't need to hear what I have to say...

...I will **prove** to you even the most successful people in America can always benefit from learning to think *more* entrepreneurial.

Because that's what we're talking about here. The failure to think *entrepreneurial* is the number one thing which is holding members back and slowing their success! Again (for the third time...)

**"There is nothing worse than someone with an *employee mindset* trying to earn entrepreneurial income!"**

Let's get to those examples...

**EXAMPLE #1:**

Judy is a 62-year-old retired teacher who is looking to earn an extra $1500 a month. In fact, in her own words she says "If I could earn an extra $1500 a month... I would be in heaven!"

This is because Judy's retirement pays her over $2000 per month. But the problem is, no one wants to hire Judy because she is 62. So Judy has a problem. She needs to earn an extra $1500 per month and no one wants to hire her.

So, like millions of other men and women in Judy's position, she began looking into various different "home-based" business opportunities.

**"In fact, you might say that it had become Judy's 'hobby' to investigate moneymaking programs."**

The sad part is that Judy's "hobby" has become an *extremely* expensive one. Not only burning up all her emergency savings but driving her **over $13,000 in**

**debt to boot**. It's at this point she received an invitation in the mail to join the **RCS Club.**

After reading the letter she called us to ask a few questions. Of course, her call is not much different than 80% of the calls we receive from prospective new members.

Because 80% of the time *(regardless of how the question is worded)* the caller is always asking the same thing,which is:

**"If I buy into your program how much money am I GUARANTEED to make?"**

This type of question is typical of someone coming from an *employee* mindset. After all, when you work as an employee you are **guaranteed a certain amount for each hour you work**. But the *entrepreneurial* world is far different...

**"Because in the entrepreneurial world you have to pull your own weight."**

This means not only do you have to take care of the customer, you are given the monumental task of *finding* the customer. And we won't get into the bigger question...

**"Why would anyone want to give you their money in order to become your customer?"**

SOUNDS LIKE A TOTAL PAIN IN THE BUTT! Doesn't it? It would be so much easier if you could just sit home and...

**GET PAID to send emails...**

**GET PAID to take surveys...**

**GET PAID to mail postcards...**

**GET PAID to stuff envelopes...**

**GET PAID to return phone calls!**

And this is why Judy had gone $13,000 in debt chasing "the dream" of earning an extra $1500 a month. Because she was trying to find a way to **earn entrepreneurial income with an employee mindset.**

Sadly, this makes about as much sense as trying to catch criminals with the mindset of a nun!

**"Back to Judy's phone call..."**

We would have loved to promise Judy she could "earn $375 a week assembling products at home" or "make $500 weekly mailing letters..." but we couldn't. Because we would be lying if we said that.

**"So, we gave Judy something even more valuable. And that was, the TRUTH..."**

We told her that in order to maintain an **"A+ Rating"** with the **Better Business Bureau** we could *never* guarantee her a monthly income.

But what we could do, is guarantee her a **specific amount of value within 30 days**... or we would refund her money.

Unfortunately for Judy, this wasn't good enough. Because according to her words "she wanted something that would provide her with a **guaranteed income."**

NOTE: this is the thinking which got her over $13,000 in debt from past opportunities. Because the moneymaking "program" Judy is looking for only exists in one place, and that is, in her mind.

**"And this is why there are so many scams peddled in the business opportunity industry."**

Because marketers have figured out not only that people buy what they **want** and not what they **need**, but that they are selling to a market which is made up 99% of people with an *employee mindset* and not an entrepreneurial one.

And this is why so many business opportunities are marketed to you in a way which makes it almost seem as if you're just going to be working at home doing an easy job like stuffing envelopes for one dollar each!

So, in the case of Judy, she was not interested in becoming a member of the real cash secrets club. Instead, she decided to keep looking for that money making program she believes exists. The good news is, after blowing over $13,000 on opportunities she figured out many things which did not work.

Of course, joining the club would have given her a huge shortcut to success, but she decided to "go it alone" and there's nothing wrong with that. We wish her well...

**"But here's the reality..."**

Millions of men and women like Judy waste thousands of dollars and years of their lives because they are not willing to change their thinking. Think about it.

When it comes to success you have two choices. Because the laws of reality are not negotiable. In other words...

**"You can try to change reality or you can try to change your thinking. You know which is easier."**

Because the reality is, Judy had talents we could have helped her turn into the $1500 per month she desired. But before we can help her do that, she has to **change her mindset** from that of an employee to that of an *entrepreneur*.

This is because before we can help her identify her talents and learn how to market them to customers she must **adopt an entrepreneurial mindset.**

She must learn to look for problems for which she can help her clients with solutions *(again, if you could GET PAID to stuff envelopes it would be easier - but this is reality. Sorry.)*

In Judy's case she was a retired teacher. This means she has skills in helping people learn how to read, write, edit and many other things. In fact, we even hire people like Judy from time to time.

You see, there is a wide range of things she could do for people and businesses to earn extra money on her own.

She could *help someone* write their first book... she could *help someone* edit a book. She could *help tutor* children at their homes... she could solve problems etc.

And in most cases, the income would amount to far more per hour than she ever earned as a teacher.

But sadly, until she **changes her mindset** from one of an employee to that of an *entrepreneur*, none of these opportunities will materialize. And it's the same for so many others...

**EXAMPLE #2:**

Robert received an invitation in the mail to join the real cash secrets club. Upon reading the letter he became very excited. In fact, he admitted to reading the letter three times!

He even called call us asking questions like "Is this for real? I mean, is this legitimate?"

Of course, we responded "If it wasn't, we wouldn't answer the phone and we definitely would not have an A+ Rating with the Better Business Bureau."

Naturally, Robert placed his order with great enthusiasm.

**"Then, about a week later he sent his package back for a refund with a long scathing letter..."**

He said the Real Cash Secrets manual was nothing but excessively over hyped worthless information. And, that he already knew almost everything in it. But his real issue was that he was looking for "real" business opportunities he could start with almost no money.

I actually called Robert and got him on the phone. The conversation was rather interesting because the reason for my call was due to the fact he claimed our advertising was incredibly misleading (according to his letter.)

I explained to him that the real cash secrets manual was designed to show new members the power of knowledge and how quickly it could benefit them.

I also explained that this was clearly detailed in the letter as well as the introduction of the manual with the following guarantee...

**"If you will invest 10 minutes a day for 30 days we guarantee you will find at least $4024 in cash value."**

I didn't want to assume he did not read the entire manual so I asked him if he did in fact read it from cover to cover. To my surprise, he admitted he did not read the entire program.

But then he went on, to explain he read enough to know that it was nothing new and just over hyped garbage. At this point, I knew there was no way that I could help Robert. But for my own entertainment, I had to ask him...

**"Exactly what type of a home-based business opportunity are you looking for?"**

His response was typical of opportunity seekers looking for entrepreneurial income but operating with an **employee mindset.** Because he stated he was looking for a business he could start from home, part-time, and have the potential to **earn $10,000.00 per month.**

He also stated he wanted to be able to start this business with under 200 bucks. *Yes (for some) this is reality-based thinking in America today...*

**"I only laugh because there was a time when I FELT THE SAME WAY!"**

I think there is a little part of us that all want to "get rich quick." It's kind of like winning the lottery. Let's move on to the final example...

**EXAMPLE #3**

Actually, this is not one story of one customer but rather, many stories of many different customers.

However, they each started out being stuck because of an *employee mindset.*

In other words, the difference between them and the other two stories I shared, are that these customers were able to **overcome their employee mindset** and move on to adopt entrepreneurial thinking (and therefore begin obtaining results.)

**"Why so many people try to sell you 'turn-key-we-do-it-all-for-you' business opportunities..."**

Because over 90% of opportunity seekers have an employee mindset they are very receptive to investing money in opportunities **which appeal to that mindset.**

Because the employee mindset does *not* want to think. The employee mindset does *not* want to solve problems.

The employee mindset does *not* want to create anything. And (if it can) the employee mindset does *not* want to work. Marketers of home-based business opportunities have caught on to this like flies on you know what.

This is why you see so many opportunities that require no work other than you investing money or maybe, mailing a postcard (and in most cases you pay someone else to mail the postcards!)

As a result, many of our new members have invested and lost money in such programs in the past.

**"While it's bad they lost money, the good news is (for those who didn't give up) they will be a little smarter and more receptive to hearing THE TRUTH when it comes along."**

As you can imagine, these are the kind of customers we help and enjoy seeing succeed.

Bill is a retired truck driver with some health issues. As a result, no one wants to hire him. Even worse, his retirement income is only $1400 per month which he can barely survive on.

To make matters worse, Bill is broke. So he has no startup capital for any type of business opportunity and he has no cash or credit cards because he got in trouble with those years ago.

Like every new member of the real cash secrets club, one day Bill received a letter in the mail inviting him to join.

He read the letter and found it interesting. As he puts it "if even 10% of what the letter said was true I'd still be coming out ahead on the investment." So he joined.

When he received his real cash secrets manual he was instantly impressed. Not just by the fast shipping but the presentation of the program and what he received. He began reading and loved the large font because it was easy to read.

Even more important, he was impressed with the information (even topics which did not apply to him but made him think of other people he knew which they did.)

He stayed up past midnight reading and taking notes of things he could do. And the next morning, he got started...

Because he's over 55, the first thing he did was go to a website he had read about which had helped seniors **reclaim over $15 billion** from programs their tax dollars originally funded. To his excitement, he qualified for more than one program.

The website he went to is **BenefitsCheckup.org**. On page 140 of your Real Cash Secrets manual are many other websites you want to check for programs and benefits you may qualify for.

# "Real Money Income Opportunities You Can Bank On."

Beginning with this issue and following through with our promise to bring you legitimate opportunities without all the B.S. you are used to seeing in the mail...

...is the **Real Money Income Opportunities You Can Bank On.**
Without further ado here's what our editors just uncovered. You may be able to tap into these home based money machines as soon as you finish reading.

Here you go...

### How to Make $40/Hour Driving People to the Airport

You've probably heard about people making a good side income driving for ride sharing companies like **Uber** or **Lyft**. What you don't know is, many airports won't let them operate there. Could be they are in cahoots with the taxi and limo operators?

But what they can't stop is people driving other people to the airport. And if you guessed 'there's an app for that' you'd be on the money.

A website called **Wingz.me** brings together individuals who want to make extra money and people wanting to save a little money getting to the airport. In fact, that's all the company does, airport rides only.

Here's how it works. Passengers go online or use the app to book a flat rate ride to or from the airport. They prepay and all you do is pick them up and drop them off or be there when their plane lands.

You can just work when you want. Some do it full-time for a nice income.

After you've been at it a while, the **Wingz app** lets you build repeat business with a **direct booking feature.** This way your excellent customer service brings you a steady stream of return passengers, as well as makes it easy for them to refer friends and family.

Often you can make more money for your time than an **Uber** driver handling many short fares. To and from airport rides are always high fare transportation and that's why many drivers can make as much as **$40 an hour.**

You don't need to worry about insurance, because if you become a **Wingz.me** driver they provide you with a $1 million dollar per incident liability insurance policy.

**Wingz** says on their website that some drivers make $2,000 a week. How much you want to drive is up to you. Some drivers just operate on the weekend, to supplement their regular income.

**Wingz.me** operates for numerous U.S. airports. If they are not currently in your area, email them and get on their list.

Or do what many enterprising individuals do, they advertise their service on **Craigslist**. You can also tell family and friends, even post flyers in your local area offering your airport transportation service.

The reason any passenger would rather use you versus a cab or limo is simply price. For what seems like forever, those industries have had a stranglehold on airport transportation and charged prices to reflect **zero competition.**

Some airports are starting to allow **Uber** and **Lyft** to operate, but **Wingz.me** has a big price advantage by offering a **flat rate.** And you know people always seem to find the best price.

Whether you hook up with a company like **Wingz.me** or create your own business and advertise locally, you can make some really good money driving people to and from the airport. Best of all, work only when you want.

To get started on this part or full-time easy to do income opportunity, visit **Wingz.me** and if they don't operate in your area, test market with flyers, emails to friends and associates and place ads on places like Craigslist.

### Advantages and Profits of Becoming a Tour Guide

Tourism is booming in America. Never before has the country seen such large segments of the population with so much disposable income.

**"More than half of the U.S. population is now over age 40."**

Some are in peak earning years. While a great many baby-boomers are retiring with more wealth than past generations.

You may even see tours in your town. In some major cities there are bicycle tours, Tours on Segway's, Walking tours, Bus tours. Even personal, one-on-one tours.

Entrepreneurs and the self-employed are taking full advantage of the opportunities to earn extra income, if not build full-time lucrative cash flow.

If you want to cash-in on this growing trend, read on how easy it is to make good money part or full time being a tour guide in your area.

Today it's easier than ever to become a tour guide because of websites like **Shiroube** and **Vayable**. On these websites you can launch your own personal tour guide business and only work when and for who you want.

These websites put you in front of the market, so tourists browsing will see your tour offer and listing, then hire you online.

If you prefer employment, as an independent guide, you can offer tours and charge from $25 even as high as $200 per person for upscale experiences.

If you become an employee for a tour company, you may qualify or work your way into a number of positions. Such as;

Assisting and receiving groups as they arrive at train stations, bus depots and airports. This position generally pays between **$10 to $15 per hour.**

An entry level tour guide, say

giving a walking tour of your town, can also expect to earn $10 to $15 an hour. As you gain experience, you'll get **$20 to $25 an hour.**

Rise to the level of a tour director and you can command as much as **$250 per day** and higher. Some tours can be several days, even weeks or a month for destination tours.

In addition to income accompanying clients on a tour can provide you with free lodging and meals.

What qualifications do you need to become a tour guide? If you work for a tour company, most will give you on the job training. Your ability to remember the history of your area, when something significant happened and ability to tell stories will keep you in demand.

Some cities will require you to obtain a license. You may even be required to take a test to determine what you really know about the places you will be conducting tours.

You can get a leg up on others competing for tour guide positions by taking courses at local community colleges or even get professionally certified through the **National Tour Association.**

In the summer, demand for tour guides goes way up. Not only in the U.S., but around the world.

In Iloilo City, Philippines, *Emilia Drilon*, an 82-year-old retired teacher, works as a tour guide on a bus, pointing out attractions as tourists motor throughout the area.

She got the job after taking a *3-day course* offered by the **Department of Tourism.**

And if you'd rather freelance, remember to check out the websites **Shiroube** and **Vayable** where you can create your own tour, post it and respond to potential clients online.

Full-time or part-time, many senior citizens are enjoying the financial benefits of being a tour guide. Chances are you will too!

To launch your very own tour business, visit **shiroube.com** and click on 'become a local guide.' Also visit **vayable.com** and click on 'list an experience' to start giving any type of tour in your area.

If you would rather work for a tour company, contact the ones in your area as chances are they are always hiring or will be soon.

### Big Money in Reselling Thrift Store Clothing

You've probably heard stories of people finding rare books, coins, art and collectibles while scrounging around a thrift store, flea market or yard sale.

Sometimes you can make a great find on a barely used clothing item. Well one young lady has done so well reselling clothing she found at thrift stores that she actually gave up her corporate job.

Currently she makes **$5,000 a month**, just reselling used clothing and accessories.

Here's how she does it. She uses an App.

Like most 20 somethings who stay glued to their smartphones, then *University of Arkansas* student *Alexandra Marquez* downloaded an app just to entertain herself for 15 minutes back in 2012.

The app is called **Poshmark**. If you have a smartphone or tablet, you can download it for free now.

If you have some lightly worn clothing all you do is snap a picture and create a listing on **Poshmark**. You use certain filters to describe it so prospects can easily find your item in searches. And you are in the business of reselling clothes and accessories.

Often women are looking for accessories, handbags, clothing and shoes that they may only wear a couple of times. So they buy for the occasion, then resell it afterward.

**Poshmark** makes it super simple to sell your items. After someone buys, you are emailed a prepaid, pre-addressed label. All you do is put it in a box and drop it at any post office or postal service mailbox. You can even notify the post office and the carrier will ring your bell and pick up the box for free.

Now 23-year-old Alexandra makes her living reselling thrift store and other clothing items on **Poshmark**.

Her keen eye noticed what people were buying, so she set out to find more of those items.

She spends three or four days a week not only visiting thrift stores and flea markets, but also buying overstock from local boutiques. And women in her area know she is the go-to if they want to sell their gently used clothing.

The clothes and accessories she offers on **Poshmark** are sold from $40 up to $250.

Her overhead is very low. She doesn't need a website. Works out of her home. And takes mileage deductions for using her car to scoot around town searching for items or going back and forth to the post office.

Even better, **Poshmark** pays both the shipping costs and credit card fees. All she pays is a small commission on anything under $15 and 20% on items over $15.

To net **$5,000 a month**, she lists about 75 new items during a typical week and ships 20 to 40 packages a week.

Now don't think you can't do this because you aren't a millennial. The fact is...

**"Almost two-thirds of Facebook users are women over age 40."**

These percentages can be projected across all social media. So download the free app by doing a search for **Poshmark**.

Start with accessories and clothing in your own home. You may be surprised the amount of income you can make doing something you would otherwise be doing anyway... shopping!

Just go to **poshmark.com** and sign-up, plus download the app. While there you may even find some clothing and accessories you want. Very easy and simple to get in the big business or at least clearing out your closet and possibly becoming the go-to for boutiques in your area to move overstock.

**"Easier Than You Think to Start A D.I.Y. Crafts and Gifts Business from Home."**

Do you like making crafts? Decorations? Clothing? Anything cool someone else may want to wear or put on their desk or wall?

Thanks to websites like **Etsy**, it's easier than ever to sell your wares. Some crafts people are making a financial killing.

Here's an example;

After *Alicia Bock* became a mother, like most new parents she started taking lots and lots of pictures.

To stay at home with her newborn, she quit her health education job. After friends and family noticed her knack for taking good photos, she started exhibiting her work at local art shows.

The reception was so good, she then jumped online and placed her photos for sale on **Etsy** in 2005. Not only do consumers buy her photos, designers and interior decorators do too.

The biggest feather in her cap came when Hollywood set designers stumbled on her work. Some of her photos have appeared in *Sex and the City* movies as well as the redecorating TV shows like *Extreme Makeover: Home Edition*.

Here's another story;

Do you like to embroider? Lots of people do it for fun or to make gifts for friends and family.

*Janick Gravel* of Canada makes a living selling her embroidered wall art on **Etsy**.

A graphic designer by trade, she had tinkered with selling handmade jewelry on **Etsy**. Sales were o.k.

But when she started selling her collection of handmade embroidered wall art, sales too off. Now she makes a living from her D.I.Y. craft sales.

Sales didn't stop there. As her reputation grew, shops in Montreal started carrying her line. Then she branched out to local craft shows.

Her advice is to make what you love. Then your passion will find its way to customers who love your work.

But wait there's more...

If you've looked for a business you can run out of your home, chances are you've seen offers to help you set up making soap at home.

Some people do it as a hobby. *Martha Stewart* has featured stories on the soap making craft on her TV show.

But did you know you could make a living making and selling your own soap?

Australian *Mei Ong* opened her soap making shop on **Etsy** in 2012. Working from her apartment in Melbourne, she makes soaps including her signature line, jewel-shaped soaps. Most customers by them for gifts. And often customers place large orders for weddings and other special occasions.

Within a year of offering her soaps online, she was mentioned in *The Oprah Magazine*.

Her soaps are a blend of oils, scents and butters and are all vegan. Her line includes bar soaps, exfoliating polish and moisturizing mousse.

Today what began as a hobby has turned into a full time self-supporting income.

The preceding success stories are just a few examples of D.I.Y. craft people making good money doing what they love.

In addition to the website **Etsy**, there are other online and offline distribution channels too. As you read in the examples above, local craft shows, even distribution through mainstream retailers offer great opportunities for you to turn a D.I.Y. craft idea into a full-time income or part-time if that's all you need and want.

To investigate this further, go to **etsy.com** and click on 'sell on Etsy.' If you don't already have something handmade you want to test market, browse everything for sale on **Etsy** and you may find inspiration and exclaim, "yea, I can do that!"

**"Make Solid Money as A Real Estate Photographer."**

Every time a house, condo, building or property comes on the market, it requires pictures. This is especially true in today's online world where virtual tours rule.

Then there is another whole subset of this DIY business, taking 'for sale' pictures for floating real estate... house boats and yachts.

How do you get into this business? Let's look at one David Filipi who operates as a real estate photographer on the website **PrimeVirtualTour.com** in *Las Vegas, NV.*

David is a member of ***Real Estate Photographers of America***. You can join too by visiting **RealEstatePhotographers.org** where you can get listed in their directory to make your availability known to your market. You'll also get the insider-pointers you need to build your business.

Realtors are happy to pay for good presentation photos of the property they have for sale.

Think of it, if the average home sells for $200,000 throwing off an average commission of $6,000, then a couple hundred bucks for some great photos is a drop in the bucket. Especially since it can help clinch the deal. And make it fast and easy for the most prospects to take an online tour.

**PrestigeVision.com** provides virtual video tours for those selling yachts. They became so successful, they branched out into virtual videos for companies selling jets to the wealthy.

As you can see, any high priced sale, whether it's a home, boat or plane, will require photography. An investment the seller must make if they want to get a deal done fast, because potential clients will find it easier to browse the offer online from anywhere in the world.

If you want, you can start small. All it takes is a digital camera and some skill. If you already take photos as a hobby, then you can quickly break-in to this lucrative field. Work when you want and for whom you want. Be your own boss.

It's not that hard to make at least $1,000 extra a month in your spare time. Remember, when sellers want to prepare a property for sale, they have a need for photos that must be met immediately. Even if there are other photographers in your area providing the same service, they won't be able to handle all the demands.

Just set up shop. Start building your network. And you can jump on the real estate gravy train just like other must-haves… notaries, lawyers, surveyors and appraisers.

A good way to build your portfolio, is to take photos for friends and family doing a 'for sale by owner.' As soon as you can show that your photos helped sell a property, you are off and running.

Plus, you can even charge additional fees helping to stage the property. No home is photo ready just because it is coming up for sale.

Real estate, boats and planes are sold every minute of every day all across America. If you have basic photography skills or are willing to take a course at your local community college or art institute, you can find a way to make solid money as a real estate photographer.

To get started in this money making opportunity, go to **realestatephotographers.org** and click on *'join real estate photographers of America.'*

If you are already friends with a local realtor and handy with a camera, you may be able to get your first gig as soon as you can print up some business cards.

**"Opportunities Ahead..."**

Stay tuned for this regular feature to bring you more real home based income opportunities.

The fact is, people just like you are finding ways everyday to break out of the "wage slave" mentality. And we will continue to report them as fast as we can.

If you feel like a hamster on a wheel, trying to make ends meet, its not entirely your fault.

**"According to a U.S. Federal Reserve survey, the individual**

**net worth of Americans has DECLINED 85% since 1983!"**

...even after taking into account home value and other major assets.

How did this happen? There are many reasons... but one thing is for sure... business owners enjoy lots of tax and gain advantages.

That's why you are a **RCS newsletter** subscriber, to beat the bankers, lawyers and politicians at their own game. Taking advantage of the same loopholes they put in for themselves.

The fact is, you need more than your income from work if you want to finally get ahead. Take the vacations you deserve, pay off debt and have the money you need for retirement.

On *page 181* of your **RCS manual** it clearly shows the advantages of having a side business or a full-time one where you make the rules.

If you are interested in learning more about **"The secret to turning debt into retirement income"** see page 271 of your "Real Cash Secrets" manual. Or call us...

**(480) 739-6000**

Til next time... keep your eye on your mailbox for the **"Q.C.S. Members Only Magazine."** Yes... your next issue will be a full blown 56 page magazine.

---

# Welcome to Your THIRD Issue of the Quick Cash Secrets Newsletter

Dear Subscriber,

Everyday you get pitches in the mail, see infomercials on TV or read about business opportunities in magazines. And everyday someone just like you buys 'pie in the sky.'

Yes, who doesn't want to make $10,000, $20,000 and up a month from a do-it-yourself business. But when they dangle the 'big opportunity' it's just a ploy. A trick to get you to bite.

What you need to focus on instead is realistic measurable gains in income. First simply put in the effort to double your income.

And this doubling of your income doesn't have to come from a side business. Sometimes you can find that money by adjusting what you are already doing.

In your Quick Cash Secrets manual, there are easily workable solutions to many things you spend money on now. Or more important, stuff you should avoid because it's a money waster.

Take multi-level marketing or as they like to call it 'network marketing.' As you can read starting on page 173 of your Quick Cash Secrets manual, network marketing has 4 dirty secrets. If you've been involved in multi-level marketing before, you no doubt have experience some of these setbacks.

But when they dangle the 'high commissions' from useless products, a new wave of fish wash money into the shysters bank accounts. Its only later they discover no one really wants the products and the whole scheme is just to get as many people as possible to buy something once. And those somethings gather dust in a closet unless the so-called distributor uses all the product themselves as their only way of getting any of their money back.

Sure there are people sitting atop those pyramids who are raking in the bucks. Just like the frauds at the top of any b.s. operation is raking it in on the backs of others parting with their hard earned money.

Pie-in-the-sky never fails to attract the unsuspecting. But as the headline of a famous financial ad proclaimed, the real money is made by 'getting rich slowly.'

So to start, make it your goal to double your income. In your Real Cash Secrets manual you'll find many nuggets to do just that.

And don't get addicted to just income opportunities. Managing money is where the rubber meets the road.

In your Quick Cash Secrets manual you'll find many ways to manage your money better. One of the best is managing debt.

There's good debt, like a mortgage on your home or income-producing property. Then their stupid debt like high interest rates on credit cards.

Many of you reading this right now are on a treadmill with credit and department store card debt. So instead of managing debt, you are racing for income to service debt where there are smart ways to wipe it away.

You'll make more money with insider-knowledge than you will with a business opportunity like stuffing envelopes. One of the oldest cons ever and it still works today.

Let me ask you, have you read every page of the Quick Cash Secrets manual? If so, how many ideas have you applied. Some of them are super simple like switching credit cards and then selling the miles. Others take some time to develop, but can be workable solutions for anyone willing to apply themselves.

To take full advantage of life-changing income opportunities...

...and remember, just doubling your income can change your life... you need to think like an entrepreneur, not an employee.

The reason you may not be thinking like an entrepreneur now is because that is the way you were conditioned. As America made great strides by the 100th anniversary of the Declaration of Independence, the Industrial Revolution took hold.

And as America grew, so did its companies. Firms where a few at the top held all the power while workers were dependent on their employer.

Then the U.S. fought two World Wars. Again, a top down management strategy. Those below had to follow orders even if it meant certain death.

Why so many Americans are struggling financially today is because they can't get away from the employee mindset. They can only apply for jobs. Show up. Get paid, take their vacation days if they can afford to go anywhere. And hope their job holds out.

The problem with the 'just do as you are told' culture is people become trained to not take risks. Even if their gut tells them there is an opportunity, they can't bring themselves to take it.

And this is a mindset mainly present in Western cultures. Here's what I mean.

Next time you go shopping or run errands, pay close attention to who is running those small business. More often than not they are first and second generation Asians, Africans, Middle Easterners, Eastern European and Hispanics.

They come to this country, pool their money together and buy a business. It may be a dry cleaner, convenience store, yogurt shop - you name it. They become their own boss and reap the rewards. Soon you'll see them driving a Mercedes. While you hope your clunker makes it to the job you hate.

Even today with Americans achieving higher education levels than ever, people still look for a 'job' and bide their time covering their ass and many never make an impact during their career.

Today through globalization and the power of the Internet, the whole top-down model is being disrupted. The front line workers who deal with customers are finding it easier than ever to see a problem others want solved and then cater to it.

This is the entrepreneur mindset. Fix something others want fixed.

And with the Internet, people can launch a website in no time. Or with cheap offshore manufacturing, just about anyone with a little money can become the next Tommy Hilfiger if they can design some fashions that resonate with the public.

But you must know this, the employee mindset system is totally rigged against you. That's why you have too much debt, have to use credit cards to pay for groceries and now can get a 10-year car loan!

All while entrepreneurs pay less in taxes as a percentage basis than you do. So why not become an entrepreneur?

What is the biggest difference between an entrepreneur and an employee?

Entrepreneurs learn how to fail. With each failure you are actually gaining a step toward success.

**Winston Churchill said it best, "Success is stumbling from failure to failure with no loss of enthusiasm."**

So you needn't be afraid of failing. Trouble is, most Americans are so cash strapped that even a little failure can send them to the pawn shop with the family jewels.

If you don't have a lot of money to risk, then what do you do?

You do research. You find the facts. You DON'T bite on get rich quick schemes.

English scholar Mary Beard puts it this way...

**"Action without study is fatal. Study without action is futile."**

Many of you reading this have bought no telling how many $37 make-money ideas and most can't tell where the manual or book is now.

You acted first without studying. Remember, that's one of the services we provide, to review so-called business opportunities so you have the facts before you act.

Now let's talk about the second sentence of the quote above, "study without action is futile."

Again, have you REALLY studied every page in the Real Cash Secrets manual? There are so many ways to make and save money, anyone who takes the time to read and then take the most important step, ACT... well there is money right in front of you.

When you have the facts, you can also avoid money and time wasters.

And we also cover in your manual lots of 'opportunities' where you should run the other way.

Still the opportunity laden marketers get the uninformed to send in their hard earned money after reading the most outlandish claims ever made.

Which brings us to another quote about research and this one comes from Mark Twain. He said...

**"Get your facts first, then you can distort them as you please."**

So before you fall for the next 'big thing', set your sites on something you can reasonably accomplish and that is doubling your income.

And remember, your Real Cash Secrets manual, the newsletters you'll continue to receive and the real money-making opportunities we've uncovered will help you get ahead.

When you discover solid information and then act on it, you can double your income. Then that income will allow you the money you need to invest in future endeavors.

There is absolutely nothing wrong with "getting rich slowly."

**"How to Hone Your Skills as an Entrepreneur..."**

Entrepreneurs think outside of the box. Employees recite what they've been told.

If you want to gain the entrepreneur mindset, you need to learn to think freely... unencumbered by limiting beliefs.

Don't be afraid to challenge what is accepted. Going against the crowd is always where the big money is.

It doesn't matter how many business opportunities you look into or even buy...

...to operate them as an entrepreneur you need;

- ✓ to understand the opportunity, you see and have a clear path to achieve it
- ✓ to be at peace that everything won't be under your control (risk taker)
- ✓ to be aware of yourself and your tendencies so they don't cloud your vision
- ✓ to be confident and not afraid to fail
- ✓ to be able to kick yourself in the butt and get going even if you don't feel like it or are afraid you might fail
- ✓ to listen to your customers as they will tell you how to sell them and what problems they want solved
- ✓ to be willing to work hard and that's why so many people fall for envelope-stuffing-scams because they want to believe they can hit the lottery in their sleep

Entrepreneurs make lots of money because they are willing to accept the facts listed above. Employees grind away hoping they can save enough for retirement. And dreamers hope the next thing they try will bring them instant riches, only to wake-up broke.

Here's a story about someone thinking and acting like an entrepreneur instead of an employee.

In fact, being suddenly faced with unemployment sparked her to stop thinking like an employee.

Like any endeavor, there is trial and error involved. But she never ever gave up.

# "Ohio Lady Loses Job Then *Doubles* Her Income."

In April of 2012 Ohio native Kristin Scott, a single mother, lost her job. Not that the loved the job so no big loss. Then she decided to research the candle making business.

After months of watching YouTube 'how to' videos on candle making, she paused her idea. But the entrepreneurial spirit kept burning, so she got back on the project.

A friend told her about another friend who was making money hand over fist with her candle business in Detroit. So she reached out and found a mentor.

Starting at her kitchen table she made the usual mistakes of mixing fragrance and wax. But she kept at it through trial and error.

Less than 6 months after losing her job, she attended her first home and garden event where she sold her candles by lighting them and letting the fragrance pull in buyers like a moth to a flame.
Then she got the brilliant idea to market her candles as massage oils. This boosted her sales dramatically.

Next she started looking for ways to lower her cost. Up until then she had been buying supplies from her mentor. Once she moved to a wholesaler she cut her costs in half.

She continued to forge ahead, not afraid to fail because grabbing a full time job would always be there should things not work out.

While on a trip to Atlanta, she and her girlfriend saw a music artist she was a fan of and she summoned the gumption to walk up and tell him about her candles. To her surprise, he said he would buy 10. Then he posted her product in his social media.

Using that success, she reached out to other celebrities and her guerilla marketing paid off. Just 3 years after starting, she opened a storefront in her hometown of Youngstown, Ohio.

What makes her candles different than everyone else making candles? Well she experimented a lot with the right balance of wax and fragrance.

She didn't wait for the market to find her, she expanded the market through contacting celebrities on social media who not only bought her candles, but shared their experience with their Facebook and Twitter followers.

Entrepreneurs are determined. And often start small. Today her income is double than the job she lost. And she hasn't peaked yet.

Her story clearly illustrates the power of one idea. As soon as you've finished reading this issue of Quick Cash Secrets, crack open you manual and spend a couple of minutes a day reviewing the ideas. It may be the best 10-15 minutes a day you've ever spent.

# "How to Become an *Electronic* Real Estate Mogul."

The Internet is the new age real estate. One big difference is, there is unlimited quantity unlike Board Walk and Park Place, if you remember playing Monopoly as a kid.

Here's what I mean. Let's say you spent your career as a carpenter or maybe a bookkeeper. Everyday all across the world, someone picks up a hammer for the first time or enter debits and credits to keep the books for a their first client.

And they would love to get some inside tips on exactly what you know so they can do what they do faster, better and cheaper.
So you start website targeting them. They come to read your articles, watch your videos, even order specialized books you created. Just like any publisher, readership means money from advertising and products sold.

Now before you scramble to put up a website and start counting the income you think you will get, keep in mind the Internet is VERY competitive. So competitive most websites get very little business.
But this creates an 'out' too. You can string together a lot of little websites so the total income is a windfall.

Research has proven, the more websites you have, the more total traffic you have. And the more website visitors, the more ways you have to link to products and services to earn a commission. Offer your own 'how to' books. And get advertisers for your website.

Take bookkeeping for instance. Some people are searching for 'bookkeeping services' and you could create a website to funnel those leads for a profit when you send them to other bookkeepers. Others are searching for 'bookkeeping courses' something you would create and sell them.

Another niche is 'bookkeeping and taxes' and this is vital information people will be searching for until their last breath on earth.

Still another niche is 'bookkeeping software'. Here you review the various solutions available and then link to their websites and you receive a commission.

The list goes on and on and so it is true for any niche you may have inside knowledge on.

Now let's say you have trouble just managing your email and the Internet is a big bugaboo you'd rather avoid. Then let me ask you this, are you on Facebook?

If you are, you know how addicting it can be. Go to any coffee shop and you'll see almost everyone with thumbs blazing on their smartphones. Looking at their Facebook as if they were standing in the hall of second grade class staring at the new kids parading by.

Did you know you can market to your list? Here's an easy example.

If you state doesn't have the stupid Internet sales tax, you can become an affiliate for Amazon.

How does that work?

You go to Amazon and sign up and what you get is commissions on stuff people buy after clicking a link in an email you send.

Let's say you check your Facebook newsfeed and people are going on and on about a new diet they heard about. You write an email about an Amazon book detailing the new diet, send to your list. A certain number of them buy and you'll get a commission.

If you have lots and lots of Facebook friends, others will pay you to make posts about their products too.

As you read this, the Internet is constantly changing. We reported last issue about some apps where people are getting good paying gigs driving folks to the airport or reselling thrift store clothes. Opportunities abound daily.

Stay tuned to future issues of Quick Cash Secrets as we are working on a jump-start training course that will make it super simple for anyone to make money on the Internet, even if you have trouble sending an email now.

## *"Putting Yourself in a Position to Win..."*

To be in a position to take advantage of any opportunity, your well-being is key. You must take steps to keep stress to a minimum. Your mind needs to be clear, so you make sound decisions. Your body needs to function so you can make your day of work in whatever endeavor you choose.

What most people do is wait until the fall apart then go to the doctor. Your doctor will likely hand out pills as if they were candy. The fact is, the U.S. prescribes more pills than all the other countries on earth.

Let yourself go too far, and you end up in the looney bin or on the operating table.

The following is a sure-fire plan for 'preventative medicine'. And it really works. How do we know?

This is the tried and true health and mind methods used by one of the world's top blackjack players. He's counted cards for 40 years and regularly walks out of the casino with tens of thousands of dollars.

If you want to read about his blackjack methods, get the book 'Burning The Tables in Las Vegas' by Ian Andersen, his pen name. He can't reveal his true identity or the casinos would bar him from playing and distribute his picture to every casino in the country.

In the book he has one entire chapter of how he prepares mentally and physically to deal with the stress of not only counting cards at the blackjack table, but also putting on the act of being just another losing gambler.

If his health tips work at his level, imagine what they would do for you as you set out to first double your income, then exponentially build your bankroll from there.

Here's how he manages to stay in top form. And keep in mind he has honed his personal routine for almost 40 years.

Maybe not everything he does will work for you. But you are encouraged to tweak your mind and body well-being habits to find the sweet spot so you can get everything you want and deserve in life.

Not only will better health habits put you in a better position to win with business opportunities, they will also make your social and family life much more rewarding.

First of all, by noon everyday he has consumed his entire daily allotment of fruits and vegetables. Dinner is the big meal with protein, which can make one sleepy. Which ensures a good night's sleep.

While at the casino, he takes a morning walk and in the afternoon a swim. This gets him as close as possible to the '10,000 steps' recommended a person take every day to stay healthy.

He avoids junk fats, like fried foods. On salads he uses oils instead of sugar, salt and preservative filled dressings.

He recommends putting flax seeds on both fruits and veggies. Flax is loaded with Omega-3 fatty acids that keep your heart and arteries running clean and clear.

Can't stand the idea of flax seeds? You can also get plenty of Omega-3's from walnuts. Also from fish like salmon.

The day before he flies to a casino, he does a one-day fast. Fasting cleans out your system and you awaken the next day with more vim and vigor than you can remember having since you were a teenager.

He won't eat anything served on the airlines. And during his stay at the casino, he eats small meals so he doesn't run the risk of feeling sluggish.
He cites a study done at UCLA School of Medicine proving calorie restriction increases lifespan. For him light meals during the day puts his mind and body into the super focus necessary to play $300 hands of blackjack.

And he never reaches for sodas or junk juice drinks, instead he drinks plenty of water, especially spring water. Or green tea which has very low caffeine.

He also supplements his diet with multi-vitamins and herbs proven to fight inflammation.

If you just get a little more conscientious with you diet you will put yourself in a position to win. Your lifestyle determines how efficient your brain works.

If you continue being a couch potato, you will have your guard down for the schemes that trick you into believing you can fold letters and envelopes during a TV mini-series and somehow wake up a millionaire.

# "Real Money Income Opportunities You Can Bank On."

## Street Team Part Time Work Pays $20-$25 An Hour

Have you ever heard of a street team? If you've been to an outdoor music or art festival, BBQ cook-off, fairs or trudged in line for a sporting event, no doubt you've seen someone working for a street team.

They may hand out samples of products from candy to cigarettes. Or they may operate in a booth for name brand clients like State Farm insurance.

Street team employment is simple. You apply for a position and if you go to major job sites like Indeed.com, you'll see lots of jobs for 'street teams.'

Companies are always sending people into large crowds to give out samples or ask survey questions. And the work is pretty much year round.

You'll see people handing out samples to tail-gaiters waiting for a football game to start.

Or you'll see them stationed under pop-up tents on parade routes, festivals and events. They hand out give-a-ways in return for email addresses so the company can promote directly to the consumer.

I've personally received free Twix candy bars at one event. And free cigars at another. In both instances, the street team employee approached me and ask did I want a sample.

Sometimes I've been approached and asked to take a short survey. It could be on tourism. On what type of insurance, I have. Just about anything.

In other cases, street team members give out samples at grocery and department stores. Have you ever been grocery shopping and seen someone offering samples of food? They don't work for the store. They are employed indirectly by the manufacturer of the product.

Here's how it works. Do a search online for 'street team jobs.' Then apply. Once accepted you'll be given various assignments.

Sometimes you'll work for the same company over and over. Other times they will rotate you between different jobs.

The pay is often $20 to $25 an hour. And you can earn bonuses by your activity level.

They measure your activity level by how many email addresses you collect. Or in the case of samples, how many pictures did you take of someone with the sample.

You'll often be given an iPad to use. As well as a GPS tracker so the company can confirm you are where they have assigned you. Or you are moving about a large crowd such as one you'll encounter at a festival or football game.

It's really simple work. And if you enjoy talking to people, you could earn some nice money in your spare time.

To get started, simple go on the Internet and do a search for 'street team employment.' You'll see links to job boards and websites of street team operators in your area. Just apply to them all and take the best offer you get.

**Work from Home as Virtual Juror**

Do you like watching shows like Law & Order and other dramas where characters end up in court?

If so, you may want to check out being a 'virtual juror' where you help lawyers test their cases. Before a lawyer presents a case in an actual courthouse setting, they want to tweak their presentation so their client has the best chances of prevailing.

Lawyers want virtual jurors from the same county where their case is scheduled to go to trial. On a website like www.ejury.com, cases will be regularly posted. You then apply to be a juror.

If accepted, you review the case material and then submit your verdict. Sometimes you will be asked to take a survey as to why you came to the conclusion you did.

The pay isn't tremendous, as low as $5-$10 a case. More complicated cases will pay more. You'll see the pay scale for the particular case you've applied, before you ask to be on the ejuror.

Its free to sign-up for www.ejury.com. Other sites may try and charge you to 'see' the cases available for you. Don't pay it. You can find out by doing a search for 'ejury' or 'virtual juror' and see any websites operating in your area.

One virtual juror reports that they found www.ejury.com very easy to use and enjoyed reading the case material. She said the extra money pays for her cable bill and Netflix account. Another said the work is easy and the case file questions are simple.

So if you are hooked on shows like Law & Order, Murder She Wrote, NCIS, etc... while you are in a commercial break, go to www.ejury.com and sign up for free. Easy-to-do extra money you can earn at home.

**Get Paid to Have Your Car Wrapped with Advertising**

Carvertise.com match drivers like you with companies who want to advertise with signage on their car.

Sometimes you will be chosen because of your commute pattern or where you shop, dine and go for entertainment.

What the advertisers want is, when they launch a campaign in a certain market or even nationwide, they want cars with their advertising strategically cruising everywhere they want to be seen.

Carvertise pays drivers from $300 to $650 per campaign. Their qualifications are you be over 21, have a car 10 years old or less and you currently drive at least 800 miles a month.

There are others companies that do the same thing, but do check out their online reviews before signing up. And never pay anyone to 'join' their site so you can get employed.

Carvertise does have an 'A' rating with the Better Business Bureau. While a competitor called Wrap-Match has an 'F' rating with the BBB.

**Make Your Car Payment from Renting It Out**

When to take a moment to think about it, most people's car is sitting idle almost 90% of the time. Unless of course you are a soccer mom.

Thanks to the peer-to-peer economy that has brought us websites like eBay, Uber and others, you can now list your car for rental.

One website called www.FlightCar.com lets you park for free at the airport when you go on a trip. While you are away, they rent your car to arriving passengers.

Currently FlightCar is in 12 major airports and is expanding rapidly. You get 10 cents and more a mile, depending on demand. While that doesn't seem like a lot, consider this.

Like any other opportunity, check it out before you sign-on. And if you have any doubts, email us for a review as its part of your membership in the Quick Cash Secrets Club.

But before you go looking for business opportunities, will you go back and review every page of the Quick Cash Secrets Manual.

Before we ever published the manual, we spent tens of thousands of dollars mailing surveys to real people just like you. People who are having trouble making ends meet in the rigged economy.

What those surveys revealed were the top things people wanted more insider-knowledge on. So take the time to review everything right in front of you. Just one idea can make or save you a bundle. If you simply try to execute the plan.

# "How To Turn

## Your Trash Into Cash."

Everyone knows you can get a little change by selling aluminum cans, cardboard boxes and even cooking oil.

But there's lots more ways to turn other trash into cash. Here's some you may have never heard of.

**JUNK MAIL**... the Small Business Knowledge Center will actually pay you for your junk mail. You read right.

Why would they do this? Well if you haven't figured it out by now, more money is spent on direct mail advertising than all other advertising combined.

And smart marketers are always on the alert for who is mailing what and how often. This way they can tell what worked well and what didn't.
All you need to do is visit their website and sign-up. Go to www.sbkcenter.com and click the 'join' button.

They send you postgage paid envelopes and all you do is fill it with junk mail and send it to them.

They estimate you can earn $20 every 6 weeks or so. Plus, they want you to forward certain emails you get too and that's another way to build up points you can redeem for major retailer gift cards.

Even better, you can refer friends and build points too.

And if you are a small business owners who are self employed can make even more money, because you receive both consumer and business direct mail.

Finally, the periodically send mystery shopper surveys where you can earn extra rewards reedeemable for give cards from over 200 popular retailers.

So stop throwing away that junk mail and sign-up at www.sbkcenter.com now.

**RECEIPTS**... market researchers will also pay you for your receipts. There are several mobile apps you'll use to take a picture of your receipt and then earn points redeemable for cash.

From your smartphone, do a search for these mobile apps where you can make money with your receipts.

**Receipt Hog**

**Ibotta**

**Checkout 51**

**GrouponSnap**

They are all easy to use and just another way to take something you would normally throw away and turn it into extra cash.

**CLOTHES**... often people will clean out their closet and drop the stuff off at Goodwill. But there are several websites where you can sell your clothing.

One is RecycleYourFashions.com and not only can you sell your clothes there, you can also buy gently worn fashions you may want.

If you have a weeding coming up and want to save some money on a dress. Or have a used wedding dress just sitting in your closte, then check out EncoreBride.com or PreownedWeddingDresses.com where bridesmaids can buy and sell.

**WINE BOTTLES & CORKS**... Designers in the arts and crafts arena will pay for your old wine bottles and corks. All you have to do to sell them is list what you have on eBay.

**CAR PARTS**... With more people trying to keep their old clunker going longer (especially if they fell for one of those 10 year car notes), keep in mind you can sell old auto parts.

Did your fuel or water pump go out? You can sell it because it will be remanufactured. And you can always get a gift card or coupon for recycling your old car battery.

You can get the most money, up to $50 for your catalytic converter.

The bottom line is, as Americans we throw away lots of stuff. Sometimes its valuable because we didn't know grandma's old antique whatever was worth really big money.
But more often than not, everything you bring into your home can often go out for money when you are through using it.

## "Americans' Income Addiction and How You Can Make Big Money Helping Them Kick The Habit."

According to a survey recently

published by Bankrate.com, 62% of Americans have have no emergency savings. They would be hard strapped to come up with an unexpected doctor bill or car repair.

There is a two-out-of three chance that you are in the same boat, as you read this.

So what happened? Are people still drowning from the economic tsunami know as the Great Recession?

Did several generations of Americans simply forget how to save if they ever knew how?

Or as we've written in these pages before, they U.S. economic system is rigged. Not only for those who have the ways and means to exploit a flawed system...

...but also for anyone who has insider knowledge. Info they can use to beat the fat cats, bankers, lawyers and lying politicians.

Certainly having the deck stacked against working people is part of the reason so few have any money set aside for emergencies. But there is a much bigger reason and fix it and anyone can thrive no matter how little they earn.

The big problem is simple. We want stuff. New cars before our old one has really gone through the paces.

We want as much house as the bankers will allow us to sign for. We want the latest electronic gadets. Today's fashions. Vacations we can't afford unless we pay on plastic.

Even if most folks hit the lottery today or gained a windfall inheritance from a relative, because they don't have a plan in place, the money runs out before the party is over.

But you haven't won the lottery and your rich unckle is still alive and rich. Yet your lifestyle continues to creep into your bank balance and then spill over to credit cards. Often to the point of putting you on the brink.

**How To Beat Income Addiction**

Simple. Pay yourself first. Before you load up on anything you can put off, save something.

Just saving a measely dollar a day will give you one-third of an $1,000 emergency savings that 62% of Americans don't have.

Now I know what you are thinking. You can't save a dime. After all, you've been proving just that your entire life.

Well in addition to cutting back, beating your income addiction so you have some extra cash by month's end...

...you can also CREATE cash with smarter debt management.

Most Americans just accept it as a fact of life that they will be up to their eyeballs in debt even as their coffin closes.

But there are ways out. You can...

**Fight Debt and Win!**

Yes, this is a shameless promotional article for the books and CD's you'll see at the end of this newsletter.

But more than a promotion, it will be a lifesaver for anyone who reads and follows the proven principals contained in the program.

Do you know why so many people can't seem to shake debt even though they desperately want to make it all go away?

They never really know their net worth. On page 101 of one of the books in the Fight Debt and Win program, the Debt Free Bible, there is a worksheet to show exactly where everything stacks up.

After taking that assessment, you then start attacking the culprits that keep you as an indentured servant.

For almost everyone, the big culprit is credit card debt. And again, its not all your fault. Here's the story why.

Soon after the turn of this century, the big banks lobbied (paid off) Congress to pass sweeping new bankruptcy laws.

Fair enough you say. Because lots of people were declaring bankruptcy then going straight to the ATM and sucking cash from their credit cards. So there were some loopholes that needed to be closed.

But the crooked bankers didn't stop there. They prodded Congress to enact legislation to make it much harder for anyone to wipe their debts clean. Even the single mom being crushed with unbearable medical bills to pay for the care of a sick child.

So what did the banks do once the new bankruptcy laws went into effect? Think back 10 to 15 years and you may remember.

Suddenly your limits as to what you could charge on your credit cards went up. Some people were even upgraded to cards they did not order.

New too-good-to-be-true credit card offers started arriving in the mail. Then almost overnight, many Americans had more debt.

Not because they are bad citizens. But because the easy money was there like herion to an addict.

**Settle Your Credit Card Debts For Pennies On The Dollar**

In the Fight Debt and Win Program there is an entire 300 page book just on settling your debt for a fraction... pennies on the dollar.

You see there are secret programs bankers, lawyers and the medical community doesn't want you to know about.

Because when you do, you can utilize programs they have in place to chop your debt down to size.

And best of all, afer you do, you can then consult with your friends and others in your community and charge them $500 for helping them save over $5,000 and get out of debt years sooner. Visit for details...

**http://ZodiPublishing.com**

# Welcome to Your FOURTH Issue of the Quick Cash Secrets Newsletter

Dear Subscriber,

Lots to cover in this issue. Know you want to get started so here you go with more news you can use to make real money, sometimes fast.

## "How Scammers Can 'Legally' Sidestep Federal Trade Commission Rules Governing Business Opportunities."

It didn't take long after the 'Great Recession' for your mailbox and inbox to be flooded with so-called work-at-home opportunities.

And as complaints started to roll in, your government took steps to protect you. Or at least this is what they thought.

As a recent article in Response Magazine proves, some of the shysters simply adjusted a few things so they could bypass the new laws.

According to the article's author, former Federal Trade Commission Attorney, William Rothbard, here's how one company was sued by the FTC and beat them.

Do a search for the Zaken Corp. and you'll see numerous rip off reports and Better Business Bureau complaints,

Now the FTC did finally put enough pressure on the Zaken Corp. as to hasten their demise. But not before they scammed thousands.

Here's how they won the first court case the FTC brought to test their new 'biz op' rules.

Zaken Corp. successfully argued and won in court that the new FTC 'biz-op' rule didn't apply to them because... and get ready for legal speak...

"The definition doesn't apply to any work-at-home offer but only those in which the seller represents (in pertinent part) that it "will … provide outlets, accounts, or customers … for the purchaser's goods or services … or buy back any or all of the goods or services that the purchaser … provides."

The short version is, Zaken Corp. successfully argued they were offering consumers the opportunity to earn a commission by locating distressed merchandise, then turning the lead over to the company who would then buy or sell the merchandise.

The court ruled for Zaken saying... "defendants don't offer a business opportunity under the rule because: a) they do not represent that they will "provide outlets, accounts, or customers" for the purchaser's goods or services"; b) they do not provide such "outlets, accounts, or customers;" and; c) the sales commissions their finders receive upon converted merchandise leads do not constitute a "buyback" of their services."

The FTC first sued Zaken in 2013 and lost that case. But continued to pursue them and in 2014 won a $25-million-dollar judgment.

What did the principals of Zaken do? They closed the business. And according to the website RipoffReport.com, the principals opened another 'biz-op' outfit in not time, at a different address under a new company name.

If you've bought any type of work-at-home offer from a company that did not disclose to you that they are involved in lawsuits or makes earnings claims they cannot substantiate, report them to the FTC as soon as you can.

# "Why People Keep Falling For 'Work-At-Home' Scams."

You get something in the mail. It makes big claims on how much you can make stuffing envelopes, making phone calls, running classified ads - you name it.

The price seems reasonable enough, usually around $30. So you send it in. You get the package. It's usually junk. You rarely try for refund and even when you do, you have to fight to get it if it ever comes at all.

And then you do it all over again. Why?

The scammers know a couple of triggers you need to hold back on before you pull out your credit card.

They know you are curious. So curious that you literally HAVE TO KNOW if this is the real deal. Because unless you order, you won't know. So order you do. And 99.9% of the time you get crap. Some don't even bother to send you anything at all. They just close down. Change addresses. And start all over again.

The other big thing scammers prey on is your lack of knowledge. And that's the whole reason we started the Quick Cash Secrets Club. To give you inside knowledge.

So you don't have to risk a dime. We'll give you the skinny on every so-called business opportunity operating today. And we'll get to the bottom of anything new that hits the market before you fork over a dime.

Making money online is another way people get suckered. Yet usually the money the 'guru' makes is not from anything more than the worthless products they sell you.

Often they don't have any valuable Internet real estate. They just send spam emails and direct mail promising you riches.

These scammers also know there is power in a lot of websites. So they will sell the same worthless product on dozens of sites they own, often tweaking the name of the product so you don't know its them again.

They operate under pseudonyms so you never can really find them. They have fake testimonials. Fake bank statements.

And if the authorities shut them down, they simply put up a new website and start all over again.

Because the scammers know how to market to the vulnerable. To ensure you protect yourself, take a look at the following risk factors uncovered by the American Association of Retired Persons (AARP).

You are likely to fall for a scam if you;

Feel lonely or spend your day isolated from family and friends,

Lose your job and don't have enough savings to tide you over,

Get clobbered by unforeseen bills such as medical, house repair or car maintenance,

Are up to your neck in credit card debt and can barely make the minimum payments.

In fact, scammers actually profile their most likely victim.

They know older people under financial pressure are more likely to have trouble spotting a liar.

They know a younger person will buy stuff to become accepted by their peers. And driving a shiny new sports car the scam promises tends to work well to separate the uninformed from their money.

They know certain states have larger percentages of older people who are having trouble making ends meet. According to Federal Trade Commission complaint data, the top states for scammers are; Florida, Texas, New Jersey, Arizona, California, Maryland, Delaware, Michigan, Nevada and Georgia.

They know lonely people are looking for 'prayers to be answered' and will reach out to scammers for anything like making money or helping them find a soul mate.

They tap into affinities. Maybe it's someone who made a presentation to your church group. Or if you are a member of a stock picking group, fishing group, knitting group - any group where they can get just a couple of members to 'buy in' so the others will feel like that is proof enough they should jump on board too.

And they know most Americans are deeply in debt, even retirees still have a mortgage and unmanageable credit card balances.

Not all offers to help you get out of debt are bogus. Mostly it's the ones promising you riches with no real clear path or plan.

The facts are, there are many legitimate ways to reduce your debt when you know how.

One of the most successful courses we've ever published is our Fight Debt and Win Program. Starting on page 271 of your Real Cash Secrets Manual is everything you want to know about the successful Fight Debt and Win Program.

Follow the course and first slash your debt. Then advertise your services and charge others $500 for real-world solutions to reducing their debt.

With 62% of Americans having less than $1,000 in emergency savings, you can see how huge the market is for debt consultants.

You can morally and ethically help people REALLY reduce debt, after you first do it for yourself. Otherwise they, and you will continue to fall for scams designed to prey on false hope.

# "The Ugly Truth About Foreign Exchange Trading."

Another big scam working daily across the globe is the FOREX market (foreign exchange trading).

If you haven't received a pitch yet, here's the story. Everyday there are several trillion-dollars in the Forex market for buying, selling and exchanging currencies.

Most of the time, traders are using leverage to potentially increase their earnings when prices go the way the bet. And that is the operative word, 'bet.'

Let's say you have $5,000 in a FOREX trading account and you leverage it 50 times so the total value of your transaction is $250,000.

If the 'price interest point' also known as a 'pip' drops by 100, you would quickly lose more than $2,000. We can go into greater detail about 'pips' but suffice to say, you want to steer clear of FOREX trading.

According to the website Quora.com which bills itself as "the best answer to any question," the most viewed Forex writer states the following and we quote...

"80% of all day traders quit within the first two years.

Among all day traders, nearly 40% day trade for only one month. Within three years, only 13% continue to day trade. After five years, only 7% remain.
Traders sell winners at a 50% higher rate than losers. 60% of sales are winners, while 40% of sales are losers.

The average individual investor under performs a market index by 1.5% per year. Active traders underperform by 6.5% annually.

Day traders with strong past performance go on to earn strong returns in the future. Though only about 1% of all day traders are able to predictably profit net of fees.

Traders with up to a 10-year negative track record continue to trade. This suggests that day traders even continue to trade when they receive a negative signal regarding their ability.

Profitable day traders make up a small proportion of all traders – 1.6% in the average year. However, these day traders are very active – accounting for 12% of all day trading activity. "

So the odds against you are 100-to-1. Yet everyday someone bites on a Forex scam offer.

Here's the ones to be on the lookout for.

**1. Signal Sellers** want to sell you information on the trades to make. They charge a fee for this service. They claim they've unlocked the holy grail to the market. If they did, they could make more money trading their own account and would not need your money.

**2. High Yield Investment Funds** take it one step further. You don't have to worry about trading. They want you to turn over your money and they will trade it for you. Many are located offshore and are nothing more than Ponzi schemes.

**3. Magic Software** promises to tell you when to buy and sell. Often this digital snake water sells for $5,000. Think of this, if there was really an algorithm to figure out the FOREX market, don't you think Goldman Sachs and the others on Wall Street would have discovered it by now?

The bottom line is; the FOREX scams work like all others. You are wooed with promises of riches with little work and a tiny investment. It's a fairy tale. Pure and simple.

And the same tactics are used to hook you on stock trading and commodity futures.

If the pros have trouble making money, what are your chances?

## *"How The Rigged Economy Clobbered Americans."*

Immediately after World War II the post war boom lifted all Americans.

Businesses were growing. Workers were doing their jobs faster, better and cheaper.

And the money that flowed into well managed businesses found its way to their employees. Workers who went out and bought stuff.

This cycle of increased productivity, more profits and active consumer spending continued well into the late 1960's.

Then the 1970's hit and America began to see increased competition. Can you remember how Toyota started grabbing more share of the U.S. auto market? And stuff once laughed at for being 'made in Japan' all of a sudden started flooding the electronic landscape.

So to deal with this competition, American corporations stopped passing on productivity gains to their workers and instead kept the money. And so began the steady slide of the average U.S. worker.

If you were lucky enough to be at the top of a corporation where you cleaned up on stock options, you did well. Or if you worked for a company that still offered a pension, you aren't hurting as bad as most others are now.

But for most Americans, their wages have stagnated, even lost value since 1979. Instead of recognizing the problem that the consumer can't afford the basic necessities, clothes, cars, appliances and houses...

...instead of seeing it as a problem, the corporate fat cats, their unscrupulous bankers, lying lawyers and crooked politicians tilted everything even more in favor of the 'investing class.'

The rich had their taxes lowered. The idea was, if those with the ability to invest could invest more, then all the money would 'trickle down' to the average worker.

The trouble is, that didn't happen. Again the system colluded against the working class. Gave them more access to expensive credit, like charge cards. Lower down payments on houses. Longer terms for car loans.

All with the purpose of keeping you in debt until you die and your relatives have to settle the debt out of what is left of your estate.

Meanwhile, the rich got richer. While most of you reading this didn't feel what was happening, like the proverbial frog in a pot coming to a slow boil. By the time you see you are cooked, it's too late.

Some of you reading this today are near retirement age. And conventional wisdom says don't claim your Social Security benefits until you are at least full retirement age (65 or 66 depending on the year you were born).

Because if you start taking Social Security benefits at age 62, your monthly check is less. And you can wait until age 70-and-a-half, your monthly benefits will be the highest you can get.

However, many Americans are so poor they have to start claiming as soon as they can, age 62. And that illustrates another example of how the system is rigged against working Americans.

If you start your Social Security benefits at age 62, you are only allowed to earn from a job $15,700 annually.

For every $2 you go over that amount, you will lose $1 in benefits the following year. Now don't fret, you don't lose the money forever. You'll have it tacked back on when you reach full retirement age.

But listen to this. You can have UNLIMITED investment income. So if you have the money to play the stock market, not only do you pay a lower tax rate than if you worked at a fast food chain, it doesn't count against your Social Security earnings test.

If you own an apartment building throwing off $30,000 a month in free cash flow, that too won't count as 'earned income.'

Yet the individual who starts collecting Social Security at age 62 and can't possibly make ends meet with their benefits (like no one can)...

...so they have to take a job. They are only allowed to earn $15,700 a year or have benefits deducted if they go over.

Are you starting to see the problem the American economy is in? Everything was rigged for the last 35-40 years against working people.

So to help them 'spend' like they used to after the post WWII boom, all kind of crazy financial products were developed like high interest rate credit cards.

Then the consumer got clobbered again. Today retirees have mortgages and credit card debt because of the rigged system.

And they, like you, are looking for a side income. A business to run out of their home. Or a business they can start on the cheap.

Here's what the prestigious *Forbes* magazine says about what the rigged economy did to America, and we quote...

"It also generated horrendous unintended financial, economic and social consequences: short-term decision-making, relentless cost cutting, staff reductions, squeezed operations, lower investment, crippled innovation, a dispirited workforce, reduced benefits and pensions for employees, mindless mergers, closed factories, off-shoring of production, increased debt, reduced ability to compete, declining rates of return on assets, rampant illegality in the financial sector, excessive financialization of the economy, and ultimately secular economic stagnation."

You need only turn on the news to see daily examples of what Forbes describes in the paragraph above.

But it gets worse. *Forbes* blames you for allowing the following to happen and not standing up and revolting.

"We as a society have come to tolerate that that extracting value from public corporations is given precedence to creating value; that financial gains from productivity improvements are not passed on to workers who generated them; that executives award themselves extraordinary bonuses for objectively poor performance; that many boards of directors have degenerated into a formalized mutual support system; that illegal stock price manipulation on a gargantuan scale is standard practice; and that economic stagnation and decline has come to be seen as, if not acceptable, inevitable. The fact that we as a society tolerate this situation means that we, too, have become a part of the problem."

So what are you to do? Get in your car and drive downtown and whack your banker in the head?

Then head over to the mayor's office and set his toupee on fire?

Or as Shakespeare wrote in "Henry VI"...

''The first thing we do, let's kill all the lawyers.''

Nope, nope and nope. What you have to do is outsmart the crooked bunch.

And the simplest way to do that is start a business of your own. That's why you joined the Real Cash Secrets Club, to get the inside scoop on legitimate businesses you can actually start on a shoestring.

Then to help you put together your meager investment to fund your new enterprise, you'll find in your Real Cash Secrets manual hundreds of ways to save on credit cards, cars, mortgages and just about anything your household budget goes toward.

Take the time to review those ideas. It only takes one idea to land you on huge savings. Money you can use to become a business owner so you can take advantage of all the tax advantages that will put more money in your pocket than working and saving ever will.

Even the office-in-home tax deduction will chop 20-25% off your rent or mortgage payment from what you'll save in taxes. Don't beat them, join them!

## "How To Unlock The Door To Wealth <u>After</u> 50 Even If You Are Deeply In Debt Now."

Author Steve Siebold who wrote the book *How Rich People Think* says its actually easier for seniors to make money hand over fist. But first they need to adopt the same belief system of self-made millionaires.

He claims people over 50 even over 70 can rake in all the money they want within 3-5 years if they will just adopt the right mindset. The older you are, the more your life experiences will work for you.

Yes, younger people are tech savvy, but that isn't what it takes to be rich. It takes experience and the ability to recognize when you can provide something of value.

But first, you need to change how you think about money. What's the right way to think so you can pave your street with gold?

As we've mentioned in this newsletter before, you have to ditch the get rich quick mentality. Sure some people cash a big lottery ticket or by chance go to work for a company where they get stock options that deliver a windfall.

One thing all the self-made millionaires Siebold interviewed had in common was, they believed they could become wealthy. Then they set out to find a way to create value, with a product or service, so they could achieve real wealth.

The rich are constantly accessing what they are doing. Is it helping them to achieve their goals or is it holding them back. And one of the main things you have to change is your beliefs about money.

Most people think of money as a 'have to' in life. They have to work in a job they don't like so they get money.

If they grew up going to a Christian church, they were drilled with "it's easier for a camel to get through the eye of a needle than a rich man to go to heaven."

Most people inherently feel money is evil. Or they have other limiting beliefs such as money is hard to come by.

It reminds me of one of the pro golfers from decades ago. It took him years to start earning real money. He related that Arnold Palmer and Jack Nicholas arrived at tournaments with their own private transportation and private chefs. This golfer took the bus and ate hot dogs. And he said, "if you eat hot dog, you play hot dog."

That's the trouble with the way most people approach money and wealth. They 'think' hot dog instead of steak.

The self-made millionaires don't use limiting beliefs like 'money is tight.' Instead they look at everything as one big game. A creative process they can win if they apply themselves.

Once you start to think of wealth accumulation as a process, you start seeing opportunities to provide goods and services to help people do something faster, better and cheaper.

The fact is, rich people are not greedy. Nor are they void of spirituality. In fact, they often use their money to help others.

But all the news is about taxing the rich. The rich control too much wealth. The rich are hurting others.

People think to make a lot of money you have to come from privilege. The best schools. Know somebody who is connected.

Anyone can get rich in America. You simply have to provide value. What is your idea, product or service that creates real value so others want to give you their money?

You can't feel guilty about helping yourself. If you can't help yourself, who will? And if you can't help yourself, you can't help others.

The rich aren't afraid to fail. They know they can lose everything and one day get it back.

They hate to waste time. You can't get time back. You can get money back. And often you can regain your health. But you can never get time back.

Rich people don't have high IQs. They just go about their business methodically. Plugging away everyday with the idea, product or service they know creates real value for the marketplace.

Break it down to the simplest value possible. If people don't want to scoop up the poop dogs leave in their yard, they can hire someone to do it. That's value, scooping poop from lawn.

From there you build wealth by scooping poop from 500 lawns.

Business schools teach creating value. But people never learn how. They stay stuck in their limiting beliefs and wage slave themselves until death.

Another surprising thing the author found out about the rich is, they are living among us. They aren't conspicuously consuming by living in a mansion. Or driving a Rolls Royce.

They are living down the street. Often unnoticed yet quietly amassing a fortune.

Just because you haven't struck it rich by middle age, doesn't mean you can't. Ray Kroc was 52 when he joined a tiny hamburger place called McDonald's. He saw the value of having one on every corner of every town on the planet.

It can happen to you. If you first just believe. Stop thinking life has left you behind. Because of the wisdom you've built up over decades, you are better able to really see what the market wants, even if it's just the market in your home town.

# "Real Money Income Opportunities You Can Bank On."

**Homeless Woman Becomes Millionaire In Two Years**

*Forbes* magazine often has offbeat success stories in their pages. And none are more gripping than Dani Johnson's story.

In just two short years, she went from living in her car while dependent on cocaine and booze, to a millionaire.

Here's her true story...

Like a lot of attractive young women, Dani worked as a cocktail waitress. She lived in Hawaii at the time after moving from California. Often that income didn't pay the bills so she found herself living in her car parked near a beach.

Yes, she had issues from childhood physical, emotional and sexual abuse. She turned to drinking and cocaine to soothe the pain.

Soon she found herself down to exactly $2 and 3¢. Hardly enough to deal with the $35,000 in credit card debt, much less food, clothes and an apartment.

By Christmas Eve of 1990, she was coming off a two-month bender. She was sleeping with 8 different guys just so they would take her out to eat.

For that Christmas, she and others working at the same cocktail lounge took a pile of cocaine to the beach for a little 'white Christmas.'

The next morning Dani woke up in a booze and drug filled haze and felt she had enough of 'life' and proceeded to drown herself in the ocean.

Then something almost magical happened. A voice inside her head coaxed her to pull herself together and climb from under the waves.

The battle with her demons was far from over, but she knew she had to do SOMETHING or slip back into the self-destruction that almost ended her life.

Still she was unable to afford Hawaii's high rents and she simply had to stop living in her car or relapse into a downward spiral that brought her near death.

Everything she had to her name was in the backseat of her car. As she rummaged to rearrange it, she stumbled upon a weight loss program she had ordered a long time ago.

She felt a way out. She turned the package over and called the publisher in the states and asked about distributing the program in Hawaii.

With almost no money, she had hand written a flyer for the product and posted it in the Post Office where everyone went.

She had no phone, so she got a $15 a month voice mail service. She had no address, so she had the product she would distribute sent to a liquor store where she knew the owner.

Three hours after posting the flyer she had 25 voice mail messages. In her first month of business, she had 40 checks in hand representing $4,000 in sales.

In her first year she made $250,000. By the second year she was a millionaire. Then she opened 18 weight loss centers in the U.S. And in 1996 sold the whole outfit to become a multi-millionaire.

If Dani can rise up from under a wave, nostrils full of salt water and near death...

...to sell an information product that made her a millionaire in two short years, imagine what potential you have.

Your life experiences, hobbies and career helped you gain lots of valuable information. Info people will pay for.

So why not package it up and sell it. And if self-publishing isn't for you, do what Dani did. Find someone else's product you can get resale rights to.

One man earns a part-time fortune selling personal protection products like stun guns and pepper spray along with personal alarms and home security.

Sound like fun?

Visit the following sites to learn more...

**http://SafteyTechnology.org**

**http://PoliceMart.com**

**http://CuttingEdgeProducts.net**

**http://TboTech.com**

It's actually easier today. Come up with a plan. Then just do it.

Even if you start with a flyer at your local laundromat, it is a start. So what are you waiting for?

### Surprising Ways Millionaires Minted With YouTube Videos

No doubt you've seen YouTube videos. Maybe someone emailed you a funny one to watch. Or you can reminisce TV characters from year's gone past. Certainly your email inbox is flooded with tons of videos where people want to sell you something.

Don't think you can make money by posting YouTube videos? It's pretty easy really.

You simply get a free account with YouTube and start adding videos. If any of them take off and get viewed many times, Google will send you a check. Because on your YouTube page will be ads and that's how both Google, owner of YouTube, and you make money.

Here's some hard to believe but absolutely true stories of YouTube video millionaires.

Grumpy Cat, is a pet with a perpetual frown. When owner Tabatha Bundesen first posted a picture on social media, it quickly went viral with lots of people adding captions like "I smiled once."

So Tabatha started posting YouTube videos and in no time, was able to quit her job as a Red Lobster waitress.

The money from people visiting her YouTube page started rolling in so fast that Tabatha hired an agent for the cat and they even trademarked the name 'Grumpy Cat.'

In addition to the highly viewed YouTube videos, Grumpy Cat also has licensing deals for t-shirts, coffee mugs, etc. and makes personal appearances at conventions like Comic Con.

Grumpy Cat isn't the only YouTube superstar cat. There's Maru in Japan who jumps in boxes. Shiro also in Japan whose claim to fame is letting the owners stack things on her.

Maybe YOU want to take your camera phone to the local animal shelter. See if you can pick something up interesting. Post it to YouTube. If it takes off, adopt the cat and hire an agent.

Let me ask you this. Do you think you are smarter than a 9 year old?

Well a 9-year-old named Evan started a YouTube channel reviewing toys. And guess what, he rakes in over $1 million a year.

A teenage girl makes lots of money with her YouTube videos showing other girls the ins-and-outs of applying makeup.

Is there something you have a passion for that you could turn into YouTube videos? It's easy enough to test. All you need is your camera phone, some ingenuity and your free YouTube account.

Go ahead and experiment with some videos. You may be surprised like the Grumpy Cat owners or the parents of the 9 year old.

### Easier Than Ever To Make A Small Fortune Publishing Your Own Books

Amazon started in the '90's to sell books. Today they sell just about every type of product including downloadable books.

And Amazon allows anyone to create their own book and upload it for sale on their Kindle platform.

Kindle lets you easily read books on your computer, tablet and even phone.

Some people give away their books as a way generate leads for something else they are selling, like selling coaching services.

The fact is, you can take your life experiences and find someone who wants to be coached on the shortcuts you've amassed over the years.

Here's a couple of success stories from do-it-yourself Amazon Kindle publishers.

*New York Times* bestselling author John Locke wrote a 'how to' book titled, *How I Sold 1 Million eBooks in 5 Months!* Maybe you want to pay the $2.99 to download the book so you can do it too.

UK citizen Mark Dawson made $450,000 in one year selling books about a fictional assassin. Even Forbes magazine profiled him about his Amazon Kindle ebook success.

Or check out author team Bob Mayer and Jen Talty who shows

you how to make money on Amazon Kindle with their $4.99 ebook, How We Made Our First Million on Kindle.

Maybe you just want to write a story your grandparents told you. A story no one has ever heard before.

Or maybe you are a school teacher who has a down pat lesson plans other teachers would buy.

Others have done more with less, why not you?

### Make BIG MONEY With An Online Course

As you've read earlier in this issue. At your ripe age, you've encountered a lot. Learned plenty. Survived crisis. You name it.

Some experiences people want to hear about. Some skills people want to learn too. And then your career. Everyday younger people are starting the same career you have decades of experience in. Share the knowledge with your on online course.

Now, you don't need a fancy website or even a website at all. In today's 'sharing economy' some people are making millions selling courses on an online educational website called Udemy.

Former math teacher Rob Percival sells The Complete Web Developer Course so people can learn how to build websites. His sales have exceeded $2.8 million.

Alun Hill made $650,000 selling courses showing the average person how to earn money as a photographer or videographer.

Currently Udemy has 22,000 courses people can take to better themselves.

What do you know others would want to learn? Even if it's about knitting or gardening, you may be surprised at how much money you'll make.

### *"Weird Business Ideas That Make Money Hand Over Fist."*

From the strange but true deparement, get aload of these actual businesses and what they sell. Maybe they will spark an idea for you to form a start-up.

**FineArtAmerica.com** sells 'fetal greeting cards." Yup you read right, FETAL greeting cards.

Want to announce a pregnency? You can show ultrasound photos of the fetus.

Yes people are actually paying $8 a card and less when purchased in quantities.

And if celebrating life with a greeting card seems a little farfetched, then how about...

**Cremation Jewelry** from PurpleCloudStudio.com where you can get both cremation urns or have your loved ones ashes made into jewelry.

You can even have your creamated pet's ashes fashioned into jewelry.

And it even gets weirder for the well-to-do. You can have your loved one's ashes made into a real diamond starting at only $3,500.

As they say, ashes to ashes and dust to dust or in the case of our next weird biz idea...

**Irish Dirt** can be bought from Independent.ie for $15 a pound.

Who buys Irish dirt? Funeral directors catering to the Irish-American custom of sprinkling the stuff on a casket.

And so you can dance a jig at the next Irish wake, why not get a...

**Sockscription** so you never have to shop for socks again.

We know how frustrating it is to always seem to fail to pair the same socks after laundry. Happens to this reporter weekly.

Well, visit BlackSocs.com, like customers in 70 countries have and get three pairs delivered three times a year for $80.

So slip on a new pair of socks, your favorite walking shoes and take the dog for an outing and don't forget to bring the...

**Doggles** which will protect pooche's eyes. You know how your dog LOVES to hang his head out of the car window.

The Doggles protect his eyes. And we know how people love their dogs as over $5 million dollars of this motor dog fashion have been sold.

Even if you don't take the dog in the car, the Doggles will protect them from excessive sunlight and debris while you are walking them to take a whiz, which brings us to the weirdest business yet...

**Human Urine**, which people buy to pass drug tests at work.

No we aren't going to take sides in the drug war. But its crazy you can smoke pot in Colorado, drive across state lines for a job interview and be denied employment because you failed a drug test.

BuyCleanUrine.com sells a pocket sized bottle for $87.38!

Maybe its time you got pissed enough at the rigged system and started your own business.

Having your own business is your sure-fire way to having the kind of life you deserve.

Wihout your own business, you will continue to get taxed to death or until death. Either way you lose.

With your own business, you can enjoy all the perks the system put in place because business people have lobbiest. Politicians have been literally paid off to give business onwers breaks.

With your own business, you can then build up cash to invest. Because unless you have 'passive' income, you have no chance of ever getting rich.

The reason many of you haven't started your own business is because you don't have the money.

So you continue to juggle credit cards to provide your most basic needs, much less ever take a vacation.

Well there is a way out. And it's the **Fight Debt and Win**. We show you the 'secret' back doors the credit card companies don't want consumers to know about.

But when you do, you'll be chopping that debt down faster than you ever thought possible. And from there, you can take your 'debt expertise' and charge friends and neighbors $500 a pop to do what you did.

Isn't is about time you *really* took control of your finances instead of them controlling you? Visit for details:

Zodi Publishing
**Q.C.S. Newsletter**
http://ZodiPublishing.com

# Welcome to Your FIFTH Issue of the "Quick Cash Secrets" Newsletter

Dear Subscriber,

## "How Rich People Think Differently Than You."

In the last issue, we discussed some of the findings from Steve Siebold's book *"How Rich People Think."*

We gave you an overview of some of the main points the book makes. Today we are going to dig a little deeper and be specific on how rich people think differently than you. And what you can do to change your mindset to set yourself up for prosperity.

People that don't have money distrust the rich. It has become a theme of political rhetoric. Granted the system is rigged. But you don't have to sit there and take it.

The same tax laws that help the rich get richer will also help you, if you bother to get the knowledge and act on it.

Rich people think not having money is a problem. Sure you can't buy happiness but you can enjoy an easier life if you have money.

Rich people plan and work to make themselves happy. People without money seek happiness from trying to save the less fortunate like them. What they don't understand is, in order to put yourself in a position to help others, you have to help yourself first.

Rich people know they must take action to get money. The average person thinks they will all of a sudden get a windfall from some get rich scheme. It doesn't work. So they buy another scheme.

There are many rich people who did not go to college, have an MBA and some even didn't finish high school. Yet the average person believes their only path to the good life is to be highly educated. The fact, specialized knowledge is what puts you ahead.

Like specific knowledge about real estate, a business you own, a how-to book you write. The list of specialized knowledge is infinite.

Someone is always looking for a way to do anything faster, better and cheaper. In your Real Cash Secrets manual you'll find lots of very specific solutions to making or saving money.

You've had the manual for a while now. How many of the ideas did you try? Only action will give you the power to have the future you want.

And more important, the power

to fail. There is specific knowledge to be found in failure.

Abraham Lincoln failed in many businesses.

Not all of Donald Trump's business have succeeded. In some cases, both he and his investors lost their shirt.

But investors keep giving him money because he wins more than he loses. And the only way he wins more than he loses is by taking action. One loss doesn't define his career or life. You learn what you can, salvage what you have left and then move onward and upward.

Some people make good money being a professional gambler. However, to exploit the tiny edge they have in blackjack, sports betting, horse racing or dice setting...

...they have to fail many, many times. Yet 51% or as high as 54% of the time they win. Do this over and over and their bankroll grows.

Most people don't have the objectivity to deal with the swings in building a bankroll. So they put it all on 'red' on the roulette wheel hoping this is their lucky day.

The winning gambler doesn't get involved in games there is no mathematical edge. **Specific knowledge is their edge.** There are millionaire poker players who only have a high school degree.

The average person looks back. They long for the time when... they had a brand new car... had a better paying job than now... owned a home that ratcheted up in value because of the property boom... you name it.

**Rich people wake up every day thinking 'opportunity.' They know with specialized knowledge and action they can make the future better than today.**

Average people think the good old days will never return. And they act accordingly.

**Rich people think of money as a tool. Managed properly, they learn to make more money with money. Build passive income with their money working all the time.**

Average people get emotional about money. Feel threatened when they come up short. Overspend on consumer items when they get an inheritance, a bonus or have a really good year.

They buy to fill emotional needs. They don't see saving and investing as a way to get rich because it doesn't give them the 'lift' they get from a shopping spree.

Rich people find an idea, product or business they are really passionate about and dive in relentlessly to make it work.

Average people are stuck in jobs they hate. Work for bosses they want to strangle. Sloth through a commute they could do blindfolded.

Because they have to pay the bills. They won't eliminate the hundreds a month for cable TV and all the premium channels, then invest that money. Instead they surround themselves with bills that forces a slave mentality when it comes to work.

Rich people set the bar high. And as soon as they achieve that goal, they place the goal post further away.

Average people have low expectations. Like making it past the end of the month. Or just holding onto a job.

Rich people are always aiming higher, then taking the specific action to reach their goal. Often just getting halfway there is way more of an achievement than most people set for themselves.

They then regroup and figure out why they only got half of what they planned and use that specific information to make changes so they can prosper next time.

Average people falsely believe they have to do something to make a lot of money. This leaves them wide open to the get-rich-quick schemes.

**They are not focused on the long term. They are striving for a short term fix to a long term problem.**

Rich people know you have to 'be' something to make a lot of money. They know you have to be a better manager, more efficient and realistic.

By focusing on being a better human being they set themselves up for success. When you change who you are for the better, it becomes easier to rake in more money than you ever imagined.

Rich people know the fastest way to make money is to use other people's money. But why do other people lend you money?

Because the individual or business has proven they know how to find the 'gaps' and take advantage of them. Gaps in what the market wants and is getting. Gaps in how the market values something and what its really worth in a few years.

Will the future worth of building make it a good investment? Has the developer made similar investments in the past with good results?

This is why the Donald Trumps of the world have investors lining up. Because his deals win more than they lose. And investors have made lots of money in the past.

Average people think they have to make money to invest. This is true to an extent.

But back to our real estate example, many people have achieved great wealth in a short period of time because they learned 'creative' financing. They know how to do deals for houses. And they continue parlaying deals until they amass a fortune.

The average person thinks they will never save for the down payment for an investment property and it becomes a self-fulfilling prophecy.

Average people don't know how to gauge a market. From real estate, to stocks, commodities. Or fashion if they own a design firm. Even a car dealer displaying the latest models from Detroit.

Average people think people buy something because they thought it through. This car has good gas mileage. Will last as long as the car loan.

Rich people know markets go up and down with people's emotions. Warren Buffet put it best...

"Be fearful when everyone is greedy and greedy when everyone is fearful."

You see the emotional behavior all the time. Something happens and makes the news and the stock markets sells off.

Or someone in the neighborhood gets the latest model car and all of a sudden, the others want a new car in their driveway too. No matter if they can afford it or not.

Rich people understand when fear or greed is driving the price of something up or down and are ready to take full advantage. Often this means doing the opposite of what everyone else is doing.

Average people often buy emotionally. New flat screen TV. More car than they need. Keeping up with the 'Joneses' keeps them in debt forever.

**Rich people live below their income level. This allows them to bank cash for emergencies that would send other in hock. Or have the money they need when a good opportunity arises.**

Average people are more focused on survival. Not getting ahead. They lament about what they don't have. And stay stuck in a negative feedback loop.

Rich people look at the world objectively. And they teach their children to do the same thing. Their children learn to have something; you must take action. Have a plan and feel really passionate about what you are doing and wealth will come.

Rich people are always looking for more knowledge. Information they can use to get ahead.

Average people are looking for entertainment. They aren't reading as many 'how to' books as they are reading entertainment publications.

**Rich people know to maintain their edge; they must always be learning.**

Average people think the rich are snobbish and don't make friends with them.

Rich people don't make friends with average people because they don't want to hear about doom and gloom. They want to talk about opportunity.

Average people pinch pennies. Clip coupons. Save what they can. And hope they will be o.k.

**Rich people are always thinking about what they can earn. They are always looking for big opportunities.**

Average people play it way too safe. Are scared to take risks.

Rich people take calculated risks. Knowing full well everything won't work out. But often just one in ten big ideas need to hit to produce great wealth.

Average people strive for comfort. Comfort food. Safe decisions. They avoid uncertainty like the plague.

Rich people know life ain't easy. Taking risks is part of the game. They find comfort in being able to find a way to sail into uncharted waters.

Rich people don't gamble with their health. They know their money can buy them the best healthcare. They know they can always get money back. And only get their health back if they have the money to afford it.

Average people feel good just having health insurance at all. Even though the deductible would put them in the poorhouse. And having basic insurance delivering basic service often isn't that much better than no healthcare at all.

Average people think they can't make a lot of money because family comes first. Their children's education. Healthcare. Living in a good community.

They feel if they spend too much time pursing wealth, they can only do so at the expense of their family life.

Rich people know they can have it all. They can make the right decisions and structure their life so everyone enjoys abundance.

As you read the preceding paragraphs, how many times did you identify with limiting thinking or beliefs?

If there is any underlying thesis of this entire article it's this...

**...the rich have a thirst for specialized knowledge, sizing up the risks and then taking action.**

They know full well every idea won't be a winner. But by honing their processes for evaluating opportunities, they know they will ultimately be successful.

# "Think You Want To Work At Home? Fantasy *Versus* The Reality."

Do you know what the 'gig' economy is? A Bloomberg Business report said 90% of Americans don't know.

Because of technology, internet, computers, tablets, laptops - more people than ever are working at home. And a 'gig' is a project. Often in a given week or month, people will do many projects for various clients. Sometimes never the same ones.

Before the gig economy, the work at home types were in real estate, sales, babysitting, artists, writers and the like.

Today people have administrative and customer service jobs at home. Run their own website. Act as consultants. Operate their own direct mail business.

But many are often shocked to find working at home isn't all it's cracked up to be. And since you are constantly considering business opportunities for working at home, this article is to give you the realties you can expect.

Yes, you can work in your PJs. But are they clean enough to answer the door when you receive a package? No one wants to see someone in their jammies with food stains from eating at your desk.

**Your friends and family don't believe you have a real job. They expect you to be available when they want to drop by. Or you can do errands for them like wait for their cable guy.**

One of the biggest myths is, you can work when you want. However many people loose site of boundaries and structure and simply work all the time. Even if its half assed, they feel if they are sitting in front of the computer, they are accomplishing something.

Another big fantasy is you don't have to deal with the office jerk-offs. Well here's some news. Your clients and their employees can be assholes. And dealing with your cell phone provider, internet service provider and other vital services can leave you scratching your head how any of them stay in business. These companies are often packed with jerks.

A reality is, you don't have much human interaction unless your spouse or children are also at home. Some people, especially in the creative field like to work that way. Others simply take a walk or combine an errand with a trip to somewhere they can socialize, such as a coffee shop.

One big unproductive fantasy is; you can drink on the job. Never a good idea, even if you had a glass or two during lunch when you were stuck in the corporate world.

A reality is, you and your spouse or significant other may start to argue. The one working at home feels cheated because the other is gone all day. Yet the one who just got home from the office is exhausted. If this happens to you, take time out to set boundaries.

Saving money from working at home is both a fantasy and reality. It depends on how you approach it. You don't spend money commuting or having to wear corporate outfits that cost money. You also get the home office deduction off your income taxes.

The dark side is; you may make emotional decisions because you feel lonely. Like shopping online too much. Or thinking you can keep moving happy hour up an hour until it's your lunch.

**Unlike a job, when you work at home you never really are off the clock. There's always emails to return. Some deadline that keeps you working past 5pm.**

**Even a project that may consumer your entire weekend.**

You can cope by also taking impromptu mini-vacations. If you feel you've hit the wall, don't sloth through and see your work suffer. Leave the house and go to a movie or the park. Or just take a walk.

Many potential work at homers fantasize about being their own boss. The key word is 'boss.' You have to do what your old boss did. Meet deadlines. Prepare schedules. Adhere to budgets. If you don't, your business suffers.

Unlike a job, when you are sick you'll still want to work because the computer is right there. The fact is, you are still sick and your work will show it.

**One reality people aren't ready to deal with is distractions. At work you put them aside because someone is looking. But working at home allows you to 'cheat' a peak at a talk show, have a long social chat online or the phone or just plain do nothing.**

Structure your time in at least 30 minute intervals. Ignore everything and just work. Then take a five-minute break. Get up. Walk around. Look out the window. Return emails. Then hit another 30 minute focused and productive time slot. You can carve out 4 hours a day like this and it will give the rest of your day for errands or busy work like dealing with the bank, internet service provider or whatever.

A reality of working at home is you have to exercise. At a job you get exercise just walking to and from your car, the train station or throughout the office.

At home you are at the computer all the time. And when you quit, you have trouble falling asleep.

At the very least, take a morning or afternoon walk or both. Do some deep knee bends before lunch. Then clock out for the nightly news and stretch and do other simple exercises you can do without the latest butt blaster or other gizmo you saw on TV at 2am when you couldn't sleep.

**The one big reality you need to understand is, to work at home you must be doing something that results in real income.**

Too many people fall for the fantasy and that is where the work-at-home schemers find and target you. **Did you know the 'envelope stuffing' scam has been going on since the 1920's?**

If you are not operating your own legitimate business, there are many websites that will hook you up with real employers who are looking for someone to telecommute.

Starting on page 171 of your Real Cash Secrets manual is a wealth of info about work, both getting a good or operating your own business from home.

And on page 173 are facts you need to know about multi-level or network marketing, second only to envelope stuffing as a way to separate you from your money and leave you just a little poorer.

The fact is, there are many legitimate ways to make money at home. You've read about some of these in the pages of this newsletters about people using apps to sell stuff, rent their car, etc.

Your business must fill a real need and solve a problem and you have to be prepared to work, so do something you like doing, otherwise you have the same misery you got with your paycheck at the office.

# "Finally, How To Beat The Fears *Blocking* Your Success."

You have a right to be fearful. The system rigged it that way so you will march in line.

Stay tied to a car payment. Have a mortgage you can never pay off. Pay high interest credit card rates while the banks borrow from the government at next to nothing. Yet jack up your rates because you lost your job in a recession they caused and then got bail out money.

They sell you fear. Fear you won't be able to cope without them. And their crazy financial products designed to make you a slave the rest of your life.

How dare you think of starting your own business. Paying off your mortgage early. Paying cash for a car. Taking a vacation, you don't have to spend the rest of the year paying off the credit card balance.

They've got most Americans paralyzed by these fears. And most never get beyond them to tackle the fears of starting their own business.

**"Fear defeats more people than any other one thing in the world."**

**-Ralph Waldo Emerson**

Your fear can actually DRIVE your business. Here's now.

**1.** Find the starting point. So you want to start a business as a consultant. You've spent years in a certain profession or trade. And today millennials can't find a job to pay off student loans they can't pay off with a job.

So you can teach them what you know. But you don't because you have never been a consultant before. What do you do?

**You find someone who is doing it. And learn from them. It doesn't have to be your particular niche. In fact, reading or hearing how someone overcame obstacles to launch a successful consulting business in any niche can give you a leg up on starting your own.**

Same is true for any business you want to start out of your home. Dog sitting. Dog exercising. Dog doo-doo clean up. Whatever. Someone is doing it successfully somewhere.

Maybe they have a book. A seminar. Or like the lady making candles we reported to you in a recent issue. She reached out to another in her state who showed her the ropes. Even sold her supplies until she reached critical mass.

**2.** You fear you don't know enough. Lucky you. Today the Internet has a 'how to' video for just about everything. Because those who post the videos make good money when people land on their YouTube page.

You can find the answers to just about anything, faster and cheaper than you could before the Internet.

Simply do what government officials do. Pass yourself off as an expert. Then learn as you go.

But unlike government bureaucrats, you'll have to eventually make money. Even if you fail, it's not a total loss. It's just one step closer to your next success.

**3.** You fear the delusion of 'safety.' The fact is, you aren't safe in your job. If you have one. The U.S. economy stopped rewarding worker productivity in the '70's.

The only safety you have is in your head. You are better off taking calculated risks.

Then relentlessly doing whatever you have to do to make your dream come true.

**"Develop success from failures. Discouragement and failure are two of the surest stepping stones to success."**
**-Dale Carnegie (1888-1955)**
**world-renowned author/speaker**

**4.** No start-up capital. You know banks only lend money to people who don't need it. Doesn't mean you won't someday reach that status.

Angel investors are hard to come by. Family and friends can't imagine why anyone would want to do what you do instead of slave their life away at a job.

Entrepreneurs jump start. Apple started in a garage. Then took a steady path to unbridled growth.

Other entrepreneurs, like one who makes tables out of reclaimed wood (www.stabletables.net) actually started with one table. Sold it. Parlayed the profits. And since 2006 business has exploded.

**Bootstrap yourself. Start small. Prove your idea. As the income grows, you can leave your regular job.** Or stop drawing down all of your retirement funds just to pay taxes on a house you can't sell because no senior can afford to both sell and pay out the wazoo to get a condo.

**"Fall seven times and stand up eight."**
**-Japanese Proverb**

**5.** People discount you. For all the usual prejudice. You're a woman. You're a man of color. You have little experience but big ideas.

Once you get rolling, delivering a great product, excellent customer service and hard work...

...the most important people will take notice. Customers!

**"As I look back on my life, I realize that every time I thought I was being rejected from something good, I was actually being redirected to something better."**
**-Dr. Steve Maraboli**
**speaker/author**

**6.** You know little about marketing. Many people do when they start a business. So they plan. They see what others have done. Did they do well with direct mail? Neighborhood fliers? A website.

You simply start. Measure. Refine. Find a way. Then rinse and repeat again and again.

**"Success is the sum of small efforts, repeated day in and day out."**
**-Robert Collier (1885-1950), American self-help author**

**7.** Being successful can be lonely. People gravitate to their peers. Worker bees socialize with worker bees. So if one person the community is the honey bee, few will want to be friends because you are successful and they are not.

And because you are successful, you aren't available for every happy hour. BBQ or swim party.

What do you do? You join the chamber of commerce. Trade associations. Any organization where you can meet and learn from like-minded people. Chances are, you'll teach something too.

**"What if I told you that 10 years from now, your life would be exactly the same? I doubt you'd be happy. So, why are you so afraid of change?"**
**-Karen Salmansohn, best-selling self-help author**

**8.** You fear your family may not understand. The fact is, all successful families pull together all the time. Not just for a business venture. But in health crises. Social adjustments.

Chances are your spouse, children and in-laws will be supportive. Lay out the risks. Tell them there may be sacrifices like you won't be trading in cars every two years like you were.

**"We will either find a way or make one."**
**-Hannibal (247-182 BC), Carthaginian General**

**9.** Not getting your money back. Let's face it, businesses do fail. It doesn't mean you are a failure. You learn. You move on.

If you had what it takes to start a business and do the very best you can, then you have what it takes to do it again.

**"A winner is just a loser who tried one more time."**
**-George M. Moore Jr. (1862-1940), Member U.S. House of Representatives**

**10.** Fearing obstacles. You can overcome an obstacle. But most people don't view it that way. They see it as a wall. A stopping point. You never stop. And even if you fail, you gained valuable experience for the next venture.

I hope you've seen some of your fears in the preceding examples. And fully understand you are not alone.

Manage these fears. Face them head on. Take the plunge. The alternative is to leave this earth in debt. Which means you'll have never, ever, really enjoyed life like you deserve.

**"The best way out is always through."**
**-Robert Frost (1874-1963), American poet**

# "Real Money Income Opportunities You Can Bank On."

The Great Recession of 2008 forced a lot of people out of work. Some never rejoined the ranks of the employed. Because they started a business.

They got bit by the entrepreneur bug or faced bankruptcy. So startup they did.

They started mostly professional services type businesses. Makes sense. Many companies had to lay off workers. So they turned to contract work.

They also started construction businesses. This is counter-intuitive because construction was the leading businesses that felt the downturn as the housing bubble burst.

Entrepreneurs started educational businesses. Everything from driving schools to any type of 'how to' anyone would pay for.

Some jumped into the wholesale and retail sector. **Taking their experience from their former employer into a business of their own.**

Manufacturing had the lowest start up rate, but many individuals built and sold stuff. Not the factory type of manufacturing we think of. But with the growth of the Internet, if you make something you can find a way to sell it directly to the consumer. Anywhere in the world.

### Create A New Product

Here's one of the manufacturing start-ups as first reported in U.S. News and World Reports.

Jeffrey Nash was 60 in 2014. He didn't make much as a retail salesperson. Hadn't saved much for retirement. And was behind on his house note.

What he DID do was create a product. A new type of baby walker called "Juppy."

He shopped it at baby product conventions. Found some interest. And did $200,000 in revenue his first year.

He now sees his senior years as one long growth curve. Income going up for the next decade. All because of his product idea.

## Cater To Growing Senior Population

Today the U.S. population has more senior citizens than ever. As of this writing, the tail end of the baby-boomers is 52.

Currently there are over 50 million senior citizens in America. And every day there are 10,000 more people hitting 65.

We are looking at decades of senior services needed for a growing population.

Maybe you have an idea for a new all-natural supplement or can private label a good one.

Or you can help seniors with financial planning. More seniors than ever are entering retirement with mortgages and credit card debt. Even student loan debt their children defaulted on. Or their own student loans because they went back to college late in life.

Here's a business you can start on a shoestring.

## Senior Home Care

You basically show up. Make sure they take their meds. Run some errands. Maybe some light housekeeping. Even play cards or watch TV with them.

To start your senior home care biz, you only need a computer, Internet connection, some brochures and a reliable car. You may sometimes take the senior to the pharmacy or doctors' appointments. Some seniors will pay for your lunch when you take them to a restaurant.

The national average for in-home senior care is about $24 an hour. If you live in a big city like Miami or New York, you can command as much as $40 an hour.

You don't need any medical training. In fact, you will alert authorities if your client has an emergency. And stay on the line until help arrives.

It's pretty easy to get started. You can post a free ad on Craigslist. Or distribute a flyer at your church.

Some senior retirement homes will let you put fliers there. Your job is the same. Sit with the elder and help them with small tasks. Or just keep them company.

If you have a website or yellow pages listing, you will likely get calls from the senior's children who live in another state. But are actively searching for help.

A big advantage you'll have over the companies that have staff is, their workers are paid very little. Often minimum wage.

You on the other hand, probably have more life experience. And can be more resourceful and helpful. Even able to converse on a wider range of topics.

Sometimes a husband and wife team can launch a senior care start up. There is enough work to employ both of them.

Another advantage you'll have of companies staffed with in home care workers, often the minimum wage workers won't show up at all.

It's not unusual for children of seniors, who live out of state, to shower an in home senior care worker with bonuses, even a higher wage, just because they found someone reliable.

You can expect to make as much as $50,000 a year. Not bad for a business you operate out of your home.

And remember, you'll get to keep more of what you make with your office-in-home tax deduction, cell phone, internet connection and even mileage on your car.

Your clients will typically range from 65 up to almost 100 years old.

You won't be required to do anything having to do with medical services other than reminding them to take their meds.

**And here's another good reason for you to look into this business model, it is actually the most in-demand job in healthcare, according to the U.S. Department of Labor.**

Because of medical advances, more seniors can live at home instead of a facility. This means a growing market for decades ahead.

Plus, you can only work part-time if you want. Often with just one client.

You don't need any formal training. But if you want to set yourself apart from others a client may be considering, you can get free training from the Red Cross. Often this training will allow you to charge a higher rate too.

## Be A Senior Concierge

An offshoot of the in-home senior care biz is being a concierge. You would offer to do things the senior can't do or if they are still working, too busy to do.

You may simply run an errand. Take care of the dog. Shop for their groceries. Drive them to and from appointments.

You will also help the children of the senior. Today both spouses have to work to make ends meet. And the last thing a family with children needs when visiting the grandparents, is to be saddled with lots of tasks the senior saved up for them to do.

No matter what the economy is doing, seniors will have a need for your concierge services. In fact, personal concierge services are currently a multi-billion-dollar industry, including the niche of seniors.

Just like in-home senior care, you can make anywhere from $20 to $50 an hour. If the senior needs your services on nights and weekends, you can charge a premium fee just like plumbers and electricians do.

If you transport seniors in your car, it's a good idea to get added insurance for business use of your vehicle.

You'll be doing a lot of services like paying bills for those whose memory is declining. Helping them with email to stay in touch with friends and family. Even help them shop online. And don't be surprised if a senior wants you to help them set up a profile on a dating website.

### Help Seniors Relocate

Another niche opportunity in the growing senior market is downsizing. Many seniors are still living in too big of a house.

They are selling the homestead and buying a condo. Or moving in with family somewhere else.

(By the way, our editors are working on a real estate training course that will show you how to profit by helping seniors avoid taxes when selling a home. Watch your mail for this opportunity.)

When you help seniors move you are removing stress. Stress they can't handle because of vision, mobility and health issues.

This business is growing so fast that the National Association of Senior Move Managers now has almost 1,000 members. Up from 30 the first year. Proof there is big money to be made.

In addition to the actual move is downsizing. You'll be the conduit between the senior and family members as what to keep from the attic, basement, spare bedroom and garage.

Just going through all this stuff and helping manage what to keep, give to family or sell is a big job in and of itself.

They simply can't take it all to a smaller residence. And what they can take needs to be packed and cataloged.

What doesn't go needs to be sold on eBay, Craigslist or divvied up among family who will cherish the heirlooms.

You can command high rates for this high touch service. Anywhere from $40, even as high as $100 an hour.

**According to the National Association of Senior Move Managers the average rate charged is $52 an hour. A good number of the move mangers make over one-hundred grand a year.**

Again, it doesn't matter what the economy is doing. The senior needs to downsize. And they or their family has the money to pay you well.

And you don't need to worry about doing any actual moving. You manage the move. Hire everyone to do specific tasks.

What you will do is;

1.) Sort thru all their stuff and help them decide what goes, goes with family and gets sold

2.) Be a liaison with charitable donations

3.) Supervise the movers and packers

4.) Help set up the new location and if it's in another state, coordinate with the senior move specialists there

Just one move, doing everything listed above, will employ you for about a month. Think about that. You'll just need 12 clients a year if you want to work fulltime.

You won't need any special insurance other than business use of your vehicle.

### Senior Safety Advisors

Because of fast growing advances in healthcare, today more seniors than ever have the opportunity to 'age in place.'

But this is not without a host of new problems. Especially the safety issue.

Seniors fall. Bump into things.

Let the neighbor's dog in because they can't see it's not their dog. Or worse, let a package delivery person in who is an imposter.

Then you have the telemarketing and door-to-door scams. All preying on the declining facilities of senior citizens.

As a safety advisor, you help the senior and their children or family, fully access any potential issues. Then launch full preventative measures for safety.

For instance, making more surfaces in the home 'slip proof.' There are a variety of products on the market to do just that.

Then there is proper set up and maintenance of security systems and medical alert systems.

What you offer is to do a survey. And you can charge as little as $50 for a small residence up to several hundred dollars for a larger home.

If you find a gap in their 'safety net' you then earn referral fees from alarm companies. Even contractors who install railings, ramps and tubs and showers easier to get in and out of.

All you do is list your services on the Internet, on Craigslist and flyers in your community. The senior's children will be contacting you mostly, because they are concerned for their parent.

You can command high fees because your survey will be extensive.

You'll thoroughly evaluate their entire home interior. Make sure cleaning products and flammables are stored safely.

You'll look outside for proper lighting, railing and stairs.

You'll survey their bathroom making sure it is easy to use based on their current mobility.

You'll look over their kitchen. Often seniors don't know some appliance isn't working properly. Or even know where their fire extinguisher is. They may keep food products long after the expiration date.

If they have a pet, is it one that won't cause the senior to trip. And can the pet get the care needed.

Then there's issues in the bedroom. Is everything accessible and working? Can they summon authorities in case of an emergency?

Most important is communications. What will happen if the phone goes out? Is there emergency exits. Are all alarms in working order and can they be heard from everywhere?

Finally, there's a safety checklist for personal safety. Is their clothing so tight that circulation is compromised? Are their socks skid proof? Are their meds easily accessible?

**Another reason this service is so in demand is government agencies encourage it. Social services too. Preventing a fall is a very high priority. As many as 40% of seniors who break a hip never live on their own again.**

With the lifespan of U.S. seniors being longer than ever, coupled with the great numbers of seniors...

...you can easily start any of the service type businesses mentioned above. Often with very little money. We're talking less than $1,000.

You may even be doing something like this now, sitting with an elderly neighbor.

**The market is growing. And has money to spend. You can expect these business opportunities to boom for the next 20 or so years. So why not take full advantage. Even if its part time, it's still good money. And a steady income.**

tune into."

Entrepreneurs who achieve wealth fast don't wait until everything is perfect. They charge ahead and perfect on the go. Or stated another way, on-the-job training.

Some of the biggest fortunes made by entrepreneurs are achieved by looking ahead. What does the market need?

As we told you in the last newsletter, a huge wave of opportunity for decades to come is to cater to the growing senior market.

Is there something you see that would fit in nicely with the expanding senior population?

If so, charge ahead. You just might come up with a big moneymaker. Life changing cash.

Because the senior population has never been this big before. And people are living longer than before. There are millions if not billions to be made solving problems for elders.

## "Medical Bill Madness And What You Have To Do To <u>*Reverse*</u> The Insanity."

If you haven't figured it out by now, the health care industry wrote the Affordable Care Act, known as Obamacare.

That's simply the way our rigged system works. Corporations help create laws that favor them and their cronies. While you get pick pocketed even when you don't have your pants on.

What's shocking to everyone with medical insurance is, people are still getting clobbered with crazy bills. We're talking tens of thousands of dollars in bills.

Sure everyone knows today's deductibles are the size of what you can pay for a used car. But what no one is ever ready for is the almost fraudulent level of billing being perpetrated by the medical community.

Case in point. One lady went in the hospital for a natural child birth. The doctors determined she would need an emergency cesarean.

When she got the bill the hospital had charged her for BOTH a natural child birth and cesarean. Double billed her for anesthesia. And crammed the bill with literally everything under the sun.

Even the most diligent patients, who clear ahead of time that their doctor and hospital is in their insurance network...

...are often saddled with all kinds of crazy charges where other health care professionals simply came in the room. And are out of network.

We're talking $3,000 here, $5,000 there. Whopping charges patients didn't see coming.

If this hasn't happened to you, a loved one, family member or friend - it's just a matter of time.

So what the hell can you do?

As we state starting on page 107 of your Real Cash Secrets manual, often you can get a better deal just by asking.

If you get whacked with an outlandish hospital bill, you can use as part of your negotiation tactics, a comparison of what a similar service goes for at other hospitals.

And often the hospital will lower your rate to what they charge insurance companies or Medicare.

Because as an individual, the first thing they do is sock you with every charge they can, knowing full well most of it is unlikely to stick. That being said, some people blindly pay the bogus charges. Especially if they are under $5,000.

The hospitals can also tap state and Federal programs to get reimbursed. You don't have to be on welfare to qualify.

If all of that fails, you can get hardnosed with a patient advocate. These fee based services, including attorneys, know how to read through the gobble-gook on your bill and strip away the confusing, even out right double dipping that occurs way too often.

If you want to go it alone, you can get unexpected medical bills lowered. Just follow these tips.

TRACK EVERYTHING - You'll get bills coming from every direction. The hospital. Doctors. Labs. And the ambulance if you required one.

You'll be well advised to pull them all into a spreadsheet. Check and double check every line of every bill for duplications.

Verify services were actually performed. And those fees are reasonable. Again, when billing individuals, the health care industry has rates far and above what they extend insurance companies and Medicare.

Even call the hospital. Because some bills may arrive 30 days or more later. Only adding more to the confusing mess.

REVIEW EVERYTHING - The billing gotchas are everywhere. For instance, you may have been released from the hospital in the morning. Yet on the bill you are charged for a full day.

If you are on meds and arrive

with them, hospitals are notorious for charging you again for your OWN meds.

Another sneaky way hospitals pad the bill is charging you for sheets and other stuff that is already included in your room rate.

FIGHT YOUR INSURANCE CO. - Insurance companies routinely deny stuff they say they will cover. They do this because a certain percentage of people won't fight. Make sure you do. Even get a lawyer to send a letter for you.

Or send your own certified letter showing you are carbon copying an attorney. Often this is enough to get the insurance company to do what they are supposed to do.

NEGOTIATE CASH DISCOUNTS OR PAYMENT PLANS - Hospitals routinely do both. Once you get the B.S. off your bill, then ask for a payment plan. Or you can get an additional discount by paying it all at once.

What happens is, you may have a co-payment, say 30%. But instead of billing you 30% and your insurer 70%, the hospital will bill you above what the negotiated rate with the insurance carrier. You can get them to back down.

As most people who've been in the hospital the last several years know, the health care industry is out of control. It's up to you to fight for yourself.

Medical debt is still one of the leading causes of bankruptcy. You can get a better deal if you follow the steps above.

Even better, consider our Fight Debt and Win Program mentioned at the end of this newsletter. Plus,

## Welcome to Your SIXTH Issue of the Quick Cash Secrets Newsletter

Dear Subscriber,

Lots to cover in this issue. Know you are ready to jump in. Here you go...

# "The 10 Pillars Of Wealth."

Twenty something Alex Becker wrote a book on how he built a multi-million-dollar business after serving in the Air Force.

By the time he was 28 years old, his total revenue was $4 million annually and his net worth was over 7 figures.

Here's some of what you'll find in his book "The 10 Pillars Of Wealth" about how self-made entrepreneurs got wealthy.

Just as we state on page 181 of your Real Cash Secrets manual, you must have both active income (from your job) and passive income (from a business, product or process) if you want to achieve independent wealth.

What holds most people back from getting wealthy is they think it's all about how much time they have to work. Nothing could be further from the truth.

Time is money. And your money can work for you while you are asleep. If you have a business, process or product that sells like crazy.

Entrepreneurs who made it big take full responsibility when things go wrong. They learn from the mistake they made.

Maybe they miscalculated the market. Hired the wrong person. Got involved with a bad joint venture.

Whatever went south, entrepreneurs who got wealthy took full responsibility for everything that went wrong. Learned from it. And used the experience to do better next time.

"If you could kick the person in the pants responsible for most of your trouble, you wouldn't sit for a month."
-Teddy Roosevelt

Entrepreneurs who are making a killing spend more time acting than planning for every foreseeable pothole they may encounter on the road to wealth.

To again quote President Teddy Roosevelt...

"Get action. Do things; be sane; don't fritter away your time; create, act, take a place wherever you are and be somebody; get action."

In the book, author Becker advises on failing faster. This way you learn faster. And get closer to achieving your goals.

And when taking action, entrepreneurs only get involved in tasks that generate money. Money is the measuring stick.

Without making money, you have no business. And no business being in business.

Successful entrepreneurs believe they will win. The self-help gurus call it 'abundance.'

It's a belief more than anything you can do.

The late self-help author Wayne Dyer stated it this way...

"Abundance is not something we acquire. It is something we

watch your mail for more detailed info about how you can Fight Debt and Win.

The average credit card debt per U.S. household is over $15,000. With the Fight Debt and Win program on your side, you can slash your own first. Then charge $500 per client to help others do the same thing.

Almost all Americans are struggling with debt. As a debt consultant, you'll have a steady stream of potential clients with problems they need solved now. Especially medical debt negotiation.

# "Real Money Income Opportunities You Can Bank On."

From the money doesn't grow on trees department...

...here's some real growth opportunities.

Do you have a 'green thumb' and enjoy gardening? Then you want to read about these real income opportunities you can do from home.

Grow SPECIALITY CROPS - and here's a list of them and what you can expect to make. Landscapers can't get enough

BAMBOO. The demand is that high. They make great indoor plants. In many Asian cultures, they call their indoor designs 'lucky bamboo.'

In landscaping bamboo makes a great screen, hedge and shade plant. And they stay green year round.

Retail value can go as high as $150 for potted bamboo plants. If you have a quarter acre of land to devote to growing bamboo, you can gross over $50,000!

As a grower, you can bank on how quick they mature, giving you inventory to sell to landscapers and do-it-yourself interior home designers.

Another in demand cash crop you can easily grow at home is GARLIC. With so many farmer's markets in urban communities plus local restaurants wanting to source close to home, the market is expanding each year.

On top of that, more health conscious Americans are adding garlic to cooking and even outright taking it for medicinal purposes.

Most local growers are commanding $2 per square foot for a garlic garden. If you have lots of land, you can grow as much as 15,000 pounds of Elephant garlic on a single acre and enjoy $6 per pound. A whopping $90,000.

If you don't have a lot of land, but a nice backyard, you can grow

FLOWERS. In fact, growing flowers is a booming business and someone at home can get started for as little as $100.

And you don't even need to grow to maturity. Lots of retailers and especially consumers will buy your starter plant.
Another good crop to grow at home are heirloom TOMATOES.

Tomatoes are the most bought vegetable. And heirlooms taste the best. In fact, sales are increasing all the time.

Put them on your menu or sell them for $4 per pound. Just one plant can yield 25 pounds a year!

What makes heirloom tomatoes so in demand is they don't ship well. So your local farmers market and groceries will buy all you can grow.

Add to that the consumer trend for naturally, locally grown food and you can see why tomatoes can turn a small plot in your backyard into a cash cow.

Another cash crop with the nickname "green gold" is GINSENG. Treasured by Asians for thousands of years, ginseng continues to find its way into a wide variety of supplements.

Taken on its own, ginseng boosts energy and libido. And Chinese medicine recommends it for its healing properties.

The drawback is, it takes over 5 years for the roots to mature.

But smart growers supplement their income by selling seeds and rootlets.

Altogether, including the mature plant, just a quarter-acre can produce as much as $50,000.

Did you know ginseng was grown and sold to help the fledging colonies revolt against the British?
Yes, ginseng helped finance the Revolutionary war.

In drought stricken parts of the U.S., a new cash crop has emerged - GROUND COVERS.

Instead of having a lawn that can't get enough water and turns brown, ground covers require far less maintenance.

You can grow these in your back yard and often bring in as much as $20 per square foot.

What's a good example of a ground cover plant? English Ivy is at the top of the list. You've probably have some growing in a neighborhood hear you.

There other in demand ground cover plants too. Just take a little trip to your local nursery and ask them what are the most popular for your area. Then grow them.

Another very profitable crop you can grow at home is HERBS. Both medicinal and cooking herbs have an immediate market.

And often you can sell the starter plants instead of waiting for them to grow to maturity.

Your herb garden will be one of the easiest crops to start. You can sometimes do it in your window sill.

Some of the most popular cooking herbs are basil, chives, cilantro, oregano and parsley.

The top medicinal herbs are lavender, calendula, St. John's wort and chamomile.

Now we go from herbs to LANDSCAPING shrubs, even trees. Grow them in your back yard and get fifty-bucks a plant started in a pot. Specialize in hard to find trees and shrubs and earn even more.

You can even call landscapers in your area and simply ask them what do they need the most, then grow it. Most often, its low maintenance plants homeowners and business want the most.

It's not hard to get started. Only a couple hundred bucks to get all the supplies you need. Even a small nursery of 1,000 square feet can hold as many as 400 fifteen-gallon containers of trees and shrubs.

This bigger grow operation will require a business license, unlike the smaller backyard plots we've discussed earlier.

But once you get it rolling, you'll have a very profitable side business. And remember, it is truly the ultimate work-at-home business opportunity.

As more health advocates point out the importance of having a diet rich in MUSHROOMS, offer a great value. Especially from a very small space.

There is constant demand at your local grocer for oyster and shiitake mushrooms.

In just a 10 x 10 space you can produce almost $30,000 of mushroom sales. Exotic mushrooms typically go for $12 a pound and since they don't ship well at all, your local groceries have to source from the area.

Here's the math. You can grow 25 pounds per square foot. So in a 10 x 10 space at $12 a pound, that's a whopping thirty-grand.

Even if you don't sell them to a local grocer, take them to your local market. They often sell out before any other product there.

You may find some local restaurants too who would buy everything you can grow for them. Restaurants want as many fresh ingredients as they can get.

You can have your first crop to market in as little as six weeks. Anything you can't sell right away, you can freeze dry and that opens up new markets too.

Another drought resistant crop you can grow is ORNAMENTAL GRASS. You can start hundreds of them in your backyard in by dividing root clumps from the 'mother' plant.

They are colorful. And some grow tall to act as a privacy screen.

Depending on your area, landscapers could be looking for a supply from a wide variety of ornamental grasses. Just pick up the phone and ask them what they need the most, then grow it.

Because more Americans are downsizing and choosing to live in smaller urban dwellings, so very small decorative plants command very high prices.

One such plant is BONSAI trees and shrubs. Perfected by the Japanese, bonsai is a method to stunt the growth of a tree, yet retain its natural appearance.

The plant is literally trained to grow lavishly in a very small space.
A seasonal offshoot of decorative plants is the table-top Christmas tree. Again, those living in small apartments and condos simply don't have the room for a full size tree. And a tiny artificial tree ruins the ambiance.

Plus, the trees are not discarded after the season. They can be kept year round, often on balconies or patios.

And speaking of balconies and patios, weaving trellis plants on to boards makes for natural privacy screens. These are always in demand.

MICROGREENS allow even apartment dwellers to get in on the farm to table movement. Or sell them at the local farmer's market.

Thanks to the culinary boom in America, microgreens are used for everything from garnish to mini-salads or added for color and texture to larger salads.

You could easily have a crop ready to market in as little as three weeks. And when you from $25 to $50 a pound for your crop, you'll surely want to continue growing year round.

Many are grown on shelves,

making it even easier for a small operation to thrive anywhere.

You may ask, what is a microgreen? Another name is baby greens. It's the in-between growth beyond a sprout, yet not a full grown plant.

Because of their 'baby' state, the flavor is often more robust. That's why they are in such demand in restaurants.

And when many microgreens are mixed together, the blend of colors as well as tastes make for an impressive looking as well as yummy salad or garnish.

The most lasting and pure gladness comes to me from my gardens.
-Lillie Langtry

We hope the home growing business opportunities above spur you to find a way to make a little extra cash, or a full-time living with your green thumb.

Just find your plant niche, start small and plow the profits back into your growing business.

# "You Can't Live Off Social Security - What To Do."

You hear the statistics almost every day. A nation of seniors not ready for retirement.

What happened? Did an entire generation simply not know how to save?

The answer is quite simple. The totally rigged system clobbered the working class.

We reported in an earlier issue of this newsletter about a study proving the average American's net worth declined 83% over the last 35 years.

And this decimation in net worth includes the value of a house and car, typically the two biggest assets of most families.

While the rigged system pounded you with taxes, the banking system changed the bankruptcy laws, then extended you more credit than you needed.

You had to use the credit cards just to make ends meet. God forbid there's an emergency. It would send most families to the pawn shop if they had anything of value to get a loan against, unless they removed their wedding rings.

So if you are over 50 or are already receiving Social Security, you have only two choices.

One, get out of debt completely. And the best way you can do that is our Fight Debt and Win Program.
In it, you'll find the step-by-step methods you can use to free yourself from debt forever.

After you fix your finances, you can then charge others in your town $500 to help them recover from debt. Everything from advertising for clients to auditing their income/expenses to coaching, is in the Fight Debt and Win Program.

The other thing you'll need to do is start a business. Don't think for a second you can expect a job to help you.

Even if you love the job you have now, how do you know the business or job will still be available a year from now. Much less 5 years from now.

Take the bull by the horns. Start your own business.

You've just read how easy it is to grow something and sell to farmer's markets, grocers and restaurants in your area.

Starting a business will give you an income stream you control, not some clueless boss who gets a raise whether the business does well or not.

Starting a business will give you lots and lots of deductions off your taxes. Things you are already paying now, like your cell phone, use of your car, office in home, even your health insurance if you are not yet eligible for Medicare - all become tax deductible.

When looking at businesses to start, stick with one with very simple business plans. Like the gardening examples in this issue.

Or as a debt consultant as we mention often.

Why do we mention being a debt consultant over and over again?

Because first, you have to get totally out of debt. Debt is a killer. A lead collar to a swimmer.

The other big reason we advocate you become a debt consultant is - almost two-thirds of Americans can't come up with $400 to handle an emergency like a car repair.

The market for being a debt consultant is huge now. And will only explode when we have another recession, which we typically do every seven years or so on average.

Where seniors make the mistake when starting a business is getting involved with a so-called opportunity that requires a lot of capital investment.

If you don't have money now, how will you come up with capital to invest? Max out your credit cards? Chew up your home equity if you have any at all?

On page 173 of your Real Cash Secrets manual it tells you to avoid at all costs multi-level marketing.

And since multi-level marketing became so associated with being a scam, they renamed it network-marketing.

By whatever name, you are forced to buy useless stuff. Because you buy into the dream that you can sell it and double your money.

But the whole network marketing business is just a ploy where thousands and thousands of people buy the junk once.

This means the people at the top rake it in, while almost everyone else has a closet full of stuff they have to use themselves if they want to get any of their money back.

Many of you reading this will probably have to start collecting Social Security benefits at age 62 instead of your full retirement age (65 or 66 depending on the year you were born).

What you may not realize is, if you start collecting benefits at age 62, you are currently only allowed to have $15,700 in 'earned income.'

And when you read how the rigged system is so totally against working people, you will become livid.

By the way, it really doesn't matter when you start collecting Social Security, at age 62, full retirement age or the mandatory age of 70 and a half years old...

...you will still receive the same total payout over your lifetime. You monthly benefits will simply be less at age 62 than age 66. Your biggest checks will be if you can hold off until age 70.

But still, the total you receive will be about the same on average. These statistics come directly from the Social Security Administration.

Well as you know, you can't live off Social Security. And if you start receiving benefits when you reach 62, you are capped at $15,700 of 'earned income.'

For every $2 in earned income over $15,700, you'll have $1 deducted from your next year's benefits.

Now the money isn't lost and gone forever, it is simply tacked back on when you reach full retirement age.

But what I'm going to tell you next will really piss you off.

Let's say to avoid going over the $15,700 in earned income you get a job as a Walmart greeter. So combined with the average Social Security benefit of about $1,100, you'll make a whopping $28,900 a year.

Whoopee! Try taking a vacation on that income, much less just getting by.

But let's say you own a fourplex apartment building and live in one unit. The other three units throw off $3,000 a month in net investment income.

Well that $36,000 a year doesn't count as earned income. Neither would any dividends you receive from stocks you own.

You could make one-million a month in investment income and it would not count against the $15,700 earned income cap for anyone starting Social Security at age 62.

Again, the system is rigged against those who work. Period.

So what can you do?

You can start a corporation. And this corporation would own the business you start. Even if it's a dog sitting and walking business, you incorporate.

The easiest corporations to start are LLCs (limited liability corporations). Then you elect to have the LLC treated as a Sub Chapter S corporation so you can take money out as investment income.

Now I know all of this sounds complicated. And most of you don't have the time and patience to slime around the Internet trying to figure out how to do this.

Don't worry. Help is on the way. Our editors are working on a book to show you exactly what to do. Step-by-step how to beat the system that is rigged against you.

It's the same thing the rich do with their endless posse of accountants and lawyers. They simply read the laws that are in place and then tailor their business dealings and investments to 'fit' the system.

You'll be able to do it too. Even better, your corporation can be owned by your self-directed

Investment Retirement Account. So in essence, you can start your corporation with a tax deductible investment.

Yes, sounds complicated. Watch your mailbox as our editors are diligently talking to the best sources of 'how to' info so you can get the step-by-step plan to do this.

In the meantime, you need to work on the other sure-fire method of putting yourself in a good net worth situation.

First, re-read starting on page 107 of your Real Cash Secrets manual the section on Debt and Credit Tactics.

Then on page 127, re-read about

Debt Negotiation. See how to lower your debt now.

And after you've read all of that, you'll have only seen a tip of the iceberg about getting out of debt. The complete system and methods can be found in the Fight Debt and Win Program. And its guaranteed to help free you from debt or you can return it in 30-days for a 100%, no-questions asked refund.

Plus... remember, after you get your debt under control, you will then be in position to help any of the other 76% of Americans struggling with debt. This is the biggest market for anything!

You can charge them $500 for a few hours' work. Just one client a week brings you $26,000 in additional income from a business you can do from home. Over the phone and via the Internet.

And keep your eye on your mailbox for more real business opportunities. If you haven't learned but one thing by now, our editors ONLY alert you to achievable opportunities.

No get-rich-quick scams. Only real businesses or side jobs you can actually do, with very little investment.

### "Know These Successful People Who Started Raking It In *After* Age 50?"

As you read this newsletter, I'm sure you have doubts that your life will ever be more than it is.

Struggling to pay off debt. Jumping from get-rich-quick scheme to another. Getting clobbered by taxes and more taxes.

And not being able to sleep at night because there is no job security any more in America.

While you pound the table telling you to just take action. Do something. Anything as long as it's a legitimate opportunity.

It's good to hear stores of others who became successful late in life. Some of these people you've heard of already.

What may surprise you is how old they were when things really began to take off.

Why are you more likely to start a successful business or create a blockbuster product late in life?

Because of your life experiences. You know what you know. And know what they don't know.

Read on for inspiration. Then vow to take action. Not high risk capital investment. Planned, calculated action designed to give you the best chance of getting a total return for very little money. Just your effort.

At age 65, 'Colonel Sanders' of Kentucky Fried Chicken fame owned a restaurant and small motel on U.S. 25 near Corbin, Kentucky.

However, his once successful business started to flounder because the new Interstate highway system about 10 miles away, drew away his foot traffic.

So the Colonel perfected is blend of seasoning and quick frying of chicken. Opened one near the Interstate. Then traveled the country selling 900 franchises.

One of the most popular children novelists ever was Laura Ingalls Wilder. Her name may not be familiar to you, but her series of children books "Little House on the Prairie" became world knows. And spawned a highly viewed TV series by the same name.

Did you know she didn't publish her first book until age 65? And after that, she wrote 11 more books in the series.

You've no doubt heard of the Zagat restaurant reviews. Did you know Tim Zagat started this business when he was 51 years old in 1986?

In 2011 he sold the business to Google for $151 million dollars.

How about Takichiro Mori. He left his position as an economics professor at age 55 to become a real estate investor in Japan. This was 1959.

By the time of his death in 1993, he was the Warren Buffet of his time with an estimated net worth of $13 billion.

Or how about the American folk artist known as Grandma Moses. She was in her 80's when she first started painting.

She picked up the brush because arthritis prevented her from doing what she loved, embroidery.

At age 76 in the 1930's she started painting. And for the next 25 years gained fame and money.

You may have never heard of Jack Cover. But his invention is in the news all the time.

In 1970, at 50 years old, after a career with NASA, Cover invented a weapon for rendering assailants incapable. His invention was the Taser.

By the time of his passing in 2009 at age 88, authorities in 45 countries were using his patented product.

Now you will certainly recognize the next story. At age 55 this famous actor ran and was elected as Governor of California. Yes, one of the most admired presidents ever, Ronald Regan.

We hope these preceding stories inspire you to don't' just sit there. Don't just take what you are being handed. Take charge. Look for an opening. Dream. Take a chance.
You never know. You could one day be featured as a success story.

### "Ingenious Strategies To *Double* Your Income."

Too many of you reading this now are stuck. In jobs you don't like that don't pay enough. Or trying to survive on Social Security benefits that are not survivable.

So you dream of getting rich quick. Taking shortcuts. When you should be thinking about a more achievable goal. Doubling your income within the next 12 months.

First, determine your skills. What is your strong suit?

Once you clearly identify that, find out if you are being paid what you are worth. Maybe there is another company in your area that pays more for the same work you are doing now. Or you could get a much higher salary by moving to a new, more lucrative town.

The website www.payscale.com can help you with not only salary comparisons but also cost of living reports. So you'll know if you move it will actually be worth it.

If you plan on staying where you work, then take on extra projects. Make suggestions for the company to do something better, faster and cheaper.

You can move up the ladder this way, as well as learn new skills that will further your career.

Even if you don't want to leave your current employer, still interview at least every 12 months. This will keep you on your toes. Let you see what's really out there. And often result in a higher paying position.

Never stop learning. Expand your knowledge base in your current job. Also look for peripheral knowledge that will help you cross over and manage another department.

Best of all, learn how to start and operate a side business. Something you can do with very little startup capital.

If you already have a business, raise prices. This is especially relevant for freelancers like writers, designers and computer related workers.

You can also become a consultant. Your skills are teachable. Or can be applied to other businesses.

Plus, you can package up your knowledge and sell it as an 'info-product.' In fact, our editors are putting the finishing touches on an educational program to teach you how to cash-in on the info-product business.

Because of the reach of the Internet and the inexpensive way you can launch a website, you can literally be raking it in faster than you ever dreamed possible.

Many have made info-products their full time business. And that's not the only way to make money with your knowledge.

You can turn a hobby into a business. Any craft you like making can now be sold fast on a wide variety of websites bringing craft people and their customers together. You've read some in these newsletters about people doing just that.

### *What Successful People Do That You Don't?*

Understand how you do anything is how you do everything. With that in mind, start your day making up your bed. And handle every small task the same way.
Learn to use your voice recorder on your phone or at least the notepad. Your mind is a beautiful thing. Often the solution to a problem or breakthrough idea will come when you are doing something else. Don't try and remember it. Document it for later.

Remember your body is you best asset. Treat it well. Workout every day, even it's just a 30-minute walk. And eat well. No you don't have to be on a strict diet. But don't load up on junk convenience food that will slow you down.

Take time to have lunch with other people who can enlighten you. It may be a co-worker from another department. An employee at a company across the street. Or just a neighbor. The fact is, those who are more socially engage enjoy life more. Learn more. And have they finger on the pulse of the market so they can innovate when the market has a problem that needs solving.

Always deliver more than you promise. This will make you the go-to whether you are an employee, consultant or friend.

Take time to just be quite. In those quite moments you will recharge. And put yourself in a position to achieve more than you think you can.

You can meditate like a lot of people do. Or just get in a room without a phone, computer or media device. Just take a few moments to chill.

"Do your work, then step back. The only path to serenity."
— Lao Tzu

Start your day thinking every positive thought you can. Anxiety comes from not living in the 'now.'

If you wake up feeling stressed, you are likely merging today with the past and projecting failure into the future.

Bring yourself back to the 'now' by getting in touch with your five senses.

What do you hear at this moment? See? Smell? Taste? Touch?

Try that simple exercise to bring yourself back to the present. You can only manage the present.

When you do, the mistakes of the past will disappear. You'll learn from them.

And by doing your best now, tomorrow will be better.

Be grateful you simply woke up to another day. Rolling Stones co-founder Keith Richards tell the audience at every concert...

"I'm glad to be here. In fact, I'm glad to be anywhere."

Don't act like you are better than everyone else. But do live like everyone should live. T

That means don't lie to people. Or cheat anyone. Steal others ideas. Avoid making excuses. Or complaining.

Be THAT person everyone wants to be and more important, be with.

Don't hide from conflict. How many times have you seen a problem become much bigger just because someone was unwilling to confront it head on?

Problems unattended only get worse. Nip them in the bud. Fix mistakes. Move forward.

Make room for your family. Dinner is a good time to connect with them daily. After all, they are why you want to be successful.

Finally, treat everyone like you would want to be treated. Don't shortchange anyone. Take time to hear many different viewpoints.

Sometimes breakthrough ideas come from where you least expect it.

Use the principals mentioned above to be more efficient. Most people aren't. That will give you a big edge in business and life.

*Congratulations! And welcome to the "Q.C.S." Club...*

# "Opportunity Review Service!"

**"A new way to discover the <u>FACTS</u> about any business opportunity you see advertised <u>WITHOUT</u> risking your <u>OWN</u> money!"**

Dear Q.C.S. Club member,

What I am about to share is more than valuable... **it is priceless!** Because it will SAVE YOU THOUSANDS OF DOLLARS in *wasted* time and money (just like it has for other *Q.C.S. Club* members!) Here's what it's all about...

**"A Service Whose Time Has Come!"**

Over the years ***Q.C.S. Club*** members have contacted us about numerous business opportunities they've seen advertised. Of course, their questions are always the same *"What is it? What do you know about it? Should I invest in it? Is it a scam or rip off?"*

As a result, we created the Q.C.S. Club **"Opportunity Review Service"** to save club members thousands of dollars in *wasted* time and money.

**"Here's how it works..."**

Every year we investigate and buy numerous business opportunities and money making programs. This includes the good, the bad and... *the ugly!* As you can imagine, we have an enormous amount of "inside information" on what's worth investing in and what is a scam or rip-off.

So, we decided to make this information available to ***Q.C.S. Club*** members for a price you can't pass up...

**"Here's how to save thousands starting TODAY!"**

As an ***Q.C.S. Club*** member all that's required is you fill out and mail the coupon below and let us know what money making programs you would like to know **THE FACTS** about. Just provide us the names of the programs *(and any advertising... if you have it).*

Mail this to us with the coupon below along with a small printing and postage fee of **only $10 per opportunity requested.** *And...*

We will send you back a **FACTUAL REPORT** on the money making programs. It's as simple as that. And, it will save you thousands of dollars. Here's what other members are saying...

*"Thank you. Your opportunity review service saved me over $3,500 by avoiding an opportunity which would have cost me a small fortune in time and money!" Bill, AR*

*"What a valuable service. I had no idea I was about to be taken advantage of. Now I feel like I have someone who can help me avoid making costly mistakes." Marcia, NY*

*"The club helped me find a real money maker while avoiding getting ripped off. Thank you". Roger, LA*

Today is your chance to get the FACTS on any money making program you are curious about! Please, mail the coupon TODAY!

*(Note: please respond TODAY as this service could be discontinued for obvious reasons. If discontinued, coupon will be immediately returned with fee. To avoid missing out, mail coupon today!)*

## <u>Q.C.S. Club</u> <u>***"Opportunity Review Service"***</u> <u>*Order Coupon!*</u>

[ ] **YES!** *Count me in!* Please send me **FACTUAL REPORTS** on each of the money making programs I have listed below. This way I can know all THE FACTS <u>without</u> risking any money! **I am enclosing $10 per opportunity requested.** Please send me reports on the following opportunities listed *(only $10 each for printing, postage & processing)*

Opp. #1:______________________ Opp. #2:______________________

Opp. #3:______________________ Opp. #4:______________________

**I am enclosing a total of $____ by [ ] Cash [ ] Check [ ] Money Order**

*(payable to: Zodi Publishing)*

**Ship my reports to:**

NAME____________________________

ADDRESS:__________________________

CITY:______________________ STATE:_____ ZIP:__________

AREA CODE and PHONE#:(______)________________________

***Mail to:***

**Zodi Publishing**
**100 Easy St**
**Unit 5590**
**Carefree AZ 85377**

# ~Action Steps I Can Take TODAY!~

# ~Action Steps I Can Take TODAY!~

# ~Action Steps I Can Take TODAY!~